PERFORMANCE
&
REALITY

PERFORMANCE
&
REALITY

ESSAYS FROM
GRAND STREET

EDITED BY BEN SONNENBERG

RUTGERS UNIVERSITY PRESS

NEW BRUNSWICK AND LONDON

Copyright © 1989 by Grand Street Publications, Inc.
All rights reserved
Manufactured in the United States of America

Library of Congress Cataloging-in-Publication Data

Performance and reality : essays from Grand street / edited by Ben
    Sonnenberg.
        p.   cm.
    ISBN 0-8135-1395-2   ISBN 0-8135-1409-6 (pbk.)
    1. Literature, Modern—20th century.   I. Sonnenberg, Ben.
II. Grand street.
PN6014.P39 1989
808.8′004—dc19   88-28301
                                                                    CIP

British Cataloging-in-Publication information available

Design by Deborah Thomas
Cover photograph of Charles Ludlum by Sylvia Plachy

CONTENTS

[*v*]

PREFACE

Cyril Connolly, who edited the London magazine *Horizon* from 1939 to 1950, told of once wanting a bookshop where he could scold the customers for not knowing Mimnermus or Sir Richard Roos. "I soon realized I'd have to have *two* shops, one across the road," Connolly said. "So I could show 'em the door and point and say, 'And if you don't like it here, you know where you can go.'"

The essays here are from but one shop, *Grand Street*, established 1981. The shops across the road all appear to belong to big chains or small specialists. I hope the essays will give pleasure and show something of the character of the magazine. Of the twenty-four essays, fourteen were assignments. The rest were offered to *Grand Street*. With three exceptions, all appear here for the first time in a book.

I thank the authors for their permission to reprint these essays. I thank Deborah Thomas who designed and publishes *Grand Street* and who designed this book.

Ben Sonnenberg

PERFORMANCE

&

REALITY

PERFORMANCE AND REALITY

Stanley Elkin

There is in literature an element of what I shall call "crossover." In primitive form it is often little more than echo, or allusion, and is borrowed from one thing and imposed on another for what might almost be homeopathic reasons, growing a sort of interest, as money grows interest—lump sum momentum like a chain letter no one has broken.

We frequently see the crossover in story titles. E. M. Forster writes *A Room with a View, A Passage to India;* Bob Coover "The Cat in the Hat for President." Joan Didion calls her novel *A Book of Common Prayer*, Thornton Wilder his play *The Skin of Our Teeth*. Indeed, it isn't only authors who consciously mine the allusive, magical properties inherent in prior names—inherent *after* the fact—history itself does it. "World War Two" is a crossover, catchy as a tune. Not sequential convenience, mind you, though that's certainly part of it, but actual art. So artful and catchy, in fact, that the one on the drawing boards, that hasn't even happened yet, is already being called "World War Three."

Writers of advertising copy and the editors of popular magazines are perhaps the most expert, certainly the most self-conscious, practitioners of this form—and it *is* a form—with its values of pun and slogan. It would be an interesting exercise to examine the titles of the news articles in just one issue of *Time* magazine. I'm too lazy to take the trouble, and too troubled to take the pains, but if I were a better person and had the character for it, I'm certain that what I would find would be a kind of cornucopia of recombinant and essentially *literary* elements—in jokes for outsiders.

But whether the source is literary or idiomatic—usually it's idiomatic—the intended effect, when it is not merely cute, is always the same—new wine in old bottles, some recycled but incremental and compounded sense of the world, the lifting of one occasion to enhance another.

Two years ago, to no one's particular notice, I thought to call a collection of bits and pieces from my previous books *Stanley Elkin's Greatest Hits*. I thought it an inspired title. The model was from the recording industry, an allusion to what, in America, has become almost a genre—*Wayne Newton's Greatest Hits, Elvis's* . . . : the habit of reissuing in a new package the popular but out-of-print blockbuster golds and platinums of established stars. Often these anthology recordings are promoted in TV commercials with the note, like a surgeon general's disclaimer on a package of cigarettes, that it's not available in stores.

My intentions had been honorable. That is, like all honorable intentions, they were born out of frustration and despair. All I ever wanted, as I tell my friends, is to be rich and famous and to live forever without pain. My title, I felt, was pure crossover ironic, not in the least cute, pure art. I have no greatest hits of course, no golds, no platinums, none of the fabulous and rare ores, elements and alchemicals of the Las Vegans; in me metallurgy reduced to mere spin-off, simple dross. Anticipating, I even tried to make the case with my publisher that we should use the other crossover phrase as well, and display the fact prominently on the jacket that the book was "Not Available in Stores." An in joke for an outsider. For me, I mean.

To this point, at least, I've been talking only along the fringes of art and fiction, my notion of crossover simplistic—allusions, slogans and puns, statutory miles from my argument. But even allusions, slogans and puns with their pentimento, almost geological layers and palimpsest arrangements do in primary colors what good fiction with its infinite palette must always try to do.

Let me tell you about the flamenco dancer.

The flamenco dancer sits in the café against the whitewashed walls, slouched in his wooden chair. While the women dance, a guitar player, his feet oddly stolid and flat-foot on the small platform, leans his ear against the back of his instrument as if he is tuning it. Another gazes impassively across the fretted fingerboard of his guitar as though he were blind. The family—it is impossible to know relationships here, to distinguish husbands from brothers, sisters from wives—a mysterious consanguinity undefined as the complicated connections in circus; only the standing, hand-clapping man in the suit, shouting encouragement like commands, seems in authority here, or the woman, her broad, exposed back and shoulders spilling her gown like the slipped, toneless flesh of powerful card players. Even the slouching brother? husband? nephew? son? is attentive but demure, the women's hair pulled so tightly into their comb tiaras you can see the deep, straight furrows of their scalp. Their arrhythmic clapping is not so much on cue as beside it, beneath it, random as traffic, signaled by some private, internal urging like spontaneous pronouncement at a prayer meeting. Yes. Like testimony, like witness. Except for this—the finger snapping, the hand claps never synchronous as applause, the occasional gutturals of the men and the abrupt chatter of the women like a musical gossip—they do not seem absorbed, or even very interested, their attention deflected, thrown as the voice of a ventriloquist, loss of affect like a dominant mood. Inside the passionate music and performance they are rigid, distracted as jugglers. The men and women, patient in their half circle of chairs as timid Johns, polite whores in a brothel, seem even less aware of each other than they are of the performers, kinship and relationship in abeyance, whatever of love that connects them dissolved, intimacy stoicized, the curious family in the cavelike room suddenly widowed, suddenly widowered, orphaned, returned to some griefless condition of independence.

And now the *bailora* completes her turn. Like some human beast, she seems to rise from the broad, tiered flounces of her costume as from a package of waves at a shoreline, the great, fabric petals of her long train swirled, heaped as seawater at her feet, her immaculate ass, hips, thighs and tits a lesson in the meaty rounds of some mythic geometry, her upper arms spreading from her shoulders like wings, angled to her forearms, her forearms angled to her wrists, her wrists and hands and fingers and long

[3]

Latin nails a squared circle of odd, successive dependencies, the stiff, queer displacement of the askew fingers like some hoodoo signal to charm the bright arrogance of the dance.

The man in the suit—when did the cigarette, burned out now, only a dead ash longer than the intact paper which supports it, go into his lips?—beats an asyndeton, paratactic, ungrammatical applause. It is that same deliberate offbeat accompaniment that earlier had almost but not quite violated the heel clicks and toe taps of the *bailora*. No matter how studiously the audience in the café tries to keep up with it they cannot fall in with this artful dodger.

Now the flamenco dancer rises from his chair. Slim and grave as a bullfighter he moves in his gypsy silks and gabardines, his trapezist's *pasodoble* entrances and heroics. Alone, it is as if he marches in a procession, deadpan as a saint, solemn as Jesus. He looks like a condemned man leading an invisible party of executioners and priests to his gallows, the host at his own murder feast. There is nothing epicene or hermaphroditic in his bearing, yet he could almost be the embodiment of some third sex, or no, some sexual specialist, a fucker of virgins, say, of nymphets and schoolgirls and all the newly menstrual. In his tight, strange clothing, the trousers that rise above the waist and close about his spine, the small of his back, the narrow jacket and vest that just meet them, leaving off exactly where the trousers begin, not a fraction of an inch of excess material, sausaged into his clothes as the girls' hair had been into their comb tiaras, the bulge of his genitals customized, everything, all, all bespoke, fitting his form, seamless as apple peel, the crack in his ass, the scar on his hip, he seems dressed, buttocks to shoulders, in a sort of tights, some magic show-biz gypsy latex.

And now he is in position on the platform, conducted there by the asyncopatic hand claps of the man in the suit.

At first he appears the perfect flamenco analogue of a bullfighter. If the women, with their elaborate hand and arm movements, had seemed to flourish banderillas and

[*4*]

brandish lances, the flamenco dancer with his minimal upper body gestures and piledriver footwork, seems to wield capes, do long, stationary passes, slow motion veronicas, outrageous down-on-one-knee *rodillas*. Indeed, with his furious heel-toe, heel-toe momentum, he seems at times to be the actual bull itself, pawing the ring of platform in flamenco rage. Bullfighter *and* bull, as the dancing woman had seemed an extension of the actual sea.

This is what the flamenco dancer looks like.

He has the face of a cruel, handsome Indian and looks insolent as a man in a tango. There are layers of indifference on his face like skin, like feature itself, some fierce inappetency and a listlessness so profound that that itself might almost be his ruling passion, some smoky nonchalance of the out-of-love. Not cold, not even cool, for these words at least suggest an *idea* of temperature, and the flamenco dancer seems to have been born adiabatic, aseptic. What, on someone else's face, might look like sneer, snarl, contempt, may, on his, signify no more than the neutral scorn and toughness on the face of a bulldog.

Now the flamenco dancer is possessed by his *duende*, his musical *dybbuk*. His is *jondo*, profound—death, anguish, tragedy. The larger issues. (Music is hard. In prose, music is very hard to do, unconvincing as lyrics, a cappella on a page. Avoid trying to render music. Avoid the sensations of orgasm. Steer clear of madmen as protagonists and likewise eschew a writer as a hero of the fiction. And it's swimming at your own risk in the stream of consciousness. "Knowing believes before believing remembers," says Faulkner in a Joe Christmas section in *Light in August*. What the hell does that mean?) And the guitarist is singing his serious *soleares*, calling his *cante* like a ragman, whining his tune like a cantor. *Davvening* despair.

> I am no longer what I was [he sings,
>   calls, whines, *davvens*]
> now will I be aga–ain
> I am a tree of sadness
> in the shadow of a waa–aall . . .

A woman was the cause
of my first downfall;
there is no perdition in the world
that is not caused by women . . .

In the neighborhood of Triana
there is neither pen nor ink
with which to write my mother,
whom I haven't seen for . . . ye–ars.

"*¡Olé!*"s pour in from the satellite performers half an
orbit behind the flamenco dancer. "*¡Olé!*"s like an agreement, a deal, an oral handshake, a struck bargain. The
done/done arrangements of serious negotiation.

And now it happens. Just now. The flamenco dancer is
doing a particularly difficult riff. This murderous tango
of a man whose body is one taut line of mood, who,
touched at one end of that body should, by the laws of
physics if not the conventions of his trade, like the strings
on the musician's guitar, vibrate at the other, but whose
art it is to defy physics, to drive his feet like pistons without ruffling a ruffle of his shirt, who *does* that, whose
ruling second skin of costume, revealing still that inch
and a half of scar, the material caught in it, in the *scar*, the
magic show-biz gypsy latex, stuck there like the long, dark
vertical of a behind snagged in the pants of a fat man rising
from a chair on a hot day, does not, does *not*, display a single qualm of muscle, not one quiver, tremor, shiver, flutter,
not one shake, not even his trousers which, snug as they
are from mid-thigh to the small of the back, are cut like
normal men's beneath that and actually hang like a gau-
cho's in a sort of a flare below the knee, not even his damn
trousers jump! It is as if *he* is the ventriloquist (you must
come back; you must return and use everything; you
must use up your material; you must move the furniture
around); it is as if *he* is the ventriloquist, only what he
throws is not his voice but his feet, his shoe leather; it
is as if *he* is the ventriloquist, has exactly on the physical plane the ventriloquist's schizophrenic detachment,

[*6*]

straight man and comic all together all at once, only it ain't only his lips which don't move, it's *everything!* His hands are stilled, his calves are quiet, his knees, the ruffles on his shirt, *all* his torso, and it's as if he really *is* detached, actually separated from the interests of his body, only his feet going on about their business like steps drawn on a dance chart.

Except, as I say, now it happens. This dark fandango of a fellow is grinning. He is grinning; not smiling, grinning; not pleased as punch; probably not even happy; but grinning, *grinning*. And not *just* grinning, not simple human cheer or the Cheshire risibles of pleased teeth, but the original, paradigmatic, caught-out, pants down, caught-in-the-act, shit-eating smirk of grin itself!

Because that is how the flamenco dancer must be rendered, I think. A man who never grins, whose profession it is to keep a straight face, who earns his bread by artful scorn, whose squared back, poseur, gypsy bearing is by ordinary the stately four-four time of toreros and graduating seniors, must be shown with his face naked, his bared teeth and grinning lips like private parts. There must be crossover, what joke writers call the "switch." There must, that is, be a grafting of one condition upon another, the episodic or eventful equivalencies of pun and slogan, the schizophrenic tensions and torsions—though unless he's a minor character the flamenco dancer may not be mad, recall—of all discrepant allegiance.

It's like this. A flamenco dancer, a tinker, a tailor, a candlestick maker, any human being, cannot be shown in fiction without quirk, wrinkle, slippage—the fall, I mean, from the photographic, all, I mean, the strictly realistic and correct dictionary parameters and ideals of grace. Which explains whiskey priests, golden-heart whores, hungover surgeons, cowardly soldiers, misers who tithe, mercenaries who develop some long-haul loyalty they cannot understand or even very definitively or coherently explain. "A man," Hemingway's dying Harry Morgan says in *To Have and Have Not*, "one man alone ain't got. No man alone now. No matter how a man alone ain't got no bloody fucking chance." Which explains, that is, all driven stereotype and fictional cliché. But the instincts of the cliché are correct; only the judgment of the writer is flawed, his critical lapse of recognition, maybe his reading habits. He is like the writer of mystery stories pursuing the idiosyncratic as relentlessly as ever his amateur detective pursued any murderer.

But I'm not talking about the idiosyncratic so much as I am about the strange—the flat-out, let-stand, mysterious. If there can be no flamenco dancer without that shit-eating grin, neither ought there to be any of the tight hospital corners of explanation. In James Agee's *A Death in the Family* there occurs perhaps one of the strangest ghost stories I've ever read. Jay, the father, has just been buried. The family returns to the house after the funeral. Here Agee discharges point of view into the disparate consciousnesses of a handful of characters. Upstairs the mother senses a presence in the room—that of her dead husband. Simultaneously, in another part of the house, their little boy feels that his father's spirit has suddenly returned. Still another relative hears an odd noise, looks around, sees nothing but is convinced that Jay has returned from the dead to comfort his mourners. Each character is certain that Jay has come back, is with them again but, not wanting to upset the others who might not understand, decides to say nothing about the visitation. Agee never explains the startling conviction of reunion each has experienced. Indeed, he never even alludes to it.

Or Anthony Powell. In his novel *From a View to a Death*, Powell draws a tight and quite conventional picture of the middle professional class. Mrs. is sixtyish, a bit dowdy, a touch past it but still civilized. Mr. is a professional soldier, a major, retired. They live an uncomplicated home life in a genteel but ordinary house a few miles from town. They drink sherry, they take *The Times*. And one morning his wife goes into town to do some shopping. I don't have the book in front of me but this, at least approximately, is what happens. "You'll be all right, dear?" "Oh, yes, I'll read I should think." "Is there anything you need?" "Cigarettes. I require cigarettes." "What, don't you have *ci*garettes?" "Well I thought I did, but it appears I'm running out." "I'll bring some from Scrapple." "Most kind. Most decent." "It's on my way. It isn't as if it wasn't on my way." "Most considerate." "And I did wish to see Scrapple. Ask after his wife." "Mnn." "What's that, dear?" "My book. I can't seem to find that book I was read-ing." "What, the one about the campaigns?" "Yes, the campaign one, that's it." She sees the book and brings it to him. "Oh," she says, "that sunlight! Much too bright on the page." "Yes. It is rather. Yes." "Shall I draw the drapes then? You could switch on the lamp." "Most thoughtful. Yes." And she draws the drapes and the major thanks her, and they kiss good-bye, and she goes out to start the car. He hears it start up and listens to her drive off and rises from the chair beside which the lamp is now burning. He puts the book about the campaigns on the seat of the wing chair so that he won't misplace it again and walks into another room. When he returns he is dressed in his wife's clothes, even her makeup, even her hat. He sits back down in the chair and reads the book about the campaigns by the light of the lamp in the drape-drawn room. That is the end of the chapter. Powell never mentions the major's transvestism again. Though we see him again. And each time we do, *each time*, observing him closely now, aston-ished by him, gradually taken with an apparently de-cent man, we think: This fellow dresses up in women's clothes; he likes to put on a girdle; he enjoys the brace of a brassiere, the squeeze of a pump. There is that faintly geological feel of crossover, character layered as a cake.

Not the idiosyncratic, not the strange, maybe not even the mysterious finally so much as the queer, protuberant salience of the obliquely sighted. What the periscope saw, what goes on in the corner of the eye, talking pictures in the kaleidoscope, eyes staring back at you, weeping, through the keyhole, the application of a close but possibly afflicted vision, as if writers were color-blind, say, or men-tal. (Because the flamenco dancers and the ghosts and the British majors (ret.) are all used up.) We endanger a species simply by mentioning it. So not the idiosyncratic, strange or mysterious, or even that queer protuberant salience of the obliquely sighted; maybe only suprise. Which I take to be some flipped-coin mix—flipped-coin because it can go either way—of the ordinary in league with the exotic, the strange displacements of the ordinary. The flamenco dancers and ghosts and majors retired are all used up, but we can never be quit of them, or they of us. We must wring them dry as a sheet, put usurer's pressures on them, dun them with obligation, hit them when they're down. And, using surprise, surprise always in some un-Hitchcockian way so that surprise is not ever expected, not ever the form itself that is, not ever looked for, some logical, non-*Jaws*ian sense of the thing. Not Boo! from a closet or Happy Birthday! from pals. Surprise inevitable as verdict, ordered as law.

I went to the Metropolitan Museum of Art. It was one of those fine, rare spring days in New York when optimism flows like an energy, when, mysteriously, there is a kind of astonishing democracy in the air, the pollen count zero and the ego and envy in abeyance, not even coveting my neighbor's wife, not coveting at all, giving everyone the benefit of the doubt, *this* old Scrooge, better than Christmas; not "You, boy! You know the poulterer on the High Street? Fetch a goose, I'll write you into the will!" Because you figure he doesn't need it, convinced everyone is a personage anyway, the pimply fellow in dirty jeans, the bag lady, the Howard Hughes type fishing coins from the gutter—all, all personages, all upperly mobile and down from the three-million-buck co-ops across Fifth Avenue, out for a breath of air, a touch of art. Your eye out for Kissinger, your eye out for Jackie.

On Eighty-first Street, personages were sprawled on the museum steps eating hot dogs, knotted saltbread, sipping soda. Two vendors, their marvelous wagons with their clever compartments like trick drawers in a desk, about twelve feet apart, cry "Hot dogs, hot dogs here," more to each other than to their customers. They do a brisk business and seem terribly amused, as if all that's at stake is the side bet they have down on who will turn over the most saltbread today.

I schlepp up the steps, pulling myself along by the railing, this privileged Porgy for whom even the bag ladies get out of the way. I climb half a mile of stairs. (I *love* art!)

Schoolkids, cross-legged on the floor, civil and serious, snug and curiously private in this public place, copy masterpieces into their sketchbooks. Joan has organized a wheelchair. I wave to the toddlers in strollers. "Hi kids," I say, amusing myself that I know what each is thinking, struggling to say. Not, "Hey look at the cripple," but "Mommy, Mommy, there goes the biggest toddler in the goddamn world!" I'm having a marvelous time, my heart in high for once. Everywhere people back from the gift shop carry Metropolitan Museum shopping bags like so much artistic grocery, and I have, in this perfect temperate zone with its ideal temperature and humidity designed for canvas and pigment, a sense of some best-foot-forward, good-willed world, as if Philanthropy were an actual order of actual politics, as much a rule of reign as the dynasties and kingdoms and tribes whose artifacts and paintings and sculptures seem somehow the place's generative treasury, not a repository of art at all but native wealth, natural resource, like Saudi oil, Zimbabwe chrome, Argentine beef. So close to the source of things, I am close to tears. It could be the giant toddler is simply overtired, on the edge of crankiness, tantrum. But nah, nah, his heart's in high, overwhelmed by the good order and best behavior of the citizens of this good country, the schoolgirls seated cross-legged on the floor, concentrating, intense, their lower lips in their teeth to get a line just right, to catch it on the tip of their drawing pens and hold it there, balancing, balancing, careful, gentle as people in bomb squads, till they can thrust it safely onto the drawing pad and be rid of it. (I will tell you something secret about myself. It's none of your business but I don't much care for music, the classics I mean, the high symphonies and opera styles, yet whenever I go to a concert I weep. It's the cooperation that gets me every time, that dedicated

[*11*]

sense of the civil—not the music but the musicians, the useless fiction of harmony they perpetuate. It is this that gets me now.)

Did I tell you it is Saturday? It is Saturday, and scattered among the lovers and schoolkids, the Fifth Avenue co-op owners, the free-lance tour guides and museum guards and gift-shop marketers and toddlers—use it; use it up—the retired majors and flamenco dancers, are fathers and sons, fathers and daughters. The children—use it; use it up—have lunched on vendor hot dogs and have mustard on their chins, the corners of their lips, bits of saltbread like a light seasoning in the wrinkles of their clothes. The kids are oddly solicitous and gaze where their dads direct their attentions with a courteous, leashed patience, not bored but the opposite, concentrating—use it; use it up— working hard as those schoolgirls cross-legged on the floor, intense themselves, as nervous about line, but it's their own expressions they're perfecting, that they must balance even longer than that memory on the tip of that drawing pen, hold and hold like a smile for an old-time photograph, breathing of course, even talking, giving and taking, exchanging ideas, opinion, but everything controlled as the climate in this place, and suddenly I recognize these kids. They are Saturday's children, and they are here by court order, by official decree, sentenced by a judge and their own mixed loyalties, serving their time like good cons, and the fathers too, sneaking a glance at their watches, wondering if it's time yet to go to the museum restaurant, time to get out altogether, figuring how much time it will take up to get a cab to the Russian Tea Room, how long the wait will be, how fast the service, which movie to take the kid to, when it gets out, timing what's left of the morning, the long afternoon, doing in their heads all the sums of visitation, rehearsing the customs of custody.

And I get an idea for a story. Perhaps it was my private joke in the wheelchair that set it off, my vision of myself as a giant toddler; perhaps it was all this, well, *behaving*, this sedate and serious steady state attention I feel all about me, the suspicion, grown now to conviction,

[12]

that no one is having a very good time; certainly my sudden awareness of the divorced fathers and their children, doing God knows what sums of custody in *their* heads, had the most to do with it, but I have an idea for a story.

It's this.

Julian's—I even have the name—parents are divorced when Julian is eleven years old and Julian's mother gets custody. The court grants Julian's father liberal visitation privileges—weekends, of course, certain specified holidays, Julian's birthday in even numbered years. And Julian will spend at least one month of his summer vacation with his dad.

Only when the story opens Julian is thirty-two years old, his mother and father in their early fifties, and Julian is dutifully waiting for his father's Sunday visit. Nothing, absolutely nothing, is wrong with Julian. Though he still lives at home, he has grown up to be an intelligent, healthy young man, decently employed, still single but ordinarily sexed, not particularly fixated on either his mother or his dad. The story will concern itself with their afternoon, Julian's and his father's, with the mutual anxieties both have about these visits, anxieties not all that different from the anxieties of the parents and children doing those secret sums of custody in their heads. Perhaps they will visit the Metropolitan, certainly they will go to the Russian Tea Room where their order will be taken by the man in the suit. I expect they will have the conversation fathers and sons usually have on such occasions, the father discreetly pressing Julian for information about his mother, and Julian politely resisting, reluctant to be either go-between or honest broker, and both, from time to time, glancing at their watches.

The story is not yet written, or even begun, but I am satisfied that it satisfies my criteria, that it has all the elements—the shit-eating grin on the flamenco dancer's face, the idiosyncratic, the strange, the mysterious, the queer protuberant salience of the obliquely sighted, crossover, and what the periscope saw, surprise, and all the rest of these strange displacements of the ordinary. 🦋

BORROWED DOGS

Richard Avedon

When I was a boy, my family took great care with our snapshots. We really planned them. We made compositions. We dressed up. We posed in front of expensive cars, homes that weren't ours. We borrowed dogs. Almost every family picture taken of us when I was young had a different borrowed dog in it. The photographs on these pages are of my mother, my sister and myself. It seemed a necessary fiction that the Avedons owned dogs. Looking through our snapshots recently, I found eleven different dogs in one year of our family album. There we were in front of canopies and Packards with borrowed dogs, and always, forever, smiling. All of the photographs in our family album were built on some kind of lie about who we were, and revealed a truth about who we wanted to be.

When I began to look at the portraits of Egon Schiele—I hadn't really known his work until the Museum of Modern Art's "Vienna 1900" show in 1986—I was excited. It seemed to me one of the highest examples of portraiture without borrowed dogs. So when I began thinking of what I might say about him, I thought I would contrast Schiele's candor and complexity with the entire tradition of flattery and lies in portrait-making.

I've always thought that Rembrandt was the master of

this kind of empty ennoblement in portraiture, and that he was the most dangerous "Master of the Borrowed Dog" simply because he is the most perfect and seductive of painters. So when I was invited to give this lecture at the museum by Kirk Varnedoe, curator of the show, I was preparing to say hard things about Rembrandt; and it just didn't seem like a swift thing to do. Since I had no other thoughts on the subject, I decided to decline.

Now, what I'm about to tell you is true in every detail.

The morning that I made up my mind not to attempt to speak in public about Schiele, I walked from my study into my bedroom (I'd been having carpenters build bookshelves under my bed), and there by the window was Rembrandt himself, standing in my bedroom in Rembrandt light. There, holding a hammer, dressed as a carpenter, was the genius himself. I reached for Kenneth Clark's book on Rembrandt and showed Rembrandt, the carpenter, the chapter on his self-portraits. The carpenter agreed that they were absolutely of him. He said, "This one, of course, when I was younger." I set up my camera, asked him to imitate the drawings I'd shown him, and did a few snapshots. (All this happened in five minutes.) Rembrandt the carpenter acted Rembrandt the painter exactly. It seemed undeniable to me that Rembrandt must have been acting when he made his own self-portraits. It was so clear. Rembrandt was telling me that he was acting when he drew himself. Not just making faces, but always, throughout his life, working in the full tradition of performance. Elaborate costumes, a turban, a beret, a cloak, the rags of a beggar, the golden cloth of a sultan, and someone's dog—really performing in a very self-conscious way.

And then I realized, thanks to Rembrandt the carpenter, that it was precisely this quality of performance that links Rembrandt and Schiele—that links all portraits, but which Schiele took to an inspiring and radical extreme. And that ought to be my real subject, just as it is the real subject of all portraits that interest me.

Because portraiture is performance, and like any performance, in the balance of its effects it is good or bad, not natural or unnatural. I can understand being troubled by this idea—that all portraits are performances—because it seems to imply some kind of artifice that conceals the truth about the sitter. But that's not it at all.

The point is that you can't get at the thing itself, the real nature of the sitter, by stripping away the surface. The surface is all you've got. You can only get beyond the surface by working with the surface. All that you can do is to manipulate that surface—gesture, costume, expression—radically and correctly. And I think Schiele understood this in a unique, profound and original way. Rather than attempting to abandon the tradition of the performing portrait (which is probably impossible anyway), it seems to me that Schiele pushed it to extremes, shattered the form by turning the volume up to a scream. And so what we see in Schiele is a kind of recurring push and pull: first toward pure "performance," gesture and stylized behavior, pursued for its own sake, studied for its own sake.

Then these kinds of extreme stylizations are preserved in form, but disoriented, taken out of their familiar place, and used to change the nature of what a portrait is.

I think this begins with hands and gesture. All portrait artists have to think about what to do with hands. It's not at all that a portrait is a kind of arrested moment in a stream of gesture. Gesture just doesn't proceed in lock step with thought. On the contrary, gesture in life always follows thought and precedes words. You extend your hand, then say, "Hello"—if you reverse the order, something else is going on. In a fixed image, there's no possibility of one act informing the other. Nor is gesture in a portrait just pantomime where you invent the right meaningful gesture. Where the hands go is intimately tied up with the whole expressive quality of design, the graphic rhythm of the image as a whole, as well as its psychological and emotional content.

So the first thing one sees in Schiele is this kind of marionette imagery. This kind of laboratory of splayed fingers that seem oblique and purposefully unrevealing—the kind of experiment you do when you try to find some random or chance or unpredictable element to break a stereotyped form.

On second look, it becomes clear that this new language of hands really affects things in a fundamental way. First of all, what started out as pantomime has become part of a larger graphic scheme—a jagged, spindled rhythm that you see as clearly in Schiele's flowers as in his figures. And then, eventually he used apparently aberrant or oblique gestures to create a whole new, meaningful language of gesture that, for me, is much more convincing than the traditional postures. Beginning in pure marionette theater, ending with an image and gesture to do with intellect—(this pulling down of the eye)—that's much truer and more beautiful than, say—to scrape the bottom of the barrel—Rodin's *Thinker*.

The ultimate expression of this kind of performance—extreme stylized behavior—is of course fashion, where everything—the entire body, hair, makeup, fabric—is all used to create a performance. So many portraits in the history of art are fashion portraits, fashion images, as in so many beautiful Klimts. Schiele understood fashion and seems to have been fascinated by it. But he also, more excitingly, chose neither to succumb to it nor reject it. In the same way that the apparently stylized and abstract language of gesture in the marionette pictures, once controlled, became the means toward a new language of gesture, it seems to me that Schiele never abandoned the theatrical conventions of fashion, but instead intensified those conventions in a way that transformed their meaning. I think the masterpiece of this particular—and particularly daring—aspect of Schiele's work occurs in the picture of himself in a jail cell. Here, in the extreme of humiliation and pain, imprisoned for the daring and power

of his work, he draws himself in an explosion of form, equal to the most extravagant ideal of fashion. No man's garment flows so lyrically in the best of times, let alone the worst.

One of the other elements of performance is, of course, the prop. And of course it's significant that Schiele in his portraits, for the most part, deprived himself of props and scenery. He used empty backgrounds. They're so spare.

As one who is addicted to white backgrounds, it seems odd to me that a gray or tonal background is never described as an empty background. But in a sense, that's correct. A dark background fills. A white background empties. A gray background does seem to refer to something—a sky, a wall, some atmosphere of comfort and reassurance—that a white background doesn't permit. With the tonal background, you're allowed the romance of a face coming out of the dark. I don't think you find portraits with white backgrounds before Schiele. Maybe in drawings. Never in paintings, with the possible exception of the white icons of Novgorod. And that, I think, is the point. It's so hard with a white background not to let the graphic element take over. It's so hard to give emotional content to something so completely and potentially caricatural, dominated by that hard, unyielding edge. And that, of course, is the challenge and importance of it. If you can make it work successfully, a white background permits people to become symbolic of themselves.

All of these things—the new language of gesture, the reversal of fashion, the daring white background—are elements that excite and move me in Schiele's work. But what really excites me in his work is what he does with sex. Of all of Schiele's pictures, the one that has come to mean the most to me is the self-portrait masturbating. It seems to me to be a real revolution in the way we imagine sex and erotic life in art. It brings together two different but deeply related things in a very stirring way. First, it's raw and truthful about sex. It reveals something previously hidden about erotic life in art. But in a more subtle way, it's truthful about the implicit eroticism of all portraiture.

I think there's an element of sexuality in all portraiture; the moment you stop to look, you've been picked up. You look in a way you're not allowed to look in life. Is there any situation in life where you can look at the Duchess of Alba for half an hour without ending up dead at the hands of the Duke? A confrontational, erotic quality, I think, should underline all portraiture. But this confrontational quality of portraiture is almost never explored, so far as I know, in explicitly erotic images. They tend to be always voyeuristic rather than confrontational.

Rather than making "sexy" images, it seems to me that Schiele began with the knowledge of the complexity implicit in the sexuality of all portraiture, and then again turned up the volume. It's as though he is saying, "You want to see? I'll give you something to look at. And my painting will look at you looking at me." Is there an image in art before this of a man, rather than a woman, masturbating? Schiele engaged in the performance of masturbation; presents it as a performance. He seems to have understood the erotic nature of all portraiture and been at once excited and revolted by it. For all the high degree of sexuality in his work, there's an interesting lack of sensuality.

All of this—all this knowledge about being a portrait painter, and about performing this act, about watching himself performing the act, and painting himself performing the act, and then about looking at the painting he made—seems, to me, wrapped up in this image. It also seems, to me, a bad performance, though a radical one. This picture fails as a metaphor from the neck up because of Schiele's youthful addiction to sentimentality in the treatment of his own face. It's in the face that we see The Loneliness of the Masturbator—this head expresses a much more banal conception than does the subtlety of this body. It seems to me to limit the picture's power by making masturbation acceptable in art only as a pleasureless act, instead of a frenzied, complicated, pleasurable, destructive wacking-off. Imagine a different Schiele head on this Schiele body.

Forgive me. I know I've gone too far. Presuming to say what Schiele should have done or might have done is out of the question. But let me end with a story that may say something about all of this: performance, gesture, fashion as performance, and the afterlife of Egon Schiele.

In 1975 I had arrived at the point in my own career where I was no longer interested in doing portraits of persons of power and accomplishment. However, there were three men whose work I admired enormously and whose portraits I wanted to make: Francis Bacon, Jorge Luis Borges and Samuel Beckett. Their portraits turned out to involve three different kinds of performance: Borges gave

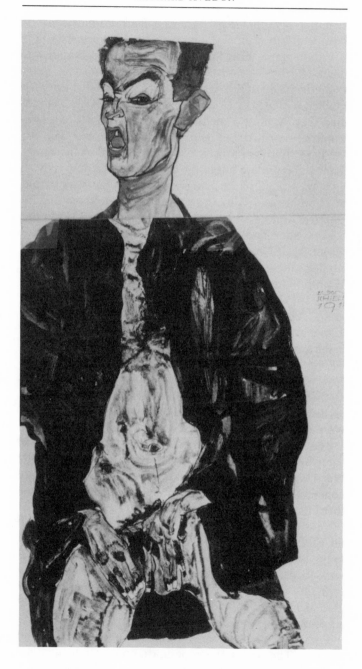

an unphotographable performance, Beckett refused to perform and Bacon offered a perfect performance.

I photograph what I'm most afraid of, and Borges was blind.

On the plane to Buenos Aires, I discovered that Borges's mother, with whom I knew he had lived all of his life, had died that evening. I assumed, of course, that the sitting would be canceled. But he received me as we had planned, the next afternoon at four o'clock. I arrived at his apartment and found myself in the dark. He was sitting in gray light, on a small settee, and signaled with his hand for me to sit beside him. Almost immediately, he told me that he admired Kipling and asked me to read to him. "Go to the bookcase and find the seventh book from the right on the second shelf," he said. I did. He told me what poem of Kipling's he wanted to hear—"The Harp Song of the Dane Women"—and I read it to him. He joined in occasionally. Did I know Anglo-Saxon? he asked next. Which would I prefer, legend or elegy? Elegy, I chanced. He explained to me, as he prepared to recite, that his dead mother lay in the adjoining room. Her hands had clenched in pain just before her death, he explained, and then he described how he and their servant had straightened out each of his mother's fingers, one by one, until her hands lay in peace on her breast. Then he recited the Anglo-Saxon elegy, his voice rising and falling in the dark room.

The first time I saw him in light, it was my light. I was overwhelmed with feeling and I started to photograph. But the photographs turned out to be emptier than I had hoped. I thought I had somehow been so overwhelmed that I had brought nothing of myself to the portrait.

Four years later, I read an account by Paul Theroux of his visit to Borges. It was my visit: the dim light, the trip to the bookcase, Kipling, the Anglo-Saxon recital. In some way, it seemed Borges had no visitors. People who came from the outside could exist for him only if they were made part of his familiar inner world, the world of poets and ancients who were already his true companions. The people in that world knew more, argued better, had more to tell him. The performance permitted no interchange. He had taken his own portrait long before, and I could only photograph that.

[24]

In 1979 I went to Paris to photograph Samuel Beckett. As we were about to walk around the corner to the camera and white paper, Beckett spoke. "This is very painful for me," he said. I chose to believe him—though the remark might have been meant in another way—and stopped the sitting before it began. I'm still not certain that I did the correct thing.

My sitting with Francis Bacon was planned for a Sunday morning in Paris. I had set up my outdoor studio on the shady side of the Musée d'Art Moderne at the Trocadero. Bacon came in a striped shirt, leather pants and a checked jacket, dressed to kill, dressed to be photographed. And we had a charming conversation about the differences between living in Paris and London. It was a sunny day, and a really lovely, civilized exchange. Then I began the portrait. I explained the nature of the diptych I wanted to achieve. I'd made a little sketch of what I hoped to do. I asked him to exchange his jacket for my plain, dark sweater. And then I asked him to bring his hand up into the portrait. If I'd asked the same of a politician or banker, or for that matter, any one of us, the tendency would be for the subject to want to look distinguished, sage, to rest a chin on a hand, or bring a hand to a forehead. Bacon immediately acted the role of the private Bacon with the greatest purity, economy of gesture, and yet filled with authentic feeling. Without my saying a word, he understood what my portrait was about, what it called for from him, and he still remained true to himself. No one could

act Bacon but Bacon. On this perfect, clear Sunday, facing the Eiffel Tower, he achieved an honorable and perfect performance. Now that I look at the picture again, I see how much this gesture of internal conflict comes out of the modern tradition Schiele began. I certainly wasn't aware of it at the time, and I very much doubt that Bacon was either. But now I like to think that while we were performing, Schiele was pulling the strings.

THE DEATH OF DREISER

Esther McCoy

For some eighteen years I had done reading and some research jobs for Dreiser, first in New York, then in Santa Monica, where I moved in 1932. The Dreisers (Helen Richardson, with whom he had lived for many years) moved to Los Angeles in 1938; the reading continued even during the two years I was a fifty-hour-a-week engineering draftsman at Douglas Aircraft.

In 1945, I had been working for a year as an architectural draftsman for R. M. Schindler, whose office was two blocks away from Dreiser at 833 Kings Road. The sun had poured through the west windows of the drafting room with such zeal that the lines from the soft (2B) pencil smeared under my hand and there were streaks of graphite on my arms. Schindler, who normally spent the afternoons overseeing his jobs under construction, came in early because the jobs had stopped—there were not even two-by-fours on the market. It was not the first time this had happened; materials were very scarce at the end of the war. He said this was a good time for me to take a week off. He disappeared into the bathroom and I left without washing my hands. The drive home was about thirty minutes, but that day it would be three hours before I washed the graphite off my elbows.

As I drove past Dreiser's house I remembered the books I had in the car for him. I meant only to drop them at the door, but when Helen answered the ring her face was strained. "Teddy had a heart attack last night. Come in."

Dreiser had rallied and the doctor had left him at home; he was coming now to see whether Dreiser should be moved to a hospital. Would I wait with her? And would Berk and I spend the night with her?

She took me to the bedroom where he was lying, very gray, wearing an oxygen mask. His long lashes lay child-like and vulnerable on his cheek. He opened his eyes. "How are you?" I asked.

He lifted the mask. "Bum."

When he was sick he wanted the safety of Helen. She

wiped the mucus from his mouth, and as she busied herself with his pillows she fell into the role of mother soothing a sick child who was bound to recover. Everything else in her manner said he would not.

I left his room and stood for minutes in the hall, looking into his study. On his desk were the talismans he had collected over the years—a tiny woodcarving of a Chinese fisherman carrying a pole with a fish on the hook, a figure of a blanket-clad American Indian with black braids that over the years had become matted, and a terra cotta Kewpie with pointed head and outstretched legs. The figures had followed him everywhere from the time I first knew him. He was superstitious about them as he was about many other things. Sometimes when I was going on a journey he would press a new penny into my hand for luck, and once I gave him a Chinese coin which he carefully put in his vest pocket. Once he had asked me to drive him to a fortuneteller in Sawtelle. "I hear she's very gifted," he had said. (When Helen handed me Dreiser's suit later to place in a cardboard box, two new nickels fell out of a pocket. I took them home and put them in a sewing kit where they may still be.)

Looking at the highbacked Italian chair Dreiser sat in to write, I had a certainty that he would never again use it. How many times I had sat opposite him in this room and other rooms as he had listened sympathetically. He was, as he had said, a featherbed.

Helen had said to me once, "You know why Teddy likes you, don't you?" and for some reason, not wanting to hear why, I had laughed, and she had joined me in laughter and so I never really knew. It was unlike me to guard myself against knowing; but I had.

Now, I sensed, it was over, and I should never again sit opposite him. I should never again see him lay out a hand of canfield and play as we talked.

The doctor came; he felt it was wise not to move Dreiser and called the registry for a nurse. A male nurse appeared presently and went at once to read the labels on the medicines by the bed.

When Helen and I were alone in the living room I tried again to phone Berk, and as he was then at home, I left at once.

I had been inside the house for little more than an hour, but without warning the day had changed. A sea wind had blown in, and a small dense white cloud raced in front of the sun, obscuring it momentarily. There was a chilly edge to the air, and I shivered under my thin blouse. As I turned onto Santa Monica Boulevard, the clouds raced faster, and there was a strange spectacle of patches of sunlight and dark as the swiftly moving clouds obscured the sun. But before I reached Doheny Drive the sun was hidden and the day was gray. The fog began to roll in, and the lights on the Christmas decorations on the streets were pink and fuzzy. Great hoops of fog rolled down Wilshire Boulevard and the buildings were gray masses. The stop-lights and headlights melted into the heavy blanket. Before I reached Westwood, all the landmarks disappeared, and the only guides were the indistinct white lines of traffic lanes. Occasionally a filling station reared up. Otherwise there was no way to distinguish between what was moving and what was standing still.

If Dreiser had seen it he would have been immensely moved. A fog that dissolves the known was as close to his concept of death, I thought, as any I could imagine. He was mystic enough that he might have chosen to die (if his passionate wish to stay and his fear of going had been less strong) under such reality-destroying manifestations. He might have been awed standing on a balcony looking down on it—but in a car, no—possibilities of accidents alarmed him. If he had been younger and there were more time, he could have supported the experience on a foundation made up of a mass of minutiae and shaped it into one of his fictional structures. They were firm and enduring structures. But alas, the middle years of the twentieth century which admired economy of materials found his work amorphous. The last quarter of the century is less bothered by loosely organized surfaces and is impressed by a strong skeleton. He sought lasting materials for his structures; he examined half a dozen cases of ambitious young men murdering pregnant sweethearts before settling on the most representative to build *An American Tragedy*.

In the dense fog I missed my own street. When I finally opened my door the only thing left to remind me of the sweltering part of the day were the streaks of graphite on my arms. Berk was hacking at the Christmas turkey; he dropped the knife and said with relief, "You do it." So I scrubbed my hands and arms in the kitchen sink and stripped the turkey, handed Berk the carcass to carry to the trash can and made sandwiches and coffee, then packed our bag before finally getting under the shower. When the phone rang I was finishing my sandwich.

It was Helen. Dreiser had just died. She said she would wait until after I came to call the undertaker. The spirit, she said, stayed in the body for hours after death. "I want someone with me who loved him when I call them."

I stood for many minutes looking at the room, seeing him there on the sofa with a young schoolteacher he had lured to California during one of Helen's absences, a perplexed young woman who knew not what awaited her as Dreiser escaped to the porch and lay down on the chaise, his tired face visible to us through the window. I could see her wounded eyes and knew that anything I said to dislodge her would make the wound deeper—Berk was better at this, he could modify her picture of herself, making her feel she was adventurous, even worldly, sending her home with a heightened self-image.

I saw Dreiser at the table where we had eaten so many meals, first with Tim and me, then Berk. He had gone with me to Tim's funeral and heard that one tiny cry of anguish squeezed out of me, and had laid his hand on Tim's painted forehead and said, "What have they done to you, Tim?" He had comforted me when we walked out into the bright spring day and I had vowed never to feel spring again.

When we returned to Kings Road, Helen was in charge of herself. She called the undertaker, and presently two men came with a gurney. As the body was wheeled to the open front door, Marguerite Harris burst in. She had been helping Dreiser edit *The Bulwark* earlier in the year, and as an old friend and now editor had assumed a proprietary air toward Dreiser that had finally led to her banishment from the house. Helen had recounted the story with fire in her eyes. "She said it was for American literature she acted. And I said you weren't interested in American literature when you were an expatriate for years in Europe."

She was a thin intense woman whose father, a Swedish maritime man, had invented a device for hoisting cargo which had made him a fortune. Once she had taken me to their estate in Darien, Connecticut, and from the porte-cochère we had walked a long flight of stairs with trophies of the hunt mounted on both walls. She once edited a "little" magazine, *Direction*, for which she had asked me to write a piece on Schindler, but she had deleted Schindler's criticism of the French architect Le Corbusier because, as she told me after publication, too late to object, "I knew Le Corbusier in Paris. I asked him to come to Darien to design a house for me on the property."

A curious scene took place at Dreiser's door. Marguerite threw herself on the body, thus stopping the exit of the gurney through the door. The men wheeling it remonstrated, but as Marguerite clung to the body, moaning, they appealed to Helen. It was Marguerite then who made her intention known. She was going to accompany the body. "That is not permitted," one of the men said, and Berk came forward to try to take Marguerite's hands. To no avail. Marguerite then made a curious boast that seemed to explain nothing. "I drove an ambulance during the war."

Finally Helen, inordinately quiet given the circumstances, said, "Let her go." To this the men protested, "It is not permitted." Helen then repeated it, "Let her go." She said it kindly but as one who was in charge.

I was stunned by her generosity. I could not help ponder the fact that Helen, who had shared him with others for over twenty years in life, was willing to share him after death. She was the one person who saw him now as a public figure rather than as a man, and during the days before the burial I saw her grace in meeting other women in Dreiser's life, some of them so stricken they could hardly speak, leaving it to Helen to keep the conversation going.

Berk and I slept on the sofa in the living room. Before we went to sleep Helen made many trips between Dreiser's study and her second floor retreat, walking past us in the living room to the stairs off the dining room, always with papers in her hand. After we got to sleep we were wakened a number of times by the telephone ringing in Helen's room or the study; if she was halfway between them she ran for the phone, then we heard her faint harried voice. A feeling of secrecy hung in the air. I supposed there were things to sort out in a hurry about her status. I had never questioned her about her life, but I assumed she was not married to Dreiser or it would have been in the papers. But for the twenty-some years I had known her she had been called Mrs. Dreiser.

By eight the next morning Helen's friends had begun to arrive. Lillian Goodman, always accompanied to affairs at the Dreisers by her young black cook, Ophelia, and always bringing in baskets of things from the car. The baskets were heavier this time, for food and grief go hand in hand. But only Ophelia today was openly grieving. Tears fell softly from her eyes as she stood at the kitchen sink peeling a raft of potatoes. Today there was no Dreiser to come in and make her laugh.

I was fitting roasts and vegetables and tidbits into the refrigerator when a voice came from outside the kitchen window. I saw a large barefoot man in fresh white cotton pants and shirt. Ophelia opened the window. His voice was soft and insinuating as he asked about the deceased. He had read the brief obituary; noting that Dreiser was a writer and had died of a heart attack, and his specialty being heart disease, he needed some questions answered for the book he was writing. Now what were his favorite vegetables? Did he eat Brussels sprouts—this vegetable had a curious effect on the heart; had he eaten beets before he was stricken, did he keep his intestines clean? Inside and outside cleanliness were important factors in the health of the heart. His study of medicine had taught him that cleanliness strengthened the heart muscles.

I stood by the refrigerator, my hand on the open door, watching the man and thinking how Dreiser would have loved it. Lillian came into the room. "Who is it?" she demanded, then, "Close the window, Ophelia," then left. "Yes, ma'am," Ophelia said, and we went back to listening to the wonderful strides medicine had made in the vegetable line. I joined Ophelia at the sink and looked into delphinium-blue eyes below almost white eyebrows and heavy white-blond hair. He was a partial albino. He said to me, "You have a sinus that will one day give you trouble unless you are taken off red fish. Tell me, did the deceased eat pomegranates?"

"Close that window!" Lillian cried as she returned to the kitchen. "Go away, old man!"

"Death comes unbidden," the man said, "but we invite it in a hundred ways."

I went to another window to watch the man walk down the drive. Then Helen came to fetch me. Her face was shiny with perspiration. "The reporters are here. I don't know what to tell them."

"Tell them to come back later."

Lillian came to whisper to me, "Did they ever get married?"

"I don't know," I said.

"But I thought she would have told *you!*"

It was sad to realize that others thought me a confidante of Helen's—and I had always assumed that Lillian, one of Helen's many singing teachers, would have the answers.

"Go and help her," Lillian begged.

I did. But I was uncomfortable, thinking I might have to see her publicly separated from a name she had used so long.

A reporter was asking her the date of her marriage to Dreiser and she refused to answer. He pointed out that when a famous man marries it is news, and no paper had carried the story.

She gave them the date, June of the previous year, 1944. Then they wanted to know whether she too had joined the Communist Party, and if she had approved of Dreiser joining.

Helen stood up to them badly. Yet when they were gone she startled me by saying that they were married in a small town in the northwest, and Dreiser had used only his first name, Herman, not Theodore.

The burial was delayed for a week, first by the holidays, then by a gravediggers' strike. During that time two camps had developed which wanted to dominate the burial service. Helen was determined that neither side prevail. The Communists were the most assertive, but the religionists proved in the end to be as strong. While Helen represented justice, she went on shopping sprees. She was abetted in this by Dreiser's niece, Vera, a very large woman with a Ph.D. in psychology, who arrived at Kings Road soon after Dreiser's death. She was an impressive figure with her long flaming red hair and stylish clothes. She and Helen arranged for a Hollywood Boulevard shop called Nancy's to be opened to them on a Sunday, and they came back with an assortment of black veils and dresses, a black fur jacket and even black nightgowns.

During this time the offices of pallbearers were evenly divided among the religious, the political and friends. And Helen and Vera went to Forest Lawn to choose a plot large enough for a space for Helen. And there were sessions with the beauticians at Forest Lawn about whether the face should be tinted or the nails polished; a sculptor was brought in to make a cast of the head and the right hand. (I have somewhere a plaster cast of the hand.) I recalled that Dreiser had once sent me to interview morticians to find out their lore and charges. After one dismal attempt, I had sent Berk in my place; he thoroughly enjoyed it but, having taken few notes, was inclined to build it into a dinner-party story rather than material for an assault on a "profession."

During the days of waiting for an end to the gravediggers' strike, Marguerite, on the religionists' side, came frequently to the house, but finding little comfort inside had gone out to the garden. Once I saw her walking, her hands thrust into the pockets of her pea jacket (a holdover from war styles which favored the military), her head sunk low in her sweater, and I had thought of Lucy Snowe, the little governess in Charlotte Brontë's *Villette*, pacing up and down the alley of plane trees sorrowing for a love that did not bloom.

Once I found her sitting in Dreiser's chair at his desk. It was a morning when Helen had phoned early to ask if Berk would accompany her to Forest Lawn where last-minute decisions were to be made; then she asked if I had any suggestions for words to go on the tombstone. I said there was perhaps something in one of his own poems and would be glad to look. Berk and I drove in together, and I went to Dreiser's study where Helen had laid out Dreiser's poems on his desk.

And there was Marguerite sitting in his chair. She was

unhappy to have me break into her reverie. I asked her help, but she was not responsive. I read several poems aloud, then as one of them reminded me of "The Red Slayer," which Dreiser had liked, I quoted a few lines ". . . if the slayer thinks he slays and the slain thinks he be slain . . ." etc., etc. Her scorn was infinite. "Such ideas no longer interested him," she said.

In the last days I had seen her turn a scornful face to Helen many times. Marguerite seemed certain that she alone understood Dreiser.

I disregarded her scorn and went on reading. Presently she told me that Dreiser had experienced a conversion while working on *The Bulwark*. She seemed on the point of going on but didn't. I wondered if she was about to tell me that she too was born again.

Berk also had a rough morning. He was appalled at the way Helen had been seduced into a lavish funeral. Among the messages that came for Helen while she was out was one from Upton Sinclair declining to be a pallbearer, explaining that he and Dreiser were acquaintances, not close friends.

It was too much for Helen. She burst into tears. "We went several times a year, at their invitation! He and Teddy had the warmest of relations!" I recalled the number of books on spiritualism Mrs. Sinclair had pressed upon Dreiser, which he had turned over to me to read. They had been heavy going.

We were standing on the front porch, leaning against the rail and facing the fine modernist Dodge house Irving Gill had designed in 1916. "Jewish architecture," Helen said.

"There is no such thing," I responded.

She had been uncomfortable at the Schindler house when Pauline Schindler had asked me to bring them to a Sunday breakfast. Helen and Dreiser were dismayed by the concrete floors on a level with the garden, the uncurtained sliding glass, the tilt-up concrete-slab walls, the unpainted redwood. Dreiser had seen the drafting room once or twice when he had come to bring me books to read. I remembered the roaring laughs of Schindler and Dreiser as they mentioned some political gaffe.

At the breakfast Dreiser had been ill at ease until we

went to sit in the garden; there he began questioning a scientist from Cal Tech who had been too shy to speak while we were at the table. I don't remember what field he was in, only that he possessed some knowledge that fascinated Dreiser and that the scientist was delighted to pass on. I do remember that we were all intensely interested in the two-way conversation—except Pauline. She interrupted more than once, but Dreiser rudely disregarded her and went on with his questions. Being disregarded, she called on others present to express opinions. "What do you say to this," she asked one guest, then another. Guests looked at their watches and remembered it was time to go. She had broken up her own party.

Once during the wait for the burial Pauline came to the Dreiser door to offer to select the music for the service. Helen declined the offer.

Finally the day came. Berk and I rode with Helen and Vera Dreiser in a long black limousine to Forest Lawn. We had worn out our grief and our patience in the details. Dreiser had liked to stand up at funerals and speak for a friend. The spontaneous words springing from love and appreciation were missing at his own funeral, as if it had been reworked so often it became over-designed.

I said to Helen, "I don't think I can go through with this." But Vera was prepared. She opened a vial, shook out a tablet, and from her purse took a flask of water and a tiny cup for me. I seemed to be the only one not up to the ordeal. I could see then why women wore black veils.

A Congregational minister spoke, somewhat hesitantly as if he were under scrutiny. He was. Charles Chaplin read the poem I had helped select from Dreiser's book, *Moods*; John Howard Lawson was very much at ease as he matched the dates Dreiser had written his books with social and political events, which interested me very much, but as he wore on he became dry and doctrinaire.

From a distance, I wonder often that ones who did not live through the intensely political '30s should seek a reason for Dreiser's joining the Communist Party. I am even more surprised that anyone should assume that he was led into it by friends. No one persuaded him; if anyone had tried I feel sure it would have made him question his decision. He wanted to make a statement about the uneven distribution of wealth, and he did. What I have wondered is why his written statement of his reason for joining was left to someone else to write; it is not in his style, and nothing sounds less like him.

After we drove back from Forest Lawn, Berk and I stood for a moment with Lillian Goodman in front of the house.

"A fine property," she said judgmentally.

I often got more of what happened from the *Los Angeles Times* after that. The safe-deposit box was opened. It was filled with gold. Dreiser had left it there after the order came in the '30s to turn gold in. A percentage of his estate was left for the education of "Negroes," which I believe was not fulfilled. Little or nothing was left to Dreiser's family, which brought me a letter from Dr. Vera Dreiser, asking my help in breaking the will. I did not answer the letter.

Helen domiciled her nephew in the apartment over the garage. He was a slight, sallow lad who was an active member of Jehovah's Witnesses, going out each day to bring people to the faith. In spite of his religious fundamentalism so close at hand, Helen became more worldly. I saw little of her for some months, then she invited me to lunch, allowing me to choose the place. I chose The Players on Sunset, at one of the tables on the terrace. She had gained quite a bit of weight, and her breath was short. She ordered a pink lady and I ordered the same thing I always had at The Players, a martini and jellied consommé and cold poached salmon; she had a salad and chocolate mousse. Then, assuming that I walked the edge, she asked me to collaborate with her on a book about her life with Dreiser. I had to decline. She named a good fee, but I resisted. I realized as I saw the beads of sweat on her pancake makeup that to sit in the sun was the last thing she wanted; she had assented in the hope of my agreeing.

One evening after leaving the Schindler office, I stopped off at her house with books belonging to Dreiser. Her nephew had seen me walk to the front door from his garage tower and came to tell me that Helen was out of town. I suspected then that the nephew was left to guard the "fine" property.

[37]

We met at another lunch, and this time she chose the place, a dark restaurant in Beverly Hills. At the table next to us was George Sanders. Helen told me she had a lover she wanted me to meet—an Indian whose name was, I believe, Firoze. He had come to America on a scholarship, had failed in his studies and Helen was now helping him look for a field which would fit his unusual talents. She thought it was in the category of "speech." They had been recording speeches he had made and she wanted my advice. I asked where he had made his speeches and the subject. He had made no speeches and he had no subject.

She showed a marked loss of breath as she described the ecstasy she had experienced when they made love. She had gained even more weight, and her double chin trembled as she continued. She asked that I come alone, without Berk, to hear Firoze's voice—this was to be a work session for the three of us.

I went. I suppose he was handsome. I could see only the flash of his very white teeth and wonder if the sparkle in his eyes came from some kind of drops. I had rarely seen anyone so vain. Helen was watching my reaction. I thought then of things she had suffered at Dreiser's hands and tried to hide my dismay. Helen told me when he left the room that he was not easy to know, and urged me not to be "put off by his good looks."

I asked so many direct questions about where he would use speech, once perfected, that Helen saw I was a novice in the area of speech. What she had not wanted to say right out, I soon saw, was that she was grooming him for Hollywood.

We met a few times after that, but it was hard to pretend that Firoze was not a charlatan. By 1950, when Berk got cancer, Firoze had had no success. Helen phoned from time to time. Berk finally recovered, and we rented our house to a visiting professor at UCLA and spent nine months in Cuernavaca, where Berk played chess every day at a barbershop across the street from the Quo Vadis funeral home. When we returned to Santa Monica, we learned that Helen had had a stroke and was then living with her sister in Oregon. I wrote her there, and her sister replied in Helen's name—a letter starting "Hello there!" When she died of a later stroke we were invited to the service at Forest Lawn. Who should come up to me but a very seedy-looking Firoze. He said, "I had no idea I was in her will, it came as a shock." He dropped a carnation in her grave. I saw him one last time. He was a contestant on the Groucho Marx show, no longer seedy. Dreiser would have been astonished to see some of his money spent on Firoze's wardrobe. And on Jehovah's Witnesses. Yes, he had been an agent for the redistribution of wealth.

'THIS GUY WOULDN'T GIVE YOU THE PARSLEY OFF HIS FISH'

Gary Giddins

I became interested in Jack Benny in the early 1970s, when I saw him live. The occasion was a New York concert appearance by George Burns, who, after several years of relative inactivity, was embarking on his highly successful comeback. Benny came along to introduce him. It took him about ten minutes and I don't remember a word he said. But I've never forgotten that as soon as he walked out—body flouncing, arms swinging to breast-pocket level, eyes glazed with stoic chagrin—I was convulsed with laughter, an effect his TV appearances had never had on me. If Burns was good, Benny was magical. During the past year my impressions of that evening have been confirmed almost nightly, thanks to the Christian Broadcasting Network. CBN harvests souls by day, but by night it lures prospective recruits with back-to-back reruns of old programs by those same wily Jewish comedians, Burns and Benny. After a year of late-night viewing, often of shows that I recalled from childhood with a rather indifferent fondness, I've become a Jack Benny zealot, recounting bits and anecdotes, hoarding pregnant pauses and martyred stares, and even composing this tract. Here was a radiantly funny man, whose humor stands up against all odds.

The fact that I can't recall anything Benny said in concert is germane, since he may be the only great comedian in history who isn't associated with a single witticism. He got his biggest laughs with two exclamations—"Now cut that out!" and "Well!"—and impeccably timed silences. When he died in 1974, I watched the news stories for samples of his jokes. There weren't any. The one bit they frequently played came from radio: Benny, out for a stroll, hears footsteps behind him. A holdup man says, "Your money or your life." Benny says . . . nothing, for a very long time. That's the joke. But it isn't the topper. The holdup man repeats his threat and Benny shouts, "I'm

Mimi Gross

thinking it over!" On the original radio broadcast, he
followed through with yet a third variation on the theme:
the holdup man gets abusive and Benny, a model of agitated innocence, responds, "If you wanted money, why
didn't you just ask for it?" Needless to say, none of this is
funny if you don't know the character of Jack Benny.
What an arduous exercise it would be to try and explain
Benny's unprecedented and unequaled success in Ameri-

[*41*]

can comedy to an audience unfamiliar with the sound of his voice or the pan on his face. Happily, that task is not yet necessary.

Everyone I know knows Benny, though the degree of knowledge depends on age. Those under forty remember him from TV; those over forty remember him chiefly from radio (specifically, a Sunday-night-at-seven ritual so widespread that in 1943 NBC declared the time slot his no matter what sponsor bought it). Benny was a comic institution for about forty years and apparently had no detractors—though Benny wouldn't have been too sure. In his later years, an insurance group eager to use him in its newspaper ads hired a marketing researcher to measure his popularity. The company was elated by the results: he was loved by 97 percent of the American public—a higher number than for anyone else. "What did I do to that three percent?" Benny wanted to know.

Yet the character he created and developed with inspired tenacity all those years—certainly one of the longest runs ever by an actor in the same role—was that of a mean, vainglorious skinflint: a pompous ass at best, a tiresome bore at near best. To find his equal, you have to leave the realm of monologists and delve into the novel for a recipe that combines Micawber and Scrooge, with perhaps a dash of Lady Catherine de Bourgh and a soupçon of Chichikov; or, better still, a serial character like Sherlock Holmes, who proved so resilient that not even Conan Doyle could knock him off. The Benny character was no less fully rounded—an obsessed fan, armed with hundreds of broadcasts, might construct a reasonably detailed biography of him. On the other hand, no one believed Doyle was Holmes, while many people believed Benny was "Benny," a phenomenon that amazed the actor as much as a literary parallel would later distress Philip Roth. A lawyer once dunned him with outraged letters for refusing to pay Rochester his piddling back wages (a plot contrivance on radio); the exasperated Benny finally wrote him, "I only hope you're making in one year what Rochester makes in one month."

Many of the veteran entertainers who pioneered on radio, exchanging a string of vaudeville theaters for millions of living rooms, were surprised by the new audience's credulity and the implications. A fan once asked Gracie Allen if Benny was really cheap; she responded, "Am I stupid?" Yet Benny, like Roth, courted trouble by injecting just enough reality into his work to confuse the issue, and by sustaining his conceit—this, perhaps, was his greatest achievement—through all the fashions that attended the Depression, the Second World War, the affluent society, and the switch to television. Once he established his image, he remained intransigently loyal to it. No but-seriously-folks closers or nice-guy apologias for him. Unlike every other comedian you can name, he never stepped out of character. He seems to have sensed early on the new medium's potential as a mirror for the more commonplace foibles of a mass audience. In any case, he emerged over the decades as a comic staple who could bind the sensibilities of several generations.

Meredith wrote of Molière that he "did not paint in raw realism [but] seized his characters firmly for the purpose of the play, stamped them in the idea, and, by slightly raising and softening the object of his study . . . generalized upon it so as to make it permanently human." Benny's fictions evolved so humanly that the actors who incarnated them ended up adopting the names of their roles. Eddie Anderson had many credits before he joined the Benny crew, but was thereafter known in private life as Rochester. Owen Patrick McNulty legally changed his name to Dennis Day after his first four years with Benny; his family convinced him to change it back, but he performed exclusively as Day. Sayde Marks, Benny's wife, assumed the name of the dumb gentile shopgirl she played and remained Mary Livingstone Benny even after retirement. Benny also underwent a name change, though not to suit a script. During his apprentice years in vaudeville, his real name, Benjamin Kubelsky, prompted two law suits—the first from a violinist named Kubelik who thought a violin-playing Kubelsky would confuse people; the second from Ben Bernie, who complained that the resulting pseudonym, Benny K. Benny, was a deception designed to cash in on Bernie's fame. ("Now Jack Osterman is suing me," Benny used to tell friends, referring to a comic of the day.)

If the Benny character looms as a kind of metafiction, it isn't in Victorian novels that its genesis is to be found. Benny virtually invented situation comedy, and like most significant innovations, his was a natural outgrowth of local traditions: the American stereotypes and modes of entertainment predominant at the turn of the century. When Benny came along, minstrelsy's ritualistic subordination of individual performers to a faceless—or blackfaceless—group was on the wane, but the idiom's conventions had a lasting influence. The minstrel olio was the first American variety show, typifying theatrical fragmentation and creating such enduring specialties as the Irish tenor (who traditionally sang the first solo) the stout announcer and buffoon (Mr. Interlocutor), sketch dialogues (Mr. Tambo and Mr. Bones), and grotesque caricatures of every racial and ethnic group.

Vaudeville, its immediate heir, freed the specialty acts from an oppressive scheme, not to mention blackface, and forced the performers to assume more individual identities. Still, nostalgia for the old minstrel troupes lingered. The first variety show ever broadcast was a 1924 performance by Dailey Paskman's Radio Minstrels, and tributes to minstrel stars regularly turned up on radio and in movies through the mid-1940s. During the broadcast première for the 1940 film *Love Thy Neighbor*, the banter between Benny and Fred Allen turned into a kind of minstrel badinage, which prompted Benny to ad-lib (and fluff!) a reference to Mr. Tambo: "We'll go right into a black routine," he said, imitating the endmen laugh, "Yuk, yuk, yuk." He had a right to patronize the old style. The best of the untethered, unmasked comics on the vaudeville circuit had long since originated more precise and inventive personae, often working in pairs—a straight man with a laugh-getter. Sketch humor had come into its own.

Into that world, enter Benjamin Kubelsky, a very young and eager violinist *manqué*. He was born on St. Valentine's Day, 1894, in Waukegan, Illinois, the son of Russian immigrants and Orthodox Jews. At six he began violin lessons and at eight was acclaimed a local prodigy; at twelve, he persuaded a friend to get him a job in a theater and worked his way up from ticket taker to usher to musician in the pit orchestra. He must have been pretty good,

[*44*]

because Minnie Marx tried to hire him as music director when her sons played the theater, an offer his parents made him decline. In 1912, Benny was expelled from high school and went on the road with a flashy pianist and veteran performer named Cora Salisbury. When she retired after the season, he teamed with another pianist and in 1916 the act of Benny and Lyman played the Palace Theater at $250 a week. They did eleven minutes of musical parody, and although *Variety* called it a "pleasing turn for an early spot," they flopped. Benny returned home when he learned his mother was dying; a year later he joined the Navy, where he devised a routine with the famous novelty composer and pianist Zez Confrey. More significantly, he also did his first monologue in a Navy show that eventually toured the Midwest. By the time he returned to the civilian circuit, Benny was concentrating on getting laughs while holding on to the violin as a prop. He was billed "Benny K. Benny: Fiddle Funology," then "Jack Benny: Fun with a Fiddle," and finally "A Few Minutes with Jack Benny."

Robert Benchley praised his cool bravado and subtlety when Benny returned to the Palace in 1924, but others panned him for what they construed as egotism and aloofness. Benny was studying other comics to learn how to sustain narratives and raiding joke books for one-liners, including occasional "cheap jokes"—e.g., "I took my girl to dinner, and she laughed so hard at one of my jokes that she dropped her tray." Nevertheless, he was regularly employed. Nora Bayes hired and romanced him, and the Shuberts installed him in the revue *Great Temptations*, on which tour he courted and married eighteen-year-old Sadye Marks. Never a major vaudeville star, Benny appeared in three unsuccessful movies and worked mostly as an emcee during the next few years. Yet he was making good money in 1930—at least fifteen hundred dollars a week—as the comic in *Earl Carroll's Vanities*, when he faced up to the fact that vaudeville was through and began looking beyond it.

Ed Sullivan gave Benny his first radio shot in 1931; he opened with, "Ladies and gentlemen, this is Jack Benny talking. There will be a slight pause while you say, 'Who cares?'" No one did, but the following summer his agent got him a job as emcee on a show featuring George Olson's band. Benny experimented with topical humor, and began kidding movies and the sponsor ("I was driving across the Sahara desert when I came across a party of people . . . ready to perish from lack of liquid. I gave them each a glass of Canada Dry Ginger Ale, and not one of them said it was a bad drink"). By summer's end, he had made a terrifying discovery. Radio consumed material faster than he could get it. A joke that might have worked for a whole season in vaud was good for only one night on radio.

In 1934, at age forty, Benny saw the promised land. His guide was a writer George Burns had introduced him to named Harry Conn, who seems to have played Herman Mankiewicz to Benny's Orson Welles. Accounts differ about Conn's contribution, since they parted bitterly a few years later, but there is no doubt—Benny himself was emphatic about it—that Conn was instrumental in conceiving the brainstorm that revolutionized radio: situation comedy based on the lives of the performers, complete with sophisticated sound effects. Instead of revue skits and strings of jokes, each show would be a variation on a constant theme: life with Jack Benny. It was Conn's misfortune to underestimate the importance of Benny's delivery, timing, personality, and script-editing in making the initial concept work. Once the idea was established, writers could be replaced, as Conn was when his demands grew unreasonable. But before that happened, he and Benny came up with many of the motifs that would become the star's trademarks: the scenes set in his home, the Irish tenor, the cheerful announcer, the dumb girlfriend, the obnoxious band leader, and the *reductio ad absurdum* of shows that depicted only a mock rehearsal for the show on the air. It was not an immediate hit; in 1934, the *New York World Telegram* named Benny the most popular comedian on radio, but two sponsors dropped him. Not until 1936 and 1937, when Rochester and Phil Harris joined the cast, did the Benny phenomenon take hold.

When Benny surpassed Eddie Cantor in the ratings in 1937 as the most popular star on radio—a position he maintained for most of the next fifteen years—he rang the death knell, symbolic and real, for vaudeville. Cantor later remarked, "He made all the other comics throw away their joke files." His popularity had no equal in radio, then or ever. Utterly stymied by Benny's success on NBC, CBS produced an ambitious series of topical dramas for the Sunday-at-seven slot, because no sponsor would buy the time. (The notion of combating popularity with quality seems rather quaint today: CBS, which bought Benny's radio show in 1948 and made a fortune with it, canceled him on TV in 1964, when "Gomer Pyle" beat him in the ratings.) As Fred Allen told Maurice Zolotow in 1950, "Practically all comedy shows on the radio today owe their structure to Benny's conceptions. He was the first to realize that the listener is not in a theater with a thousand other people but is in a small circle at home. . . . Benny also was the first comedian in radio to realize that you could get big laughs by ridiculing yourself instead of your stooges. Benny became a fall guy for everybody else on the show." Or as Benny put it, "The whole humor of Jack Benny is— here's a guy with plenty of money, he's got a valet, he's always traveling around, and yet he's strictly a jerk."

Some jerk. Everyone knows a few things about radio's Jack Benny: he was eternally thirty-nine, cheap, bald, self-admiring, drove a dilapidated Maxwell (is there any other kind?), lived alone with a valet named Rochester, and had irresistibly blue eyes. With the possible exception of the last, none of this was true of the real Jack Benny; in fact, he had to eliminate the bald jokes when he moved to television. Henri Bergson wrote, "The comic comes into being just when society and the individual, freed from the worry of self-preservation, begin to regard themselves as works of art." Benny honed that generalization to a lunatic specificity: he made himself a clown by acting the part of an artwork. No matter how many humiliations he had to endure, his self-esteem remained untouched; like cartoon characters who fall off cliffs, are momentarily flattened, and quickly restored, Benny and his vanity were emboldened by adversity. The better the audience knew that, the less he had to do for a laugh. *He* was the laugh. All he had to do was trigger a few buzzwords. A carnival pitchman promises him a quarter if he can correctly guess Benny's age, and guesses thirty-nine.

Benny simply gazes helplessly, and the audience is right with him, agonizing over his hopeless choice between the quarter and his vanity.

He opened one television show by striding center stage and calmly announcing, "Well, here I am again, standing in front of millions of viewers, completely relaxed, and not a worry in the world. Now, some critics will attribute this to my years of experience; others will say it's the temperament of a true artist. Personally, I feel that it's nauseating confidence." Right away, the audience likes him. Yet he continues in a mode of fake candor, as though he were stepping out of character: "My psychology in starting out with a remark like that is to get you people to dislike me immediately. Then when you realize you're disliking a nice, harmless, elderly man, this gives you a guilt complex. Guilt leads to sympathy, sympathy leads to laughter, and laughter leads to applause. And then when the applause is over, you go home and I go to the bank. That's when I laugh."

Money, and Benny's affection for it, was his most successful leitmotif, one that required some courage to pursue, since it underscored the most persistent of negative Jewish stereotypes (and yet another convention of minstrelsy). Of course, by carrying it off so well, Benny helped to dispel penuriousness as an anti-Jewish barb. Still, this was a matter of concern to him. In 1945, at the height of the fad for radio contests, his show offered a prize to the listener who could best explain "Why I Hate Jack Benny" in twenty-five words or less. Benny approved the idea, but worried about inviting anti-Semitic responses and asked that they be pulled. Of 270,000 entries, only three were offensive. Benny's Jewishness, in the context of his comedy, is a rather complicated issue, and the manner in which he broached it suggests the degree to which the Jews of his generation felt, in Bergson's phrase, "freed from the worry of self-preservation."

Before 1900, Jewish grotesquerie was a familiar ingredient in the entertainment world, but Jewish humor that wasn't self-deflating simply didn't exist on the American stage. "There were plenty of excellent Jewish performers," according to vaudeville's chronicler Douglas

Gilbert, "but they were doing Dutch, blackface, or singing and dancing acts. Some of them were good Irish comedians. Indeed, Weber and Fields at one time did a neat
Irish act." Gilbert traces the emergence of Jewish humor
to the Mauve Decade success of one Frank Bush, whose
doggerel included:

> Oh, my name is Solomon Moses I'm a bully Sheeny man,
> I always treat my customers the very best what I can
> I keep a clothing store 'way down on Baxter Street,
> Where you can get your clothing I sell so awful cheap.

But no single performer can liberate a people's pragmatic
instinct to keep their ethnicity under cover. Something
more, a confident sense of assimilation, is necessary. Years
later, Al Jolson seemed to personify and answer that
need: first he changed his name and hid behind blackface, then he wiped it off to emerge as a celebrity whose
renown in the Jazz Age was rivaled only by that of Babe
Ruth and Charles Lindbergh. As Jack Robin (in *The Jazz
Singer*), he was the Augie March of his time—a fast-
talking all-American hustler who could discard or employ
his Jewish roots with equal facility. Which isn't to say that
Jewish entertainers weren't apprehensive about their gradual acceptance as Jews; even in the Hollywood of the
'30s and '40s, Jewish producers avoided Jewish subjects
and Jewish actors played Italians.

Benny's ambivalence about Jewish humor runs throughout his program. Mary Livingstone, who variously turned
up as his wife, girlfriend, or just another prickly opponent,
had no Jewish characteristics. Benny drew directly on
his own Jewishness only rarely. In a TV episode, he audi-
tions actors to play his father in a movie to be based on
his life. One actor identifies himself, with a thick burr, as
Kevin O'Houlihan. Benny stares haplessly into the camera
before blurting, "NEXT!" On a radio show, guest star Bing
Crosby told of how he'd been rejected by a country club
for being an actor. Benny ad-libbed, "How would you like
to be an actor *and* a Jew?" To his friends, he was the
quintessential Jewish monologist. The harmonica vir-
tuoso Larry Adler, who toured with him and considered
himself a disciple, told me that Benny "not only epitomized

[*49*]

Jewish storytelling and intonation, but showed everyone else how to do it." That intonation comes across more clearly in off-camera interviews and, oddly enough, his highly amusing letters—some of which are collected in Irving A. Fein's *Jack Benny: An Intimate Biography*—than on the air. Nevertheless, the Benny program employed two Jewish dialecticians—Sam Hearn in the early years, and later the more enduring Mr. Kitzel (played by Artie Auerbach).

A harmless, middle-aged man who speaks with a chirpy Ellis Island twang and wears a glassy-eyed smile, Mr. Kitzel is the *only* recurring character who doesn't treat Benny like a jerk. No matter how harrassed he is, Benny is always delighted to hear Mr. Kitzel's "Hallo, Mr. Benny," and to play straight man for his corny jokes. Mr. Kitzel isn't nearly as funny as the other cast members, but for Benny he represents one bright moment amid a regimen of humiliations. On an early TV show, Benny takes the Beverly Hills Beavers, a boys' club, to the carnival. Mr. Kitzel plays a utility man, who keeps turning up in different guises—first selling hot dogs, then in a gorilla suit, and so forth. The show ends when the boys want to see the belly dancer, and Benny says he doesn't think it would be right. We zoom in on the dancer's face, and hear Mr. Kitzel's voice as she lip synchs, "It's all right, Mr. Benny, it's only me." Benny turns an amazed smile to the camera, shrugs his shoulders, and leads the pack into her tent.

Benny was probably wise not to make too many direct Jewish allusions. After all, his alter ego embodied enough standard Jewish stereotypes to effect not only the anti-Semitic backlash he feared but intimations of the self-denigrating humor of early vaud. He toted a violin, ogled himself like a girl, mistreated the help, and hid his money in a dungeon surrounded by a moat. Yet he played the role with such originality and brio that his failings seemed at once too particularized and too broad to represent an ethnic group. His moot sexuality is a good example. In a TV episode, he explains to Rochester why the studio wants to film his life: "I wasn't exactly the first choice, but they found out mine was the only life they wouldn't have to censor. [Intent pause] Darn it!" Though he was eternally youthful (else the age jokes wouldn't have seemed quite

so crafty), and, at least in his early years, a great success
with women, Benny so convincingly embodied the ineffec-
tual fop that he became a professional neuter—sexless
even when playing opposite Carole Lombard in his best
film, *To Be or Not to Be.*

On radio, Benny was sexually anchored by Mary; on
TV, he became slightly hysterical (floozy Barbara
Nichols played his occasional date). He was surrounded
by sexuality that was vulgar (Phil Harris), sly (Rochester), and placid (guest couples such as the Ronald Col-
mans on radio or the Jimmy Stewarts on TV). But Benny
remained a naif, a momma's boy without a momma, or,
more precisely and odd, a momma's boy with a black male
servant for a momma. Yet unlike Johnny Carson, who, for
all Benny's obvious influence on him, is sexually cold and
untouchable, Benny was warm and intensely physical—
constantly patting the hands of his female guests and
wrapping his arms around the shoulders of his male
friends. (Benny prefigured the "Tonight" show host in his
movie *The Big Broadcast of 1937.* He played a radio host
named Jack Carson who boosts his ratings by having a
couple get married on the air, à la Tiny Tim.)

Most of Benny's character traits evolved accidentally.
If a certain joke worked one week, he played a variation
on it the next. The age jokes, for example, didn't start until
he was fifty-five, and a nurse in a sketch asked him his
age; he paused and said thirty-six. It got a big laugh, so
he remained thirty-six for the rest of the season. The following year, he was thirty-seven; in the next, thirty-eight.
He decided to freeze at thirty-nine because it's a funnier
number than forty. Of course, his most fertile subject was
his stinginess, an angle that produced countless variants.
Here is a small garland of them:

He pays his agent nine percent.
He keeps Mary's fur in his refrigerator: it's "a better deal
  than the storage company."
He plays a one-hundred-dollar Stradivarius—"one of
  the few *ever* made in Japan."
For fifteen years, he drove a 1927 Maxwell—sound effects by Mel Blanc—which he reluctantly sacrificed

to the wartime need for scrap metal. Reborn as a bomber, it made the same sputtering noises.

When traveling, he pawns his parrot rather than leave it at the pet shop at seventy-five cents a day.

He stays at the Acme Plaza in New York—the basement suite, which "underlooks the park."

The act of pulling a dime out of his pocket produces suction.

He discovers his tux is stained. Rochester: "That's what you get when you rent a dress suit." Benny: "Well, let's be careful who we rent it out to."

When Fred Allen visits him in the 1945 movie *It's in the Bag*, Allen finds a hatcheck girl in the closet and a cigarette machine in the living room. "This guy wouldn't give you the parsley off his fish," Allen mutters.

Benny's secretary calls a cab for him, and is told it'll take two hours. "Are they that busy?" he asks. "No, they say they'd like time to think it over."

A terrorist throws a rock through Benny's window with a note that warns, "Get out of town before it's too late." "Hmmm," Benny muses, "just a note, no ticket."

At the race track, Benny says, "I hope I win, I can sure use the money." Mary: "Why? You've never used any before."

On TV, Benny lives in characteristic middle-class, sitcom modesty—his house and those of his movie-star neighbors could easily be exchanged for the dwellings on "Father Knows Best" or "Leave It to Beaver." On radio, however, his vault is somehow located in a subterranean passage, protected by a drawbridge, a moat, a creaking door, a guard who hasn't seen daylight since the Civil War, and finally a combination safe. "You must have a million dollars in the vault," Mary assures him when he worries about money. "I know," he says, "but I hate to break up the serial numbers."

Benny's cast of characters was fine-tuned by the same hit-and-miss system that produced his most enduring conceits. Some performers remained with him for decades. The most celebrated was Eddie Anderson, a vaudeville star whose appearance as a Pullman porter in a 1937 episode was so successful that he was brought back as Benny's valet. He continued as Benny's long-suffering but shrewd and frequently impertinent sidekick until he retired twenty-one years later. As Rochester Van Jones, Anderson delivered a brazenly hoarse counterpoint to Benny's spry chatter, and usually got the best lines. On his day off, Rochester might don an outrageously gaudy smoking jacket, sprawl on a chaise sipping mint julep and smoking a cigar, refusing even to answer the phone. But he earned those days. Rochester had to dip his typewriter ribbon in grape juice because Benny wouldn't replace it. When Benny tried to talk him out of installing his own phone, assuring him he could use his, Rochester said, "I know, boss, but look at it this way. Suppose the house is burning down and I haven't got any change?" They didn't quite love each other; but they were thoroughly at home in each other's company. One Christmas, Rochester asked a department store clerk to help him choose a gift.

Clerk: What kind of man is your boss? Is he the athletic type?

Rochester: No.

C: The intellectual type?

R: Well, no.

C: The executive type?

R: Hmmm, no.

C: Perhaps the outdoor type?

R: NO!

C: Well, perhaps he's the playboy type.

R: (laughs)

C: I'm afraid there isn't very much left.

R: That's him!

It was a source of pride to Benny and his staff that when the NAACP and other groups condemned the portrayal of blacks in the media in the 1950s, there was no protest about Rochester. Nor could anyone doubt Benny's personal feelings: in 1940 he refused to perform or board in segregated establishments, and in 1968 he returned $17,000 rather than fulfill a touring contract that would have taken him to South Africa. Yet his public image was utterly nonpolitical. Indeed, his refusal to link his comedy to serious issues made him especially valuable in the 1960s, when everyone else made a show of taking sides. Benny continued to fulfill the comedian's contract to focus on manners rather than morals. I've been able to find only one instance of his making a political statement: "I am neither a Democrat nor a Republican. I'm a registered Whig. If it was good enough for President Fillmore, it's good enough for me. Now don't laugh about President Fillmore. After all, he kept us out of Vietnam."

I don't imagine there will ever be another generation of entertainers who can sustain the loyalties of successive generations as Benny and a handful of his contemporaries did. President Kennedy is said to have been eager to meet Benny because he recalled the Sunday evening ritual in the 1930s when his father made the whole family sit around the radio. The tempo of life, the dissolution of family entertainment, and the increasing disposability of popular culture have imposed new imperatives and standards. Does this mean that Benny himself will simply fade away? Will the very character-induced economy that enabled him to get laughs simply by staring into the camera undermine the effectiveness of his programs when the character is no longer widely known? One innovative cultural critic, John A. Kouwenhoven, has suggested that the strengths of American art lie in its open-endedness, in its fulfillment of Emerson's dictum that man is great "not in his goals but in his transitions." Situation comedies, like other American variations in high and low culture—including skyscrapers, jazz, *Leaves of Grass*, comic strips, the Constitution, and soap operas (to use some of Kouwenhoven's examples)—derive their integrity not from a notion of finalization but from process and continuity. They are designed with interchangeable parts, to be altered and disposed. What survives is the motivating idea, the germinal core.

Benny himself was a remarkably adaptable figure in the entertainment world, taking every technological twist and popular fashion in stride and refusing to wallow in sentimentality and nostalgia. Yet his radio shows are largely inaccessible to contemporary tastes, as are virtually all radio shows from the pre-TV era—except to satisfy those same maudlin longings Benny rejected. The TV shows are another story, chiefly because we still live in a television age. Ironically, despite the visual humor and the irresistible physical presence of Benny, they are not as richly made as the radio series. But they will suffice to keep Benny from becoming primarily a show-business metaphor—much as films kept Will Rogers and W. C. Fields from becoming mere metaphors respectively of cracker-barrel wisdom and inebriated impudence. In the relaxed ambiance of Benny's TV skits, a singular clown holds his ground—"completely relaxed, and not a worry in the world." The viewer who hasn't been primed on the fine points of Benny's world will pick them up soon enough; though even a naïve viewer may find Benny's preposterous carriage and delivery sufficient to evoke a deeply, and perhaps unexpectedly, satisfied smile. It's not the situations in Benny's comedy that compel attention; it's Benny himself—or, more accurately, Benny qua "Benny"—a peculiarly durable character.

On Not Knowing the Half of It
My Jewish Self
HOMAGE TO TELEGRAPHIST JACOBS

Christopher Hitchens

In the early days of the December that my father was to die, my younger brother brought me the news that I was a Jew. I was then a transplanted Englishman in America, married, with one son and, though unconsoled by any religion, a nonbelieving member of two Christian churches. On hearing the tidings, I was pleased to find that I was pleased.

One of the things about being English, born and bred, is the blessed lack of introspection that it can confer. An interest in genealogy is an admitted national quirk, but where this is not merely snobbish or mercenary, it indulges our splendid and unique privilege of traceable, stable continuity. Englishmen do not have much time for *angst* about their "roots," or much of an inclination to the identity crisis. My paternal grandfather had a favorite joke, about a Wessex tenant in dispute with his squire. "I hope you realize," says the squire, "that my ancestors came with William the Conqueror." "Yes," returns the yeoman. "We were waiting for you." It was from this millennial loam that, as far as I knew, I had sprung. I had long since lapsed my interest in family history as being unlikely to prove any connection to title or fortune. For something to say, I would occasionally dilate on the pure Cornish origins of the name Hitchens, which had once been explained to me by A. L. Rowse in the course of a stuporous dinner at Oxford. The Celtic strain seemed worth mentioning, as representing a sort of romantic, insurgent leaven in the Anglo-Saxon lump. But having married a Greek (accepting confirmation in the Orthodox Church with about as much emotion as I had declined it in the Anglican one) and left England, I never expected any but routine news from the family quarter.

My brother's account was simple but very surprising. Our mother had died tragically and young in 1973, but her mother still lived, enjoying a very spry tenth decade. When my brother had married, he had taken his wife to be presented to her. The old lady had later complimented him on his choice, adding rather alarmingly, "She's Jewish, isn't she?" Peter, who had not said as much, agreed rather guardedly that this was so. "Well," said the woman we had known all our lives as "Dodo," "I've got something to tell you. So are you."

My initial reaction, apart from pleasure and interest, was the faint but definite feeling that I had somehow known all along. Well used to being taken for English wherever I went, I had once or twice been addressed in Hebrew by older women in Jerusalem (where, presumably, people are looking for, or perhaps noticing, other characteristics). And, though some of my worst political enemies were Jewish, in America it seemed that almost all my best personal friends were. This kind of speculation could, I knew, be misleading to the point of treachery, but there it was. Then, most provoking and beguiling of all, there was the dream. Nothing bores me more than dream stories, so I had kept this one to myself. But it was the only one that counted as recurrent and I had also experienced it as a waking fantasy. In this reverie, I am aboard a ship. A small group is on the other side of the deck, huddled in talk but in some way noticing myself. After a while a member of the group crosses the deck. He explains that he and his fellows are one short of a quorum for prayer. Will I make up the number for a *minyan*? Smiling generously, and swallowing my secular convictions in a likable and tolerant manner, I agree to make up the number and stroll across the deck.

I hesitate to include this rather narcissistic recollection, but an account of my reactions would be incomplete without it, and I had had the dream recently enough to tell my brother about it. He went on to tell me that our grandmother had enjoined us to silence. We were not to tell our father who, we knew, was extremely unwell. He had not known that he had a Jewish wife, any more than we had known we had a Jewish mother. It would not be fair to tell him, at the close of his life, that he had been kept in the dark. I felt confident that he would not have minded

[57]

learning the family secret, but it was not a secret I had long to keep. My father died a matter of weeks after I learned it myself.

The day after his funeral, which was held in wintry splendor at the D-day Chapel overlooking our native Portsmouth, whence he had often set sail to do the King's enemies a bit of no good, I took a train to see my grandmother. I suppose that in childhood I had noticed her slightly exotic looks, but when she opened the door to me I was struck very immediately by my amazing want of perception. Did she look Jewish? She most certainly did. Had I ever noticed it? If so, it must have been a very subliminal recognition. And in England, at any rate in the *milieu* in which I had been brought up, Jew-consciousness had not been a major social or personal consideration.

We had family grief to discuss, and I was uncertain how to raise the other matter that was uppermost in my mind. She relieved me of the necessity. We were discussing my father's last illness and she inquired his doctor's name. "Dr. Livingstone," I replied. "Oh, a Jewish doctor," she said. (I had thought Livingstone a quintessentially English or Scots name, but I've found since that it's a favorite of the assimilated.) At once, we were in the midst of a topic that was so familiar to her and so new and strange to me. Where, for a start, were we *from*?

Breslau. The home of B. Traven and the site of a notorious camp during the *Endlossung*. Now transferred to Poland and renamed Wroclaw. A certain Mr. Blumenthal had quit this place of ill omen in the late nineteenth century and settled in the English Midlands. In Leicester, he had fathered thirteen children and raised them in a scrupulously orthodox fashion. In 1893, one of his daughters had married Lionel Levin, of Liverpool. My maternal grandmother, Dorothy Levin, had been born three years later.

It appeared that my great-grandparents had removed to Oxford, where they and their successors pursued the professions of dentistry and millinery. Having spent years of my life in that town as schoolboy and undergraduate and resident, I can readily imagine its smugness and frigidity in the early part of the century. Easy to visualize the retarding influence of the Rotary Club, and perhaps Freemasonry and the golf club, on the aspirations of the Jewish dentist or hatter. By the time of the Kaiser, the Levins had become Lynn and the Blumenthals Dale. But I was glad to learn that, while they sought to assimilate, they did not renounce. Of a Friday evening, with drawn curtains, they would produce the menorah. The children were brought up to be unobtrusively observant. How, then, could such a seemingly innocuous and familiar tale come to me as a secret? A secret which, if it were not for the chance of my grandmother outliving both my parents, I might never have learned?

Dodo told me the occluded history of my family. "Oxford," she said, materializing my suspicions, "was a very bad place to be Jewish in those days." She herself had kept all the Jewish feasts and fasts, but I was slightly relieved to find that, aged ninety-two, she was staunchly proof against the claims of religion. "Have any of your friends ever mentioned Passover to you?" she inquired touchingly. I was able to say yes to that, and to show some knowledge of Yom Kippur and Chanukah, too. This seemed to please her, though she did add that as a girl she had fasted on Yom Kippur chiefly to stay thin.

The moment had arrived to ask why this moment had arrived. Why had I had to bury my father to get this far? On the mantelpiece was a photograph of my mother, looking more beautiful than ever, though not as beautiful as in the photograph I possessed, which showed her in the uniform of the Royal Navy, in which she had met my father. I had been interrogating this photograph. It showed a young, blond woman who could have been English or (my fancy when a child) French. Neither in profile nor in curls did it disclose what Gentiles are commonly supposed to "notice."

"Your mother didn't much want to be a Jew," said Dodo, "and I didn't think your father's family would have liked the idea. So we just decided to keep it to ourselves." I had to contend with a sudden access of hitherto buried memories. Had my father shown the least sign of any prejudice? Emphatically not; he had been nostalgic for Empire and bleakly severe about the consequences of losing it, but he had never said anything ugly. He had been a stout patriot, but not a flag-waver, and would have found racism (I find I can't quite add "and chauvinism") to be an affront to the intelligence. His lifetime of naval service had taken him to Palestine in the 1930s (and had involved him in helping to put down a revolt in my wife's neighboring country of Cyprus in 1932), but he never droned on about lesser breeds as some of his friends had done in my hearing when the gin bottle was getting low. If he had ever sneered at anyone, it had been Nasser (one of our few quarrels).

But I could recall a bizarre lecture from my paternal grandfather. It was delivered as a sort of grand remonstrance when I joined the Labour Party in the mid-1960s. "*Labour,*" my working-class ancestor had said with biting scorn, "just look at them. Silverman, Mendelson, Driberg, Mikardo . . ." and he had told off the names of the leading leftists of the party at that period. At the time, I had wondered if he was objecting to *German* names (that *had* been a continuous theme of my upbringing) and only later acquired enough grounding in the tones of the British Right to realize what he had meant. Imagining the first meeting between him and my maternal grandmother, as they discussed the betrothal, I could see that she might not have been paranoid in believing her hereditary apprehensions to be realized.

And then came another thought, unbidden. Oxford may have been a tough place to be a Jew, but in the European scale it did not rank with Mannheim or Salonika. Yet my parents had been married in April 1945, the month before the final liberation of Germany. It was the moment when the world first became generally aware of the Final Solution. How galling it must have been, in that month, to keep watch over one's emotions, and to subsume the thought of the Breslau camp in the purely patriotic rejoicing at the defeat of the archenemy.

"Well, you know," said Dodo, "we've never been liked. Look at how the press treats the Israelites. They don't like us. I know I shouldn't say it, but I think it's because they're jealous." The "they" here clearly meant more than the press. I sat through it feeling rather reticent. In January

of 1988, the long-delayed revolt in Gaza had electrified
Fleet Street, more because some ambitious Thatcherite
junior minister had got himself caught up in it than for
any reason of principle. The following Sunday, I knew,
the *Observer* was to publish a review of *Blaming the Victims*, a collection of essays edited by Edward Said and
myself. This book argued correctly that the bias was
mostly the other way; even if, as Edward had once put
it so finely in a public dialogue with Salman Rushdie,
this was partly because the Palestinians were "the victims
of the victims." I didn't know how to engage with my
grandmother's quite differently stated conviction. But
when I offered that the state she called "Israelite" had
been soliciting trouble by its treatment of the Palestinians,
she didn't demur. She just reiterated her view that this
wasn't always the real reason for the dislike they—"we"—
attracted.

Well, I knew *that* already. The Harold Abrahams character in *Chariots of Fire* says rather acutely of English
anti-Semitism that "you catch it on the edge of a remark."
Whether or not this is more maddening than a direct insult I could not say from experience, but early in life I
learned to distrust those who said, "Fine old Anglo-Saxon
name" when, say, a Mr. Rubinstein had been mentioned.
"Lots of time to spare on Sundays" was another thoughtless, irritating standby. This was not exactly *Der Sturmer*,
but I began to ask myself: had I ever let any of it go by?
Had I ever helped it on its way with a smart remark?
Had I ever told a joke that a Jew would not have told?
(Plenty of latitude there, but everybody "knows" where
it stops.) In this mood I bid farewell to my grandmother
and, leaving her at her gate, rather awkwardly said,
"*Shalom!*" She replied, "*Shalom, shalom,*" as cheerfully
and readily as if it had been our greeting and parting
since my infancy. I turned and trudged off to the station
in the light, continuous rain that was also my birthright.

Enough of this, I suddenly thought. A hidden Jewish
parentage was not exactly the moral equivalent of
Anne Frank, after all. Anti-Jewish propaganda was the
common enemy of humanity, and one had always re-

garded it as such; as much by instinct as by education. To claim a personal interest in opposing it seemed, especially at this late stage, a distinct cheapening of the commitment. As the makers of Levy's rye bread had once so famously said, "You don't have to be Jewish." You don't have to be Jewish to find a personal enemy in the Jew-baiter. You don't have to be a Palestinian to take a principled position on the West Bank. So what's new? By a celebrated and practiced flick of the lever, your enemies can transfer you from the "anti" column to the "self-hating." A big deal it isn't.

Well, then, why had my first reaction to the news been one of pleasure? Examining my responses and looking for a trigger, I turned back to *Daniel Deronda*, which I had thought when I first read it to be a novel superior even to *Middlemarch*:

> "Then I *am* a Jew?" Deronda burst out with a deep-voiced energy that made his mother shrink a little backward against her cushions. . . . "I am glad of it," said Deronda, impetuously, in the veiled voice of passion.

This didn't at all meet my case. It was far too overwrought. For one thing, I had never had the opportunity to question my mother. For another, I had not (absent the teasing of the dream) had Deronda's premonitions. My moment in the Jerusalem bookshop, accosted by a matronly woman, did not compare with his *rencontre* in the Frankfort synagogue. On the other hand, the response of Deronda's mother did seem to hit a chord:

> "Why do you say you are glad? You are an English gentleman. I secured you that."

Another memory. I am sitting on the stairs in my pajamas, monitoring a parental dispute. The subject is myself, the place is on the edge of Dartmoor and the year must be 1956 or so, because the topic is my future education. My father is arguing reasonably that private schooling is too expensive. My mother, in tones that I can still recall, is saying that money can be found. "If there

[62]

is going to be an upper class in this country," she says forcefully, "then Christopher is going to be in it." My ideas about the ruling class are drawn from Arthurian legend at this point, but I like the sound of her reasoning. In any case, I yearn for boarding school and the adventure of quitting home. She must have had her way, as she customarily did, because a few months later I was outfitted for prep school and spent the next decade or so among playing fields, psalms, honors boards and the rest of it. I thus became the first Hitchens ever to go to a "public" school; to have what is still called (because it applies to about one per cent of the population) a "conventional" education, and to go to Oxford.

Until very recently, I had thought of this parental sacrifice—I was ever aware that the costs were debilitating to the family budget—as the special certificate of social mobility. My father had come from a poor area of Portsmouth, was raised as a Baptist, and had made his way by dint of scholarships and the chance provided by the Navy. My mother—well, now I saw why questions about her background had been quieted by solemn references to Dodo's early bereavement. And now I wish I could ask my mother—was all this effort expended, not just to make me a gentleman, but to make me an Englishman? An odd question to be asking myself, at my age, in a new country where most of my friends thought of me as "a Brit." But an attractive reflection, too, when I thought of the Jewish majority among my circle, and the special place of the Jews in the internationalist tradition I most admired. It counted as plus and minus that I had not had to sacrifice anything to join up. No struggle or formative drama, true, but no bullying at school, no taunting, not the least temptation to dissemble or to wish otherwise. In its review at the time, *The Tablet* (what a name!) had complained of *Daniel Deronda* that George Eliot committed "a literary error when she makes Deronda abandon, on learning the fact of his Jewish birth, all that a modern English education weaves of Christianity and the results of Christianity into an English gentleman's life." Nobody would now speak with such presumption and certainty about "the results of Christianity," but insofar as this abandonment would not be an act of supererogation on my part, it was by now impossible in any case. In other words, the discovery came to me like a gift. Like Jonathan Miller in his famous writhe in *Beyond the Fringe*, I could choose to be "not a Jew, but Jew-*ish*."

Or could it be that easy? I had two further visitations of memory to cogitate. At the age of about five, when the family lived in Scotland, I had heard my mother use the term "anti-Semitism." As with one or two other words in very early life, as soon as I heard this one I immediately, in some indefinable way, *knew what it meant*. I also knew that it was one of those cold, sibilant, sinister-sounding words, innately repugnant in its implications. I had always found anti-Jewish sentiment to be disgusting, in the same way as all such prejudices, but also in a different way, and somehow more so. To hear some ignorant person denouncing Pakistani or Jamaican immigrants to Britain was one thing—there would be foulmouth complaints about cooking smells, about body odors and occasionally about sexual habits. This was the sort of plebeian bigotry that one had to learn to combat, in early days as an apprentice canvasser, as a sort of Tory secret weapon in the ranks of the Labour vote. But anti-Semitic propaganda was something else. More rarely encountered, it was a sort of theory; both pseudo and anti-intellectual. It partook of a little learning about blood, soil, money, conspiracy. It had a fetidly religious and furtively superstitious feel to it. (Nobody accuses the blacks of trying to take over international finance, if only because the racists don't believe them capable of mounting the conspiracy.) When I came across Yevtushenko's poem *Babi Yar* at the age of sixteen, I realized that he had seized the essence of the horror I felt; the backwardness and cunning that could be mobilized. I memorized the poem for a public reading that my school organized for the Venice in Peril Fund, and can remember some lines even now without taking down the Peter Levi translation:

> No Jewish blood runs among my blood
> But I am as bitterly and as hardly hated
> By every anti-Semite
> As if I were a Jew.

That seemed to me a fine ambition, even if easily affected at a civilized English boys' school. I know that it was at about that time that I noticed, in my early efforts at leftist propaganda, that among the few reliable allies in a fairly self-satisfied school were the boys with what I gradually understood were Jewish names. There was occasional nudging and smirking in chapel when we sang the line "Ye seeds of Israel's chosen race" in the anthem *Crown Him*. What did it mean, *chosen*? Could it be serious? I hadn't then read *Daniel Deronda*, but would have shared his stiff and correct attitude (antedating his discovery) that:

> Of learned and accomplished Jews he took it for granted that they had dropped their religion, and wished to be merged in the people of their native lands. Scorn flung at a Jew as such would have roused all his sympathy in grief of inheritance; but the indiscriminate scorn of a race will often strike a specimen who has well-earned it on his own account. . . .

Oh, I was fair-minded all right. But strict fair-mindedness would suggest the conclusion that it didn't *matter* who was Jewish. And to say that it didn't matter seemed rather point-missing.

The second memory was more tormenting. Shortly before her death, and in what was to be our last telephone conversation, my mother had suddenly announced that she wanted to move to Israel. This came to me as a complete surprise. (My grandmother, when I told her fifteen years later, was likewise unprepared for the revelation.) Now I ransacked that last exchange for any significance it might retrospectively possess. Having separated from my father and approaching middle life, my mother was urgently seeking to make up for time lost and spoke of all manner of fresh starts. Her praise for Israel was of the sort—"It's a new country. It's young. They work hard. They made the desert bloom"—that one read in the Gentile as well as the Jewish press. The year was 1973 and the time was just after the Yom Kippur war, and in trying to moderate her enthusiasm I spoke of the precariousness of the situation. This was slightly dishonest of me, because

I didn't doubt Israel's ability to outfight its neighbors. But I suspected that any mention of the Palestinians would be a pointless expense of breath. Besides, I wasn't entirely sure myself how I stood on that question.

In June 1967 I had sympathized instinctively with the Jewish state, though I remember noting with interest and foreboding a report from Paris, which said that triumphalist demonstrators on the Champs Elysées had honked their car horns—*Isra-el vain-cra!*—to the same beat as the OAS *Algé-rie Fran-çaise!* My evolution since then had been like thousands of other radicals; misery at the rise of the Israeli Right and enhanced appreciation of the plight of the Palestinians, whether in exile or under occupation. Several visits to the region meant that I had met the Palestinians and seen conclusively through those who had argued that they did not "really" exist. By the time that I moved to the United States, the Left and even the liberals were thrown on the defensive. In America at least, a major part of the ideological cement for the Reagan-Thatcher epoch was being laid on by the neoconservative school, which was heavily influenced by the Middle East debate and which did not scruple to accuse its critics of anti-Semitism. My baptism of fire with this group came with the Timerman affair, which has been unjustly forgotten in the record of those years.

Even though Jacobo Timerman had been incarcerated and tortured *as a Jew*, his Argentine fascist tormentors were nonetheless felt, by the Reagan administration and by the pre-Falklands Thatcherites, to be fundamentally on our side. (This in spite of the horridly warm relations between the Buenos Aires junta and the Soviet Union.) They did not count, in the new *Kulturkampf*, as a tyranny within the meaning of the act. As a result, Jacobo Timerman had to be defamed.

He was accused of making up his story. He was reviled, in an attack that presaged a later hot favorite term, of covert sympathy for "terrorism" in Argentina. He was arraigned for making life harder, by his denunciation, for Argentina's peaceable Jewish community. (This charge was given a specially ironic tone by the accusation, made in parallel, that he had overstated the extent of anti-

Semitism in that country.) Although some of this slander came from the Francoist Right, who were later to appear in their true colors under the banner of General Singlaub and Colonel North, the bulk of the calumny was provided by neoconservative Jewish columnists and publications. I shall never forget Irving Kristol telling a dinner table at the Lehrman Institute that he did not believe Timerman had been tortured in the first place.

I was very much affected by Timerman's book *Prisoner Without a Name, Cell Without a Number,* partly because I had once spent a few rather terrifying days in Buenos Aires, trying to get news of him while he was *incommunicado*. Not even the most pessimistic person had appreciated quite what he was actually going through. As I read the account of his torture, at the hands of the people who were later picked by Reagan and Casey to begin the training of the *contras*, I was struck by one page in particular. An ideologue of the junta is speaking:

> Argentina has three main enemies: Karl Marx, because he tried to destroy the Christian concept of society; Sigmund Freud, because he tried to destroy the Christian concept of the family; and Albert Einstein, because he tried to destroy the Christian concept of time and space.

Here was the foe in plain view. As that pure Austrian Ernst Fischer puts it so pungently in his memoir, *An Opposing Man*: "The degree of a society's culture can be measured against its attitude towards the Jews. All forms of anti-Semitism are evidence of a reversion to barbarism. Any system which persecutes the Jews, on whatever pretext, has forfeited all right to be regarded as progressive."

Here were all my adopted godfathers in plain view as well; the three great anchors of the modern, revolutionary intelligence. It was for this reason that, on the few occasions on which I had been asked if I was Jewish, I had been sad to say no, and even perhaps slightly jealous. On the other hand, when in early 1988 I told an editor friend my news, her response was sweet but rather shocking. "That should make your life easier," she said. "Jewish people are *allowed* to criticize Israel." I felt a surge of annoyance. Was that the use I was supposed to make of it? And did that response, typical as I was to find it, suggest the level to which the debate had fallen? It seemed to me that since the Middle East was becoming nuclearized, and since the United States was a principal armorer and paymaster, it was more in the nature of a civic responsibility to take a critical interest. If Zionism was going to try to exploit Gentile reticence in the post-Holocaust era, it might do so successfully for a time. But it would never be able to negate the tradition of reason and skepticism inaugurated by the real Jewish founding fathers. And one had not acquired that tradition by means of the genes.

As I was preparing for my father's funeral, and readying a short address I planned to give to the mourners, I scanned through a wartime novel in which he had featured as a character. Warren Tute was an author of *The Cruel Sea* school, and had acquired a certain following by his meticulous depiction of life in the Royal Navy. His best known book, *The Cruiser*, had my father in the character of Lieutenant Hale. I didn't find anything in the narrative that would be appropriate for my eulogy. But I did find an internal monologue, conducted by the Master-at-Arms as he mentally reviewed the ship's complement of HMS *Antigone*. The Master-at-Arms dealt in stereotypes:

> He knew that Stoker First Class Danny Evans would be likely to celebrate his draft by going on the beer for a week in Tonypandy and then spending the next three months in the Second Class for Leave. He knew that Blacksmith First Class Rogers would try and smuggle service provisions ashore for his mother and that Telegraphist Jacobs was a sea lawyer who kept a copy of Karl Marx in his kitbag.

Good old Telegraphist Jacobs! I could see him now, huddled defensively in his radio shack. Probably teased a bit for his bookishness ("a copy" of Marx, indeed); perhaps called "Four Eyes" for his glasses and accused of "swallowing the dictionary" if he ever employed a long word. On shore leave at colonial ports, sticking up for the natives while his hearty shipmates rolled the taxi drivers and the whores. Perhaps enduring a certain amount of ragging at church parade or "divisions" (though perhaps not; the British lower deck is if anything overly respectful of "a man's religion"). Resorted to by his comrades in the mess when there was a dispute over King's Regulations or the pay slips. Indefinitely relegated when promotion was discussed—a Captain Jacobs R.N. would have been more surprising than an Admiral Rickover. In those terrible days of war and blockade, where the air is full of bombast about fighting the Hun, or just fighting, Telegraphist Jacobs argues hoarsely that the enemy is fascism. Probably he has rattled a tin for Spain; collected bandages in the East End for the boys of the International Brigade (whose first British volunteers were two Jewish garment workers). When the wireless begins to use the weird and frightening new term "total war," Telegraphist Jacobs already knows what it means. The rest of the time, he overhears the word "troublemaker" and privately considers it to be no insult.

My father never knew that he had a potential Telegraphist Jacobs for a son, but he hardly ever complained at what he did get, and I salute him for that. I also think with pleasure and pride of him and Jacobs, their vessel battered by the Atlantic and the Third Reich, as they sailed through six years of hell together to total victory. Commander Hitchens, I know, would never have turned a Nelson eye to any bullying. They were, much as the navy dislikes the expression, in the same boat.

As I believe is common with elder sons, I feel more and more deprived, as the days pass, by the thought of conversations that never took place and now never will. In this case, having had the Joycean experience of finding myself an orphan and a Jew more or less simultaneously, I had at least the consolation of curiosity and interest. A week or so after returning from the funeral in England, I telephoned the only rabbi I knew personally and asked for a meeting. Rabbi Robert Goldburg is a most learned and dignified man, who had once invited me to address his Reform congregation in New Haven. He had married

Arthur Miller to Marilyn Monroe (converting the latter to Judaism), but resisted the temptation to go on about it too much. After some initial banter about my disclosure ("Aren't you ashamed? Did you see Rabin saying to *break their bones?*") he appointed a time and place. I wanted to ask him what I had been missing.

It may be a bit early to say what I learned from our discussion. The course of reading that was suggested is one I have not yet completed. No frontal challenge to my atheism was presented, though I was counseled to re-examine the "crude, Robert Ingersoll, nineteenth-century" profession of unbelief. Ever since Maimonides wrote of the Messiah that "he may tarry," Judaism seems to have rubbed along with a relaxed attitude to the personal savior question, and a frankly skeptical one about questions of wish-thinking such as the afterlife. A. J. Ayer once pointed out that Voltaire was anti-Semitic because he blamed the Jews for Christianity, "and I'm very much afraid to say that he was quite right. It *is* a Jewish heresy." When I had first heard him say that, I thought he might be being flippant. But as I talked more with Rabbi Goldburg, I thought that Judaism might turn out to be the most ethically sophisticated tributary of humanism. Einstein, who was urged on me as an alternative to Ingersoll, had allowed himself to speak of "The Old One," despite re-fusing allegiance to the god of Moses. He had also said that the old one "does not play dice with the universe." Certainly it was from Jews like him that I had learned to hate the humans who thought themselves fit to roll the dice at any time.

Rabbi Goldburg's congregation is well-to-do, and when I visited them as a speaker I had been very impressed by the apparent contrast between their life style, for want of a better term, and their attitudes. I say "apparent contrast" because it is of course merely philistine to assume that people "vote their pocketbook" all the time, or that such voting behavior is hard-headed realism instead of the fatuity it so often is. The well-known Jewish pseudo intellectual who had so sweetly observed that American Jews have the income profile of Episcopalians and the voting habits of Puerto Ricans was an example of

[70]

Reaganism, of what Saul Bellow once called "the mental rabble of the wised-up world."

Anyway, what struck me when I addressed this highly educated and professional group was the same as what had struck me when I had once talked to a gathering of Armenians in a leafy suburb in California. They did not scoff or recoil, even when they might disagree, as I droned on about the iniquity and brutality, the greed and myopia that marked Reagan's low tide. They did not rise to suggest that the truth lay somewhere in between, or that moderation was the essential virtue, or that politics was the art of the possible. They seemed to lack that overlay of Panglossian emollience that had descended over the media and the Congress and, it sometimes seemed, over every damn thing. Over drinks afterwards I suddenly thought: Of course. These people already know. They aren't to be fooled by bubbles of prosperity and surges of good feeling. *They know the worst can happen.* It may not be in the genes, but it's in the collective memory and in many individual ones too.

Was this perhaps why I had sometimes "felt" Jewish? As I look back over possible premonitions, echoes from early life, promptings of memory, I have to suspect my own motives. I am uneasy because to think in this way is, in Kipling's frightening phrase, "to think with the blood." Jews may think with the blood if they choose: it must be difficult not to do so. But they—we—must also hope that thinking with the blood does not become general. This irony, too, must help impart and keep alive a sense of preparedness for the worst.

Under the Nuremberg laws, I would have been counted a Blumenthal of Breslau and the denial of that will stop with me. Under the Law of Return I can supposedly redeem myself by moving into the Jerusalem home from which my friend Edward Said has been evicted. We must be able to do better than that. We still live in the prehistory of the human race, where no tribalism can be much better than another and where humanism and internationalism, so much derided and betrayed, need an unsentimental and decisive restatement.

SALAMMBÔ
THE CAREER OF AN OPERA

Francis Steegmuller

Salammbô was Gustave Flaubert's second published novel, the story of a devout Carthaginian princess and her seduction by a giant Libyan warrior, Mâtho, who had stolen from her care the zaïmph—the sacred veil of the moon goddess Tanit (the Phoenician Venus). It was issued in Paris in 1862, five years after the success and scandal of *Madame Bovary*.

On March 29, 1983, the Teatro di San Carlo, the famous old opera house of Naples, was the scene of a curious world premiere: the first "realization in scenic form" of a series of six operatic scenes which Modest Mussorgsky had been inspired to compose a hundred and twenty years before, after reading a Russian translation of *Salammbô* in 1863.

After sporadic work, Mussorgsky abandoned the project of composing an entire *Salammbô* (actually he had intended to call his opera *The Libyan*, with Mâtho given the principal role); and he later incorporated parts of the music in *Boris Godunov* and elsewhere. But his original pages of *The Libyan* were not unknown. In 1884 Rimsky-Korsakov published an arrangement for two sopranos and two altos, with piano accompaniment, of the "chorus of the Priestesses of Tanit" in Mussorgsky's Act Two; and in 1930 all the scenes were gathered together and published by the Russian musicologist Pavel Lamm. In November 1939, during ceremonies commemorating the centenary of Mussorgsky's birth, two other scenes from *The Libyan* were sung at the Moscow Opera; and quite recently, in 1980, as "revised and reconstructed" by the Hungarian composer Zoltán Peskó, Mussorgsky's *The Libyan*, now rechristened *Salammbô*, was given in concert form in Turin, Rome and Milan by an international cast of singers and the orchestra of the RAI (Radiotelevisione

Italiana), with Peskó directing. Recorded live, the beautiful Milan performance is available in a well-documented album (Fonit Cetra; Columbia Masterworks M236939).

It was the same Peskó "revision and reconstruction" of Mussorgsky's fragmentary score, again conducted by Peskó, that was given at the Naples premiere "in scenic form." Once again an international cast of singers was engaged; and the choral work was divided among three groups: the chorus of the San Carlo, the children's chorus of the Naples church of Santa Chiara, and, as guests, the Philharmonic Chorus of Prague. The stage director was the Russian Juri Lyubimov.

All this was announced in good time in the Neapolitan daily newspaper, *Il Mattino*. When preparations for staging were well under way, however, there came from Moscow the news that the singers engaged for the two principal roles had suddenly, without explanation, been refused exit visas. After a frantic search, substitutes were found: the American mezzo-soprano Annabelle Bernard, who learned her role of Salammbô in Russian in two weeks; and the Bulgarian basso Boris Bakov. (The third principal singer, who appeared in all performances, was also an American, the baritone William Stone.) As rehearsals progressed, tension developed between the adult Neapolitan choristers and their Czech guests concerning respective roles and positions on stage—a situation eventually resolved (according to enthusiastic articles in the *Mattino*) amid embraces and tears, armfuls of roses, and toasts in Italian champagne. The premiere took place as scheduled; and critics and public alike, while applauding the singers, the orchestra, and the overcoming of difficulties, were surprised by certain elements of Lyubimov's staging.

The production opened with Lyubimov himself, made up to resemble portraits of Mussorgsky, seated at a piano, stage right, in the throes of composing his score; at the left stood a slender figure, with pince-nez and cane, in white linen suit and white straw hat, intended to represent Flaubert (in fact he resembled photographs of Che-

[73]

khov); while over all this were broadcast, in Russian and French, incomprehensible passages from the letters of the author and the composer concerning their respective parts of the work. (In real life, Flaubert never knew of Mussorgsky's opera, and probably never heard of Mussorgsky.) These elements of the opening scene, and many subsequent details, were fully comprehended only by those in the audience who had been cued by the indispensable *Mattino*. ("They could at least dust the stage floor," one subscriber grumbled to her neighbor; but those who had done their reading knew that Lyubimov had had portions of the floor strewn with sand, "to give a sense of the North African desert.")

Equally puzzling to many was the periodic rise and fall, on hinges manipulated from below, of other sections of the stage floor. (One had learned—again from the inevitable *Mattino*—that these pendulations were supposed to invoke the opening and closing of pages of a book.) When erect, the panels formed low walls behind which the choristers stood while singing. In the novel, Carthaginian children, chosen by lot, are cast as a living sacrifice into the fiery furnace of the god Baal, to ensure a Carthaginian victory over the barbarians besieging the city. In Naples, the horror of this scene was somewhat tempered by the inability of some of the child choristers to restrain their glee, as, seemingly pushed by the officiating high priests from behind the raised panels, they clearly enjoyed the fun of dropping down to their doom through the gaping hole that had appeared in the stage floor of the San Carlo.

The production ended with two heavily symbolic scenes invented by the director: Flaubert was seen to embrace Mâtho (his own creation) and then to act as executioner, slitting Mâtho's throat (concluding the novel by assassinating his own hero?); and Mussorgsky's piano, *sans* composer and strewn with sheets of staff paper, was spotlighted on an otherwise empty stage (his abandonment of his score).

One left the San Carlo with the suspicion that one had not seen what is sometimes professionally called a "traveling" production; and that for dramatization of *Salammbô* one had best remain content with the celebrated brief sequences in *Citizen Kane*.

Between the two events—Flaubert's publication of his *Salammbô* in 1862 and that curious presentation of a series of neo-Mussorgskian scenes from the novel on the stage of the San Carlo well over a hundred years later—there was born, and perhaps died (no one can be sure), yet another *Salammbô*, one that was truly "grand" opera. This one eventually took Flaubert's characters to the stage of the Metropolitan Opera House during its seventeenth season at Broadway and 40th Street, having arrived there via Brussels, Paris, Cairo and New Orleans. A number of interesting personalities were connected with its career.

Flaubert always refused to permit dramatization of *Madame Bovary*, considering it, as he said in one of his letters, "not a subject for the stage." The prohibition seems to have been respected by his niece and heir, Caroline Commanville (Mme Franklin Grout), who was otherwise avid in profiting from her uncle's literary remains. Eventually, however, after Caroline's death in 1931 and the entry of all Flaubert's works into the public domain in 1944, the floodgates opened; and in various languages there now exist stage, film, radio, television and operatic versions of *Bovary*.

Probably no one has seen or heard them all; but a few might be cited. In one Parisian stage adaptation the role of Emma Bovary was played by a Slavic actress with a strong native accent, a whim of casting "justified" by the director as symbolizing Emma's fantasies of exoticism in her provincial Norman milieu. Darius Milhaud composed the score for a 1934 film version of the novel directed by Jean Renoir. In an early scene of an American film released that same year, Emma (Jennifer Jones, costumed *en amazone*) and her lover Rodolph (Louis Jourdan) are shown riding their horses through groves of California live oaks; and toward the close Charles Bovary (Van

[75]

Heflin) is heard to inquire of his dying wife, "Kin ya hear me, Emma? Kin ya hear me?"—rustic syllables possibly adopted by a capable actor at the behest of the director in deluded deference to Flaubert's delineation of poor Charles as a rube; or perhaps mere inadvertence.

As for opera, readers will remember that Emma heard only one lyric performance in her life—"*Lucie de Lammermoor*," sung in a Rouen theatre, an experience that caused her to "vibrate to the very fiber of her being" and sent her into "palpitations"; whereas in more recent times Emma has herself become a soprano, in French, Italian and German operatic versions of her story. None of these, any more than the other adaptations, has yet proven Flaubert mistaken in his view that the story should remain a novel.

Flaubert recognized that in contrast to *Madame Bovary*, much of the flamboyant, crowded *Salammbô* was essentially theatrical—indeed, potential stage material of the most grandiose kind; and two years after its publication he asked his friend Théophile Gautier, who had reviewed the novel with Romantic enthusiasm in *Le Moniteur*, to mine it for an opera libretto. Gautier had written scenarios for a number of exotic ballets, including the well-known *Sakountala* and *La Péri*, as well as a novel laid in ancient Egypt, *Le Roman de la momie*; and to Flaubert he must have seemed the ideal librettist for his Carthaginian epic. But years went by and nothing came of it. Gautier was constantly busy with other projects; and perhaps the extravagance of Flaubert's novel daunted even him. As a possible composer for *Salammbô*, there was talk of Verdi, but nothing came of that, either; and Berlioz, though tempted, decided that the subject was too close to that of his *Troyens*. One applicant for the commission seems to have been Samuel David, who had won a Prix de Rome (a two-year stay at the Villa Medici) and was now musical director of the synagogues of Paris. In the end it was Ernest Reyer, a friend and several times collaborator of Gautier's, a friend also of Flaubert's and an admirer of his more exotic works—*The Temptation of Saint Anthony* and *The Legend of St. Julien the Hospitaler,* as well as *Salammbô*—who obtained from Flaubert the exclusive right to compose a score. Despairing of Gautier as librettist, Flaubert turned to Gautier's son-in-law, the poet Catulle Mendès; but Mendès procrastinated, and what he finally came up with was impossible. In June 1879, less than a year before his death, Flaubert wrote to a friend: "I have broken with Catulle Mendès, and Reyer is going to take Barbier and get busy with *Salammbô.*" But apparently even the experienced Paul-Jules Barbier, who had written the libretti of *Faust* and *Roméo et Juliette* for Gounod, foundered on the teeming *Salammbô.* Yet another candidate was Philippe Gille, future librettist of Massenet's *Manon* and Delibes's *Lakmé.* Finally, Reyer found his librettist in a good friend, Camille du Commun du Locle, ex-director of the Opéra Comique.

In the early 1860s Giuseppe Verdi had been commissioned by Émile Perrin, then the manager of the Paris Opéra, to compose the opera we know as *Don Carlo,* to be sung in French for a Parisian premiere. When the librettist, Joseph Méry, died in 1865, the completion of the writing was entrusted to Perrin's thirty-three-year-old nephew and secretary. This was DuLocle. The son of a sculptor in Orange, he was a graduate of the prestigious École des Chartes with a degree in paleography and a Prix de Rome. He was something of a dandy. His letters reveal him as witty and charming. By the time *Don Carlo* was produced in 1867, DuLocle, Verdi and Verdi's wife had become affectionate friends. The following year DuLocle traveled in Egypt with Auguste Mariette, the Egyptologist; and on his return—to quote from a letter written him by Verdi—"You gave me four little printed pages without the name of the author, telling me that the Khedive would like an opera on that subject, since it was Egyptian." The "author" was Mariette, and the four-page story, called *La Fiancée du Nil,* was the germ of *Aïda.*

The ensuing story has its celebrated place in the an-

nals of opera: how DuLocle persuaded Verdi to accept
the Khedive's commission and persuaded the Khedive,
through Mariette, to pay Verdi the large fee of 150,000
francs in gold (50,000 as an advance); his work with Verdi
in writing a libretto in French prose, which was then transposed by Antonio Ghislanzoni into the Italian verse that
is sung today. (It was retranslated into French by Du-
Locle and the musicologist Charles Nuitter for French
production.)

DuLocle continued to be useful to Verdi through the
Egyptian and Italian premieres of Aïda in the winter of
1871–72; and letters between the two men are always
affectionate. Meanwhile, DuLocle was pursuing a Parisian
career which, while it initially brought him prestige, was
destined for disaster. In 1871 he was appointed co-director
of the Opéra Comique. In 1874 he became its director,
and at his invitation Verdi conducted there a series of performances of his Requiem. Sympathetic to contemporary
composers, DuLocle commissioned a number of works—
among them Carmen, which he produced in 1875, declar-
ing it a masterpiece.

But it soon became clear that this man of talent and
taste did not possess the qualities of an executive. Carmen
was a fiasco, condemned by critics (even Reyer was lukewarm about it, and devoted most of his review in the
Journal des Débats to recounting the original Merimée
story); the finances of the theater fell into confusion; to
prop up the tottering company DuLocle made use, with
Verdi's permission, of the funds advanced by the Khedive
and confided by the composer to DuLocle's care. The
money was irretrievably lost; DuLocle's health broke
down; and in 1876 he resigned, at the age of forty-four.
The next year, his poem André Chenier was awarded a
prize by the French Academy. Under the name of "Ca-
millo" he wrote musical articles for the magazine XIXème
Siècle, but he seems never again to have been regularly
employed. For a time he spent his winters in Rome and
summers at Avranches in Normandy; and eventually he
retired to the island of Capri.

[78]

There he spent the rest of his life. Of small stature, his humor embittered, he became known among the English residents of the island as "The Acid Drop" and among the Capresi themselves as "'U Francesiello"—"the little Frenchman." A drawing done when he was sixty-three shows him sharp-featured, elegant, wearing a tarboosh, perhaps in memory of his Egyptian days. Verdi forgave him, and suggested a reunion in Genoa. But although Du-Locle corresponded with him, and translated into French the first two acts of *Otello*, he seems never to have left his island. He died there in 1903, at seventy-one, and is buried in the foreigners' cemetery.

It was from Avranches, in 1879, in reply to Reyer's plea, that DuLocle agreed to write a five-act libretto for *Salammbô*, in eight "tableaux," following an outline prepared by Flaubert himself.

In a gossipy article in the Parisian newspaper *Le Figaro*, Ernest Reyer was once described as being "tall and *'moustachu,'* " wearing the red rosette of the Légion d'Honneur and looking like "a young general who had risen rapidly in the service." Reyer had, indeed, risen rapidly in the service—of music. A *marseillais*, born in 1823, his real and full name was Louis-Étienne-Ernest Rey. As a young man he lived for some years with an uncle who was a government official in Algeria, and there he acquired a taste for orientalism. At the time Flaubert gave him the operatic rights to *Salammbô* he was fifty-six—a prolific composer, an informed musicologist, librarian at the Paris Opéra (a more or less nominal post, to which he seems to have paid scant attention), and a critic writing for various newspapers, especially *Le Journal des Débats*, where a predecessor had been Hector Berlioz. (The older composer and the younger were friends and mutual admirers.)

As the article in *Le Figaro* pointed out, the titles of most of Reyer's principal works, in addition to *Salammbô*, begin with the letter S: *Le Selam*, a "symphonie orientale" with chorus, inspired by Gautier's poem of the same name;

Sacountala, a ballet score, libretto by Gautier; *La Statue,* an *"opéra comique"*; and *Sigurd,* a "grand" opera on a Wagnerian theme but with a not at all Wagnerian score. (Leaving one to wonder whether he might have been less interested in Flaubert's novel had it been christened either *Carthage* or *The Mercenaries,* titles which Flaubert had at various times considered.)

Reyer was not loved among his fellow composers. In his reviews he "slashed away with an iron pen," as *Le Figaro* put it, "savaging anything written in the sweet old-fashioned way." As a premature Wagnerite he had been sneered at; and during the Franco-Prussian war the press reminded readers that in 1862 he had dedicated his opera *Erostrate,* which had its premiere in Baden-Baden, to the Queen of Prussia (later Empress Augusta). In addition to Wagner and Berlioz, his favorite composers were Gluck, Beethoven, Mendelssohn, Schumann and Brahms. (It is said to have been his love of German music that caused him to change his name from the Hispanic-sounding Rey to the Teutonic Reyer.) When Verdi, about whose earlier works Reyer had not always written kindly, heard that the critic had accepted the Khedive's invitation to attend the Cairo premiere of *Aïda,* he wrote good-humoredly to his publisher, Giulio Ricordi, that he was "looking forward to hearing the wrath of God." But Reyer wrote respectfully of *Aïda,* and profited from the occasion to travel up the Nile—another link between him and Flaubert, whose Egyptian tour had been one of the most intense experiences of his early life.

Indeed, another French musicologist, Hugues Imbert, writing about Reyer in his *Nouveaux Profils de Musique* (1875), found many resemblances between the two men. "It isn't only in his literary aspirations, in his taste for orientalism and ancient legend, in his hatred of the bourgeoisie, that there exists a very marked affinity between Ernest Reyer and Gustave Flaubert. The two men resemble one another in certain physical attitudes and particularities. Reyer is less theatrical in manner and more contemporary in aspect; but his thick moustache, his rather stiff carriage, his curt voice, sharp glance and brusque handshake . . . remind one of a Flaubert on somewhat smaller scale."

To DuLocle in his troubles, Reyer had always been loyal. In more than one of his articles he paid tribute to DuLocle's range of accomplishments; and he was one of the few to remind the public that although Ghislanzoni's might be the only name to appear as librettist on the posters advertising *Aïda*, it was DuLocle who had written the original text.

Reyer was delighted by the two sample scenes for a *Salammbô* libretto that came to him from DuLocle. "They whetted my appetite," he later wrote. "A few months later the text was finished, and the first pages of my score were written very quickly." Reyer might well have been pleased. DuLocle's five-act text is an expertly contrived compression concentrating (as Flaubert had suggested in his outline) on the Salammbô-Mâtho infatuation and providing an excellent launching pad for the required series of solos, duets, choruses and spectacles. For a time, Flaubert prudishly balked at depicting, on stage, the climactic breaking of Salammbô's ankle-chain (symbol of her virginity); but Reyer persuaded him to give way. It was Flaubert who had suggested DuLocle's finale, in which Mâtho, made captive, breaks his bonds and joins Salammbô in suicide by dagger. (In the novel, Salammbô dies of emotion after seeing Mâtho torn to pieces by the mob and his heart held aloft by the high priest as an offering to the sun.)

But Reyer very soon interrupted his work on the score: Flaubert's sudden death from apoplexy on May 12, 1880, caused him to lose heart for the task—"destroyed his courage," as he himself said. Putting *Salammbô* aside, he returned to a score that he had similarly left incomplete some years before—the opera *Sigurd*, with a libretto adapted from the *Niebelungenlied* by DuLocle and Alfred Blau. Flaubert's niece, always sharp, and displeased by what she saw as Reyer's defection, promptly set about commissioning a scenario for a *Salammbô* ballet, with a score to be written by Léo Delibes; but Reyer, alerted, reminded her of the exclusivity Flaubert had given him, and she desisted. *Sigurd* was completed in 1883; and on January 6, 1884, at its premiere at the Théâtre de la Monnaie in Brussels, it was hailed as by far Reyer's finest work, a masterpiece. Reyer had been on poor terms with the management of the Paris Opéra—hence the Brussels premiere; nevertheless, *Sigurd* opened in Paris the next year, with equal success. From its Brussels premiere through the celebration of its fiftieth anniversary performance at the Monnaie in 1934, *Sigurd* was sung there eighty-nine times. In Paris it remained in the repertory through its two hundred and forty-ninth performance in 1935. There are numerous recordings of portions of its score.

Greatly contributing to the success of *Sigurd*, and achieving a personal triumph in the role of Brunhilde, was the twenty-seven-year-old French mezzo-soprano Rose Caron, who had joined the Brussels company—it was her first engagement by a major house—two years before. In Mme Caron, Reyer not only found his perfect Brunhilde, but, looking ahead, saw his next heroine as well. He returned to *Salammbô*. After five years' work he completed it, having composed the leading role with Mme Caron always in mind. "I gave her my manuscript score," he wrote later. "Her rare intelligence enabled her to grasp my every intention. I made her understand how I myself conceived the role: she embodied it. The first time she sang it for me I was dazzled, fascinated. The little room in which we were working suddenly took on the proportions of a vast stage. I saw the decor, the costumes; and with only me present, at the piano—this will scarcely seem credible—she sang as though she were singing for an audience of two thousand, all waiting to burst into applause."

"*Salammbô* will be sung wherever Mme Caron is singing," Reyer declared when asked his plans. "No Mme Caron, no *Salammbô*." Those remarks were directed against the management of the Paris Opéra, which had not renewed the contract Mme Caron had been given following her Parisian debut in *Sigurd*. The Théâtre de la Monnaie agreed to welcome Mme Caron back; and it was thus in Brussels that the Reyer-DuLocle *Salammbô* finally had its premiere, on February 10, 1890—almost ten years after Flaubert's death and almost eleven after DuLocle had delivered the libretto.

That premiere was a triumph. But it was principally a triumph for Mme Caron, and for Reyer as composer of those portions of the score that were sung by her. On the real stage of the Monnaie she repeated the splendid performance that had so dazzled him in the little rehearsal room; and the applause he had imagined there was, in the opera house, deafening.

Flaubert had experienced acute difficulty in attempting to give life to the characters in his novel. At an early stage of the work he had written to a friend: "I would give the demi-ream of notes I have written during the last five months, and the ninety-eight volumes I have read, to be, for only three seconds, really moved by the passion of my heroes." For "heroes" one may read, in particular, "heroine"; and Lucien Solvay, the music critic of the principal Brussels evening newspaper *Le Soir*, who had read that lament in one of the then recently published volumes of Flaubert's correspondence, found that Flaubert's longing would have been fulfilled had he heard Mme Caron's interpretation of what Reyer had written for her:

> Where the composer triumphs is the way he has conceived and conveyed the character of the heroine—whose weakness Flaubert was so aware of in the novel. In the opera, her character surges up, takes form, captures the limelight and becomes heroic and touching as never before. This role, one might say, *is* the opera: it is the poetry, the charm, the seduction of the work. In it the composer's inspiration is refined and elevated: it soars; into it he has put all his emotion, his entire soul.
>
> Mme Caron is the *ideal* Salammbô. To speak of the discretion, the eloquence, and the charm of her interpretation of the role would add nothing to that single adjec-

tive, which embraces all possible analyses. And the ovations given her only emphasized the power of her art, so personal and so profound.

Tribute was paid by the critics to much, though not to all, of Reyer's score. "Whether one calls *Salammbô* a compromise between the old school"—the critic was referring to Gluck, Beethoven and Reyer's other admired elders— "and the young [Wagner and Berlioz], or a work of 'transition' is of little importance: this is a beautiful work, very worthy and very honorable, a great effort—and a great success." The rest of the cast was also praised, and the orchestra, and the very lavish production (said to have cost three hundred thousand francs). One critic objected that the costumes, gorgeous as they were, "had no local color." In fact, Flaubert himself, for all his phenomenal research, had had to do much guessing as to the nature of Carthaginian costume: it seems that no one had ever recorded what a pre-Christian Carthaginian looked like, and he had done his best by examining sparse remains from Phoenicia, Carthage's mother country.

Although it never achieved the popularity of *Sigurd*, *Salammbô* was to remain in the Brussels repertory for many years. Mme Caron sang it there frequently (forty-six times during its first three seasons); and after her retirement it was revived for a number of other singers. By the end of the 1927–28 season, its last, it had been sung at the Monnaie seventy-two times.

Following Mme Caron's success as *Salammbô* in Brussels, she—and Reyer with her—became reconciled with the management of the Paris Opéra, and she returned to sing in the one hundredth performance of *Sigurd* there on December 30, 1891. But plans for a Paris premiere of *Salammbô* miscarried; a delay ensued; and it was only on May 16, 1892, under a new management, more friendly to Reyer, that the opera had its Paris opening. Except for the addition of a ballet danced in the camp of the Mercenaries—a scene which Reyer considered absurd but was

[*84*]

persuaded to write in order to give employment to the Opéra's "rats" (that group of young ballerinas much portrayed by Degas)—it was a repetition of the sumptuous Brussels production; and in Paris it triumphed again. In a long, chauvinistic review in *Le Figaro* by the critic Charles Darcours (so ecstatic as to suggest some paid arrangement of propaganda for the new management), *Salammbô* was greeted as signaling the emergence of the Opéra from a period of stagnation and representing the return of truly French opera to France:

> As for M. Reyer's harmonic system, it is of a totally French quality, and derives not at all from the Wagnerian school, which so many of our young composers are trying to imitate today. As far as harmonic invention is concerned, M. Reyer so preserves his own personality that one would think he had never seen or heard any work of the German master. If one wanted to seek a more valid affiliation, one would have to say that M. Reyer proceeds more from Berlioz than from anyone else.

Mme Caron was hailed as "the most remarkable lyric tragedienne we have heard in our greatest theatre. . . . The tragic actress who achieves such effects by *simplicity* is a great artist."

That was printed in the May 17, 1892, issue of the newspaper.

What happened overnight—or, more likely, had been hatched in advance—is one of the minor mysteries of the history of late nineteenth-century French journalism. Someone—possibly a member or partisan of the ousted regime of the Opéra—"got to" the management of *Le Figaro*; and the following article, signed "Matho," appeared in the issue of May 18.

MME CARON INTIME

In the near future, Parisians are going to have several more opportunities to applaud, as they did two evenings ago, the superb interpreter of *Salammbô*. They are curious, and are asking for a few intimate details concerning this artiste who is now suddenly a star. So let us lift, for a few moments, the *Zaïmph*, the mystical veil shrouding this Salammbô, as in the opera it shrouds the goddess Tanit whose servant she is.

Mme Caron is thirty-five years old. She was born Rose Meunier, the daughter of simple *meuniers* [millers], and she attracted no notice whatever during her studies at the Conservatory of Music. When she graduated, in 1878, she won no prizes, and being utterly without resources and a highly moral young woman she sought desperately for an engagement.

The moment was not propitious for her, it being a period when a harsh personality was seldom taken as a mark of distinction; and a Sunday-afternoon recital—the usual way of bringing oneself to public attention—was utterly beyond her possibilities. Furthermore, Mlle Rose Muenier seemed to be ill-endowed physically: her features were sharp, her figure was not gracefully rounded; her arms were long and thin. At this moment of desperate poverty a suitor appeared and was accepted—as a last resort. This was M. Caron, formerly conductor at the Théâtre des Nouveautés, a pianist-accompanist, an obscure musician, physically deformed—a hunchback—but intelligent and shrewd. Artistically intuitive, he sensed in the young woman a great unsuspected artistic potential; he guided her through new studies, advised her and directed her, despite the very obvious incompatibility of their personalities; and the result of this labor was her engagement by the Théâtre de la Monnaie in 1882.

Henceforth Mme Caron was well equipped to make her way in the theatre: she was ready for success.

What is more, from the moment she appeared on the stage in Brussels her past defects were hailed as marks of distinction, and she charmed everyone as woman and as artist. Her facial expression, by turn tender and stern, terrifying and touching; her majestic carriage, at once stately and restrained; her voice, powerful and of perfect pitch; her exquisite diction; the great art she displayed in her gestures and her costumes—everything about her was seductive; and very shortly, as Brunhilde, she won unanimous applause and was hailed as an incomparable lyric *tragédienne*.

. . . Her successes have in no way changed the modesty of her character and the simplicity of her life. Until very

[86]

recently Mme Caron, who was divorced in 1886, but has nevertheless retained the name of her husband (now *disparu*), lived in a quite modest apartment in the rue Saint-Philippe-du-Roule, with her mother, her sister and her two-year-old daughter. The great artiste is at present installed, with those members of her family, in larger and more comfortable quarters.

For the most part, the biographical details in "Mme Caron Intime" are accurate. Properly spelled, her maiden name was Meuniez; at the Conservatoire she was awarded a *"troisième accessit"* (honorable mention third class). After leaving the conservatory she studied with Mme Marie Sasse (a well-known soprano, the first Selika in Meyerbeer's *L'Africaine*): perhaps that was part of M. Caron's "guidance."

The article requires little comment. Except, perhaps, to point out that the word *disparu*, literally "disappeared," is a common euphemism for "dead." Had M. Caron died? Clearly, in 1886, the year following his wife's first Paris triumph in *Sigurd*, he had been discarded. Perhaps the offensive tone of "Mme Caron Intime" was intended as disingenuous frankness, an illustration of the case of an ugly duckling? Under the wand of a good fairy—poor M. Caron—the unpromising young woman blossomed— not necessarily into beauty, but into art?

One of Mme Caron's admirers, both for her voice and her acting style, was Edgar Degas, that great delineator of the operatic scene both onstage and backstage. In his youth Degas had seen the legendary Rachel at the Comédie Française; and in 1885, after attending a performance of *Sigurd* at the Paris Opéra he wrote to his friend Ludovic Halévy: "Madame Caron's arms are still there—those thin and divine arms, which she knows how to hold aloft for a long time, without affectation, and then lower without haste. When you see them again you'll exclaim 'Rachel, Rachel,' as I do." In 1890 Degas traveled to Brussels to hear Mme Caron in *Salammbô*: one wonders whether the exotic costumes of the women singers in that opera may have reminded him of his own early canvas, *Mademoiselle*

Fiocre in the Ballet "La Source" (now in the Brooklyn Museum).

Salammbô was sung at the Paris Opéra one hundred and ninety-six times. Its most recent performance took place on February 26, 1943, during the German occupation of the city.

During a long career, Mme Caron sang in many other operas, among them *Fidelio, Iphigénie in Tauris, Faust, La Juive, Lohengrin,* and *Otello,* the last presumably in the French translation partially made by Camille DuLocle. But Salammbô is the role for which she was renowned. Something about the Carthaginian princess—and, no doubt, the particular sympathy existing between singer and composer—called forth her best powers. Many other sopranos have sung the role, but in opera history it remains hers. She seems never to have recorded any of its music. (The portion of this *Salammbô* known to be on a disk is the "Air des Colombes" ["Song of the Doves"], sung by Marguréite Mérentié, who in 1907 had been one of Mme Caron's successors in the title role at the Opéra.) There remains a joint tribute to Mme Caron by the grateful composer and librettist of the opera: a sonnet by Du-Locle, entitled *Rendezvous,* set to music by Reyer and published in 1896, dedicated to her by both men. After retiring from the stage, Rose Caron was for some years, like her own teacher before her, a vocal coach in Paris. She died there on April 9, 1930. On June 28, 1983, there was offered at auction in Paris the original autograph score of *Salammbô* for piano and voice—those pages from which Mme Caron had, in a "little room," first movingly sung the role for Reyer. The composer had had the manuscript bound in red morocco, with Mme Caron's initials embossed in gold on both covers; he had written a grateful message on the title page, and presented it to the soprano the night of the triumphant premiere at the Paris Opéra. Now, ninety-one years later, it was sold for twenty thousand francs.

Salammbô was Ernest Reyer's last opera. After its Paris

premiere he wrote to both the conductor and the chorus master of the Opéra, thanking them and the artists under their direction for their roles in having made his opera a success. *"Les artistes de l'orchestre de l'Opéra se sont surpassés,"* he wrote; and as for the chorus, *"Ces excellents artistes ont été à la hauteur de leur renommé"*; and he saw to it that both letters were published in *Le Figaro.* Then, within a few years, and with *Sigurd* and *Salammbô* both in the repertoire, he retired to Le Lavandou on the Mediterranean coast, not far from his native Marseilles. There he died on January 15, 1909, at the age of eighty-six. His statue now stands in the square. A number of his critical articles have been gathered from the files of the newspapers in which they originally appeared, and published in two volumes. He wrote well.

Thus the composer of *Salammbô* lived to know that his opera was produced, in January, 1901, in Cairo, in the same theatre where he had attended the world premiere of Aïda, at the Khedive's invitation, thirty years before.

By that time *Salammbô* had even crossed the Atlantic, making its North American debut at the French Opera House (Théâtre de l'Opéra) in New Orleans on January 26, 1900. And a few months after the Cairo engagement it opened at the Metropolitan Opera House in New York, on March 20, 1901.

As was usual in those days, most of the singers in both American productions were Europeans, and some members of the casts had previously sung their roles in Brussels or Paris, and perhaps in Cairo as well. Stage managers were imported; in New Orleans, where almost the entire company was French, the scenery, too, was advertised as "coming from France"; and in New York it was constructed in the Metropolitan's workshop from models provided by Paris.

But if the two American productions were alike, and not least in resembling their European originals, their receptions were marked by dissimilarities—dissimilarities that possibly illustrate differences between the New Or-

[89]

leans and the New York manner of both witnessing and reporting an evening of opera. Even the advance advertising in the New Orleans press (in this case the *Daily States* for January 25, 1900) had a provincial air about it:

FRENCH OPERA

Grand Gala Performance.

With Entirely New Scenery Imported from France, Rich Costumes, Gorgeous Mise-en-scene.

THURSDAY, JAN. 25, 1900
Twenty-eighth Subscription Performance.

For the First Time in the United States
REYER'S MASTERPIECE.

SALAMMBO.

Grand Opera in 5 Acts and 8 Tableaux.
Words by Camille du Locle. Music by
E. Reyer.
Grand Ballet. Grand Triumphal March.

The French Opera House, on Bourbon Street, had opened in 1859. (It would be destroyed by fire on December 2, 1919, with almost total loss of its contents, including documents: its history is known only piecemeal, chiefly from contemporary newspapers.) There was no resident company: each November the city welcomed an ever-different, but always predominantly French, troupe; the season ran until Mardi Gras; choruses were locally recruited. From 1895 to 1904 the impresario of the French Opera House was a Monsieur François Charley, who always arrived from France a few days before his singers. Little is known about him beyond the fact that local audiences were in the habit, when particularly pleased by some sensational feature in a production, of shouting his name: "Charley! Charley!" Then they would settle down to look and listen, ready to give equally generous, if more conventional, applause to singers and orchestra. It was an endearing form of enthusiasm which had no close parallel in the more formal atmosphere prevalent—at that time—in New York.

One might cite, by way of example, the closing moments of the first New Orleans performance of *Salammbô*. Following the original Brussels production, it had immediately become "traditional" for the wretched Mâtho, a bound and tortured captive, to meet his end by being forced by the infuriated mob to roll down a long flight of steps, landing at Salammbô's feet, and there breaking his bonds and joining her in self-slaughter by sword or dagger. In New Orleans this sensational denouement, "the 'clou' of the performance," as one newspaper called it, was greeted by a roar of delighted "Charley!"s and hailed in the local English-language press as "simply grand" and in the French, along with the rest of the performance, as "*décidément phénomenal.*" Whereas the *New York Times*, a year later, would merely remark dryly that "Mr. Saleza [the New York Mâtho] fell down the steps in the last scene with a realism that would have moved the heart of Mr. James A. Herne or Mr. W. D. Howells." (By 1974 the New York press had become less self-possessed, to judge from its rapturous acclamation of Martti Talvela's downstairs tumble in the last act of *Boris Godunov*.)

Similarly, the New Orleans *Times Democrat* for January 20, 1900, wrote of M. Bouxmann, who sang the role of Giscon, the Carthaginian general: "His horseback entree of the first act was the most successful horse episode of the local stage. The basso pushed away the attendants, who wished to hold the animal's head, drew him up with the hand of a trained horseman, sang from the saddle, turned and rode away without dismounting." Whereas the *New York Times* would merely list "Mr. Gilbert," the Metropolitan's Giscon. Possibly, in the New York production, he was not even mounted.

New Orleans journalism of the period is reproduced here not to mock, but to indicate that at least as reflected in a variety of their newspapers, the citizens of that city, famous for its music seasons, were content to listen to opera enthusiastically without requiring analysis. New Orleans journalistic forays into criticism seldom amounted to more than "The grand ballet as presented in the fifth tableau is simply wonderful and brought forth cries of Charley, Charley from all corners of the vast auditorium." Or, at most: "The Tanit leitmotif is the ribbon binding the various musical pictures into a harmonious album. It is the simplest of melodies, recalling in a distant way the plaintive 'Mavourneen, Mavourneen' in the Irish master-piece, another proof that 'art knows no country.'"

It is surprising, perhaps, that so music-loving a city should have been content with that kind of printed com-ment. But the case was stated frankly in the newspaper called *L'Abeille de la Nouvelle Orléans* (*The New Or-leans Bee*) in its review of *Salammbô* on January 28th: "It should never be forgotten, even in the lyric theatre, that the eye plays a more important role than the ear, and that the spectator has more enjoyment from what he is seeing than what he is listening to." Perhaps, in discussion among themselves, some Nouvelle Orléanais may have enjoyed going deeper.

The review of the New York premiere of *Salammbô* in the *New York Times* of March 21, 1901 (with the beauti-ful Lucienne Breval as the heroine), is unsigned, as is a brief sequel printed on the 23rd. Both were undoubtedly written by William J. Henderson, the *Times* music critic for many years. Henderson's detailed analysis is in a realm of writing quite apart from that of the New Orleans press. Its first paragraph sets the tone maintained throughout: one that combines generosity and objectivity with a flicker of irony:

> Although no one is likely to fall into the error of mis-taking *Salammbô* for a work of the first order, the splendor of its scenic plan, the gorgeousness of the attire gener-ously provided by Mr. Grau [Maurice Grau, the Metro-politan's manager], and the theatrical vivacity of some of its scenes will surely set the quidnuncs talking. Such a magnificent production was never before seen on the stage

[92]

of the Metropolitan, and it has seldom been equalled in the theatres of this country. . . . Miss Breval wore gorgeous gowns and ran the gamut of her semaphoric poses. She acted with French knowledge of routine, but her singing was not a source of joy. She has most of the vices of the French school with few of its virtues.

And there follows a critique of Reyer's score, far more disinterested and more penetrating than the Belgian or French reviews. "Everything sounds suitable, proper, appropriate, but nothing sounds inevitable. It might easily have been done some other way and sound just as well. . . . On the whole, it may be said that this is the work of an industrious, ambitious, well-schooled composer, who wrote operas because in France the stage is, as it ever has been, the goal of every musician's hope, but not because the fountains of his imagination overflowed. *Salammbô* commands some respect, even admiration, but it neither touches nor thrills."

Henderson's review and its sequel constitute the best journalistic writing that has been done on Reyer—on his qualities and his limitations. It is the equal of Reyer's own writing on the work of other composers and other performances, and constitutes an excellent introduction for anyone making a study of Reyer's career.

Salammbô was sung at New Orleans seven times in 1900, and at the Metropolitan three times in 1901. Those were its only American seasons, and apparently its only performances outside Belgium, France and Egypt.

But the opera had had one earlier brief run—one that is perhaps more appropriately recorded out of chronological order, since it was preeminently a Flaubertian, rather than a specifically musical, episode.

Flaubert had seldom spoken favorably of the citizenry of Rouen, his birthplace. "Detestation of the Rouennais is the beginning of taste," was one of his maxims. The day he learned of the death of his old friend Théophile Gautier he wrote to his niece: ". . . I crossed the city on foot, meeting three or four Rouennais. The spectacle of their vulgarity, their overcoats, their hats, what they said and the sound of their voices, made me want to vomit and weep at the same time." The special targets of his detestation were the prosperous cotton manufacturers and their families who composed a large part of local "society" and who either ignored his books or professed to be scandalized by them.

Certain of the more enlightened bourgeois and professional Rouennais, however, had in fact been Flaubert's friends; and in 1890, the tenth anniversary of his death, a group of these formed a committee and turned their attention to collecting funds for a monument in his honor, to be erected outside the recently built Municipal Library. The campaign succeeded, and a memorial was commissioned from the sculptor Chapu. (It took the form of a bronze bas-relief, combining a portrait head of Flaubert with a seated female figure of Truth "inscribing his name in the book of Immortals.") The dedication ceremony was scheduled for Sunday, November 23, 1890.

But Flaubert's friends had persuaded local politicians that the mere unveiling of a statue was insufficient tribute to an artist whose international renown was beginning to equal that of Rouen's other famous sons—the great Corneille and the tragic Géricault; pressure was brought to bear "at high levels" in Paris; and the Ministry of Public Instruction and Fine Arts ordered, most exceptionally, in Flaubert's honor, a series of seven performances, at the Théâtre des Arts in Rouen, of Reyer's *Salammbô*, in advance of its Paris production. Bowing to circumstances, Reyer rather reluctantly agreed to cooperate, and the Rouen premiere took place on Saturday, November 22, 1890, on the eve of the dedication of the bronze memorial. The leading role was sung by Mlle Eva Dufrane, a soprano from the Monnaie. After the curtain had fallen on the final act it rose again, and Mlle Dufrane, standing beside a large portrait of Salammbô's creator, sang a "hymn to Flaubert" written for the occasion by Eugène Brieux and composed by Alexandre Georges.

As the *Figaro* said the next day, Rouen audiences were

known to be *"très difficiles"*: conscious of being thought
provincial, they insisted on "being shown." (Indeed, in
nineteenth-century French theatrical circles the expression "All aboard for Rouen" signified expectation of the
worst.) But at the Rouen premiere of *Salammbô*, "Although at first the audience was a trifle reserved," the
Figaro said, "it quickly warmed up. . . . The Management
had decorated the entire theatre with garlands of ivy and
camellias, as is the fashion at Nice. The Théâtre des Arts
resembled a triumphal arch, under which *Salammbô* finally made its glorious entrance into France."

At five o'clock on the cold, nasty morning of the next
day, Sunday, November 23, 1890, the novelist Edmond de
Goncourt, sixty-eight years old, had to leave his warm bed
in Auteuil and catch an early train to Rouen. As an old
friend of Flaubert's, he was to deliver the principal address at the unveiling of the monument. At the station he
joined a few other literary men, among them Guy de Maupassant, whom Flaubert had loved and called his "disciple," and Emile Zola, who had called Flaubert "master"
and whose naturalist novels Flaubert had admired with
some reservations. Goncourt notes in his celebrated *Journal* how ill Maupassant looked that day. "As the train
crossed the Seine near Rouen he pointed to the river, and
said, 'That's where I used to go rowing and where I caught
what I have today.'" (Maupassant referred to the boat-
ing parties of his youth and to the syphilis, then entering
its tertiary stage, which would kill him two and a half
years later, at the age of forty-three.)

In Rouen the party from Paris joined a group of local
and departmental dignitaries at a lunch given by the
mayor. Goncourt was nervous. "I was afraid that by the
tenth sentence my speech would be strangled in my lar-
ynx." But on the platform, to his surprise, he experienced
merely a "tremolo in the legs." Despite a freezing rain and
a wind that made him glad of his fur overcoat and
whipped the pages of his manuscript, all went well; and
after affectionately praising Flaubert and his work he pre-

[95]

sented the memorial, on behalf of the committee, to the city of Rouen.

It was accepted by the mayor, who smilingly assured the audience that there was no truth to the "rumor" that Flaubert had detested his fellow Rouennais, or vice versa. And the remainder of the program included "a speech about twenty-five times longer than mine," Goncourt noted, "by a member of the Rouen Academy, so proliferating in clichés and absurd language as to guarantee him a drubbing by Flaubert on Resurrection Day." Then the band struck up and the company dispersed.

Maupassant disappeared, "to visit a relative." Before taking their train, the other Parisians foregathered in a restaurant for a dinner that inevitably included the Rouen specialty, *canard à l'orange*, a dish for which Goncourt confesses he had "but middling esteem."

In Paris once more, Goncourt made his customary entry in his *Journal*. In his speech, written before seeing the Flaubert monument, he had spoken of it as "an eloquent Allegory . . . to which the sculptor has brought all his skill, all his talent." Now in his *Journal* he wrote differently. "To be frank, the monument by Chapu is a pretty bas-relief made of sugar, in which Truth *a l'air de faire ses besoins dans un puits*."

Flaubert, a practitioner of what is euphemistically known as Gallic humor, would have enjoyed Goncourt's words about the seated commemorative figure "attending to her intimate needs." Nevertheless Flaubert, who might perhaps have been expected to scorn the belated tributes of official monuments, had himself, late in life, fought for just such a memorial to his fellow-writer and Rouennais friend, Louis Bouilhet—admonishing a reluctant municipality that "Whoever passes by this monument will remember that here was a man who, in these materialist times, consecrated his life to literature."

Michael Walzer's 'Exodus and Revolution'

A CANAANITE READING

Edward W. Said

Michael Walzer's *Exodus and Revolution* (Basic Books) is principally a contemporary reading of the Old Testament story. Yet it also touches on revolutionary politics and biblical and narrative interpretation; and it refers to the relationship between secular and religious realms, between "paradigms" and actual events, between a particularly Jewish and a more generally Western history. This may seem rather a heavy load for so small and apparently modest a book, but it is a major part of its interest, and indeed of Walzer's skill as a writer, to say things with an appealing simplicity while in fact alluding to many considerably more complex issues. The result, however, is not so much an unsatisfactory as an unsatisfying book, though I hasten to add that Walzer sets his reader's critical faculties very intensely to work, surely a testimonial to how provocative his subject is.

The essential lines of Walzer's argument are quickly rehearsed. Unlike narratives of recurrence and return, the Exodus story is linear, Walzer says, and moves from bondage and oppression in Egypt, through the wanderings in Sinai, to the Promised Land. Moses is not an Odysseus who returns home, but a popular leader—albeit an outsider—of a people undergoing both the travails and novel triumphs of national liberation. What we have in Exodus, therefore, is the "original form of progressive history"— and, Walzer adds, while other slave revolts in antiquity established no really new or influential type of political activity, "it is possible to trace a continuous history from Exodus to the radical politics of our own time."

Walzer's exposition is interspersed with references to later events and to thinkers explicitly indebted to Exodus. Readers of his first book, *The Revolution of the Saints*, will not be surprised to see some of the seventeenth-century Protestant radicals discussed there referred to again in *Exodus and Revolution,* in addition to various American Black leaders of the civil rights movement and Latin American liberation theologians. Two of the main features of this constellation of affiliated political ideologues are, first, that they all draw upon divine authority for "radical hope" even as they stress "this worldly endeavor," and second, that none of them is theoretically systematic or, in the literal sense, revolutionary. Rather, Walzer says, these traits express what he is himself committed to, "the Jewish account of deliverance and the political theory of liberation."

Specific to both of these is the covenant, which in the Old Testament is made with God but which Walzer reinterprets as "a founding act" that creates "a people" and the possibility of "a politics without precedent in [the people's] own experience." More advantages of the covenant are that "the people" become a "moral agent." Thus for the people, solidarity with the oppressed is a moral obligation. Less pleasant (and less easy to gloss over) is the people's candidly stated need to defeat counterrevolution—that is, worshippers of the Golden Calf and, in the Promised Land, the unfortunate native inhabitants who by definition are not members of the Chosen People. Walzer's main point, however, is that culmination of Exodus in the attainment of a Promised Land is really the birth of a new polity, one that admits its members to a communal politics of participation in political and religious spheres. It isn't entirely clear what useful or positive role God can play in these spheres, once they have become the social property, so to speak, of the citizenry in a secular state; Walzer's indifference to the problem is odd, but one can at least understand it.

Walzer concedes that Exodus politics—the phrase is his, and he uses it to distinguish a particular political outlook and style—can lead, as indeed it has led in Jewish and Christian history, to messianism and millenarianism. These riotous chiliastic movements are very distant from the relatively sober and apparently attractive notions professed by believers in the kind of Exodus politics endorsed by Walzer. He also concedes that the best part of the

Exodus experience occurs at the beginning; problems of many sorts, all of them self-made, come in immediately after that to qualify, and perhaps even cancel, the beginning's promise. In any event, according to Walzer, we are fully entitled to reject anything about Exodus that smacks of mere territorialism, since what matters is the "deeper argument" proposing "that righteousness" (and not the coarse act of holding the Promised Land) "is the only guarantee of blessings." In applying these notions to modern Zionism, Walzer seems to align himself with those Israelis who want a compromise over the territories occupied by Israel since 1967, and he cites Gershom Scholem in support of the view that Zionism is not a messianic movement but a historically—as opposed to religiously—redemptive one.

Along the way Walzer offers a number of insights that expand and illuminate the Bible's relatively speedy narrative course. Of these his commentary on "murmurings"—the anxieties, difficulties and restive stirrings among the Jews being forced to actions beyond ordinary tolerance—is the freshest and most perceptive. But, as with much else in this work of one hundred and fifty pages, one wishes for more detail and amplification in its author's account of modern styles of radical politics, particularly when he draws rather challenging distinctions between Moses's Levites and Lenin's vanguard party as élite leaders of a popular movement. The former he says can be "read" as avatars of social-democratic leadership, whereas the latter quite obviously cannot. Yet the evidence he offers for such a charitable reading (unlike Lincoln Steffens's, who thought Leninism and Exodus supported each other) is comparatively meager; it doesn't in itself convince one that Moses's kindness or his lawgiving magnanimity are enough to inhibit later clerical bloodthirstiness and zeal. Nevertheless, Walzer's readers are likely at first to go along with many of his suggestive, rather than exhaustive, arguments because they are, I think, inherently attractive.

A "relaxed and easygoing vision" of reality, said Ronald Dworkin of one of Walzer's previous books: the same vision is very much in evidence in *Exodus and Revolution*. Homey, egalitarian, melioristic, as in the book's final sentences, a summary of

what the Exodus first taught, or what it has commonly been taken to teach, about the meaning and possibility of politics and about its proper form:
— first, that wherever you live, it is probably Egypt;
— second, that there is a better place, a world more attractive, a promised land;
— and, third, that "the way to the land is through the wilderness." There is no way to get from here to there except by joining together and marching.

As you read Walzer and mull over his various agreeable conclusions and affirmations, you begin to wonder how the world has become so malleable and so possible a place. Not that Walzer actually *says* it is a possible place; on the contrary, he insists on its complexity and difficulty at almost every opportunity. No: what bothers you is the world of Walzer's discourse, the verbal space in which his discussions and analyses take place, as well as the political locale isolated by him for reflection and hypothesis. Then you begin to realize how many extremely severe excisions and restrictions have occurred in order to produce the calmly civilized world of Walzer's Exodus. In itself, the strategy of *découpage* is unavoidable. Every author who pretends to rationality obviously has to do some cutting and delimiting in order to manage his or her subject, but although these tend to occur offstage, they are certainly well within critical reach, and require fairly close inspection if the main onstage action is to be fully comprehended.

Walzer's "relaxed and easygoing" work is the result of a very curious and, to my mind, extremely problematic antithetical mode, insistent and uncompromising in places, indifferent and curiously forgiving in others. Take as perhaps the most obvious instance the cluster of descriptive references with which he endows Exodus: it is Western, Jewish, liberating, complex, this-worldly, linear, clear. Compared with that of Lewis Feuer's *Ideology and the Ideologists* (referred to once in a passing note by Walzer), the Exodus of Walzer's study is tremendously circumscribed; Feuer is anxious to show the presence of the Exodus "myth," as he calls it, in *all* revolutionary ideology, Western and non-Western, progressive and reactionary alike, the more easily to reveal its multiple shortcomings.

But the grounds for Walzer's assertions of Exodus's various discrete and positive qualities are kept obscure and, I think, unexamined. Why is Exodus "Western," for instance? Why is it of use to seventeenth-century English revolutionaries? to some Latin American liberationists and not to others? to some Black leaders but not to others? Walzer has no answer that is not tautological, and he does not really propose the questions.

The effect of Walzer's chatty style is to disarm those who might look for evidence, argument, proof and the like—particularly in the writing of an author whose numerous strictures on Michel Foucault (*Dissent*, Fall 1983) includes the objection that Foucault's studies are "often ineffective in what we might think of as scholarly law enforcement—the presentation of evidence, detailed argument, the consideration of alternative views." Nor can *Exodus and Revolution* be taken as a poetic or metaphoric excursus through an Old Testament text. Walzer's political and moral study is addressed to us "in the West" and his prose is dotted with *us*'s and *ours*, the net result of which is to mobilize a community of interpretation that relies for illumination upon a canonical text believed to be central, true, important as giving "permanent shape to Jewish conceptions of time." And, he adds, "it serves as a model, ultimately, for non-Jewish conceptions too." *Ultimately* in this sentence plays a crucial tactical role, as of course does the plural in "Jewish conceptions of time." Walzer signals that there are in fact more issues than can be dealt with by "us" here and now; if we had the time, we could ultimately discover how important Exodus was as a model for various nonspecified non-Jewish views of temporality. *Ultimately.*

Let me call this tactic inclusion by deferral, in order next to bring in its accomplice, avoidance. Remember that at the same time that he uses these tactics, Walzer is making very strong assertions about revolution, progress, peoplehood, politics and morality: it is not as if he were just an avoider and a deferrer. In fact, a fog is exhaled by his prose to obscure those problems entailed by his arguments but casually deferred and avoided before they can make trouble. The great avoidance, significantly, is of history itself—the history of the text he comments on, the history of the Jews, the history of the various peoples who have used Exodus, as well as those who have not, the history of models, texts, paradigms, utopias, in their relationship to actual events, the history of such things as covenants and founding texts.

Walzer spends no time at all on what brought the Jews to Egypt (in Genesis) nor on the great degree of wealth and power which because of Joseph they achieved there. It is quite misleading simply to refer to them as an oppressed people when Genesis 46 and 47 tell in some detail of how "they had possessions therein, and grew, and multiplied exceedingly." The Old Testament gives the strong impression that the Jews had come to Egypt, an earlier promised land, at the invitation of Pharaoh to seek their fortunes, that is, as compradores; when Egypt fell on hard times, so too did the Jews, and because they were foreign they were the targets of local rage and frustration. This history is hardly comparable with that of American Blacks or contemporary Latin Americans. I suspect that Walzer uses the rhetoric of contemporary liberation movements to highlight certain aspects of Old Testament history and to mute or minimize others.

The most troubling of these is of course the injunction laid on the Jews by God to exterminate their opponents, an injunction that somewhat takes away the aura of progressive national liberation which Walzer is bent upon giving to Exodus. The greatest authority on the history of class politics in the ancient world, G.E.M. de Ste. Croix, Fellow of New College, Oxford, says the following in his monumental study, *The Class Struggle in the Ancient Greek World*:

> I do not wish to give the impression that the Romans were habitually the most cruel and ruthless of all ancient imperial powers. Which nation in antiquity has the best claim to that title I cannot say, as I do not know all the evidence. On the basis of such of the evidence as I do know, however, I can say that I know of only one people which felt able to assert that it actually had a divine command to exterminate whole populations among those it conquered; namely, Israel. Nowadays Christians, as well as Jews, seldom care to dwell on the merciless ferocity of Jahweh, as revealed not by hostile sources but by the very

literature they themselves regard as sacred. Indeed, they continue as a rule to forget the very existence of this incriminating material.

Not only does Walzer refuse to meet these matters head on; what little he does say slides away from the facts, as we shall see in a moment. He also cuts out from consideration all of the material in Numbers and Leviticus (extensions of Exodus) in which we find Jahweh urging revoltingly detailed punishments for offenders against His Law. It seems to me inescapably true that during moments of revolutionary fervor, *all* the monotheistic religions propose unforgiving, merciless punishment against actual or imagined enemies, punishments formulated by perfervid clerics in the name of their One Deity. This is as true of early Islam as it is of Pauline Christianity and of Exodus. Simply to step past all of that into a new realm called "Exodus politics" will not release you from the problem. In other words, it seems unlikely to expect that the kind of secular and decent politics Walzer salvages from Exodus could co-exist with the authority of the sole Divinity plus the derivative but far more actual authority of His designated human representatives. But that *is* what Walzer alleges. Walzer also claims rather lamely that commandments like "thou shalt utterly destroy them" should not be taken literally. Similarly, he avers, "the original conquest and occupation" of the land plays only "a small part" in Exodus politics. It is difficult to know here what Walzer is talking about, so anxious is he to disconnect from, and yet connect with, the essential parts of Exodus that have inspired the text's later users, from Indian-killing Puritans in New England to South African Boers claiming large swatches of territory held by Blacks. Maybe it is true (although Walzer provides no evidence) that the conquest of Canaan was "more like a gradual infiltration than a systematic campaign of extermination"; but he seems unperturbed that for the Jews "the Canaanites are explicitly excluded from the world of moral concern." This does not suggest a very elevated model for realistic politics, and it isn't clear how the dehumanization of anyone standing in Moses' way is any less appalling than the attitudes of the murderous Puritans or of the founders of *apartheid*. To say that "thou shalt utterly destroy them" is a command that "doesn't survive the work of interpretation; it was effectively rescinded by talmudic and medieval commentators arguing over its future applications" is, I regret to say, to take no note of history *after* the destruction of the Temple in which Jews were in no position at all collectively to implement the commandment. Therefore, I think, it is Walzer who is wrong, not "the right-wing Zionists" in today's Israel whom he upbraids for being too fundamentalist. The text of Exodus *does* categorically enjoin victorious Jews to deal unforgivingly with their enemies, the prior native inhabitants of the Promised Land. As to whether that should be "a gradual infiltration" or "a systematic campaign of extermination," the fundamental attitude is similar in both alternatives: get rid of the natives, as a practical matter. In either case, Israel's offending non-Jewish population is "excluded from the world of moral concern" and thus denied equal rights with Jews.

Walzer offers no detailed, explicit or principled resistance to the irreducibly sectarian premises of Exodus, still less to the notion of a God as sanguinary as Jahweh directly holding them in place. Walzer accepts those unpleasant but surely not simple facts as givens, and then goes on to protest that he finds in Exodus a realistic, secular paradigm for "radical politics." Not being as amphibious as Walzer, the unbelieving or atheistic reader, such as myself, cannot so quickly adjust to this odd new element, which combines sacred and profane in equal doses. In the positivist calendar, Auguste Comte unsurprisingly accorded Moses the dubious privilege of having founded the first theocracy. As a salve for the secular conscience, however, Walzer again and again offers the startling propositions that Exodus is nevertheless really secular and progressive, is about liberation and against oppression. According to him, no other text has either the priority or the force of this one, and, to repeat, "it is possible to trace a continuous history from the Exodus to the radical politics of our own time."

As we have seen, Walzer's "continuous" lines come from

what remains after inconvenient fact and divagations have
been lopped off all around them. His dismissal of the
Helots' struggle against their Spartan overlords is an example of how one such fact, which considerably lessens
the uniqueness of Exodus's liberationist power, gets eliminated. Helots, Walzer says, didn't leave "us" an account
of what they meant by deliverance, as if in itself leaving
"an account" qualified you for entry into the rolls of honor.
Only the Jews in Exodus did, which is why they were
ultimately the model for radical politics. The sturdily
anti-clerical de Ste. Croix, however, enables us to dismiss
such an exaggerated comparison as the preposterous ahistorical cant it is by stating not only that the Helots were
far more unfortunate as "state serfs" than any other ancient people, but that they were legendary in classical
antiquity and after for articulating their unified struggle
"to be free and an independent entity."

Once you begin a catalogue of the exceptions to Walzer's claims for Exodus, much less remains of his argument
about the book's paramount importance for future movements of liberation. Vico, Marx, Michelet, Gramsci, Fanon
either mention the book not at all or only in passing. Many
Black and Central American theorists do mention it; but
a great many more do not. Certainly Exodus is a trope
that comes easily to hand in accounts of deliverance, but
there isn't anything especially "Western" about it, nor—
to judge from the various "non-Western" tropes of liberation from oppression—is there anything especially progressive that can be derived from its supposedly Western
essence. All oppressed peoples dream of liberation after
all, and most tend to find rhetorical modes for mobilizing
themselves, imagining a better future and justifying to
themselves the vengeance they intend to take not only on
their former masters but also on their future underlings.

Given recent history, one would have thought that Walzer might have reconsidered the whole matter of divinely
inspired politics and coaxed out of it some more-sobering,
perhaps even ironic, reflections than the ones he presents.
With examples readily at hand of a crazy religious leadership at the head of substantial political movements in
Israel, Lebanon and Iran (all of them pulling references

out of their common monotheistic tradition in order to eliminate opposition) can he be seriously recommending that we use Exodus as "realistic" or "progressive"? Yes, he can. Perhaps it is the Exodus narrative itself he finds appealing as a work of art. If so, he says hardly anything about it that hasn't been said more artfully by various literary theorists—Northrop Frye, Frank Kermode, Paul Ricoeur, Hayden White, scholars whose uses of the Bible are exhilarating in their technical as well as aesthetic ingenuity.

No: Walzer's Exodus offers the opportunity for him to assert and stress the inaugural priority of a text as a matter of consolidation and conviction, not of persuasion or of proof. As for the relationship between Exodus and its subsequent users, Walzer included, that, like so much else about this curious contemporary performance, is hinted at in telegraphic allusions. The theoretical question of how ideological texts like Exodus relate to actual events (cf. Gramsci's famous 1917 treatment of the Bolshevik revolution, "The Revolution Against 'Das Kapital'") is not even considered. Then too Walzer's insistence on seventeenth-century Puritan ideology, which he cites as confirmation of Exodus's millennial power, denudes the phenomenon of its fascinating seventeenth-century context in the period's politicized philo-Semitism, recently studied in "Philo-Semitism and the Readmission of the Jews to England, 1603–1655" (Clarendon Press, Oxford, 1982), a monograph by David S. Katz. Walzer also ignores the quite potent negative reaction against Moses and Exodus to be found in the writings of some Puritan figures, as he does also Moses' quite fanciful apotheosis in writers like the eighteenth-century Bishop Warburton. Above all, I think, Walzer's work relegates the notion of a genuinely secular political option to nullity; he seems to be saying that only the salutary inflections in Exodus could bring forth a wholesomely progressive politics, thereby sweeping the board improbably clean of zealotry, vicious sectarianism, tyrannical theoretical systems and the sheer disorderly tumble of historical events. Reading Walzer, you could not know that a whole ideological radical literature, Western and non-Western, had offered millions of adherents ideas for which his reading of Exodus makes no allowances. Why is Walzer so undialectical, so simplifying, so ahistorical and reductive?

The first answer is that he really is not. His argument in *Exodus and Revolution* has an altogether different, and quite complex, trajectory from the one presented to a surface reading.

To begin with, Walzer is deeply and symptomatically anti-Marxist: he will have none of the labor theory of value, of relations of production, of historical materialism. Informed by his espousal of what he calls Jewish (that is, religious) conceptions of time, the anti-Marxism in Walzer is not difficult to understand. Yet Walzer continues to aver his radicalism as well as his attachments to a "secular and realistic politics," the basis for which he locates in Exodus.

Now there is nothing in *Exodus and Revolution* to suggest that Walzer's attitude toward current Jewish studies is a very developed one. From what I know of Jewish studies as a field most influenced by Gershom Scholem and today having some bearing on literary theory, it doesn't seem to me that Walzer even tries to make a contribution to the field, or to engage with other scholars working in it. I say all this tentatively because, on the one hand, Walzer doesn't offer his readers very many clarified insights as to his fundamental interests in the hermeneutical problems of canonical texts, and because, on the other hand, the Jewish material in Walzer's work is made to pull in the chariot, so to speak, of a resolutely political (and not philosophical) agenda, its path marked by repeated words and phrases: *progressive, moral, radical politics, national liberation, oppression.*

Considered as a group, the provenance of these is not Exodus. The terms enter American and European political vocabulary after the Second World War, usually in the context of colonial wars fought against movements of national liberation. The power of "liberation" and "oppression" in the works of those Third World militants like Cabral and Fanon, who were organically linked to anti-colonial insurrectionary movements, is that the concepts were later able to acquire a certain embattled legitimacy in the discourse of First World writers sympathetic to anticolonialism. The point about writers like Sartre, Debray and Chomsky, however, is that they were not mere echoes of the African, Asian and Latin American anti-imperialists, but intellectuals writing from within—and against—the colonialist camp.

Although most commentators recognize that that period is now practically over (largely because the anticolonial movements were victorious), only a little attention has been devoted to the ideological aftermath in Europe and America. A "return" to Judeo-Christian values was trumpeted; the defense of Western civilization was made coterminous with general attacks on terrorism, Islamic fundamentalism, structuralism and communism; a pantheon of aggressive new culture heroes emerged, including Norman Podhoretz, Jeane Kirkpatrick, George Will and Michael Novak. Much retrospective analysis of the colonial past focused on the evils of the newly independent states—the corruption and tyranny of their rule, the betrayed promise of their revolutions, the mistaken faith placed in them by their European supporters. The most striking revisionist has been Conor Cruise O'Brien, whose total about-face found him an entirely new audience (to some degree already primed by the Naipaul brothers) extremely eager to hear about the evils of black or brown dictators and the relative virtues of white imperialism. Other former anticolonialists like Gerard Chaliand contented themselves with chronicling the history of their disappointments.

The revival of anti-imperialist and liberationist language in discussions of Nicaragua and South Africa is one major exception to this pattern. The other major exception has been the rhetoric of liberal supporters of Israel. I speak here of a rather small but quite influential and prestigious group which, since 1967, has conducted itself with—from the perspective of students of rhetoric—considerable tactical flexibility. All along, in the face of considerable evidence to the contrary, members of this group have tried to maintain Israel's image as a progressive and wholly admirable state.

Consider that all of the Third World national liberation groups identified themselves with the displaced and dispossessed Palestinians, and Israel with colonialism. Historically, Zionist writers did not generally describe their own enterprise as a national liberation movement; they used a vocabulary specific to the moment of their vision of history—in the early twentieth century—which, while it contained important secular elements, was primarily religious and imperialist. The concepts of Chosen People, Covenant, Redemption, Promised Land and God were central to it; they gave identity to a people scattered in exile, they were useful in getting crucial European support and in the setting up of institutions like the Jewish National Fund, and, as is the case in all such situations, they were a focus for heated discussion, intense partisanship, contested political theories. After the Second World War the appeal of Zionism to the British Labour Party, the Socialist International, or to any number of Western liberal supporters—in whose ranks, surprisingly, one could find anti-imperialists like Sartre and Martin Luther King— was determined by European sympathy with the dominant Weizman–Ben-Gurion (and not Jabotinsky-Begin revisionist) trend within Zionism. This trend was perceived as socially progressive and morally justifiable in a form that Europeans and Americans could immediately understand. When R. H. S. Crossman, Paul Johnson or Reinhold Neibuhr spoke of Zionism (and later of Israel), it was because the Jewish presence in Palestine was viewed as an extension of like-minded undertakings in Europe, and, much more significantly, as restitution for the horrors of European anti-Semitism. Arabs were routinely seen as corrupt, backward, irrelevant.

After 1967, it became difficult to portray the Israeli occupation armies in Gaza, the West Bank, Sinai and the Golan Heights as furthering a great social experiment. And it has not often been noted how strange the anachronism, how ironic the disjuncture, that enabled the emergence of a new and eccentric colonial situation at exactly the same time that classical colonialism was being defeated nearly everywhere else. Eccentric because while they were settler-colonists like the French or British in Africa, Israeli Jews were different in essential ways: they had a traditional tie to the land, they had an unimaginable history of suffering, they were by no means an overseas offshoot of a metropolitan Western power. In 1967 however, the American intervention in Vietnam was at its height, and so for progressive supporters of Israel it became directly imperative to separate Israel in the Occupied Territories from America in Indochina, and to find coherent reasons for excusing the first while condemning the second.

Walzer played a pioneering role in this effort. With Martin Peretz (to whom *Exodus and Revolution* is dedicated) he wrote a landmark article in *Ramparts* (July 1967). Its title, "Israel Is Not Vietnam," comprehended half a dozen points, all of them showing the way in which Israel was not like France, the United States or Britain in their nasty colonial adventures. The article did not change the opinions of too many on the Left—to whom the article was explicitly addressed—and Peretz later withdrew his financial support from *Ramparts*. In any event, the article is important not only because Walzer used his Left credentials to speak with and to the Left, but also because the piece codified the mode of analysis he would later use.

The steps Walzer takes are worth listing. One: he finds a contemporary situation that could, if it isn't immediately addressed, affect Israel's standing adversely. In *Exodus and Revolution* it is the discredited appearance both of Jewish fundamentalism and continued colonial rule over many Arabs and Arab land. Two: he does that initially by appearing to condemn something close at hand, which progressives can also condemn without much effort and for which an already substantial consensus exists. In *Ramparts* it was Western colonialism; in *Exodus and Revolution* it is Zionist extremists like Gush Emunim and Rabbi Kahane. Three: he shows how certain rather provocative aspects of Jewish and/or Israeli history and/or related episodes in, say, American or French history, do not all fit the condemned instances, although some obviously do. Thus since Kahane, like Begin and Sharon, does not resemble Moses, Moses' stature as a fine leader is enhanced and hence he qualifies along with contemporary Israelis like Gershom Scholem and members of the Labor Party. Four (the really important intellectual move): Walzer formulates a theory, and/or finds a person or text—provided that none is too general, too uncompromising, too theoretically absolute—that provides the basis for a new category of politico-moral behavior. The book of Exodus interpreted as Walzer does fits the need quite perfectly, especially by allowing him to appropriate the language of national liberation and apply it anachronistically to the ancient Jews. Similarly, as we shall see presently, Albert Camus's position on French colonialism is made by Walzer to stand for the role of the "connected" intellectual. Five: he concludes by bringing together as many incompatible things as possible in as moral-sounding as well as politically palatable a rhetoric as possible. The desired effect is that both the generosity and the "relevance" and not the inconsistency of the procedure will be noted.

Operations of this sort cannot survive critical analysis. *Exodus and Revolution* proves their fallibility in all sorts of ways. The nagging question is how Walzer can continue to claim that his positions are progressive and even radical. He seems unconscious of the degree to which Israel's military victories have affected his work by imparting an unattractive moral triumphalism—harsh, shortsighted, callous—to nearly everything he writes, despite the veneer of radical phrases and protestations. The results have often been extraordinarily disturbing, but not, apparently, to him; here and there a disquiet will briefly disturb his style, but all in all Walzer is at ease with himself, and always has been. In 1972, for example, he argued that in every state there will be groups "marginal to the nation" which should be "helped to leave." Saying that he had Israel and the Palestinians in mind, he nevertheless conducted this discussion (that coolly anticipates by a decade Kahane's bloody cries of "they must go") in the broadly sunny and progressive perspectives of liberalism, independence, freedom from oppression. In his book *Just and Unjust Wars*, he insists on the difference between the two kinds of war, yet finds excuses for Israeli recourse to such actions he otherwise condemns as preemptive strikes and terrorism. His political articles in Peretz's *New Republic*, especially during the 1982 Israeli invasion of Lebanon, are full of such tactical paradoxes. In 1984 he rewrites the history of the Algerian war by praising Camus, the archetypal trimmer, for his loyalty to the *pied-noir* community (one of "the two Algerian nations," as Walzer calls them), for his rejection of "absolutist" politics, and for his unwillingness completely to condemn French colonialism. Walzer's unstated thesis is that the one hundred and thirty years of Algerian enslavement and consequent demands for Algerian liberation were somehow *less* of a moral cause than that of Camus's community of French settler-colonialists.

But Walzer's recuperation of Camus's lamentable waffling is even more interesting as an example of the relentless application of step four (the creation of a new category of politico-moral behavior). An essay by Walzer which appeared in the Fall 1984 issue of *Dissent*, the socialist magazine he edits with Irving Howe, reveals a good deal more about Walzer in the process than it does about Camus. Walzer says that Camus was impressive because "he was committed to a people, the FLN intellectuals to a cause." I shall leave aside for now the astonishing highhandedness of this judgment on the Algerian resistance and return to it later. According to Walzer, the people Camus wrote for were his own, and insofar as it has been viewed as the critic's role to write of his/her own people as "the others," Camus, to his immense credit, does not fit the prescription. So much, by way of backhanded dismissal, for Benda's *trahison des clercs*. Camus wrote of what was intimate for him as "a connected social critic," connected, that is, to his people, the colonizing *pieds-noirs* of Algeria. Thus he was effective in touching their consciences in ways that intellectuals who have taken critical distance from the people could not be. Moreover, Walzer adds, Camus, the writer of "intimate criticism," was always aware of how what he wrote might expose his family "to increased terrorism." Therefore he was sometimes reduced to silence, even though "the social critic can never be alone with his people; his intimacy can't take the form of private speech; it can only shape and control his public speech." In short, much more than those French intellectuals like Sartre and Aron, who condemned French colonialism outright, Camus the temporizer and political "realist" was heroic. He remained, in Walzer's approving formulation, *"what he was."*

The backing and filling as well as the complaisant

sophistry mobilized for this redefinition of the responsible intellectual's role are quite remarkable. Not only does Walzer advocate just going along with one's own people for the sake of loyalty and "connectedness": he also begs two fundamental questions. One: whether the position of critical distance rejected by Walzer could not also, at the same time, entail intimacy *and* something very much like the insider's connectedness with his or her community? In other words, are critical distance and intimacy with one's people mutually exclusive? Two: whether in the end the critic's togetherness with his/her community might be less valuable an achievement than condemning the evil they do together, therefore risking isolation? These questions raise others. Who is more effective as a critic of South African racial policy, a white South African militant against the régime, or an Afrikaaner liberal urging "constructive engagement" with it? Whom does one respect more, in the accredited Western and Judaic traditions, the courageously outspoken intellectual or loyal member of the complicit majority?

Much of Walzer's recent political and philosophical writing validates the notion of a double standard, one applied to outsiders, another to the members of the intellectual's own community or, to use an important word for him, sphere. Ronald Dworkin was right to say, in the *New York Review of Books* (April 13, 1983), that Walzer's moral theory depends on "a mystical premise" that "there are only a limited number of spheres of justice whose essential principles have been established in advance and must therefore remain the same for all societies." In a sense, *Exodus and Revolution* is a book about the establishment of such a sphere for the Chosen People who are inscribed in a Covenant and owners of a Promised Land presided over by God. Hence one's realization that Walzer's idea about "Exodus politics" turns out to be very snobbish and exclusive indeed.

Walzer has regressed to an odd position on the concept of equality. He has modified it by saying that social goods ought to be considered as having different valences within their separate spheres (education, medicine, leisure, office), not in absolute terms. The key terms once again are "members" in and "strangers" to a community, and although Walzer does not refer to Jews and non-Jews, it is difficult not to arrive at the conclusion that his reflections as a Jew on Israel have "shaped and controlled" his other thought. Thus, for him, the views that members have rights that strangers don't, or can't have, comes from the very same political ground on which Israel, as the "state of the Jewish people"—and not of its citizens, twenty percent of whom are not members of "the Jewish people"— is constructed. An additional complication, unattended to by Walzer's philosophy, is that whereas any Jew anywhere is entitled to Israeli citizenship under the Law of Return, no Palestinian anywhere, whether born in Palestine before 1948 or not, has any such right. I refer here to over two million Palestinian refugees, those people (with their recent descendants) who like the Canaanites were originally driven out of their native land by Israel on the premise that they were "explicitly excluded from the world of moral concern."

Yet the secular facts are not so neat, so clear and so simple, for "spheres" do not just exist, nor do they simply acquire the authority of natural facts, nor are they accepted uncomplainingly by "strangers" who feel their rights have been denied. Spheres are made and maintained by men and women in society. My feeling about Walzer is that his views on the existence of separate spheres have been shaped not so much by Israel as by those of Israel's triumphs which he seems to have felt have been in need of defense, explanation, justification. If Jews were still stateless, and being held in ghettos, I do not believe that Walzer would take the positions he has been taking. I cannot believe that he would say, for example, that communities have the right to restrict land ownership or immigration so that Jews (or Blacks, or Indians) couldn't participate equally in an absolute sense. Not at all. But now that Israel holds territories and rules inferior people, he does not question such practices against non-Jews. Rather he speaks about the intimate connectedness of Camus and the role of "members" in a state, as well as that of people marginal to it. As for the root problem: why the discrimination instituted by Jews in power should be any more just than the discrimination against Jews by non-Jews in power—that elicits no comment.

It would be wrong and unfair to single out Walzer in all this, since the adjustments and the compromises he has made are part of a general retreat among Left and liberal intellectuals during the past few years. We are at the point now where it is nearly impossible to discern individual themes within the chorus of revised views that blares out from the pages of formerly Left or liberal publications like the *New Republic*. Nowadays religion and God have returned, along with realism; utopia and radicalism are dirty words; terrorism and Soviet communism have acquired a kind of metaphysical purity of horror that eliminates history entirely; competition and the laws of a free market have replaced justice and social concern.

Certainly the peculiarity of Walzer's position (about which, with a few exceptions, he has not been stridently polemical) is that it is still advanced, and honored, as a Left position. It is at bottom a position retaining the vocabulary of the Left, yet scuttling both the theory and critical astringency that historically gave the Left its moral and intellectual power. For theory and critical astringency, Walzer has substituted an often implicit but always unexamined appeal to the concreteness and intimacy of shared ethnic and familial bonds, the realism, the "moral" responsibility of insiders who have "made it." Still, as I have said, if like the Canaanites you don't happen to qualify for membership, you are excluded from moral concern. Or, in Walzer's other surprisingly disparaging, dismissive judgment, you are relegated to a mere cause, like the FLN intellectuals.

If this is the difference between Exodus politics and the politics of causes, then I'm for the latter. For not only does Exodus seem to blind its intellectuals to the rights of others, it permits them to believe that history—the world of societies and nations, made by men and women—vouchsafes certain peoples the extremely problematic gift of "Redemption." Another of the many endowments Walzer bestows on Exodus insiders, Redemption, alas, elevates human beings in their own judgment to the status of divinely inspired moral agents. And this status in turn minimizes, if it does not completely obliterate, a sense of responsibility for what a people undergoing Redemption

[*115*]

does to other less fortunate people, unredeemed, strange, displaced and outside moral concern. For this small deficiency Walzer has a reassuring answer too: "to be a moral agent," he says, "is not to act rightly but to be capable of acting rightly." While it is not blindingly clear to me how national righteousness—a highly dubious idea to begin with—derives from such precepts, I can certainly see its value as a mechanism for self-excuse and self-affirmation.

Little of such writing derives from "radicalism" or from "righteousness." Walzer's Exodus book is written from the perspective of victory, which it consolidates and authorizes after the fact. As a result, the book is shot through with a confidence that comes from an easy commerce between successful enterprise in the secular world and similar (if only anticipated) triumphs in the extra-historical world. As to how radicalism and realism square with Walzer's astonishing reliance upon God, I cannot at all understand. I have no way—and Walzer proposes none—for distinguishing between the claims put forth by competing monotheistic clerics in today's Middle East, all of whom—Ayatollah Khomeini, Ayatollah Begin, Ayatollah Gemayel (and there are others)—say that God is indisputably on their side. That the Falwells, the Swaggerts, the Farrakhans in America say much the same thing piles Pelion on Ossa, and leaves Walzer unperturbed, urging a remarkable amalgam of God and realism upon us, as we try to muddle through.

But the one thing I want Walzer to remember is that the more he shores up the sphere of Exodus politics the more likely it is that Canaanites on the outside will resist and try to penetrate the walls banning them from the goods of what is, after all, partly their world too. The strength of the Canaanite, that is the exile position, is that being defeated and "outside," you can perhaps more easily feel compassion, more easily call injustice injustice, more easily speak directly and plainly of all oppression, and with less difficulty try to understand (rather than mystify or occlude) history and equality. I have read Walzer for many years and have always admired his intellect, although I have fundamentally disagreed with his politics. I have always wanted to say to him that the defense of spheres and peoplehood based on exclusion and displacement of others who are deemed to be lesser is not what intellectuals ought to be about. I have also wanted to say that ideologies of difference are a great deal less satisfactory than impure genres, people, activities; that separation and discrimination are often not as estimable as connecting and crossing over; that moral and military victories are not always such wonderful things. But having read him again recently, I now realize that *Exodus* may be a tragic book in that it teaches that you cannot both "belong" *and* concern yourself with Canaanites who do not belong. If that is so, then I thank Walzer for showing me that, and allowing me—and I hope others—to remain unconvinced by what he says, and to resist.

The Great Celtic/Hibernian School

Brigid Brophy

With no more than a grain of truth, though a grain that mythology sprouts on, it is said that an Irishman in danger of drowning is liable to call, "I will drown and nobody shall save me." English people in earshot, myth continues, politely stop trying to save him because they construe him to have declared himself bent on drowning and resistant to all rescuers.

I encountered the drowning Irishman during an English grammar lesson at school (in England). He was mentioned only *exempli gratia*, but he has ever since lodged in my imagination as a spiritual portrait of Oscar Wilde.

Between the end of February and May 25, 1895, it seems when you contemplate the cataclysm, Wilde went down, as drowning people are reputed to do, thrice. He called at his London club, the Albemarle Club, and the porter gave him, in an envelope, the visiting card which the Marquis of Queensberry had left there for him ten days earlier. The card is reproduced in H. Montgomery Hyde's biography of Wilde. The words engraved or printed on it are "Marquis of Queensberry." Above that in handwriting is, "For Oscar Wilde posing as a Somdomite." Instead of mentally deleting the interpolated *m* in the first syllable, as he would have truly deleted it had he been correcting proof, and then forgetting the incident, Wilde read through the error to the intended insult or accusation, which Queensberry, despite the apparently legalistic caution of the veil he draped over it with "posing," had—in haste, anger, unfamiliarity with the act of writing or distaste for it—rendered a nonsense word. What, after all, would you do were you indeed to pose as a somdomite?

Wilde received the card as the culmination of several attempts by Queensberry to fling a gauntlet in his face and thus drive him away from Queensberry's son, Lord Alfred Douglas, whom Wilde was in love with. Wilde instituted the libel action by which British custom and law had replaced dueling. Queensberry was entitled to plead

that his seeming libel was in fact justified. The evidence
he produced in court made it inevitable that he would be
acquitted of libel and that criminal charges would be
brought against Wilde. Between the acquittal of Queensberry and the arrival of the police at the Cadogan Hotel to
arrest Wilde, there was time for Wilde to embark for
France, where he would be secure from prosecution. He
did not go. He stood trial and the jury failed to agree on
a verdict. He stood trial again. His second trial ended on
May 25 in a verdict of "Guilty" and the sentence of two
years' imprisonment with hard labor.

The sentence did not cease to cause pain when Wilde
had served it. Released after two years, he lived in voluntary, impoverished and sometimes pseudonymous exile in
various parts of continental Europe. He was estranged
from his two sons, who were nine and eight years old
when he was imprisoned. Lest his notoriety shadow their
future, they were given another surname. Constance
Wilde, his wife, who traveled from Genoa in Italy to visit
him in Reading Prison in England so that she might tell
him gently of his mother's death, did not see him again
after that. She died in Genoa in 1898, of a creeping spinal
paralysis, at the age of forty. "If we had only met once,"
Wilde wrote to Carlos Blacker on the subject of her death,
"and kissed each other." Wilde died in Paris in 1900, when
he was forty-six.

The Irishman who drowns because his feeble ma-
nipulation of English does not make his desire for
rescue explicit is by no means a literal portrait. In a society that confused heterosexuality with morality and
obedience to the law, Wilde made some of his desires too
clear for safety. His fictions, *The Picture of Dorian Gray*
and *The Portrait of Mr W.H.*, were wielded against him
in the libel action because they disclose the play of Wilde's
imagination and intellect on the homosexual themes with
which half of Wilde's bisexual temperament was in sympathy. Likewise, in *An Ideal Husband*, Lord Goring dis-
closes the inevitably homosexual component in narcissism (and in the mythical ancient Greek whose name it
commemorates) when, just before contemplating his and

his buttonhole's reflection in the mirror, he remarks to his butler, who has prepared the buttonhole for him: "To love oneself is the beginning of a lifelong romance."

Lord Goring and Mabel Chiltern (to whom he is, by the end of the play, bound to become an ideal husband) are the two dramatic *personae* of Wilde's creation who most tellingly incarnate not only his own wit but the charm and the generosity of spirit manifest in his letters. Lord Goring is thirty-four but, as he tells his father in an expression borrowed from women, "I only admit to thirty-two—thirty-one and a half when I have a really good buttonhole." Wilde gave his age in the libel proceedings as thirty-nine and, without help from a picture which, like Dorian Gray's, could age by proxy, or even from a green carnation for a buttonhole, was obliged in the witness box to admit to forty.

His mental arithmetic may have been shaky, though in fact you probably need mental agility if you are to flatter yourself about your age, but Wilde was fully in command of the English language—and, for the matter of that, of the French and the ancient Greek. Had he needed, there were many people to whom he could make requests like the one he wrote from Paris in 1891 to the literary adviser of the English publishing house that was about to issue *Dorian Gray* in volume form: "Will you also look after my 'wills' and 'shalls' in proof. I am Celtic in my use of these words, not English." That may, however, be the boast of an Irishman whose mother was a well-known Irish patriot who published under a name that consisted of the Italian word that means "hope." The publishers in whose proofs Wilde's Irish idioms were to be corrected were Ward, Lock. Wilde's letters repeatedly refer to them as "Ward & Lock." He quasi proof-corrected the very name of his publishers, clearly holding that two surnames should not be linked by a mere comma.

The finest biography of Wilde is still that given in the editorial connective passages and the scholarly notes in Rupert Hart-Davis's marvelous 1962 edition of his letters, which is triumphant in its knowledge and sense of the period. Richard Ellmann's 1987 narrative biography

Oscar Wilde (Knopf) is more couth (except in calling Hatchard's bookshop a bookstore) than its predecessors. It is detailed on Wilde's North American tour and provides a more coherent account of Wilde's prison experience than he could in his letters, where he avoided describing kindness to him that broke or grazed regulations. Ellmann and Hart-Davis disagree whether Queensberry was the ninth or the eighth marquis. Both prefer "Marquess" to the spelling he chose for his card.

When Wilde was in it, Reading, as the address on his letters indicates, was a prison. Wilde made it a gaol for the title of his *Ballad*. Ellmann rightly recognizes Coleridge as the poet in whose patterns *The Ballad* is chiefly cast but, although he traces his influence on the plot of *Salomé*, does not recognize in the diction of *The Ballad* the presence of Heinrich Heine.

Of the photographs reproduced in the Ellmann volume, one that is not familiar from other books about Wilde is most difficult, to the verge of impossibility, to accept. A big, rather plump man in drag stoops towards a severed head that is lying on a platter on the floor. (The head is conveniently photographed from the back, so you cannot guess what kind of mock-up it is.) The caption identifies the picture as "Wilde in costume as Salome." As such the photograph was no doubt collected (in Paris) and the Salome has a facial likeness to Wilde. However, Wilde believed his *Salomé* to be a dramatic masterpiece. He was mistaken. It took the graphic genius of Aubrey Beardsley, whose illustrations to it depict Wilde's face in a full moon as The Woman in the Moon, to make *Salomé* into a masterpiece, and the operatic genius of Richard Strauss to make it into another. With more justification, Wilde was proud to have written *Salomé* in French as a vehicle for Sarah Bernhardt, which she accepted. Even had his fantasies inclined him towards drag, which despite Beardsley's joke I doubt, I do not think Wilde would have taken part in a send-up of his play.

Wilde's knowledge of Greek was pursued through his public schooling near Enniskillen, Northern Ireland. Classics, the study of Latin and ancient Greek language and literature, were still the core of the public school curriculum. Perhaps Wilde's dexterity with paradox began when he had to grasp that in the British educational system a public school was one closed to all girls and to any boys whose families could not pay the fees. His Greek in particular waxed, winning him praises and prizes during his undergraduate career, first at Trinity College, Dublin, and then at Magdalen College in Oxford, where he was a demy. The word, which, like the paper size, is pronounced "de-MY," is used in that one college at Oxford to describe the holder of a foundation scholarship or grant.

Someone who studied classics had not only to translate from the two ancient languages into English but to render an English political speech or newspaper article or passage from a poem in the prose or the metrical verse of one of the ancient languages in the style of the ancient author most suitable to the subject matter. The knack needed was that of the parodist or even the forger. Wilde, who was in 1891 to write an essay, *Pen, Pencil and Poison*, that concerned forgery, was so adept at the exercises required of classics undergraduates that he took a first both in Honour Moderations, the examination that Oxford classics undergraduates sit in their fifth term, and in Greats, the final examination whose subjects include philosophy, chiefly of the ancient Greek kind.

The knack of the gifted classics student is probably what the Oxford Union detected in Wilde when it discerned plagiary in his first volume of English verse. It was, however, with entire originality that, as a writer of stories and, above all, of plays for the London theater, Wilde devised a new English form for the epigram, which is in Greek simply an inscription or a poem short enough to be one, usually cast in the elegiac meter (in the Greek sense), and for the aphorism, which in Greek is simply a definition.

On his deathbed, mute but not quite unconscious, Wilde was conditionally baptized by a Roman Catholic priest. Conditional baptism is usually administered to adults who seek reception into the Catholic Church in case there has been a previous baptism—whose form, however, may not have been valid in Catholic terms. According to Ellmann, the precaution was not needed. Wilde was baptized as an infant by an Anglican clerical uncle but when he was four or five years old he and his elder brother were, at their mother's request, baptized again, this time by a Roman Catholic priest. Ellmann associates Wilde's experience as a little boy with the quest of both Jack and Algernon in *The Importance of Being Earnest* for Anglican adult (and possibly second) baptism. The Wilde children's double baptism into conflicting versions of the Christian faith was probably the surest method Speranza could think of to bring up her sons to be thoroughly Irish.

Despite his manful intellectual struggles to perceive Jesus Christ as the supreme exemplar of self-sacrifice, Wilde was, I think, more impressed by Socrates as he is reported or fictionalized in dialogues by Plato. In *The Decay of Lying*, where he used his sons' first names as the names of the speakers, Wilde tried to mold the Platonic dialogue into a narrative-discursive English form, halfway between story and play.

Wilde's remaining in London to stand criminal prosecution is explicable only, I think, by the fact that Socrates was tried on criminal charges of importing new deities and intellectually corrupting young men. He was found guilty by a jury of his fellow Athenians and condemned to death. Although it would have been easy for him to flee across the border, he put forward the argument, which needs neither faith nor theology to explain it, that if you live in a democracy and have not persuaded your fellow citizens to change the laws, then you are morally obliged to obey them. So he remained in Athens and in prison and drank the lethal poison that was provided so that he should be his own executioner.

Wilde and Bernard Shaw, the two greatest late-nineteenth-century (and, in Shaw's case, early-twentieth-century) writers of English, were born within two years of each other in Dublin. Wilde's father, a noted and knighted eye-and-ear surgeon, operated on Shaw's father to correct his squint, overcorrected and left the patient with a squint in the other direction. (Shaw gives a brief account. Ellmann, who seems ill-read in Shaw, ignores it.) In London, where both men were all-purpose critics and playwrights, they constituted what they called the great Celtic school and gave their London plays alternate opus numbers like musical compositions. In his inscription to Shaw in the copy he gave him of Op. 1, *Lady Windermere's Fan,* Wilde called the school Hibernian, a term which, unlike Celtic, has an exclusively Irish meaning. The idea of opus numbers probably came from Shaw, who had an acute musical ear and considerable expertise. Yet Wilde had the surer touch in seeking the literary keynote on which to end an act or a whole play.

Wilde ran risks with "renters," male prostitutes who often exacted money beyond their stipulated fee by blackmail afterwards. Shaw, a socialist economist whose socialism recognized the rights of his fellow animals of species outside the human, wrote *Widowers' Houses* (his first contribution to the "school" and therefore its Opus 2) about the rents of slum property. Perhaps the school began to disintegrate when the six-foot-three Wilde, whose addiction to food as well as to cigarettes glints through *The Importance,* became too portly to be able to wear with dignity the knee breeches he had once adopted as aesthetic clothes for men, but noticed that the six-foot Shaw remained bone-thin in his Jaeger suits.

In *The Importance,* Wilde created a work of art as vigorous and nearly as moving in its symmetry as Mozart's *Così fan tutte.* Shaw's sole gross critical blunder was not to perceive that its seriousness and beauty lay in its design.

During his after-prison exile, Wilde's concern with prison reform and the introduction of compassion to the penal system made him a socialist on almost the municipal Shavian pattern. After his death, Shaw recognized an unaustere saintliness in Wilde's generosity, which was the equal of Shaw's own.

That strange play, *Saint Joan,* which when it was produced in 1924 was acclaimed as Shaw's greatest and which is nearly his worst, expresses some of Shaw's thoughts about Wilde after his death. Perhaps Shaw's imagination or his audience's could realize the 1420s only as Pre-Raphaelite tableaux. It is the Epilogue that makes *Saint Joan* moving. Joan, condemned by as scrupulous a court as Wilde's was, is accorded immortality by the church that condemned her six centuries earlier. There is a little in her canonization and her admirers' refusal to wish her resurrected of Shaw's recognition of Wilde as an incomparably great and incomparably tiresome writer.

Yet it was in 1906 in *The Doctor's Dilemma* that Shaw accepted Wilde's tiresome aesthetic faith. At the same time, making his dramatic points, as Wilde congratulated him on doing in Op. 2, out of "the mere facts of life," he laments the death of consumption in 1898, when he was twenty-eight, of Wilde's illustrator, friend and caricaturist, Aubrey Beardsley, who becomes the dying consumptive painter, Louis Dubedat. Before he dies, Dubedat pronounces the creed that both Beardsley and Wilde really did believe in, the final two mellifluous and moving clauses in which are Shaw's acceptance of the sanctity of aestheticism: "I believe in Michael Angelo, Velasquez and Rembrandt: in the might of design, the mystery of color, the redemption of all things by Beauty everlasting and the message of Art that has made these hands blessed. Amen. Amen."

WHAT HENRY KNEW

Jean-Christophe Agnew

"Hawthorne's career was probably as tranquil and uneventful a one as ever fell to the lot of a man of letters." Such was the judgment with which the thirty-six-year-old Henry James opened his critical biography of Nathaniel Hawthorne in 1879, a judgment founded largely on his reading of Hawthorne's six posthumously published notebooks. Taken together, James thought, the notebooks revealed a life "strikingly deficient in incident, in what may be called the dramatic quality." And though James confessed his gratitude for the meager biographical detail the notebooks had yielded him, having read and reread them carefully, he remained "at a loss to perceive how they came to be written." As far as he could see, Hawthorne's notes recorded only "common and casual things," not "opinions," "convictions" or "ideas pure and simple." What indeed could Hawthorne's purpose have been, James wondered out loud, "in carrying on for so many years this minute and often trivial chronicle?"

Glib and condescending as this judgment may appear today, it was at the time regarded as even more patronizing for its having issued from the pen of a writer only just released from his own literary apprenticeship. Yet the question of Hawthorne's notebooks and of James's lofty dismissal of them lingers nonetheless, even for those readers who have never so much as glanced at them. The question lingers because in the years following his "little book on Hawthorne," James himself came to place the *process* of authorship—the careful gathering of impressions and their gradual conversion into art—at the very heart of his own life and work. Against an age that sought to mystify the role of the artist, either by stigmatizing or sacralizing it, James consistently emphasized the artist's self-dignity, self-obligation and self-discipline—what a later age would call, with perhaps equal mystification, professionalism.

Never did James put his case for a "trained, competitive, intelligent, *qualified* art" more forcefully than, in 1884, in his indignant rebuttal to Walter Besant's moralizing lecture on "The Art of Fiction." There, the "Master" rejected every test of a novel save that of its execution. "The execution belongs to the author alone," he insisted; "it is what is most personal to him, and we measure him by that." As "executant" the novelist was to consider himself free of the narrow-minded Grundyism to which Besant would have had him submit. In fact James used the occasion of his response to repudiate every one of Besant's instructions to the aspiring novelist, "with the exception, perhaps, of the injunction as to entering one's notes in a common-place book." The exception was not for ironic effect. For James, notebooks were the writer's workshop, his alembic; the greater the writer, the more cosmopolitan and capacious his vision, the less commonplace his common-place book.

So what, then, of James's own notebooks? How do they measure up to the strictures laid upon Hawthorne and Besant? The question has stood open for some time, as I've suggested, but it has been given new life with the recent publication of two books by Oxford University Press. The first is Leon Edel's and Lyall H. Powers's edition of *The Complete Notebooks of Henry James*; the second is Michael Anesko's new study, *"Friction with the Market": Henry James and the Profession of Authorship*. In one sense these two books could not be further apart, given the fundamentally psychological orientation of Edel and Powers and the equally prominent sociological interest of Anesko. But in another sense, the three authors are boon companions, for they share the conviction that revelations are to be found in the apparent ephemera of a writer's career: the casual notes, jottings and memoranda of daily life. Whatever their differences, Edel, Powers and Anesko would have us expand our working definition of the writer's notebook to encompass just that "minute and trivial chronicle" which so puzzled James when it appeared under Hawthorne's hand. The results of this more generous view of the James archive are indeed revealing, but revealing as much about ourselves as about him.

F. O. Matthiessen and Kenneth Murdock first published *The Notebooks of Henry James* in 1947. Their edition comprised the nine manuscript notebooks (running from 1878 to 1911) deposited at Harvard's Houghton Library together with preliminary sketches for three stories, including *The Ambassadors*. The book received a rather frosty welcome from Edmund Wilson in the pages of the *New Yorker*. Playing James to James's Hawthorne, Wilson acknowledged the *Notebooks* to be "a document of prime importance" but then complained of the "oddly mechanical" turn of mind they disclosed. Despite occasionally moving passages, especially those describing James's two visits to America in 1881–2 and 1904–5, the notebooks most often displayed James's characteristic detachment, his "tendency to contrivance," and his arbitrary sense of motive—in short, his capacity "to keep his whole process of thought on the surface of his mind." At the same time Wilson chided Matthiessen and Murdock for their numerous editorial interventions in the text. Most irksome, he thought, were the many interpolated critical commentaries that compared the details of James's provisional emplotments with the eventual forms they took in his published novels, plays and tales. Why, Wilson wanted to know, should the two editors have imagined that their readers would "find it more interesting to read such comments . . . than to know what Henry James spent in staying at clubs and hotels?"

Wilson never explained just what interest these expense accounts might have held out to him, but it is difficult not to see the current, "complete," "authoritative" and "definitive" version of the notebooks as Edel's and Powers's effort to meet Wilson's objections to the first edition. First of all, the notebooks have been republished without commentary, apart from occasional biographical and bibliographical references. Second, a chronology of James's life and work (whose absence Wilson had lamented in the first edition) has been included. Third, the editors have extracted the two notebooks covering James's American visits (which Wilson had earlier singled out for praise) and have placed them in a separate section entitled "American Journals." Finally, Edel and Powers have added some one hundred fifty pages of information drawn from James's pocket diaries for 1909 through 1915, his cash accounts and his address books. Armed with *The Complete Notebooks*, one can now confidently account for James's movements on August 8, 1911 (disembarking at Liverpool "and in great heat"), and if pressed sum up his assets and liabilities at the time.

But in knowing these things, what is it that one knows? And what is to be made of such knowledge? Leafing through the pocket diaries, for example, one discovers that on James's sixty-eighth birthday, he was taken to the Bronx Zoo, but that on his seventieth, he was invited to 10 Downing Street. Are the two events to be read as confirming James's sense of the differences between New World and Old, between Nature and Culture, between Present and Past? Are these "events" at all, or do they become so only by virtue of their placement within a life no less "strikingly deficient in incident" than Hawthorne's? After all, James himself did not seem to mark the day of his birth in his private diaries, nor was he above an occasional fib about his age. "I am 37 years old," he confided to his notebook in 1881. The editors' notebook says thirty-eight, however. Curious, to be sure, but are these the kind of details that make a collection "a document of prime importance"? Is this what is meant by "complete" and "definitive"? Perhaps, but as James himself remarks in the First Notebook, "The *whole* of anything is never told; you can only take what groups together."

Unfortunately, there is little in the vast canon of Jamesian criticism to indicate just how one might go about "grouping" the disparate kinds of evidence that Edel and Powers have gathered together in *The Complete Notebooks*. That failure might be explained in a variety of ways, but Michael Anesko would probably attribute it, I suspect, to the tendency of Jacobite scholarship to lock the events of James's life and work into various heroic narratives of success and failure. It is only after the passage of time and the accumulation of a "wealth of information," Anesko reminds us, that the historian is in a sufficiently detached position to make out the true limits of a writer's historical context and to interpret those limits with "greater objectivity."

Now if *The Complete Notebooks* are any indication, we are presently awash in information about Henry James, and so I imagine that it was with some confidence that Anesko set about his task. Conceived of as "an essay in the sociology of literature," *"Friction with the Market"* attempts "to reconstruct the social and economic context of the reproduction of fiction, and to bring that reconstruction to bear on the interpretation of one author's work." As such, the study, like *The Complete Notebooks*, can be taken as a deliberate answer to Edmund Wilson's original call for an accounting of Henry James's material life. But where Edel and Powers would partition the worlds of James's daybooks and notebooks, Anesko would join them. Yet the juncture is neither seamless nor complete, for he regards the young James's imagination as oscillating between the worlds of Necessity and Art, Market and Muse, Public and Private, or, in other words, between "the din of commercialism and the silence of oblivion."

In one of the most original and arresting readings of the book, Anesko finds this vocational tension figured in the portrait James draws of the young Isabel Archer browsing—as James himself had done so often—in the family library at Albany. The volumes she eventually chooses, however, are read not in the library but in an adjoining "office," which Anesko treats as a symbolic link mediating between the protective enclave of literature and the exposed stage of commerce that lies just beyond a mysterious, locked door cut into the office's outer wall. Isabel "had never opened the bolted door," James writes, "nor removed the green paper . . . from its side-lights; she had never assured herself that the vulgar street lay beyond it." This image, Anesko argues, symbolizes something more than Isabel's innocence; it also serves as an architectural metaphor for James's own professional situation—a spatial expression of the question that plagued him throughout his early career, namely, "how to open an intercourse with the world."

Considering the frequency with which the imagery of doors and windows appears in James's celebrated "house of fiction," Anesko's argument seems plausible enough. But in a rare stab at intertextuality, he also finds James's professional predicament prefigured, as it were, in Hawthorne's striking image of a bolted shop door similarly cut into the "office" of the house of seven gables. The connection seems fragile at best, unnecessary at worst, for it is clear that, whatever its literary antecedents, the Open Door becomes for James (as for his friend and McKinley's secretary of state, John Hay) a master trope for commerce—for what James describes as "friction with the market."

The remainder of Anesko's study reconstructs the yearly income James managed to wrest out of the literary marketplace as well as the toll such trade exacted upon the fiction of his middle years. That income, it turns out, was not inconsiderable, and it is one of the principal virtues of Anesko's study that it finally lays to rest the cherished fable of Henry James as a writer who earned his money the old-fashioned way, by spurning it. As Leon Edel was the first to point out and as Anesko tirelessly confirms, James earned a comfortable, if not extravagant, living from his writing in the years between 1876 (when he moved to Britain) and 1893 (when he came into a modest inheritance). And what is more, he delighted in the money his writings fetched from publishers. "I am getting to perceive that I *can* make money," he wrote his mother in 1880, "and the idea has undeniable fascination." The irony was of course that money's fascination for James deepened in direct proportion to its denial.

Such paradoxes are a feature of James's fiction, however, not of *"Friction with the Market."* Instead, Anesko forages among James's surviving letters, records and receipts in order to discover not just James's annual income from writing but the strategies he used to maximize it. The portrait of the Master that emerges as a result is that of a shrewd professional author who parlayed his early popular successes and his expatriate status into a solid, transatlantic literary career. Denied the rewards of a runaway "best seller"—a term coined only at the turn of the century— James consoled himself with the profits reaped from the dual serializations of his novels and tales. Moreover, by establishing his residence in Britain, James was able to secure his book royalties abroad while carefully timing the appearance of his stories so as to bring in the greatest returns from fretful, competitive publishers on both sides of the Atlantic. By the mid-nineties, James was dealing with ten different publishing houses. The day had definitely passed when a single patrician publisher could claim the "courtesy" of an author's trade.

A decent literary income was not synonymous with popular success, however, as James learned to his chagrin during these same years. The interminable magazine serializations of *The Bostonians* and *The Princess Casamassima* during the mid-eighties brought James money, certainly, but they brought little good will; public response to the initial chapters dipped quickly from indignation to indifference. Anesko devotes three chapters to an interpretation of these two "troubled narrative[s]" and to *The Tragic Muse*, the last of James's "topical" novels. The readings ventured are neither particularly new nor particularly compelling; they merely give to familiar Jamesian themes (private/public; art/life; beauty/necessity) a vague vocational coloring. Like other critics before him, Anesko regards the flaws in these works as symptoms of James's labored efforts to fit himself to some imagined Procrustean bed and of the resentments he came to feel as a result of his failures. James chafed at the formulaic accommodations he had made in these works, and his discomfiture is visible both in the novels and in the notebooks. *The Bostonians*, Anesko concludes, "was an inadvertent epic of his [James's] own disaffection from the literary marketplace."

For all the author's aspirations to a new, more objective reading of James's lifework, then, his readings offer little more than a sociological corrective to Edel's intensely psychological account. Despite some flattening out of contrasts, for example, Anesko's narrative strongly resembles

Edel's story of James's immersion and withdrawal from the workaday world. Indeed, as if in unconscious mimicry of this biographical movement, the narrative itself seems to lose power as it approaches the "treacherous years" of the 1890s, when James embarked upon his disastrous experiment in the theater. The whole experience—a kind of marketplace *Walpurgisnacht*—would seem to cry out for an extended treatment, but the author unaccountably glosses the episode in his introduction in order to conclude his book with a rather desultory discussion of James's arrangements for the grand New York Edition of his works; the point being, presumably, that behind the studied aloofness of James's late phase, he was still deferring to the cost-conscious demands of his publishers.

"Friction with the Market" is a thoroughly researched and gracefully written study of Henry James's professionalization, but as an essay in literary sociology, it is disappointing. It is one thing to connect one's chosen social forces or "determinants" (Anesko's term) to content, quite another to connect those same forces to form—figurative, rhetorical and narrative form. James may well have accommodated his publishers when choosing the titles for his New York Edition, for example, but he also took the edition as an opportunity to rewrite and reframe his earlier work in a prose and with a purpose that were, to put it mildly, uncompromisingly his.

Still, to say (as I am) that James took *formal* possession of his content is not to say that he thereby removed his trademark from trade itself. That James bolted the door of his later style against the vulgar expectations of the literary marketplace is, if anything, an indication of the deepened interest he felt such denials conferred upon his prose. In the theater of James's mind as in that of his work, a door closed in the first act is invariably a door opened in the last.

Theatricality is one of the distinguishing features of all of James's fiction but especially of his later works. The "scenic vision," as he called it, stamps virtually everything in his writing, from his thematics to his imagery to his emplotments. At the same time, as Anesko notes, "From his earliest days James equated the theater with money-making." Here, in his association of theater and market, James would seem to offer a key, if not the door itself, to the mysterious confluences (and frictions) between the literary and social forms that structured his life and work—the key, in other words, to the conceptual wall dividing the worlds of his daybooks and notebooks.

Edmund Wilson toys briefly with this key—in 1947—when he remarks on the contrived and mechanical feel of James's overweening preoccupation with plot in the note-books. Writing of James's successive treatments of a single story, Wilson complains that "James considers the various ways in which the drama might be made to work out as professionally and as uninspiredly as if he were a maker of trade goods for popular magazines." Surprised perhaps by the harsh tenor of his own response, Wilson immediately softens his judgment rather than develops its implications. But the implications remain nonetheless. With the exception of the so-called American Journals (which James later used for *The American Scene, A Small Boy and Others,* and *Notes of a Son and Brother*), the notebooks are almost entirely taken up with the mechanics of plotting. "Make your little story, find your little story, tell your little story," he exclaims in 1894, "and leave the rest to the gods!" In the end of course, the "divine principle of the Scenario" becomes his god. Two years later, he confesses "none too soon—that the *scenic* method is my absolute, my imperative, my *only* salvation."

The evidence of this devotion is everywhere visible in the notebooks. An entry will generally begin with a situation or premise, typically a nugget of gossip mined from a lunch or dinner engagement listed in his pocket diary. Month in, month out, the pages record what James elsewhere calls "the hum of borrowed experience"; no dialogue or description, only a methodical elaboration of an original *donnée* until all of its logical possibilities have been worked out to his satisfaction. There are few direct impressions of personal experience and little in the way of the "opinions," "convictions" or "ideas pure and simple" he missed in Hawthorne's notebooks. Occasionally, as in his successive treatments of the plot for *The Wings of the Dove,* James's prose rises to match the intensity of the moral quandaries into which his narrative experiments are projecting his characters. But for the most part James concentrates on the composition and choreography of his "scene."

Composition and choreography, scene and scenario: The terms describe the two sides of the mobile pictorialism that is James's "scenic method"; they describe as well the forms through which that method absorbs and transmutes James's own marketplace anxieties into fiction. In the first instance, James appropriates and arranges characters and things as "compositional resources." They become a novel's givens—the stage "properties," so to speak—whose initial configuration *is* the narrative's premise: both the social contract of the fictive world in which the characters operate *and* the literary contract to which the reader is expected to stipulate. This is James's static, commodified, proscenium vision of the world, a still life suitable for framing.

Still, James's fictions are never immobile. The pictures they present are always moving ones, and it is in the notebooks that one finds James patiently choreographing that movement. Change invariably breeds uncertainty and curiosity among his characters, allowing James to orchestrate their search for knowledge (and power) in such a way as to make them appear the agents of a novel's eventual narrative and compositional symmetries. These symmetries may be aesthetic or moral or both, but they are in every case negotiable reciprocities and appear as the product of the characters' own mutual positioning.

Nowhere is this dynamic principle more evident than in the extensive notes James makes for *What Maisie Knew.* Its scene first appears to him as an "intensely structural, intensely hinged and jointed preliminary frame." That flexibility allows him to trace and retrace a complex sequence of entrances and exits, which at the same time marks an equally intricate pattern of merger and acquisition among the characters. The ostensible object of this dramatic and possessive struggle is Maisie, the "luckless child of a divorced couple," who is condemned to rebound "from racquet to racquet like a tennis ball or shuttlecock" while the incestuous circle of parents, step-parents, and guardians slowly widens. As her awareness grows, Maisie becomes the subject rather than the object of the action, and it is she who makes the final moral and compositional decisions in the tale. Introduced as "the thoroughly pictured creature," Maisie becomes by the end a virtual proxy for the author.

Not surprisingly, then, James once again chooses the imagery of doors to figure his drama of knowledge, of worldliness. "Everything had something behind it," he has Maisie think to herself early on; "life was like a long, long corridor with rows of closed doors." At these doors, she learns that it is "wiser not to knock," and it is indeed only by opening specific doors, or threatening to open them, that Maisie eventually confirms the illicit parental relationships she has only fleetingly suspected. Doors thus represent for James something more than the question of "how to open an intercourse with the world," or at least a far more sexually charged notion of intercourse than Anesko, for one, seems prepared to acknowledge. The scene of James's "scenic" method is in this respect not just theatrical or commercial but primal.

Even the notebooks, mechanical and contrived as they may seem, occasionally betray the pressure of these mingled emotions. Recoiling from the humiliating failure of his plays, for example, James consoles himself in 1893 with the thought of returning to his novels and tales. "I should like to dip my pen into the *other* ink," he writes, "the sacred fluid of fiction." Literature, he reminds himself, "sits patient at my door." True enough, but to open that door was scarcely to close off the questions or feelings forced upon him by the "horrid theatric trade." If Anesko's study demonstrates anything, it is the extent to which publishing transformed itself during these same years into a flourishing, mass-market enterprise and, correspondingly, the extent to which Henry James—diffident and squeamish failure that he proclaimed himself—actively colluded in this process. Yet without an appreciation of the peculiarly theatrical and sexual associations that James brought to this new marketplace, one misses the full force and meaning of the "frictions" he found there, frictions that he then promptly registered, in heightened, almost rarefied form, of course, in his work.

But should literary sociology be required to bear the burden of explaining the form as apart from the fact of an author's fiction? Need it pursue the intersection of literary biography and history any further than, say, the writer's choice of topics or thematics? Plainly I think that it should and that Henry James's major phase—during which he published some seventeen books—is as good a place as any to start.

Now, though *"Friction with the Market"* generally scants the later years of James's career, it is still entirely possible to construct an explanation for some of its formal peculiarities in a way consistent with the economic context Anesko sketches out and, in some measure, with the documents collected by Edel and Powers. One need only point, for example, to the convergence of various material and technological changes in James's life during the 1890s: the Syracuse inheritance, which provided him a financial safety net after 1893; the Anglo-American Copyright Agreement, which expanded the transatlantic competition for authors after 1891; the simultaneous emergence of the literary agent—two of whom James employed—to further mediate the bargaining process; James's loss of serialization opportunities owing to new mass-market pressures; his decision to dictate his works to typists, the effect of which can be seen both in the increasing ornateness of his prose and his decreasing interest in the notebooks. And so on.

All these developments can be used to explain James's willingness to adopt a style guaranteed to pinch the "huge, flat foot of the public" and thus to close the door on a market he had previously courted. But these circumstances cannot explain why, having thus insulated himself from the frictions of the market, James should have made those same frictions the animating energy tempering both the form and content of his novels and, in a sense, of his life. It is worth recalling here that it was to the aspiring sculptor, Hendrik Andersen, that James first wrote of the beneficial effects of his "friction with the market." For it was to Andersen too—this time as enchanting love object—that James wrote of his plan to "take very personal possession of you." In his letters as in his notebooks and novels, the market may be found inscribed in the very forms in which James's fertile imagination chose to express itself.

Literary sociology must rise to this formal challenge, I submit, if it is to offer its readers something more than a mere mirror of their own professional preoccupations. True, the indignant Jacobite may well sniff at Anesko's careerist portrait of James, but the book's resolutely vocationalist emphasis perfectly conforms to our own current obsession with the secrets of credentials, money management and networking. In this connection, it is not at all difficult to imagine the next generation of published literary ephemera as including a full inventory of an author's Rolodexes, spread sheets and tax returns.

So what? one can imagine Edmund Wilson responding. Who needs yet another "book-length study" (as Anesko puts it) of the games of knowledge and power in James's later work? Good questions, and if what is at stake in them is no more than a trade-off between the aridities of a certified audit and those of a formalist literary reading, then I am in sympathy. But insofar as Henry James's formal choices did in fact meld with the marketplace conventions and concerns which they otherwise seemed to hold at a distance, then I am less persuaded by Wilson's and Anesko's impatience. The marketplace relations of knowledge and power, however aestheticized, are not simple "games." At the present moment, when both press and public confess themselves bemused by the jargon of "covert action" and "plausible deniability," James's marketplace fictions speak altogether intelligibly to our predicament. And they speak in this way not because they transcend history but because they are so deeply steeped in it. To read James's novels in their context is to begin to understand why we, in our context, can grant almost incantatory power to the question: "What did he know and when did he know it?"

To be sure, this is a rather large canvas on which to project the lessons of the Master. But consider, then, the more modest tableau of the book trade: the market with which the two books under review are in one way or another concerned. It is no secret that the organizational and technological transformations of publishing that Anesko locates in the 1890s have been reproduced and amplified in the 1970s. Chain bookstores, computerized inventories, attorney-agents, negotiable subsidiary rights, talk-show tours, and movie tie-ins—all have led to what Thomas Whiteside calls the "blockbuster complex." Nothing would have been more sobering to Henry James, I suspect, than to compare the income he earned for his "little book on Hawthorne" of 1879 with the $3.2 million figure negotiated in 1979 for the paperback rights to Judith Krantz's *Princess Daisy*. But then James would have doubtless boggled at the number of books presently incinerated to heat the warehouses to which they have been returned unsold. This is friction at an entirely new order of magnitude.

Yet the distance between James's Maisie and Krantz's Daisy may not be as great as it first seems. The operative words among literary agents these days are, according to Whiteside, "orchestration," "choreography" and "packaging." Books are now staged as much as they are written; they are moving pictures before they ever reach the screen. "Everything in this world has turned into show business," Felix Rohatyn reports. "You package all these things. That's the reality of the marketplace." If so, it is a reality James would have recognized because, practically and imaginatively, he had helped to create it. And for that reason, it is a reality that he can still help us to understand. "Small boy," "son" or "brother," whatever diminutive label he chose for himself, there is still room for wonder at what Henry knew.

IN THE THICK OF EUROPE

Penelope Gilliatt

Film may be the youngest art, but Polish films are born old, like many children before school regresses them. The signal movies of Poland seem to carry in them the whole knowledge of their country's history: partitions, carvings-up at peace conference after peace conference, an outlet to the sea, no outlet to the sea, other languages' names for birthplaces Poles have fought for, the dates of Kosciusko and the two battles of Tannenberg, the symbolism of Stanislaus II and Lublin and the Chopin Revolutionary, the double meaning of Poland's Roman Catholicism, the multiple meaning of Danzig-Gdansk. Without wit of the order that stares out death, the many-times-devastated Poles could not have survived. Wit, and their wit in particular, has the speed that short-circuits the bigots and bureaucrats whom Poles historically have needed to vanquish. Wit is a cipher. Wit is a password. Poles survive by codes.

One of the first times I went to Poland, in 1954, a Polish friend explained the Polish Problem to me in full. "It is an excellent country, but badly located." The friend was the great film director Andrzej Munk, who was killed in a car crash in Poland in September 1961. He was a skeptic with a halo of stiff hair that stood up like a sink brush, a thoughtful and laconic man with the wryness that seems to be the bile and blood of Poland. I remember he was driving me somewhere in Poland the summer he died. We were going along a tiny, filthy road full of garbage, like a lane in London before the Great Fire of 1666. It was called Stalin Street. "When the old man was still in the chair," said Munk, "an edict went out from Moscow saying that the main street in every satellite country was to be named Stalin Street. Luckily," gesturing to the reeking little road, "this was called Main Street in the sixteenth century."

Often the work of émigré Poles gives the feeling that Polishness is not to be tampered with: Jerzy Skolimowski's work, for one. Long involved with films in Paris and England, he wrote with Roman Polanski the script of *A Knife in the Water* (1961) when both were still in Poland. A fraction of a generation younger than Munk, and so too young to have fought in the Warsaw Rising, Skolimowski wrote and made in London in 1981 a totally Polish comedy, *Moonlighting*. An unskillful liar called Nowak, played by Jeremy Irons, is sent to England with three non-English-speaking coworkers to do a building job on a mews house in London for a well-off boss who commutes between Poland and England. Nowak is presented as being apolitical, though there is no such thing in Poland or anywhere else. Their stingy employer, benefiting from the minute value of the Polish zloti, has paid them in their local currency to finish the conversion in four weeks and doled out £20 as their recreation budget. In a few days, they have blown the lot plus another and deviously acquired £20 on a glazingly desirable secondhand color TV that busts at once. Nowak alone can understand the English headline news of military upheaval in Warsaw, martial law and the confrontation between the government and Solidarity. Under time pressure to keep his dog-tired trio at work, he pretends to them that they have had five hours sleep when they have had only three, pretends that all is well at home, pretends that they are getting messages from their wives through calls he takes at a public phone box lengthily occupied by an exasperatingly prissy Englishwoman of the sort who would say "Sorry" to a vicarage chintz sofa if she had bumped into it. With the four weeks running out fast, he revives his team with a hot bath in plumbing not yet surrounded by any of the luxe circumstances ordered from Warsaw. Natural pine paneling, exposed brick walls, the usual posh-primitive mews look of '80s London. Nowak takes to petty crime, returning a second shoplifted turkey for cash when he has already shoplifted a first. English decency sometimes surfaces, but Skolimowski has a beady eye for lofty local nastiness. A nosy neighbor with the bearing of someone retired from a tea station in India enters into combat about stealing the *Times*. And all the while, there beats under this accomplished story of desperation parading as a lark Jeremy Irons's sad knowledge kept from his infinitely exhausted colleagues that the Poland they are longing to go back to is not at all the place they left.

The pang of exile. It is there in Roman Polanski's *The*

Tenant (1975), with Polanski playing a French citizen called Trelkowsky who has repelled people all his life. He seems to be a tenant with a short lease on his own carcass. His very face has the rawness of a quick study for a finished work, marking his big, Cruikshank features and leaving expressiveness to be filled in later. He moves into an apartment left empty after a suicidal girl's recent tenancy. Polanski conveys the sense that the hero is assessing his own activities as if he were a landlord longing to serve an eviction notice. One morning Trelkowsky wakes up in drag, his vacant frame now occupied by the girl suicide's personality; his mental self-banishment has become a physical notice to quit. This is an odd film, marred by Polanski's taste for the double dare, made poignant by Polanski's split between his Polishness and his quest for the Hollywood he was to end up in with such metaphorical exactness. His talent has always roped in the wanton: it seems most coherent in his first (and home-based) feature, A *Knife in the Water*, made in Poland. The film is a scalding original, alert, nettled, about three people in a situation full of lazy dangers. A bored married couple, the sort of people who thrust each other out of the driving seat without speaking, pick up a chillingly self-reliant boy on the way to a sailing weekend. The boy is intrigued by the enterprise of sexually conquering both, partly because he resents the perpetual showing off about sailing. The ensuing politics are intentionally too clever by half. Polanski's amusedly distant view of himself led him in this and later films into endless, brilliant wrangles between his French and his Polish identities, his atheism and his Catholicism, his sophistication and his valuable lack of guile. Few artists have been more finger-marked by homesickness.

Polanski graduated from the Polish Film School at Lodz, founded in 1947 after a seedling start in Cracow by a group of *cinéastes* trying to put the devastated industry back on its feet. The first generation of graduates included Andrzej Munk and Andrzej Wajda, who have been called the obverse sides of Polishness: Munk the unbudgeable ironist, Wajda the expansive romantic. Munk was trained as an architect, Wajda as a painter. Where Munk broods over the ground plans and palpably spends months in doubt about whether the structure will really stand, Wajda makes flourishes, elated with his dazzling gift, which has developed wonderfully alongside Poland's history.

Munk directed with craft. No one with a less studious sense of nonsense would have jousted as he did with the authorities over *Cross-Eyed Luck* (1960), a bitterly funny parallel to *The Good Soldier Schweik*. Only the ending failed to get through, which he put there in the hope that it would be cut, in the old ploy to keep the rest. In the un-cut version, the luckless hero is arrested in a lavatory, not because of the man whom he has killed but because he is suspected of having written vulgar, seditious messages on the walls. The censors' objection was to the indignity of such a setting for a government arrest. I think Munk misjudged the value of the scene: later censors let it stand, and its sedateness is funny.

In 1957, Munk made *Eroica*, alone in its antiheroic atti-tude to the Warsaw Rising. In the first half of the film, marked "*Scherzo alla Polacca*," a flourishing spiv has joined the Resistance, but his surge of *gloire* soon ebbs and he leaves for the country. His wife is entertaining a Hun-garian lieutenant, who sends him back to Warsaw with a message that the Hungarians are ready to quit the Axis in exchange for Russian recognition. Behaving often with unwilling intrepidity and for some time totally sloshed, seeing a battle through a pastoral haze of stolen Tokay, the legate eventually finds the Hungarian offer refused: and to avoid being alone with his wife now that the cuck-olding lieutenant has fled, again bravely joins the Re-sistance.

The scherzo is full of glancing blows, but because the protagonist is no soldier, military self-regard could still survive. The second part, marked "*Ostinato Lugubre*" and set in a Polish officers' P.O.W. camp, is about the copper-bottomed hero class. After the Rising, a fresh batch of natural leaders is sent to the camp, joining the relics of the 1939 campaign and quickly adopting their intricate fiction of not letting oneself go. The myth that keeps backs stiffest is the myth of the courageous Zawistowski, said to have escaped, but in fact ailing in a loft above the washhouse. Only three officers know he is alive: the secret is kept out

of shame rather than security, and when he commits suicide the Nazis, in much the same spirit, provide an old
boiler to smuggle out his body. Their hunt for him has
been too public; their own military dignity is at stake. The
legend survives. *Eroica* is comic and searing, full of ungrateful wit and acted with tight, wry style, but what one
admires most is the intellectual order beneath it. Munk
was a genuine satirist, rash-spirited and level-minded.

As strongly as Skolimowski's, Polanski's, Munk's, or any
other Polish filmmaker's, Andrzej Wajda's work is steeped
in Polishness as well as in knowledge of censorship's workings through the centuries and how to save from its maws
what is crucial. Through the code substitutions possible
in fiction about the War—Nazis for Russians, loyalty for
perfidy—Wajda was a challenger from the first. He began
his career with an astonishing trilogy about Warsaw in the
war. His codes were all too factually based, with Polish
youth shown in division after the 1944 Warsaw Rising. In
A Generation (1954), *Kanal* (1956) and *Ashes and Diamonds* (1958), he showed us the harrowing split in the
young Poles' aims that was nursed with such doleful care
by Moscow. The division lay between the idealists who believed (as they will always do) in a specifically Polish
Socialism run from a Warsaw still to be "liberated," fated
to be represented by the Soviet-run government waiting
to move in from Lublin, and the equally fervent young
fighters in Warsaw's Home Army, represented by the Polish Government-in-exile in London and libeled by Soviet
rumor as collaborating with the Nazis. Taking their time
for others' blood to be shed, the Moscow politicians sat out
the battle in safety across the Vistula. The Yalta conference's settlement of Polish affairs remains highly debat-
able, however arcane it has become in the memory of the
rest of the world, and Wajda's great trilogy rests for its
full irony on historical recall of the already divided Allies'
last-gasp expediencies.

Though Wajda is so often summed up as Munk's temperamental opposite, there are specifically Polish qualities
in their work that are much alike. Their films show the
same worn energy, a humor that plays dead but always
gets up for more, and a skepticism that probably has to do
with geography: that "badly located" country. Wajda

started film work as the great Aleksander Ford's assistant on *Five Boys*. The fact that the influential Ford agreed to act as "artistic supervisor" on Wajda's projected *A Generation* gave it immediate license. Wajda himself, and everyone connected with the trilogy, had fought as a young patriot in Warsaw. *A Generation* is set in Wola, a working-class part of the city. There are two protagonists: one a dour proletarian not to be deflected, one a troubled, baffled man switching from one position to another. *A Generation* has to mouth some crass characterizing slogans to fit in with the tenets of the times, but there is no doubt where Wajda's support lies: with the destined man who sees ambiguity. Played by Tadeusz Janczar, on the run from the Germans after a relief operation in the ghetto, he dodges into a stairwell and runs higher and higher up the steps till he is barred by an iron grille. Climbing up it, he jumps to his death. This is not to say that Wajda sold his other lead character short. Played by Tadeusz Lomnicki, one of Poland's most varied actors, he becomes heroic through his straightforwardness, his modesty and his gentleness in a love affair. Wajda is one of the very few filmmakers who seem never to have seen any reason to divide those two basic energies in humanity, the urge for constancy expressed in loving and the urge for change expressed in revolution.

Wajda's training as a painter prints his films in the memory. From *A Generation*, for instance, there is a shot of Janczar running in a white trenchcoat that isolates him from the grey surroundings and seems to mark him down as doomed. From *Kanal*, there are unforgettable scenes in the sewers that were the only route that could be taken by cut-off members of the Home Army to withdraw to the center of Warsaw where the insurgents were still holding out. The sewers are labyrinthine, booby-trapped by the Germans and stinking. They are stocked with a most Polish set of characters, including a daredevil and a demented flute-playing composer. At the end, as in *A Generation*, the only way out of this Bosch garden is suicidal: the daredevil finds an exit that leads straight to waiting German soldiers, the steadfast valiants find an exit barred by a grille. *Ashes and Diamonds* is set on the last day of the war in Europe. Exhilaration, depletion. Every aspect of life is confused.

The film commemorates a razed state of mind. It is about young nationalists who have had no youth but assassination, about heroes of the rising suddenly hunted down by fellow socialists as Fascists. Other heroes, lately their fellows in the last-ditch struggle in the sewers, are lining up with the bureaucrats sent to rule by their late ally and historic oppressor, Russia. The perversions seem total. Celebration incredibly turns into new emergency. The debonair Zbigniew Cybulski plays one of two patriots who arrive at a banquet with orders to kill a Russian-trained Pole. Two wrong men are killed, and the Cybulski character is himself shot in a chase through a yard full of laundry. The figure that looks like a child playing ghost in a sheet gets a hand free to feel his own blood and smells it with an inquisitiveness near amusement. Poles understand the notion of "cool" far more vitally than we do: it is a means of survival in Poland.

The theme of the Occupation, always treated with complexity by Poles because enemy Nazis became enemy Russians in the no-win replacements cruelly common after victory waltzes, has always been a permissible theme for Soviet censors, purblind to double meanings. Munk's finest piece of work, *Passenger*, left unfinished at his death and completed from his own working drawings by his associate director, is about a woman's faulty memory of Auschwitz. Munk wasn't interested in the kind of direct narratives about the war that are the commonplace of film production in all Communist countries. He had already done something quite different in *Eroica*, with its iron-nerved mockery of his country's cherished military romanticism, and *Passenger* is not so much about concentration camps as about everyone's capacity to think of the unthinkable by stylizing it.

A smart, hard-faced woman is a passenger on a liner to Southampton; she is married now to a Pole who was an émigré during the war, and she had always told him she had been a prisoner at Auschwitz. The face of a woman on the gangplank suddenly throws up more of the truth, because it is a face she thinks she remembers from the camp. But the images of life at Auschwitz are still distant and horribly beautiful, naked girls run into a ring of the

S.S. like a *corps de ballet* instead of human beings going to the gas chamber. The reality has turned into a mime, a jumble of bleached-out scenes with the words lost. As the film goes on, the stranger's face jabs into her memory like a needle into the brain of a frog. The woman admits first that she was an overseer and not a prisoner at all, and then even her protested kindnesses to the woman turn out to be the way her subconscious now chooses to doll up the most furious sexual malice.

I doubt whether Munk intended that to be the whole truth either. The people who put his work in order have rightly left it in a state where it is still ambiguous and in places almost rubbed out, like the face of a statue under water. It is a hallucinatory film.

When Benois was working in London after the war on a production of *Petrouchka* that was to revive his original designs of many decades before, he was asked why he was making the colors brighter now. "Because that's the way people will remember them," he said. Polish films made now that bring a long telescope to the war reflect the tricks with scale and vividness that memory plays. Andrzej Baranski has lately made an engrossing picture called *Woman from the Provinces* (1985) from the vantage point of 1982. Through forty years, it looks back to the war with the mind of a now sixty-year-old woman, Andzia, played by Ewa Dalkowska. For once we see the Holocaust as it touched a village even then contained and peaceful. The details of regional life in Baranski's quiet record have the poetry of the everyday, as they have in Chekhov. Andzia, a plump, hard-working countrywoman who is a seamstress in her spare time, is widowed in the film, courted and remarried. She has a boredom threshold higher by so many miles than American film-characters' that she seems to belong to another planet. Matter-of-fact though she is, she feels passionately about the pigs she has raised. When she finds her second husband busy at pig slaughter, she grows incensed. "Why didn't you ask me? I raised thirty-two pigs before we married." There is a wealth of pig-raising experience behind her and he has no right to trample on it, this amiable second husband, Felix, who pleases her by mixing her morning fruit juice with alcohol, a good start to what always promises to be an excellent day, though she has seen bad enough in her time. In the war, through time jumps, we see the same calm village roads idly patrolled by the Gestapo, who are absorbed by a little into the community. Before a herding up for concentration camp, we catch concern in a Nazi face or two, a fuddle about whether anyone is senior enough to do this. The villains are also villagers by now; Heil Hitlering has become routine. The natural country view of life and death is so obviously at odds with the Nazis' that there is no sentimentality in Baranski's record of the Germans' fugitive hesitancies.

Andzia is one of those people who never throw anything away, because "it will come in." In the war, she puts together her bits and pieces by oil lamp. Scraps of fur become a jacket, strips of carpet become belts. Her treadle sewing machine rumbles on. In peacetime, she has electric light. Nothing else seems much changed. Yes, there wasn't a lot of food in the war, but she worked in a military kitchen, and German plates had a feast left on them. A woman of firm character, she lives in no blur of radiance, even in peacetime. Small rows erupt. She objects to the fog of shaving suds that men back into for musings about nothing. She objects to the ridiculousness of Felix's fear that a television will explode. These are new days. Yes, it was terrible forty years ago; unforgettable; but still, there are some things she can't quite remember. For indelibly alien atrocities, substitute the union of country commonplaces emphatically recalled.

Wajda, working from the same angle of code in the wonderful *A Love in Germany* in 1983 as a French–West German coproduction, based the script on a Hochhuth novel. The entrancing Hanna Schygulla plays a German small-town shopkeeper, Paulina, during the war. She has a forbidden affair with a Polish prisoner-of-war named Stani (Piotr Lysak), who helps her in the shop. Her husband is on the Eastern front. She has a small son, fecklessly allowed to watch her seducing Stani. The details are packed, domestic, extraordinary because ordinary: a child sucking a lollipop with a swastika on it, S.S. announcements that "our propaganda is consistently undermined by the Church" delivered in a quavery fashion because this is, after all, a small town, and only junior Gestapo staff are on duty. Paulina takes risks, buys contraceptives in a gossipy shop for pastoral love scenes with Stani, betrays Stani's deliberate nonrecognition of her before the authorities in the naïve belief that her love will conquer all. A postwoman whom we expect to be a heartless cow delivers a death announcement with a look of convincing sadness. There is an excellently conceived character of a beautiful traitor who can't stand Paulina: mostly, one feels, because she can't bear her sunny muddle. A near-farcical, totally tragic onset of instructiveness interrupts the carrying-out of a hanging: men including the S.S. discuss the comparative pain of hanging by which part of the neck and by what length of rope. Stani and Paulina are eventually seen by us in hindsight as being at odds because of his loving scorn of her scattiness. It is the scorn of someone who knows and obeys the rules. Her anguish is the anguish of someone who didn't notice she was breaking them. *A Love in Germany* is a piercingly grown-up work.

Wajda's densely political *Man of Marble* is a big film that takes cogent risks. He made it, finally, in 1977, after many fruitless trips to Ministers of Culture housed at the Palace of Culture and Science that stands in the razed, hastily rebuilt Warsaw. The hated palace was a present from Moscow and it looks like a wedding cake. Poles are happy to hear the Free West's jaded saying that a wedding is the first step to a divorce. *Man of Marble* is set in 1970, the year of the Gdansk shipyard strikes and the fall of Gomulka's government. Many workers were killed, and the year is ineradicable from the memory slates of all Poles, though reports of the revolt were suppressed at the time. Shot mostly in color, the film has black-and-white sequences with the look of newsreel footage, some of them actual. A young girl film director, Agnieszka—a quick, decisive beauty played by Krystyna Janda—sets out to reconstruct a truthful picture of the Stalinist past, made opaque by twenty years of shifting propaganda. Her project becomes the one flashback kernel of the picture. Its main character, Birkut (Jerzy Radziwilowicz), is a Stakhanovite bricklayer who aims to lay an inconceivable number of bricks an hour at Nowa Huta, the model socialist steelworks of the new Poland. Birkut, sweetly credulous under his muscle, believes with all his heart that new speed records in bricklaying will help his countrymen to rebuild the nation faster. His friend Witek tries to warn him that he may be making enemies, as his speed endorses the government's exhortations to work harder for a system that by no means all Poles accepted. There is a saddening incident when a saboteur, wrongly suspected to be Witek, passes him a burning brick and maims his hands. The hero, condemned to using hands bandaged so that they look like a pampered little dog's white paws, has become too well-known an individualist for comfort and a sham trial sends him to jail. It is only with October 1956 and the end of Stalinism that Birkut and Witek are released. But the young film director is still hamstrung: what she has unearthed is still politically "sensitive," in the dreadful metonymy of our times that makes the pain in Birkut's hands stand for harm to the Party. She is refused more film stock and told her half-made film lacks figurative shape, as if an amputated story could do anything else. The crucial question raised by Wajda is not so much exactly what happened to Birkut as whether it is possible at all to trace the fate of a discarded hero as ideology changes. *Man of Marble* is about the hunting down of an entry on some missing points-of-view list. It is also about the close relationship between the workers and the intelligentsia in Poland, a relationship that hardly exists in English-speaking countries but that abounds, as we saw in the Czech spring of 1968, in some Eastern European countries.

Wajda went on from the tampered-with ending of *Man of Marble* (Poles and foreigners at the Cannes Film Festival have seen at least four versions, none of them what he meant) to make *Man of Iron* (1981), after the disappearance of Birkut, who has been commemorated in some terrible pieces of socialist realist sculpture. The film fills out what Wajda was not allowed to say, or perhaps did not permit himself to say until he had more time to reflect. It opens with the series of strikes that brought Lech Walesa to power. Winkel, once radical, is now a hard-drinking TV journalist, sent to Gdansk to gather material for a program to discredit strikes. He is told not to go after the names but after the anonymous antiheroes. And

Agnieszka, *Man of Marble*'s film chronicler, is now married to Birkut's son Tomczyk, who is to go on to be one of the leaders of the 1980 strike. A couple of years before, in a Gdansk church, the couple marry before two witnesses: a woman crane operator whose dismissal was partly responsible for the 1980 strike, and Lech Walesa. It is a curious scene. By the use of a celebrated real man, in a way that would be seen as self-promoting in countries like ours, an authenticity is bestowed that carries a stamp of, to us, a forged reality. But this is Poland, and there is the benediction of something truthful here that has nothing to do with celebrity as we think of it, just as Walesa's raw and ineloquent Polish has conferred a seal of legitimacy on his leadership. The film ends with the fall of the government and the official recognition of Solidarity, a time of optimism that Wajda undercuts with a remark by an old-line C.P. member, who says, "It's only a scrap of paper, signed under pressure." All Poles have a great deal of history under their belts. Spectators will have Munich in mind, among other such scraps of paper.

And again the war looked at in memory by Wajda, this time in 1970 in *Landscape After Battle*. It comes from a short story by Tadeusz Borowski, who survived Auschwitz and Dachau and the postwar displaced persons' camps only to commit suicide at the age of twenty-nine. The film's grief is shielded by its beauty as if one were looking at a Greek sculpted head sealed off by protective wax as it juts its chin against tragedy. The film is about a young poet named Tadeusz, played by Daniel Olbrychski with the sweet freedom from impatience that one paradoxically associates with the very, very old. He loves a Jewish girl who has pretended to be a Catholic. As he wanders through the landscape of postwar Europe, he seems to be murmuring to himself again and again the advice he gives to his Polish love, a refrain that he has to repeat to himself in thought to persuade himself that it might be true. "To love, one must forget," the advice goes. Sometimes it seems to him only to hold good if he makes it "To survive, one must forget." But to forget is impossible, because it is so vastly insufficient a response to what he has seen. The catch goes round and round in his head, the melody chasing its tail like a phrase in a fugue. It finds no quiescence in coming back to the tonic, just as a catch can find no home note. Poland's experience has no finalities. The jubilation of the prisoners dancing a strange, silent gigue after their release from concentration camp is quelled after a time in one of the most sorrowful scenes of all Holocaust movies. People turn back to the confines of the camp because confinement for incalculable years has been their only sanctuary. And then the transportation to D.P. camp by American officials whose harassed benevolence is only a little different, in this film's memory, from the passing moments of compassion that Wajda convincingly shows us in the faces of the S.S. Occupation by Germans, Russians, even by their liberating allies: in Poland's history of perpetual invasion, the nationality of the invader is one of the prevailing replacement codes by which Polish movies slip messages urging stoic protest under the cell doors locked by successive censors. Towards the end of the film, there is a repeated tableau of an ancient battle fought on a stage for the displaced-person troops, synonymous with the Nazis' prisoners. One suddenly recognizes in the staging of the famous battle of Tannenberg, when Poles and Lithuanians fought the Teutonic Knights in 1410, the 1919 battle fought at Tannenberg between Russians and Germans. Every battle will always happen again. Polish films tell us this with an equanimity that uniquely extends solace. Wajda's wonderful film hangs in the memory like a prayer rug. Its coloring—it has no formal narrative—is the coloring of Polishness, made permanent by the Poles' religion, by their love of literature, by the language that Poles have kept intact for all the crazed lines of their boundaries in history. And most of all, perhaps, by their sense that there is no end: in the meaning of history's philosophy, not religion's. No end to the arguments about purposes justifying measures, or about the thin line between compromise and selling out, a line that is discussed in a key scene about the effects of martial law in post-Solidarity Poland in a film literally called *No End* (1984). The film is directed by Krzysztof Kieslowski, who wrote the arrestingly intelligent script. The major action is between types of radical lawyers; there is an argument between an old defense lawyer and a hunger striker in a prison cell that must count as one of the most urgently subtle in all courtroom movie scenes.

No end, no end. "I can't go on, I won't go on, I go on." Beckett's words, but a characterizing Polish thought. Poles of all people know that there is no end to, for instance, revolution, any more than there is to its attrition. Rebellious intent will go on souring into ambition, populism into élitism, the forthright into the craven. Wajda's huge epic *Danton* (1982) incenses academics left and right because it induces accusations of false parallelisms. This Polish-French coproduction has managed to infuriate Paris academics and raise a ban in Poland. People who cleave to Büchner's *Danton's Death* are maddened. People who cleave to the original stage play, a Polish repertory piece by Stanislawa Przybyszewska, object to Jean-Claude Carrière's every added line. The fact that the Robespier-ristes (all of whom are seen as crazed zealots and fops, and most of them men on the make) are played by Polish actors, while the populist, plain-spoken Dantonists are played by French actors, is probably at the root of the Polish official decision to push this big work under the car-pet. Danton (Gérard Depardieu) is a giant ape of a man shaking the zoo bars of Paris sophistication. He is plainly the man to Wajda's best liking, but the edgy Robespierre (Wojciech Pszoniak) emerges as a figure of tragic depen-dence on mannerism. It is the public, in the Committee of Public Safety and in the streets, who get short shrift, al-ways swayed by the last speaker and mouthing a babble of French Mummerset or Polish rhubarb-rhubarb. But per-haps Wajda chose well in confining his film to the history of a few intimates, for this is the truth of the French Revo-lution. Quite unlike the Russian, it was a colossal event brought to pass by a very small group of men who all knew each other, a European upheaval peculiarly contained within France's capital city, and one that moved with such speed that the young friends who initiated it became with-in four years one another's lethal enemies. If one sees Dan-ton as Walesa and Robespierre as General Jaruzelski, one is probably falling into the trap of censors' analogies and academics' footnotes. The intelligent achievement of

Wajda lies in subjecting his huge topic to the disciplines of a string quartet without omitting the Revolution's key paradoxes, such as Danton's belief that its violent factionalism betrayed the Revolution's propelling purpose. A clear message semaphored here to his countrymen: the stands taken in Poland must never follow suit.

GETTYSBURG

Arthur C. Danto

> *Then the whole of things might be different*
> *From what it was thought to be in the beginning,*
> *before an angel bandaged the field glasses.*
> John Ashbery

Pity-and-terror, the classically prescribed emotional response to tragic representation, was narrowly restricted to drama by the ancient authorities. In my view, tragedy has a wider reference by far, and pity-and-terror is aroused in me by works of art immeasurably less grand than those which unfold the cosmic undoings of Oedipus and Agamemnon, Antigone, Medea, and the women of Troy. The standard Civil War memorial, for example, is artistically banal by almost any criterion, and yet I am subject to pity-and-terror whenever I reflect upon the dense ironies it embodies. I am touched that the same figures appear and reappear in much the same monument from village to village, from commons to green to public square, across the American landscape. The sameness only deepens the conveyed tragedy, for it is evidence that those who subscribed funds for memorials, who ordered their bronze or cast-iron or cement effigies from catalogues or from traveling sales representatives, so that the same soldier, carrying the same musket, flanked by the same cannons and set off by the same floral or patriotic decorations, were blind to the tragedy that is, for me, the most palpable quality of these cenotaphs. That blindness is a component of the tragedy inherent in the terrible juxtaposition of the most deadly armaments and ordnance known up to that time, with what, under those conditions, was the most vulnerably clad soldiery in history.

The Civil War infantryman is portrayed in his smart tunic and foraging cap. Take away the musket, the bayonet and the cartridge case, and he would be some uniformed functionary—messenger, conductor, bellhop, doorman. This was the uniform he fought in, as we know from countless drawings and photographs that have come down to us from the Civil War. Armed, carrying a knapsack, he moved

[155]

Michael Train

Civil War Memorial, Newton, New Jersey

across the battlefield as though on dress parade. But the weapons he faced were closer in design and cold effectiveness to those standard in the First World War, fifty years in his future, than to those confronted by Napoleon's troops at the Battle of Waterloo, fifty years in his past. What moves me is the contradiction between the code of military conduct, symbolically present in his garments but absent from his gun. We see, instead of the chivalry and romanticism of war as a form of art, the chill implacable indifference to any consideration other than maiming and death, typical of the kind of total combat the Civil War became. That contradiction was invisible when the memorials were raised, and it is its invisibility today that moves me to pity-and-terror.

The rifled musket—one with a helically grooved bore giving a stabilizing spin to the bullet and making possible a flat trajectory—was known in the eighteenth century, but it was used then primarily for hunting. The smooth-bore musket was military issue. There is an affecting Yankee pragmatism in the fact that the citizen-soldiers of the American Revolution should have used their hunting weapons to such effect against the celebrated "Brown Bess"—a smooth-bore musket with its barrel shortened and browned—that the rifled musket had to be adopted by British and European armies. But the Brown Bess had been Wellington's weapon in Belgium, in the style of warfare conducted on the classical battlefield, with disciplined infantry firing in ranks at short distance: a row of blasts from these muskets, as from deadly popguns, could be pretty effective in stopping or driving back an opposed line. Even the rifled musket, at that time, used the round ball. The elongated, cylindro-conoidal bullet was invented only afterward, by Captain John Norton, in 1823, and though it has been acclaimed as the greatest military invention since the flintlock, Wellington could not see how it improved on the Brown Bess, as indeed it did not if battle were conducted as Wellington understood it. The elongated bullet, with its lowered wind-resistance making its charge much more powerful, was understood by Sir William Napier as profoundly altering the nature of infantry, turning the infantry soldier into a "long-range assassin." Napier intuited that a change in the conduct of battle at any point would entail a change at every point—like what Heidegger calls a *Zeugganzes*—a complex of instruments, men and arms forming a total system which functions *as* a totality. Napier's objection implies the very code that the Civil War uniform embodies, and defines a certain moral boundary, the other side of which is not war so much as slaughter. Rifling, the Norton bullet and the percussion cap, established as superior to the flintlock by 1839, certainly changed the face of warfare. There was no room in the new complex for the cavalry charge, as had to be learned in the Charge of the Light Brigade in 1854, and relearned in the Civil War. In any case, the standard Civil War issue was the 1861-model Springfield rifle: percussion lock, muzzleloading, .58 caliber, shooting a 480-grain conical Minié bullet. It was effective at a thousand yards, deadly accurate at three hundred. The smooth-bore was of limited effectiveness at one hundred to one hundred twenty yards. Civil War soldiers faced the kind of fire that made obsolete the way they were used by generals who learned about battle at West Point and had studied the Napoleonic paradigms. The guns faithfully depicted in the Civil War memorial statue made the style and gallantry of the men who carried them obsolete. Even the brass button would be a point of vulnerability in battles to come.

The 1903 and 1917 Springfield models were used by American infantry in the First World War. Increased muzzle velocity flattened trajectory, the ammunition clip, easy to change, speeded charging the magazine. But those rifles were fired over the cusp of trenches and the steel helmets protected the riflemen's heads. Of course, helmets have existed since ancient times and, in fact, were worn by Prussian and Austrian observers at Gettysburg, though more for ostentation than protection. They were brightly polished. "The sword carries greater honor than the shield" could be repeated by a military historian in very recent years, giving a reason why Robert E. Lee should have achieved greater honor through losing glamorously than his opponent, George Meade, earned through winning stolidly, by fighting a defensive battle. Lee had been mocked as "The King of Spades" when he used entrenchments at Chancellorsville. The steel helmet reduced injuries in the First World War by about seventy-five percent. The casualties at Gettysburg, for the three days of the battle, totaled about 51,000, of which 7,058 were outright deaths. The Roman legions were better protected, and their sanitary conditions were better than those prevailing in the 1860s. A wound in the July heat festered and went gangrenous quickly. There were 33,264 wounded. The wagon train that carried the Confederate wounded away under driving rains on July 5 was seventeen miles long. Over ten thousand were unaccounted for, and I suppose their bones would still be turned up at Gettysburg had the battlefield not become a military park. In any case I am uncertain they would have worn helmets if they had had them, for they were men who lived and died by an exalted concept of honor. You went to your death like a soldier, head held high under your jaunty cap. "As he passed me he rode gracefully," Longstreet wrote, years after, of Pickett leading his stupendous charge, "with his jaunty cap raked well over on his right ear and his long auburn locks, nicely dressed, hanging almost to his shoulders. He seemed rather a holiday soldier than the general at the head of a column which was about to make one of the grandest, most desperate assaults recorded in the annals of war." Longstreet thought the great charge a terrible mistake. He thought Lee wrong from the start at Gettysburg. Lee was deaf to Longstreet for the same reason that mourners and patriots across America were blind to the message of their memorials. Longstreet is my hero.

I recently trudged the battle lines at Gettysburg. The scene of that great collision had, according to the architectural historian Vincent Scully, been transformed by the National Park Services into a work of art, and I was curious to see, in the first instance, how the locus of agony and glory should have been preserved and transfigured under the glass bell of aesthetic distance into a memorial object. An interest in memorial art and in the moral boundaries of war would have sufficed to move me as a pilgrim to what, since the Gettysburg Address, we have thought of as consecrated ground. But I had also been enough unsettled by a recent remark of Gore Vidal's that had come up in the civil strife between *Commentary* and the *Nation*, in regard to Norman Podhoretz's patriotism, to want to think out for myself whether, as Vidal claimed, the American Civil War is our Trojan War. Podhoretz had pretended to a greater interest in the Wars of the Roses than in the Civil War, and this had greatly exercised Vidal, whose family had participated on both sides and thus had internalized the antagonisms that divided the nation. The Trojan War was not of course a civil conflict. A better paradigm might have been the epic wars between the Pandavas and Kauravas, as recounted in the *Mahabharata* and given moral urgency in the *Bhagavad Gita*, where the fact that it is a *civil* war was deemed by the great warrior, Arjuna—until he was persuaded otherwise by the god Krishna—a compelling reason not to fight. No one's remembered ancestors participated in the Trojan War when it in fact was their Trojan War in the sense Vidal must have intended, when the Homeric poems had emerged out of the mists to define the meaning of life, strife, love and honor for a whole civilization. The Civil War, if it were to be our Trojan War in that sense, would have to be so even for those whose families were elsewhere and indifferent when it took place. It has not received literary embodiment of the right sort to affect American consciousness as the *Iliad* affected Greek consciousness (Troy affected Roman consciousness through the *Aeneid*). And so a further question that directed me was whether the artistic embodiment of a battlefield into a military park might serve to make it our Trojan War in the required way, where one could not pretend an indifference to it because it was now the matrix of our minds and our beings.

Like Tewkesbury, where the climactic battle of the Wars of the Roses took place in 1471, the name Gettysburg has an irresistibly comic sound, good for a giggle in music hall or vaudeville. It could, like Podunk, serve as everyone's name for Nowheresville, the boondocks, the sticks. It was one of hundreds of "-burgs" and "-villes" named after forgotten worthies (James Gettys had been given the site by William Penn), indicating, before the place "became terrible"—Bruce Catton's phrase—simply where life went on. Gettysburg in 1863 was the seat of Adams county and a poky grove of Academe, with a college and a seminary. But Gettysburg was no Troy: the battle was *at* but not *for* Gettysburg. When Lee withdrew on July 5, its 2,400 inhabitants had ten times that number of dead and wounded to deal with, not to mention mounds of shattered horses: the miasma of putrefaction hung over the town until winter. Gettysburg became host to a cemetery large in proportion to its size, though there is a strikingly prophetic Romanesque gatehouse at Evergreen Cemetery, which gave its name to Cemetery Hill and Cemetery Ridge, and which seemed waiting to welcome the alien dead: you can see artillery emplacements in front of it in a surviving photograph. You can count the houses in Gettysburg in another photograph of the time, looking east from Seminary Ridge. That the battle was there, between Cemetery Ridge and Seminary Ridge, was an artifact of the war. Gettysburg was not somebody's prize. Longstreet called it "ground of no value." It was a good place for a battle, but though it is clear that there had to be a battle someplace soon, it could have happened in any number of other burgs or villes. Meade, knowing there was to be a battle, would have preferred Pipes Creek as its site. Lee was heading for Harrisburg, a serious city and the capital of the state, and decided to *accept* battle instead, knowing he would have to do so somewhere, and Gettysburg, by geological accident, was as good a place as any to fight.

In his novel *Lincoln*, Gore Vidal puts Mary Lincoln in the War Room with her husband. She is supposed to have had, according to the novel, a certain military intuition, and Vidal describes her looking at a map, pointing to the many roads leading in and out of Gettysburg, and saying, in effect, My goodness—whoever controls Gettysburg controls everything. Perhaps this in fact is intended to underscore Mary Lincoln's acute frivolity: if it meant, really, to show how the mind of a general got lodged in the pretty head of the President's wife, it simply shows the limits of Vidal's own military intuition. Gettysburg was not that kind of place. It was not, for example, like Monte Cassino, anchoring a line because it controlled roads up the Italian peninsula, so that when it fell, its defenders were obliged to fall back to the next line of defense. Gettysburg really *was* nowhere, of no importance and no consequence: like Waterloo it was illuminated by the sheer *Geworfenheit* of war. The essence of war is accident.

This is how it happened to happen there. It was known
in Washington in late June that Lee was somewhere in
Pennsylvania, but not known where he was exactly. Despite the telegraph and the *New York Times*, there is a
sense in which men were as much in the dark in regard
to one another's whereabouts as they might have been in
England in the fifteenth century, fighting the Wars of the
Roses. Lee had heard rumors that the Army of the Potomac
was somewhere east of him, but he had no clear idea of
where. This, too, was a matter of accident. In classical
warfare, the cavalry served as the eyes of the army. But
Lee's glamorous and vain cavalry leader, Jeb Stuart, was
off on a toot of his own, seeking personal glory. He turned
up only on the last day of the battle of Gettysburg, trailing
some useless trophies. Buford, a Union cavalry general,
sent out to look for the suspected Confederate troops, more
or less bumped into General Pettigrew's brigade marching
along the Chambersburg Pike into Gettysburg to requisi-
tion shoes. They collided, as it were, in the fog, and each
sent word that the enemy was near. Buford perceived that
it was good ground for a battle and sent for reinforcements. Lee perceived that it was a good *moment* for battle
and began to concentrate his forces. It happened very fast:
the next day was the first day of the engagement, July 1.
    Here is Longstreet's description of the site:

> Gettysburg lies partly between Seminary Ridge on the
> West and Cemetery Ridge on the South-east, a distance
> of about fourteen hundred yards dividing the crests of
> the two ridges.

This is a soldier's description, not the imagined description
of a novelist's personage: you can deduce the necessary
orders to infantry and artillery from Longstreet's single
sentence. The battle seethed and boiled between the two
ridges, as if they were its containing walls. Gettysburg
had the bad luck to lie partly between the ridges. It had
the good luck to lie between them *partly*. There was only
one accidental, civilian death: the battle took place, main-
ly, to the south of the village. The ridges formed two
facing natural ramparts, as though two feudal lords had
built their walls within catapult distance of each other.

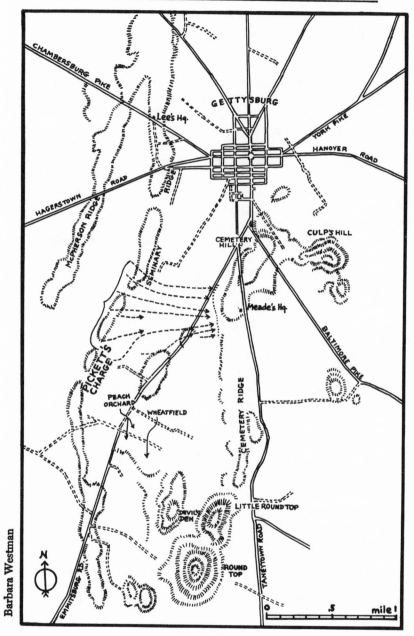

Barbara Westman

GETTYSBURG
July 3, 1863
2:30 P.M.

To visualize the terrain, draw a vertical line and label it Seminary Ridge. This is where the Confederate Army formed its line, along the crest. They seized it after a heated battle with Buford's forces which, despite reinforcements, were driven fourteen hundred yards east to Cemetery Ridge. Now draw a line parallel and to the right of Seminary Ridge, only curve it to the right at the top, to form a sort of fishhook. This was the shape of the Union line, indeed called "The Fish-hook," on July 2 and 3. (Gettysburg is a dot between the lines, just about where the hook begins its curve.) Where the barb would be is Culp's Hill. Farther back along the shaft is Cemetery Hill. At the eye of the hook is Big Round Top, at a distance of about four miles from Cemetery Hill. About half its height, and upshaft, is Little Round Top. The four hills served as battle towers. The rampart itself slopes to the west to form what is designated a *glacis* in the vocabulary of fortification. It was a formidable defensive position, but Seminary Ridge too would have been a formidable defensive position. "If we could only take position here and have them attack us through this open ground!" Lee's chief of artillery, Porter Alexander, recalled having thought. "We were in no such luck—the boot, in fact, being upon the other foot." A defensive war was not what had brought Lee north and onto enemy territory. He had to attack if there was to be battle.

Longstreet did not think there needed to be battle. Standing beside Lee, he surveyed the Union position with his field glasses for a very long time, turned to Lee and said,

> If we could have chosen a point to meet our plans of operation, I do not think we could have found a better one than that upon which they are now concentrating. All we have to do is throw our army around by their left, and we shall interpose between the Federal Army and Washington. We can get a strong position and wait, and if they fail to attack us we shall have everything in condition to move back tomorrow night in the direction of Washington.

"No," said General Lee—the words are famous and fateful—"the enemy is there and I am going to attack him there."

Perhaps Longstreet was wrong: Meade was as cautious a man as he. Why need Meade have attacked them, even though between Washington and its army? Lee's supply line was long and vulnerable, and Meade might have ringed any position he would take and wait out a seige. Still, wars are fought not so much by generals as by governments, and Longstreet knew that Washington would pressure Meade to attack, needing a victory and in fear for Washington itself. And Lee was probably right: if he could crush Meade's army here, where it was, he would have free access to Washington or Baltimore or Philadelphia. He needed or thought he needed a *brilliant* victory. He had invaded the North not for conquest but to astonish. And he could sustain a defeat as Meade could not. If Meade were defeated, pressure to negotiate would be exerted on Lincoln by the Peace Party in the Union. There might be foreign recognition. And morale would have been disastrously lowered since the Union had just undergone a series of brutal defeats. He might, on the symbolic date of July Fourth, achieve independence for the South. Whereas if he lost at Gettysburg, well, he could have swaggered back to his own territory, as after a dashing raid, trailing glory. Besides, rounding the Federal left would have baffled his troops, who had driven the enemy back to that position. Morale is a precious factor, a form of power. Lee would have to *smash* the Union left. He would have to take Little Round Top, as he nearly succeeded in doing on the second day of battle.

A battlefield has something of the metaphysical complexity of a work of art: it stands to the terrain on which it is spread as a work of art stands to the physical object to which it belongs. Not every part of the physical object is really a part of the work of art—we do not take the weave of canvas into consideration in identifying the meaning of a picture, for example, since there is no coherent way in which we can read the roughness of his surfaces into, say, the iconographic program of Tintoretto's Scuola di San Rocco. We rarely consider the fact that a surface is dry when interpreting a painting. Richard Wollheim, in his recent Mellon Lectures, borrowed from phenomenology the useful term "thematization," and would use it to say that not every part or property of the physical object is "thematized" by the work. Doubtless the concept can be taken further—I am seeking to thematize the contradiction, which most would not even see as there, in Civil War memorial statuary. But what I want to say here is that battle thematizes certain features of the terrain, transforming them into what soldiers call "ground." At Gettysburg, the flanking hills of the Federal line were thematized in this sense on the second day of battle; Cemetery Hill and the sweep of field and meadow between the ridges were thematized on the third and last day. It is doubtful the two ridges would have been so thematized in an imagined encounter between Napoleon and Wellington: their artillery would not have reached far enough, and besides, the explosive shell had not been invented in 1815. (Its invention meant the end of the wooden battleship.) What would be the point of lobbing cannon balls across the fields? One follows the structure of battle by grasping successive thematizations. War is a deadly artist. A battlefield is already more than halfway to a work of art.

On July 2, Lee strove to take either or both Culp's Hill and Little Round Top. Meade's defensive line along Cemetery Ridge would have been untenable had Lee succeeded: he would have had to draw back to Pipes Creek, and it would have been a defeat. The fighting that afternoon was fierce but uncoordinated—each commander had difficulties with his generals—and the outcome of the engagement was sufficiently ambiguous that Lee could interpret it as a victory. Still, no thanks to General Daniel Sickles, the tempestuous Federal general who had left Little Round Top undefended, both the contested hills remained, it may have seemed precariously, in Union hands. Had Meade's engineering chief, Gouverneur Warren, not happened to see that no one was holding the crest at Little Round Top and on his own authority diverted troops to its defense in the very nick of time, the outcome of that day's fighting would have been different.

It is worth contemplating Little Round Top from the perspective of weaponry. Little Round Top was called "the Rocky Hill" by the Confederates—armies improvise a nomenclature with their thematizations. Its slopes are strewn with heavy boulders of the kind that, piled up, gave

[*166*]

the name "Devil's Den" to an adjacent site. It is full of ad hoc shelters and one-man fortresses, and offers an object lesson in the military imagination. It cried out for a kind of weapon—the grenade—which was to be indispensable to infantry in the World Wars but which was considered extinct at the time of the Civil War because of the increase in range and accuracy of muzzled arms. Grenades had been intensely employed in seventeenth-century tactics (when a grenadier was a special physical type, like a shot-putter). It came into its own again in the Russo-Japanese war. The field mortar, with its high trajectory, would also have done wonders at Devil's Den, with its freestone breastworks and God-given sniper nests. Civil War battle seems to have been imagined as something that takes place on a field, between massed armies. The grenade and mortar, conceived of as suited to storming fortresses, were inscrutable in 1863, even though all the technology was in place for the manufacture of the lightweight grenades that re-entered the armory half a century later. The weaponry determined the order of thematization, and particularly the field between the ridges on which Pickett's charge was to take place on July 3 was something generals understood or thought they understood. Longstreet knew they did not.

On July 3, Lee had determined to attack Meade's center. This was his reasoning: Meade, he believed, would infer that Lee was seeking to turn his flanks and would renew the attack on the anchoring hills. So Meade would move reinforcements to right and left, leaving the center weak. Meade's reasoning was this: Lee would reason as he in fact reasoned, so the right thing was to reinforce the center. In classical warfare there is a kind of language—armies communicate through guns (as the United States and the Soviet Union today communicate through nuclear testing): a cannonade announces a charge. All that morning the Federal officers and men watched the enemy concentrate its artillery—150 guns focused on the Union center. "A magnificent sight," according to Henry Hunt, Chief of Artillery on the Union side: "Never before had such a sight been witnessed on this continent, and rarely, if ever, abroad." The Union employed about 200 pieces in that battle, and a duel opened up at about 1 P.M. that lasted nearly two hours: nothing on that scale had ever taken place before. But the state of explosive chemistry in the mid-nineteenth century raised severe cognitive problems for the Confederate force. What was used then was black gunpowder, which created dense smoke. The exploding shells cast a smoke screen over Cemetery Ridge, concealing from Confederate artillery chief Porter Alexander that he was shooting too high, and that his shells were falling behind the Union line. By accident, he hit a dozen caissons of ammunition to Meade's rear. Union Major General Hunt decided to conserve ammunition for the attack to come, and ordered fire to cease. Alexander took this as a sign that he had silenced the Federal guns, and signaled Pickett to move forward. Smoke still hung blackly over Cemetery Ridge, but at a certain moment-of-no-return a breeze lifted it and Pickett's men saw, in Allan Nevins's words, "the full panoply of Union strength in its terrifying grandeur, a double line of infantry in front, guns frowning beside them, and reserves in thick platoons further back." Until that moment, none of Lee's officers had any real idea of what power had been building up behind the sullen ridge. Had his cavalry been operative, Lee would not have charged. He fought blind.

It was in Pickett's grand charge up the slopes of Cemetery Ridge that the tragic contradiction between arms and uniform became palpable. Pickett's superb veterans, fresh in this battle, marched according to a magnificent code into a wall of fire. It was the brutal end to an era of warfare, the last massed charge. The triumph of slaughter over chivalry gave rise to Sherman's horrifying march through Georgia and South Carolina, to total war, to the fire-bombing of Dresden, to Hiroshima and Nagasaki, to the rolled grenade in the full jetliner. "It was the most beautiful thing I ever saw," exclaimed Colonel Fremantle, a British observer at Longstreet's side. The sentiment was widely shared. Pickett's charge was what war was all about in that era, it had the kind of beauty that made Lee remark, at the Battle of Fredericksburg, "It is well that war is so terrible—we should grow too fond of it." Longstreet wrote: "That day at Gettysburg was one of the saddest in my life." I think he was more or less alone in this feeling. I do not think Gettysburg was perceived as the awful defeat it was by the South, at least not then, since news of Grant's victory at Vicksburg had not yet come, nor do I think it was received as a great victory, least of all in Washington, or by Lincoln, who cared only that Meade should press his advantage. What no one could see, just because the doors of the future always are closed, was that beauty on that occasion was only the beginning of terror.

The bodies were rolled into shallow trenches, and the armies moved off to other encounters. Some 3,500 Union dead are today neatly buried in concentric arcs alongside Evergreen Cemetery. Seventeen acres were set aside for this, weeks after the battle, and it was here, before the landscaping was altogether completed, that Lincoln delivered the address which is so enshrined in the national consciousness today that it requires an effort of severe deconstruction to perceive it as a cry of victory as gloating as anything that issued from the coarse throat of Ajax. The Gettysburg Battlefield Memorial Association was chartered in 1864 and began acquiring land which was absorbed into the National Military Park established, without debate so far as I can discover, by an act of Congress in 1895. In 1933 it came under the jurisdiction of the National Park Service, which transformed it in an unforgiving way. There is an historical preservation I applaud but a political overlay that distresses me.

It is always moving to visit a battlefield when the traces of war itself have been erased by nature or transfigured by art, and to stand amid memorial weapons, which grow inevitably quaint and ornamental with the evolution of armamentary technology, mellowing under patinas and used, now, to punctuate the fading thematizations of strife. The first cannon to be fired at the Battle of Gettysburg stands by the memorial to Buford near MacPherson's Farm, like a capital letter to mark the beginning of a ferocious sentence. Four cannons form Cushing's battery stand, like four exclamation points, to mark its end at the point where Pickett's men penetrated the Union line only to be surrounded. General Francis Walker uses a Homeric metaphor to describe Pickett's charge:

As the spear of Menelaus pierced the shield of his antag-
onist, cut through the shining breastplate, but spared the
life, so the division of Pickett, launched from Seminary
Ridge, broke through the Union defense, and for the
moment thrust its head of column within our lines, threatening destruction to the Army of the Potomac.

When I was a soldier, I was often struck, as by a paradox,
that at the very moment that artillery was pounding somewhere, somewhere else men and women in soft clothing
were touching glasses and carrying on flirtations; and that
before and after this moment, but in this place, the peaceful pursuit of human purposes would go innocently forward, that families would picnic where men were being
killed. And I was overwhelmed after the war by the thick
peace that had settled back over places I had seen sharded:
Salerno, Velletri, Cassino, Anzio. There is that sense today
at Gettysburg, as tourists consult their maps and point
across to not very distant hills and ridges, or listen to
patient guides rehearse the drama of those three days in
July 1863. The statue of General Lee, on his elegant horse,
Traveller, stands just where Lee himself stood, and faces,
across the open field traversed by Pickett's division, to
where an appropriately less flamboyant effigy of Meade
looks west from Cemetery Ridge. The copse of trees that
Lee had singled out as the point to head for still stands
not far from Meade's statue, segregated by an iron fence,
as if a sacred grove. Ranks of cannons point across, from
ridge to ridge, and the sites are strewn with touching,
simple monuments, placed by the units that were there
so that it would always be remembered that they were
there. The most florid monument celebrates the Pennsylvania presence (there are 537 Pennsylvanians buried in
the National Cemetery, and 867 New Yorkers—the largest
representation by state there). There is an art history of
Gettysburg to be written, but the meaning that comes
through, even without it, is that a momentous collision
occurred here, and that it was connected with the high
and generous feelings that are appropriate, after a battle,
between those who fought it.

The Parks Services pamphlet of 1950 recommends an

itinerary with fourteen stops—it maps onto the Stations of the Cross if you have an appetite for numerical correspondences. It is chronological. You begin where the battle began, at MacPherson's Ridge at 8 A.M. on July 1. You now follow a trail south along Seminary Ridge, and you may pause in front of Lee's statue and recite the thought Faulkner insisted was in the breast of every Southern boy: it is, there, eternally "still not yet two o'clock on that July afternoon in 1863." Edging the Peach Orchard, where Sickles formed a reckless salient and lost a leg, you mount Round Top and head north to The Copse of Trees and Meade's headquarters. You pause at the cemetery and end, not quite appropriately, at Culp's Hill. In 1950, as today, you would leave 1863 from time to time and enter the present, for the acreage of the Battle Park is intersected, here and there, with fragments of mere unthematized Pennsylvania, along whose roads tractors and trucks drive past restaurants and service stations on one or another civilian errand. The almost cubist interpenetration of past and present, war and peace, is semiotically moving in its own right.

The itinerary of 1950 was dropped from revised editions of the pamphlet, in 1954 and 1962, and today the visit has a different structure. Today you enter the park, amidst many monuments, along "High-Water Mark Trail." There are no Confederate markers among the celebratory monuments: instead, there is "High-Water Mark Monument," erected by "us" to show how far "they" reached. It was not really a high-water mark. There was no flood: this was not Genghis Khan, but one of the gentlest occupations the world has ever seen. It was, exactly as General Walker put it, a spear point which penetrated but did not slay—a Homeric poet would have supposed a god or goddess deflected the weapon. Lee was the spearman—Menelaus, if the analogy appeals (except Menelaus triumphed). If we construe the Military Park as a monumentary text, it now reads *not* as the history of a great battle between heroic adversaries, but as the victory of the Union. The text begins where the victory was won. As a text, the park is now a translation into historical landscape of the Gettysburg Address. Small wonder it "fell like a wet blanket," as Lincoln afterward said. Small wonder the Harrisburg

Patriot editorialized the "silly remarks" this way: "For the credit of the Nation we are willing that the veil of oblivion shall be dropped and that they shall be no more repeated or thought of." Half the men who fell there did not fight for what Lincoln said was achieved there, and of those who might have, Lincoln's were not in every case the reasons they were there. It was an inappropriate political speech on an occasion that called for generosity, vaunting and confessional. The language is concealingly beautiful, evidence that Auden is after all right that time worships language "and forgives/Everyone by whom it lives."

I can understand, or might be able to understand, how a literary scholar, though patriotic, might find the Wars of the Roses of greater interest than the American Civil War, even if he should have no special concern with the ambitions of Lancaster and York. Henry VI, the subject of an early tragedy of Shakespeare, founded Kings College, Cambridge. But the main reason, I should think, for being interested in the civil wars of the fifteenth century in England is connected with one main reason for being interested in our Civil War. The Wars of the Roses were of an unparalleled brutality and were fought by mercenaries. It was total warfare, and the sickening experience of having one's land run over by one's countrymen but acting like brigands and in the royal pay lingered for centuries in British consciousness. Henry VI also founded Eton, on whose playing fields the British Empire is said to have been won by practices governed by the rules of fair combat and respect for the opponent. The unspeakable conduct of battle on the Continent—think of the Thirty Years War—until the eighteenth century, when Anglicization began to define the moral outlines of military conduct, must have confirmed the legacy of the Wars of the Roses in the English mind.

My sense is that the high-minded perception of the soldierly vocation is embodied in the uniform, the insignia, the flags and the vulnerability of the militia depicted in sculpture of the Civil War. The other form of war is embodied in the weapons. If there is a high-water mark in the history of modern war, it was in Pickett's gallant and foregone assault. It has been growing darker and darker ever since. I am not certain this is a basis for seeing the Civil War as "our" Trojan War. In a sense, something is not a Trojan War if it is *ours*: the Trojan War speaks to what is universal and human, regardless of political division and national culture. I am not certain that the idea of Union has any more meaning than or as much meaning as Helen of Troy, as justification for pitched combat. If the Civil War is to address humanity as the Trojan War does, it must itself be addressed at a different level than any that has so far been reached. Gettysburg is a good place to begin.

ADAMS STALKING JEFFERSON

Garry Wills

> *Dear old Jefferson! Never was there a
> more delightful ground for people to
> argue about! We discuss him here by
> the day together, just as though he
> were alive. We can fight about him as
> ardently as ever. He is supremely use-
> ful still (he and Hamilton) as a sort of
> bone for students of history to mumble,
> preparatory to getting their teeth.*
>
> Henry Adams to
> Hugh Blair Grigsby, 1877

All through the nine-volume *History* that is his masterpiece, Henry Adams kept nagging in a bemused way
at Thomas Jefferson, with an irony more telling than in-
vective. Much of America's intellectual history can be
seen as the tale of Henry Adams stalking Jefferson. For
years he could tell others that he had "settled down for the
winter, and Mr. Jefferson is feeling the knife." Only toward Jefferson, of the great historical figures he studied,
did Adams have an attitude of accounts to be settled,
claims to be threshed out, debts called in. For him, there
was business still to be done with Jefferson, as there is
for us.

Some of the passion Adams brought to his treatment of
Jefferson, at first rather unfocused and irrational, came
from regional bias and family pride. The third President
of the United States had abused as well as replaced the
second President, John Adams, Henry's great-grandfather,
and then dismissed from diplomatic service the man who
was to become the sixth President, John Quincy Adams,
Henry's grandfather. Jefferson always came first when
Henry was listing the inherited Adams enmities: "Jefferson, Pickering, Jackson, and the legion of other life-long
enemies whom my contentious precursors made"(*Letters*).

But a feud is a boring assignment, even for those more
willing to accept ancestral chores than Adams was. A
family grudge does not yield very promising intellectual

returns, and Adams was an economist of his intellectual investments. If he devoted most of his historical energies to the study of the Jeffersonian presidents, it was not to appease any gods of the hearth in Quincy or Boston, but to advance himself in Washington and New York, in the new centers of political and financial power. He studied the past to equip himself, if he could, for the present and the future.

And for this the Adams heritage could itself be the enemy. All the Adamses, Henry claims, had quarrels with the city and the region that made up their political base, with Boston and with New England—and Henry added to these a further resistance of his own to family burdens. Teaching colonial history at Harvard in the 1870s, he resented the expectation that he would be a family defender, and snapped at a student: "John Adams was a demagogue" (Ernest Samuels, *The Young Henry Adams*, 1948). Much of *The Education of Henry Adams* is the story of failed attempts to escape the gilded impediment of his birth. He was in a spiral of perpetual quarrel with dead or deadening relatives on all sides. Giving a reluctant consent to the request for a reprint of *Mont-Saint-Michel and Chartres*, he did so because it was "less Adamsy to consent than to refuse." But then he reflected that opposition to family pressure was itself a kind of refusal. So the act was more "Adamsy all round" after all. This was not the man to send out on any such simple family business as a vendetta.

Rebelliousness took the form, in Adams, of a yearning toward the South, toward that more licentious atmosphere that Quincy gave him indolent hints of in the summer. The one part of his bloodline whose importance he systematically exaggerated was his "quarter taint of Maryland blood," derived from Louisa Johnson, who married John Quincy Adams. Henry knew her in his childhood and revered her as "the Madam . . . presiding over her old President . . . hardly more Bostonian than she had been fifty years before" (*Education*, 1906, 1918). Because of her, Henry could claim to be "half exotic," and to her—with her extravagant father claiming large estates in Geor-

[*175*]

gia—he traced "those doubts and self questionings, those hesitations, those rebellions against law and discipline" that prompted him.

Such promptings turned him always toward her South— eventually toward Cuba, where he helped foment a revolution; toward Tahiti, where he painted the nude women; most often toward Washington, that sleepy Southern village that offered him summertime Quincy on a year-round basis. "The want of barriers, of pavements, of forms; the looseness, the laziness; the indolent Southern dialect; the pigs in the streets; the negro babies and their mothers with bandanas; the freedom, openness, swagger, of nature and man soothed his Johnson blood" (*Education*). He even liked Washington in August, a desperate achievement. In his book on medieval cathedrals, Adams pitted the cold Norman north against the more feminine refinements of Chartres. New England was Norman America, rigid and on defense like Saint Michael on his mount, surrounded by a coil of waters. Over and over in his work Adams depicts the New Englander being slowly covered with thin ices of introspection or calculation, ices that first inhibit, then forbid spontaneous action.

For action, one had to move south—toward laxity perhaps, toward actions ill-considered, but where action and instinct were still possible. Adams referred to his home in the north as "Scotland." Virginia was, by contrast, America's Italy. He gravitated toward Virginians from the time when, as a Harvard student, he became a friend of "Roony" Lee, the son of Robert E. Lee (at whose Arlington mansion Adams was dining the day President-elect Lincoln reached Washington to be inaugurated). As a teacher at Harvard, Adams avoided the filiopietistic expectations of his colonial history course by turning it over, as soon as possible, to his graduate student, Henry Cabot Lodge. He tried to go even further, and let Lodge teach a course in national history complementary to his own, where Lodge would expound Hamiltonian views while Adams championed the Republicans, Jefferson's party.

In his biography of John Randolph, Adams imagined the childhood of a spoiled Virginia horseman, contrasting it with a New Englander's schooling. This was a first draft, drawn twenty-five years beforehand, for the opening chapter of the *Education*, built on the contrast between Henry's own Quincy summers and his Boston winters, where it is clear that his heart is on the side of freedom and the muskrat chases.

More striking yet is the way Adams made the alter ego in his first novel a widow of one Virginian Lee and the confidante of another. With the latter she visits the Lee mansion in Arlington, now empty and surrounded by military graves. "Madelaine Lee" has exhausted the resources of the North, for thought, philanthropy and commerce, when she goes south to Washington in search of passion and power, a dangerous trip but irresistible, a move Adams made repeatedly, in varying moods of hope or apprehension or pugnacity. He went back and back to the capital to be reanimated, if only with derision. He never looked around the houses he grew up in for his heroes, but among the men of action and impulse who had served Washington and Jefferson.

If law could once be united with the indulgences of the South, America would have struck the proper balance in Adams's eyes. And once, at least, law *had* reigned there— in George Washington. Adams, who grew up on Mount Vernon Street, never doubted that Washington was the touchstone of America. Everything it might be had to be tested against what it had been under him. This was not simply because John Adams had been Vice President to Washington, or John Quincy Adams held appointed office under him. Washington stood as far above mere family pride, in Adams's mind, as above the personal meannesses of party. Although Henry's grandfather was "the President" in his family's conversations, Washington was always *the* President in his writings.

And after Washington, a long way after, came neither of the Adamses in his list of great early Presidents, but another Virginian. "Washington and Jefferson doubtless stand pre-eminent as the representatives of what is best in our national character or its aspirations," Henry wrote in his biography of Albert Gallatin (1879). Jefferson presented, on his own reduced scale, the same anomaly as Washington, a *normative* Virginian, a beacon of law from the region of license. Washington, while posing a moral challenge all but unanswerable, presented no intellectual problem. He left men wondering how they could attain again that upper air he breathed. But what he meant was clear to everyone, even though he was placed at some unbridgeable remove from them.

Jefferson was another matter entirely. What did Jefferson *mean*? It was a question to which Adams would give many complementary, sometimes contradictory, answers. Mostly tentative answers. Always approximating ones.

> A few broad strokes of the brush would paint the portraits of all the early Presidents [including, obviously, the two Adamses] . . . and a few more strokes would answer for any member of their many cabinets; but Jefferson could be painted only touch by touch, with a fine pencil, and the perfection of the likeness depended upon the shifting and uncertain flicker of its semitransparent shadows. (Henry Adams, *The History of the United States of America During the Administrations of Thomas Jefferson and James Madison*, 1889–91)

Washington was a study in light, Jefferson a study in shadow—a "study," from the age of Whistler, since the historian has turned, in this famous passage, to the resources of the painter. The "fine pencil" was the detail brush in a nineteenth-century atelier. Adams was posing for himself the kind of problem he set the heroine in his second novel: "Esther was surprised to find what a difficult model she [Catherine] was, with liquid reflections of eyes, hair and skin that would have puzzled Correggio" (*Esther*, 1884). Adams, deeply impressed by the power of portrait painters, agreed with Timon of Athens: "These pencill'd figures are / Even such as they give out." He avoided sitting for Sargent: "I knew too well what he would do to me, and I was too much of a coward." He had even better reason to respect the "pencil" of Gilbert Stuart, who fixed the images of the early Adams, especially in his miraculous painting of John Adams at ninety. When Henry published his two eighteenth-century biographies, he drew heavily on the visual evidence supplied by Stuart:

[*178*]

The nobler traits, shown only to those he loved, were caught by Gilbert Stuart in a portrait painted in this year, when [John] Randolph was thirty-three. Open, candid, sweet in expression, full of warmth, sympathy, and genius, this portrait expresses all of his higher instincts, and interprets the mystery of the affection and faith he inspired in his friends. (*Randolph*, 1879)

Set side by side with the heads of Jefferson and Madison, this portrait [of Albert Gallatin] suggests curious contrasts and analogies, but looked at in whatever light one will, there is in it a sense of repose, an absence of nervous restlessness, mental or physical, unusual in American politicians; and, unless Stuart's hand for once forgot its cunning, he saw in Mr. Gallatin's face a capacity for abstraction and self-absorption often, if not always, associated with very high mental power; an habitual concentration within himself which was liable to be interpreted as a sense of personal superiority, however carefully concealed or controlled, and a habit of judging men with judgements the more absolute because very rarely expressed. The faculty of reticence is stamped on the canvas. . . . (*Gallatin*)

Unfortunately, Adams did not trace the interplay of "contrasts and analogies" in Stuart's paintings of the three principal figures in Jefferson's administration. He seems to imply that Gallatin's self-containment and lack of "nervous restlessness" would be contrasted with at least one of the Virginian's portraits. The leaning of the neurasthenic Madison on his table for support in the Boudoin portrait may be what he was thinking of. No such trait can be found in the Edgehill portrait of Jefferson, painted by Stuart in 1805. The model is not turned three-quarter profile, like Gallatin or Madison—a pose that of itself suggests "concentration" on some intermediate distance. President Jefferson, in the midst of his troubles with the judiciary and the press, stares us full in the face, without evasion, with a kind of infuriating benignity. "No troubles here," the mild eyes seem to say. "No mysteries either. Apply elsewhere." That was his con, and Stuart seems to fall for it. Did his hand, after all, forget its cunning?

[*179*]

The limpid gaze of the Edgehill portrait is as transpicuous as Jefferson's prose style, whose easy flow washes all difficulties away. Reassuring Gallatin at a time when his administration was racked with strife, Jefferson warbled off any worries:

> Our Administration now drawing towards a close, I have a sublime pleasure in believing it will be distinguished as much by having placed itself above all the passions which could disturb its harmony, as by the great operations by which it will have advanced the well-being of the nation. (*Gallatin*)

The rockier the obstacles, the smoother the flow of Jefferson's words around or over them. He had no gift for being troubled—even, Adams kept suspecting, for being troubled by the truth. What is such a cool man doing in such a hot spot? Has he just not noticed?

These questions especially plagued Adams, with his view of the ardent South, the land of passion and instinct and spontaneous reactions. Washington had passions so powerfully reined in that his moral musculature stood out under the tension. But Jefferson seemed effortless in his appeals to sweet reason. Did he have no wrestle at all with his emotions? Adams finds it easier to forgive John Randolph the most vicious outbursts of passion than to admire the serpentine gliding of Jefferson toward his goals. There was something feline and—always an important point with Adams—something feminine in Jefferson's wiles. In that sense, maybe Stuart's hand was not fooled, after all, since the Edgehill portrait gives us a disarmingly feminine, almost grandmotherly, image of the embattled President. Adams was surely working from Stuart's picture when he described "this sandy face, with hazel eyes and sunny aspect" (*History*).

> He fairly revelled in what he believed to be beautiful, and his writings often betrayed subtle feeling for artistic form—a sure mark of intellectual sensuousness. He shrank from whatever was rough or coarse, and his yearning for sympathy was almost feminine. (*History*)

Many have noticed how readily the words Adams uses of Jefferson could be applied to himself. Writing to his brother in the Union Army, Henry contrasted the diplomatic skills he was learning with Charles's experience on the field: "My hand could at best use a rapier. It is not made for a sabre. I should be like a bewildered rabbit in action, being only trained to counsel" (*Letters*). Four years after the war, he was still contrasting their attitudes toward life:

> I will not go down into the rough-and-tumble, nor mix with the crowd. . . . You like the strife of the world. I detest it and despise it. . . . You like roughness and strength: I like taste and dexterity. (*Letters*)

This sounds remarkably like the man who "built for himself at Monticello a château above contact with man," for whom "the rawness of political life was an incessant torture" (*History*).

These points of similarity, which should have made for sympathy, were not trivial. Adams aptly treated his picture of Jefferson in artistic terms, because both men were artists, "intellectual sensualists" trying to make the outside world conform to inner rhythms and demands of form. Jefferson studied prosody as earnestly as Adams shortened and lengthened his sentences on a scheme. They both collected art and tried to form the tastes of those around them. Jefferson designed curtains; Adams painted the nude women of Tahiti; but neither were dilettantes. Both saw profound political, social and religious significance in the arts. Madelaine Lee, in *Democracy*, carries her Corot to Washington as a kind of talisman, a touchstone to measure the difference between real depth and mere muddle. Jefferson brought back his "Guido Renis" from France with a serious political purpose, "to improve the taste of my countrymen, to increase their reputation, to reconcile to them the respect of the world & procure them its praise" (*Papers*).

Above all, both men were engaged in the theory and practice of architecture. If Jefferson built his "château" apart on Monticello, Adams cooperated with Richardson in building his Romanesque observation post across from the White House on Lafayette Square. In *Esther*, Adams made the test for a modern religion its ability to create a church that would engage the present-day world, reorient the lives of those passing through or near it, impose a style that all its surroundings must obey—a thing Catholics had accomplished with their cathedrals of the Middle Ages, and one that Jefferson could still accomplish with his university; but which the churches, by the nineteenth century, were failing to do.

Both Adams and Jefferson expected a great deal from architecture, and from life. They tended always toward hyperbole; each dearly loved a superlative. With a taste for extremes, they saw the best and worst impending daily. What Adams said of Jefferson, his brother Charles had often said of Henry: "He was curiously vulnerable, for he seldom wrote a page without exposing himself to attack. He was superficial in his knowledge, and a martyr to the disease of omniscience" (*History*). Their artistry subjected both men to the temptation of ignoring things not responsive to their patterns of thought. Henry came to guard himself against his own exuberance by the constant curb of irony. He tempered hyperbole with litotes, which gives his prose its crabcrawl indirection. But Jefferson's prose remained limpid, it flowed without check or recoil, with an easiness of diversion that had to be kept entirely innocent of irony if it was to work. And innocent of other things, too. "Mr. Jefferson's weakest side was his want of a sense of humor" (*Gallatin*).

This ignorance of the world's doubleness gave Jefferson an imperviousness to doubt that astounded Adams. Jefferson had no sense of the grotesque, of the underside to things, of the self-mocking limitations that accompany the highest aspirations. There were to be no gargoyles at the completed Monticello. Jefferson, for all his outward alertness of mind and nimble gifts of observation, lacked powers of introspection. He could change his mind without knowing he had done so. What seemed to others like betrayals of an earlier position seemed but inevitable corollaries to Jefferson.

His flexibility came from the great simplicity of his character, not from deceit. He could achieve Machiavellian effects without Machiavellian intent. Remarkably free of inner demons, he found pure evil only in his enemies, at whom he could no more laugh than at himself. In a sense, he gave them too much credit. He thought Hamilton was more interested in monarchy, in an abstract principle of error, than in getting power under any serviceable name.

Trying to "do a Stuart" of Jefferson's mind, Adams kept stumbling on the mystery of the man's simplicity. As Wharton, the painter in his novel, tells Esther: "I can't paint innocence without suggesting sin, but you can, and the church likes it." Jefferson somehow conveyed his own innocence to Americans, and the nation liked it. That was the great fact of the American character, and thus of American power in the modern world. All the ugly and heterogeneous elements of medieval culture had been held together, at key moments, by the harmonizing power of the Virgin. In the same way, the myth of Virginia—of a fresh start for the human race on this continent, in communion with a rectifying nature—was maintained, above all ugly and heterogeneous elements (including slavery), by the sunny countenance of Jefferson:

> European and American critics, while affirming that Americans were a race without illusions or enlarged ideals, declared in the same breath that Jefferson was a visionary whose theories would cause the heavens to fall upon them. Year after year, with endless iteration, in every accent of contempt, rage, and despair, they repeated this charge against Jefferson. Every foreigner and Federalist agreed that he was a man of illusion, dangerous to society and unbounded in power of evil; but if this view of his character was right, the same visionary qualities seemed also to be a national trait, for everyone admitted that Jefferson's opinions, in one form or another, were shared by a majority of the American people. . . . Jefferson's personality during these eight years appeared

to be the government, and impressed itself, like that of Bonaparte, although by a different process, on the mind of the nation. In the village simplicity of Washington he was more than king, for he was alone in social as well as in political pre-eminence. (*History*)

For Adams, to puzzle out the meaning of Jefferson was to decipher the code of America itself as its people pushed westward, became a nation and formed an empire. The Sphinx that lay at the entry to that land and its secrets wore the deceptively mild expression of Thomas Jefferson. Adams was just enough like the man he studied to be usefully irritated by the things that set them apart. If he could understand those, Adams rightly sensed, he might see at last why he was so different from his fellow Americans, an exile in his own land, where even the shy and aristocratic Jefferson had been at ease.

It was a formidable task for Adams, which explains the long years he expended on it, the years of his own prime. In Jefferson, Adams had his great theme—the one that would make him the American Gibbon if only he could understand its course and significance. Modern critics of Adams have begun to understand, after Yvor Winters's perceptive essay of 1943, that Adams was at his greatest not in his last works, during what Ernest Samuels called his "major phase," but in the most sustained effort of his middle manhood, the *History* he labored at throughout his forties (the same years Gibbon was at work on the *Decline and Fall*). And the great challenge of the nine volumes of his history is the constraining need to understand Jefferson. His portrait of Jefferson, gradually built up there, is his masterpiece, the point where he proved he could "do a Stuart" of a man's mind.

It was a work for which he was particularly fitted and yet specially crippled. It would involve an act of antipodal understanding. For that reason, he could see the profound contradictions in what others took as obvious or nonproblematic. He dragged everything about the man into the clearest light, since he was painting a kind of reverse or inverted self-portrait. The misfit from one great American tradition was looking at a misfit from the other original tradition, wondering why *that* misfit prevailed. The inheritor and betrayer of the New England tradition studied the inheritor and betrayer of the Virginia tradition, and only realized after long perusal that Jefferson had been successful because he never realized he had departed from his earlier creed, never grasped the point that political transactions alter the person engaged in them so that he is a different person by the time he gets what he wants (or fails to). For all his deviousness, there was no duplicity in Jefferson; he moved from one stage of his politics to the next, without any overlap where the new could rub along in uncomfortable simultaneity with the old. He did not even have the wry self-consciousness of the shrewd clergyman:

> The strain of standing in a pulpit is great. No human being ever yet constructed was strong enough to offer himself long as a light to humanity without showing the effect on his constitution. Buddhist saints stand for years silent, on one leg, or with arms raised above their heads, but the limbs shrivel and the mind shrivels with the limbs. Christian saints have found it necessary from time to time to drop their arms and to walk on their legs, but do it with a sort of apology or defiance, and sometimes do it, if they can, by stealth. One is a saint or one is not; every man can choose the career that suits him; but to be saint and sinner at the same time requires singular ingenuity. For this reason, wise clergymen, whose tastes, though in themselves innocent, may give scandal to others, enjoy their relaxation, so far as they can, in privacy. (*Esther*)

In Jefferson, Adams was watching the performance of a political clergyman who did the equivalent of standing on one leg, year after year, without atrophy of limb or mind; and this strange power of his was a national characteristic, as well. He legitimated the nation's drive westward by disguising it. He disarmed criticisms of central power under the illusion that he was disarming that power itself. He destroyed the Federalist party by appropriating the Federalist program, and was only able to accomplish this because he honestly did not know he was doing it. He seemed the master of events while events were mastering him; but the American people, by sharing his illusions, mastered a continent. Taken on his own terms, Jefferson should not have succeeded, but he did; his terms, like all terms, got transmuted by the irresistible forces of history he thought he was steering as they skewed him from his own meaning. It is a tale of accumulating ironies that somehow knit together a nation—the reverse of Gibbon's story of human perversity unraveling the Roman Empire.

Gibbon coolly fought his way down with the Empire, savaging its invaders—Christian, Turkish, mercenary—as long as he could. Adams builds the American empire up from its own incongruous materials, watching it triumph over its champions' own intentions. His is not a national epic in the style of Parkman or Bancroft, but a comedy of errors. It is comedy in the classic sense, that it has a happy ending, but without the Aristotelian requirement that its agents be less than noble (*phauloi*). His protagonist is noble, though Adams makes it clear that the highest achievements can only be won at the cost of some absurdity, for nations as for churches. Yvor Winters notes that Adams uses humor more than any other great historian, even the sardonic Gibbon; but he was wrong to think this was an incidental flavoring to his work. It is the structural secret of it. As Adams wrote to John Hay, "T. Jefferson, between ourselves, is a character of comedy. John Adams is a droll figure, and good for Sheridan's school, but T. J. is a case for Beaumarchais; he needs the lightest of touches, and my hand is as heavy as his own sprightliness" (*Letters*).

Despite the typical self-deprecation of that last phrase, it took all Adams's wit to see that Jefferson's achievement was an accumulation of all the jokes that Jefferson himself could not see. His hopes had come true because his principles proved false—a massive tower of ironies, made not shaky but more solid by its contradictions. The Jeffersonians' inventions turned on their contrivers' heads, and still let the contrivers win. Jefferson's Embargo, meant to prevent war, racked the nation into the need for war (as relief if nothing else), and Mr. Madison's war was won, though lost. The Republicans could do nothing right, and

[*186*]

none of that mattered. Larger circumstances had determined that America should prevail.

It took great self-discipline for Adams to get this story right, for the last joke, after all, was on him. Jefferson, blindly idealistic, had been practical by the test of events: disliking the political cockpit, he had not only descended into it but reigned there. Adams only described Chartres; Jefferson built Monticello. Jefferson actually made the history Adams could only record, and the making of it brought popular acclaim, as the writing of it never would. It is his awareness of these things, a self-awareness as he weighs Jefferson's peculiar lack of self-scrutiny, that makes it so intriguing to watch Adams watching Jefferson, mirroring kindred enmities in a silver-on-white tracery of inversions. It was only out of his own weaknesses as well as strengths that Adams, treating Jefferson with the fascination of a compulsively baffled rival, could give us a portrait of uncanny intimacy and unflinching candor; puzzled by him, pulled toward him, pushed off; by instinct brought back to riddle out, touch by touch, Jefferson's significance—which he felt was Virginia's meaning, and America's (if any). No one else has done Jefferson justice, to use that worn phrase in its full sense. If the justice dealt out is sometimes rather harsh, it is less than the sentence Adams served upon himself—and most harsh when it is most like his self-judgments. It takes one to know one.

HEMINGWAY'S VALOR

David Bromwich

It is the sentences that first draw a reader in to Hemingway's writing:

> They were old eyes now but they were in a young man's face gone old as driftwood and nearly as gray.

Then, further in, the longer sentences:

> All of the operations of bull raising to one who loves bull-fighting are of great fascination and in the testings one has much eating, drinking, companionship, practical joking, bad amateur cape-work by the aristocracy, often excellent amateur cape-work by the visiting bootblacks who aspire to be matadors, and long days with the smell of cold, fall air, of dust and leather and lathered horses, and the big bulls not so far away looking very big in the fields, calm and heavy, and dominating the landscape with their confidence.

And as the paragraphs are built up, each to its separate climax, a varied pace and steady rhythm mark a path as intricate as the emotional turnings with which both co-operate:

> The room was long with windows on the right-hand side and a door at the far end that went into the dressing room. The row of beds that mine was in faced the windows and another row, under the windows, faced the wall. If you lay on your left side you could see the dressing-room door. There was another door at the far end that people sometimes came in by. If any one were going to die they put a screen round the bed so you could not see them die, but only the shoes and puttees of doctors and men nurses showed under the bottom of the screen and sometimes at the end there would be whispering. Then the priest would come out from behind the screen and afterward the men nurses would go back behind the screen to come out again carrying the one who was dead with a blanket over him down the corridor between the beds and some one folded the screen and took it away.

Narrative has to give information, of course. But if that is all one believes it can give, then Hemingway's manner will seem just a manner.

The passages I have quoted are from *Islands in the Stream, Death in the Afternoon* and *A Farewell to Arms*. The scenes that they capture—the glimpse of the eyes of a dying sailor; the casual festivity of a bullfight practice; the routines of a hospital room, seen with the huddled watchfulness of a soldier who will not die—have all been measured distinctly and consideringly, and the prose registers a fine keeping with the progress of separate recognitions. Yet Hemingway is often said to have been a *monotonous* writer. Doubtless, to those who make this charge, it implies that there was a small, self-enclosed, set of "experiments" which were always notably his. Meanwhile, a larger set was waiting to be tried, and he affected to ignore it. The sort of experiment in question, however, merely exemplifies an ideal of virtuosity. It pays off in the excitement of certain works, and in conceptions more than in works. But none of these is expected to link up with the larger pattern of a career; the worth of such a pattern, indeed, is what is being challenged. That would have been one problem with virtuosity, from Hemingway's point of view. Another was the hope it seemed to suggest that originality might go hand in hand with technical progress over a single artist's life. Crediting no such ideal for himself and no such hope, he aimed to write a prose as variously informed as his chosen idiom would allow.

Among the personal graces of the sentence about the bullfight practice, one notices first how the comma in "cold, fall air" (often, as Hemingway knew, the color effect of inferior writers) is earned by the modifications of feeling involved, and then made good by the full breath that the pause opens up. There is an almost languid pleasure in the extra *and* that follows; and in the play of "lathered" against the noun before it. The sense of alert complicity in an enfolding habit of life has been sharpened already by the jostling rhymes of *long-smell-fall*. One is thus prepared to feel that the big bulls are "not so far away" for them to look "very big" after all, as the eye dwells on them; and as it dwells on the ordinary fields, they take on the dignity of a landscape, with a dominant mood that belongs alike to the author and his subject. In the very different workmanship of the soldier's report from his bed, the cramped neatness of the room emerges plainly from the syntax that divides the whole ward into clauses evenly spaced: "and another row, under the windows, faced the wall." One has been shown in just in time to learn what awaits one here—"If you lay on your left side . . . If any one were going to die." And the mingled hope and fear are drawn from the felt force of the unsaid: every euphemism that this patient must have heard seems to be contained in the one he could not possibly have heard, "the one who was dead." Through the latter part of the description, the "men nurses" return like an uncertain omen; and when the death comes it is in the careful file of doctors and priest, in the right-angle turn "down the corridor between the beds," until all euphemism is reduced to a gesture: "and someone folded the screen and took it away."

As all of these passages testify, sensations matter to Hemingway before people do. This seems to me a necessary and not an incidental feature of his writing, for it relates to two aspects of his identity as an author: the unconfiding self-trust of his heroes; and the interest he shares with them in death as a climax of life's moments. But that is to frame his concern melodramatically, as he himself rarely does. It would be fairer to say that death interests him not as the end of sensations but as a limit drawn close around them. It gives them a meaning, as an outline gives definition to a picture. As for what this has to do with a career of writing, an answer may be pieced together from certain comments in *Death in the Afternoon* and *Green Hills of Africa*. In the latter book Hemingway remarks somewhat cryptically: "I have a good life but I must write because if I do not write a certain amount I do not enjoy the rest of my life." This may appear to admit his need, as a commercial writer, to produce a consistent style with a signature. His work, he would then be saying, is done to supply a craving for fresh stimulants in life itself—a life which his writing simply reflects, and to which it is subordinate. But that is not what Hemingway meant. Rather, his work, for him, has the quality of a *made thing*, which he of all others has added to life. The result is seemingly pointless. Nevertheless, it endures because it is alive with purpose, as life itself is not. So he must write in order to be released back into his experience and then go on, without knowing why he does, until enough traces collect for him to deposit again in the form of writing. Experience, as such, gives the pleasure that he lives for; writing, as such, does not; but the two are mutually dependent in this way.

People who find a purpose in their very lives Hemingway seems to regard with intense but distant admiration. His portrait of Robert Jordan, the hero of *For Whom the Bell Tolls*, is an attempt to show the forming of such a person by events. It does not quite succeed because Hemingway could never credibly realize the weight of external circumstances on an individual. Still, his respect for this kind of character rested on a belief that there were other disciplines as complete as that of writing. A version of that belief (partly hidden, then dramatized, with an effect of unmotivated sentiment) may be traced again in his identification with Colonel Cantwell, the hero of *Across the River and into the Trees*. Cantwell's virtuousness is understood as an almost public fact; a thing it would be tedious to rehearse in detail. With him, the shaping circumstances pass from view entirely. But here as elsewhere in Hemingway's writing, the error of tact betrays, not a lapse of taste, but the keenness of a too implicit artistic intelligence.

One of his later stories, "The Denunciation," renders with unexampled adequacy the discipline of life that he cares for outside art. Patrons of the Madrid restaurant Chicote's always keep coming back, to renew a sense of companionability which they can find nowhere else. This feeling has much to do with the antifascist struggle, but, as the narrator sketches the place, it comes to represent a wider trust in human solidarity. Sitting at a table one evening talking to a friend, he spots at a table across the room an old patron, Luis Delgado, who has not turned up at Chicote's since he went over to the Fascists. It is a puzzle why he should risk this exposure now. Maybe he was feeling reckless or high-spirited, or nostalgic for the intimacy at Chicote's. Or, maybe, he has come to spy. A waiter, looking on, grows nervous and asks the narrator, who as a journalist is nearly one of the authorities, whether it is not now his duty to report Delgado to the security police. That would lead to his arrest and probably to his being put to death. But the waiter is a good republican and a businessman. The narrator, however, answers with less decision than he is expected to show. He can see the rightness of betraying Delgado, the traitor. But he has a scruple. An action like that goes against the feel of the place, and perhaps even of the cause: the very things that have brought him and, for all he knows, Delgado back to Chicote's on this evening. The waiter does make the call anyway, and Delgado is arrested.

It is, till now, hardly more than an anecdote. But, as an afterthought, the narrator phones the security police from his hotel, to check up, he says, on Delgado, adding that it was he that made the first call. The final paragraph reads:

> All we old clients of Chicote's had a sort of feeling about the place. I knew that was why Luis Delgado had been such a fool as to go back there. He could have done his business some place else. But if he was in Madrid he had to go there. He had been a good client as the waiter had said and we had been old friends. Certainly any small acts of kindness you can do in life are worth doing. So I was glad I had called my friend Pepe at Seguridad headquarters because Luis Delgado was an old client of Chicote's and I did not wish him to be disillusioned or bitter about the waiters there before he died.

The suggestion is that the teller of this story has a finer sense of duty—the sort of duty that leads back to a common good—than the waiter and all others who obey the rules of citizenship or the logic of social virtue. His conduct in telling the lie is, in fact, like the artist's in its concern with a nonutilitarian design. Yet it remains unlike the artist's in that it has no self-regarding origin or end. For him, "the rest of my life" is all there is.

So far, what I have said about Hemingway would hold true of some other writers, starting perhaps with Stendhal. But in no other writer does one find the same curious fit between a sense of a calling and a choice of both style and subject. Hemingway's books are about light, air, wind, "the folklore of the senses"; and they mean to instruct. One can learn from reading them how to clean a fish; where a bad hunter is satisfied to have placed a shot; the parts of the stadium a matador will most avoid on a gusty day; what wines to savor and what to imbibe in quantities; and why a man is sometimes excited by a woman who cuts her hair short. Outside their proper story, all of these data may look stark, pretentious or absurd. Once placed, they are beyond ridicule. But the depth of Hemingway's interest in such things would seem to be archaic rather than modern. That is to say, he makes them all appear strangely substantial, as they can be only in a phase of culture where poetry and knowledge are one. The modernity comes in with his personal motive for finding them important. For they are his by choice and not by inheritance. They alone establish that he, he especially, was here and had a place in the general life. In the absence of these things, he would be lost.

The significance of the mere record of things done or felt, both to Hemingway and the characters who echo his tacit motive, was clear as far back in his work as "Big Two-Hearted River." A Nick Adams or a Jake Barnes is alive while he feels the change of his pulse, or the warmth of the day on his skin. And Hemingway's usual practice is simply to assume that his readers know the anxiety that prompts such testings from moment to moment. Until the publication of *The Garden of Eden*, one would have said that he refused, in principle, ever to reflect aloud on what his writing aimed to achieve. But the force of his repetitions brought out two irreducible beliefs: that experience is a loss, a deformation of oneself; and that one can guard against it by perfecting a craft, or a code of practical wisdom, or by writing a masterpiece. These were secrets of the laboratory, not to be published in the parlor, though, when faced by the literal-mindedness of his researches, Hemingway was capable of showing a delicate self-mockery. Among the barroom scenes of *Islands in the Stream* is an exchange in which the hero, Thomas Hudson, a painter, is asked to tell about "the happiest time you remember"; the prostitute who makes the request (and who somehow knows that Hudson is Hemingway's stand-in) adds the interesting warning, "And not with smells." He replies: "It has to have smells." But certain prejudices about style—about the devices that can help or hinder the weaving of life into something stronger than life—have for Hemingway an authority fully as great as that of the things he describes. There has never been a writer whose love scenes were as apt as his to divagate, between endearments, into pedantic corrections by the lovers themselves of each other's grammar and usage.

About the nature of writing and the characters of writers, Hemingway has a lot to say in *Death in the Afternoon,* most of it solid sense and some of it extraordinary. The argument he used to persuade himself that bullfighting was an art turned upon its purposeful ordering of a tragic spectacle—"the education of the bull," up to the moment of recognition that comes with its death. It is an understood artifice that a bull who starts by knowing too much cannot be fought in any case. Grant this, says Hemingway, and all that concerns you is the pure line that is traced by the moving figures of the matador and the bull. The analogy seems to be with ballet. In both, because the work goes on in a live medium, real mastery can occur only a few times in one lifetime. But as Hemingway points out, there is a further disadvantage in bullfighting. Even when the art is perfect, it makes an impression only while it is happening. In this it is the opposite of writing, which is dead once committed to the page, but exists to be renewed in the experience of the reader. In a remarkably sustained passage of *Death in the Afternoon,* Hemingway reflects on the shadowy immortality that comes to the matador, whose fame, compared to the painter's or poet's, is as sure as it is evanescent.

> If it were permanent it could be one of the major arts, but it is not and so it finishes with whoever makes it, while a major art cannot even be judged until the unimportant physical rottenness of whoever makes it is well buried. It is an art that deals with death and death wipes it out. But it is never truly lost, you say, because in all arts all improvements that are logical are carried on by some one else; so nothing is lost, really, except the man himself. Yes, and it would be very comforting to know that if at his death all the painter's canvases disappeared with him, that Cezanne's discoveries, for example, were not lost but would be used by all his imitators. Like hell it would.

Suppose a painter's canvases disappeared with him and a writer's books were automatically destroyed at his death and only existed in the memory of those that had read them. That is what happens in bullfighting. The art, the method, the improvements of doing, the discoveries remain; but the individual, whose doing of them made them, who was the touchstone, the original, disappears and until another individual, as great, comes, the things, by being imitated, with the original gone, soon distort, lengthen, shorten, weaken, and lose all reference to the original. All art is only done by the individual. The individual is all you have and all schools only serve to classify their members as failures. The individual, the great artist when he comes, uses everything that has been discovered or known about his art up to that point, being able to accept or reject in a time so short it seems that the knowledge was born with him, rather than that he takes instantly what it takes the ordinary man a lifetime to know, and then the artist goes beyond what has been done or known and makes something of his own.

The artist, then, who makes a permanent object and the artist who executes a single performance have in common a peculiarly intense individuality. The only thing that favors the creation of a text over the surpassing of every spectator's expectations of every previous contest is that it allows a falling away of the creator's own "unimportant physical rottenness." But according to Hemingway, that makes a tremendous difference; for, as he observes, "Memory, of course, is never true."

Yet both kinds of art produce examples of personal energy; and a single idea of tradition will cover both. Hemingway's conception here is not less subtle than T. S. Eliot's in "Tradition and the Individual Talent." But he does rely on a less congenial figure of thought. The works in a tradition, says Eliot, form an ever-enlarging "constellation" which shifts slightly with the addition of the "really new" work. By contrast, Hemingway admits only an individual idea of tradition itself and is inclined to look at the whole aggregate of original works as an unfinished sequence of *choices*. Each marks a separate path and a separate sacrifice; and the character of each is defined by what it omits. A great writer is differentiated from others, he remarks in another place, by selecting more readily than they the knowledge that can become uniquely his. "There are some things which cannot be learned quickly and time, which is all we have, must be paid heavily for their acquiring." So the great writer who "must pay," like the others, "a certain nominal percentage in experience," seems to have "a quicker ratio to the passage of time." The meaning on which all these dicta converge, that art gains from a forfeit of experience, is not what one would expect to find in Hemingway. It seems better suited on the face of it to a writer like Henry James. That Hemingway should so insist on it in a book that deals with bullfighting suggests that his pursuit of this minor art had just the personal motive he sought to disclaim.

When he first saw a bullfight, Hemingway recalls, he disliked the *banderillas*, which "seemed to make such a great and cruel change in the bull" by enforcing "the loss of the free, wild quality he brought with him into the ring." Only later did he learn to appreciate that their effect was to sober the bull and make him aim more surely; until, at last,

> when I learned the things that can be done with him as an artistic property when he is properly slowed and still has kept his bravery and his strength I kept my admiration for him always, but felt no more sympathy for him than for a canvas or the marble a sculptor cuts or the dry powder snow your skis cut through.

These last analogies are incongruous; the climactic image is shocking. But, evidently, in any spectacle like this, Hemingway is bound to feel the same detachment and fascination in the presence of the unimportant physical rottenness which drops away when something from life is turned into something in art. In a bullfight, that happens before one's eyes; with the restriction that it can happen only before one's eyes. Hemingway returns to the bullfights again and again, notwithstanding his awareness of the restriction. His affinity for the spectacle, as he makes us understand, is based on temperament after all, and not on his definition of a major art. He writes in the same vein, in *Green Hills of Africa*, of "freezing myself deliberately inside, stopping the excitement as you close a valve, going into that impersonal state you shoot from." For what compels his attention, not as the scene of all great writing but of his, is the instant organization of life that can happen with death.

Other artists have other subjects and greater ones. Hemingway wanted, he says, to study bullfighting for the discipline it would give his writing, but he adds that it is a narrow sort of discipline. To learn how to describe a death accurately seemed within his grasp in his late twenties. To approach a great subject, such as the change of heart that may alter a whole life, was beyond his powers then. His touchstone here was Tolstoy, whom, at the end of his career, he knew he had still not begun to rival. If one asks why in all the years between he never properly aimed at that kind of mastery, the answer will be unenlightening. It takes us back to the sheer force of his affinity for something narrower. But Hemingway's regret at having allowed a temporary focus of his craft to become the subject matter of his art may be deduced from another episode of *Green Hills of Africa*. After a particularly clumsy and brutal day's hunt, he thinks for a while about the different pleasure he might feel if, "instead of trailing that sable bull, gut shot to hell, all day, I'd lie behind a rock and watch them on the hillside and see them long enough so that they belonged to me forever." But this is a choice he is never able to make in any of his books. Even the artist-hero of *Islands in the Stream*, when asked, in the middle of the Second World War, to paint an apocalyptic satire of Cuba, prefers instead to hunt Nazi submarines; the sailor in the very first sentence I quoted will at last be photographed like any other big kill, to prove that the right materials were used to create the finished work. So for a moment the human body too becomes only "the dry powder snow your skis cut through."

Indeed, given his absorbing interest in this way of seeing, the question about Hemingway might just as well be turned around. How did he manage to hold himself back from it as much as he did? One explanation for his restraint, I think, is that the very specialization of his subject gives him a counter-charm against its inhumanity. Thus his belief that the matador is himself a work of sculpture issues in something more than aesthetic concern with the sort of people who are matadors. Both in *Death in the*

Afternoon and its sequel, *The Dangerous Summer*, all the more interesting fighters are subjected to a continuous moral inquest by their chronicler. It is sometimes assumed that Hemingway's usual hero is a man of supreme courage, beyond challenge by his rivals or by the multitude who observe his doings from the security of their noisy perch. But his books contain no such character: the stereotype is in fact a composite creature, with traits drawn from a few of his characters, from an unrewarding side of the author himself and from his shallower comments outside of his books. As it happens, one of the heroes of *Death in the Afternoon* turns out to be the matador Gallo, whom Hemingway appreciated at once for his method of attack and the frankness with which he tempered bravado with prudence.

> He was a great bullfighter and the first one to admit fear. Until Gallo's time it was thought utterly shameful to admit being afraid, but when Gallo was afraid he dropped muleta and sword and jumped over the fence head first. A matador is never supposed to run, but Gallo was liable to run if the bull looked at him in a peculiarly knowing way. He was the inventor of refusing to kill the bull if the bull looked at him in a certain way, and when they locked him up in jail he said that it was better that way, "all of us artists have bad days. They will forgive me my first good day."

Hemingway's feeling for the valor there may be in a completed work, or in the artist who is condemned to be the work himself, does not finally depend on either facing a defeat or carrying off a victory.

But a man like Gallo belongs to the comic side of things; a tragedy has to have a tragic end; and Hemingway tells us whenever he can that this is where his interest lies. Still, among the most memorable scenes of his fiction are several in which he seems to confess the unassimilability of his view of life and death. Thus in *Islands in the Stream*, Thomas Hudson is made to say an oddly charitable thing about the dying sailor:

> "Don't bother him," Thomas Hudson said. "He's a good Kraut."

[*198*]

"Sure," Willie said. "They're all good Krauts when they fold up."

"He hasn't folded up," Thomas Hudson said. "He's just dying."

It is Hudson's crony, Willie, who plays up to the old painter by invoking the ethic of the great death; and he is firmly rebuked. The worst moral fault with which one can charge Hemingway as a writer is that he sometimes does show people like Willie in a favorable light.

Why did that have to happen? Writing as personal as Hemingway's, and as closely bound to the writer's hopes for himself, is liable to all the influences of resentment, apathy or defensive fear which can create "a transition of the soul." It is as if at times Hemingway's sympathies were forced into a thin channel. He is then capable of equating imaginative survival with survival, and survival itself with life. It is plain such a mood could end in sadism but my feeling is that in Hemingway it seldom does. Rather, it confirms a tendency already noticeable in his work, by which, in order to be sure of a hidden power in himself, he has to serve as the witness of a privation. Whenever this pattern asserts control of his imaginings, he is close to nihilism—that is, to a liberty of action founded on a want of belief. There remains the anomaly that, for him, the action, once taken, must be justified by a principle of morality.

Hemingway is probably the most striking instance in modern art of a man for whom the motives and the justification of action have suffered this kind of permanent division from each other. But he is clear about why so often the action that appeals to him is violent action. This follows, as he says in *Death in the Afternoon*, from "the feeling of rebellion against death" which can only be had by killing: "Once you accept the rule of death thou shalt not kill is an easily and a naturally obeyed commandment. But when a man is still in rebellion against death he has pleasure in taking to himself one of the Godlike attributes; that of giving death." When, therefore, an artist chooses to give death, it confirms his sense that all life, apart from his work, is a drawn-out siege against the *nada* that it will not conquer anyway. On the other hand, the man of action

[*199*]

will choose to give death more often, because his life embodies a less acceptable fate. Only by excluding things
from life can he prove the solidity of the choice he represents; those exclusions lie about him in the dead forms of
the beasts he has killed. They might just as plausibly be
the corpses of the men he has killed or otherwise forced
to submit to his design. Hemingway's objection to war,
so far as one can tell from his writings, was only that it
took such acts of power off their proper individual basis.

I have been taking a concentrated but I hope a truthful
view of Hemingway's subject. The result may be to make
him more strange than he had seemed, without making
him appreciably more sympathetic. There are, however,
precedents for the withdrawal from ordinary living, the
sense of experience as foreign rather than given, which he
required in order to accomplish his work. One, as I have
suggested, is James; and the comparison is worth pursuing
a little. The dramatic situations that both writers care for
are apt to center on a moment of sudden reduction or
literalization; though for both a story is dramatic enough
if the reader is kept uneasily thinking about the mere possibility that such a moment will occur. The surprise may
come either through a reversal or an intensification of the
habits of daily existence. But it has a moral: that the
exalted pleasures and sensations of life (what James likes
to allude to in a word like "impression") arise from, and
are answerable to, some particularly coarse fact. Hemingway's pride in the fact and James's embarrassment at it
mark a trivial difference beside the agreement they share
about its significance. In Hemingway, it is true, one is
always on the brink of a small discovery, and it usually
has to do with the body; whereas James constructs whole
works to delay such a discovery, and when it does come it
comes in a discussion of money. To borrow the slang of
these literalists, Hemingway's writing is about what the
body can take; James's is about what the money will bear;
but in both cases this is something they show all the time
and can never quite say. The sum of the books that got
written, it must be added, is less satisfying in Hemingway's case than in James's, but not because his gifts were
slighter. The reason is rather that, given so choice an
asceticism, he still sometimes wanted to have his life both

ways. He wanted, himself, to serve as a sure witness to the very experience he had to break with, a witness whose report would have the irreducible clarity of a fact. It is this that gives his fiction (in episodes where a slow revenge is extorted from a worthless soul) and his first-person journalism (in passages that weigh the author's sacrifice of raw materials for a sublime effect) their occasional overtones of greed. The greed is always calculated and always intelligent, but in the defeated manner of a guardian of already cherished monuments.

M ine is the first generation in which it has been fashionable to revile Hemingway. Like Byron, he is held strictly to account for the conceit that bound his writing to his celebrity. Unlike Byron, he lacks the protection of self-irony. Some part of this reaction he certainly earned: there are whole tracts of his life in which nothing edifying can ever be sought. But the recent and familiar picture of him is so oddly limited that it now seems necessary to recall the distinct fame he enjoyed in the '20s and '30s. At that time he was known, above all, as "a writer's writer"— a character differing markedly from the creator of a signature. He was not the preceptor for a school of masculine pleasures, and not the property of the American Literature that since has claimed him. He came to prominence with the European *avant-garde* of the twenties, for whom *Ulysses* was the great work of a new age of literature. Hemingway thought that Leopold Bloom was the highest invention of that book (the judgment neither of a sportsman nor a prig), and he was one of the few contemporaries about whose writing Joyce in turn spoke with consistent respect. The idea that he looked on writing as something to be done between rounds of social éclat—that, in short, he pretended not to be a writer—is the most falsifying report about him and the easiest to expose. In this respect indeed, the type he fits is Johnson and not Byron. He thought of the dull business of composition as a trial requiring all one's nervous faculties.

There used to be people who dismissed Hemingway because they had loved his books in their youth. Now my impression is they do it because they have read a little, and heard some unpleasant things, and that is that. But

[*201*]

somebody is reading him. The past two years alone have seen the publication of a long biography by Jeffrey Meyers and an expanded version of *The Dangerous Summer*, the bullfight articles that Hemingway wrote for *Life* in 1959. Before that, there had been a comprehensive biography by Carlos Baker, and *Islands in the Stream*, a posthumous abridgement of the trilogy on the sea which Hemingway drafted in the late 1940s. Then last year Scribners published *The Garden of Eden*, a section, heavily edited, of the autobiographical novel which formed his other big project of the years after the Second World War. And now comes a third full-length biography, *Hemingway: the Life and the Work*, by Kenneth S. Lynn. Compared to Baker's *Life*, this one has rather uneven proportions; about half of it deals with Hemingway in the twenties. This shows anyway that Lynn's interest began with the work and not the life; that it ends there too is fortunate, and uncommon in a modern biographer. Meyers's *Hemingway*, well informed as it was, seemed to have been written from a quasi-moral disapproval of Hemingway, and it punished him with strenuous quotations from his enemies. Lynn plainly likes his hero, without being credulous about him. His book is not going to displace Baker's; yet it has its own distinction as a thoroughly qualified revision of a legend. Here is an example of the sort of thing I mean. In the First World War, Hemingway served as an ambulance driver and was wounded in exactly the manner described in *A Farewell to Arms*. He received a medal for heroic conduct because, as an Italian friend is made to tell Lieutenant Henry, this was a time when medals went out freely to the men fresh from America. Hemingway never seriously pretended (except once, in a speech to students at his old high school) that he had gone back to the front, as his hero does, or that he had enlisted early to fight with the Italian shock troops and stayed through the Caporetto retreat. Nevertheless, some of these things do happen in *A Farewell to Arms*, and the story about Hemingway himself made the rounds; it was repeated by critics, and not fully challenged by Baker; and it appears now as part of the "note on the author" in the paperback edition of the novel. Lynn is exceptional among Hemingway's biographers in not trusting his books as a fair index to his life. He does, I think, tend to read Hemingway's life back into his books, but that is another matter.

It is hard not to see his life in any case as a great *subject* for a biography. After hearing its facts rehearsed often enough, one starts to think they are "representative"; and then the idea of some one being representative seems more mysterious than it ever did. It has nothing to do with being all mankind's epitome, or even the special case favored by a few. What his life most suggests is the power of the exception to make us forget the rule—a power that lasts for a generation or more, until different readers come in search of a different hero. Lynn also brings us back to two aspects of Hemingway's development that have not before received the emphasis they deserve. First, the degree to which the passion of his life was involved to the very end with the father he loved who killed himself and the mother he hated who lived on: the father, a good doctor and anxious husband, who took him hunting and fishing, on house calls and emergency visits, and made him a grownup early; the mother, a devout believer in culture, who taught him that acting respectably and writing cleanly would be "money in the bank." Equally, in this account as in no other, we are made aware how stunning, recurrent and finally disastrous were the series of physical injuries that Hemingway sustained throughout his life, from the wounds to his leg and head in the war to the two plane crashes he suffered in 1954, on a last trip to Africa. These accidents, though they do not explain his long spells of depression, must have lengthened the shadow in which his recoveries were always expected to begin. Also, they made him brave with his fortune: at any moment it could seem already to have done its worst. The bare recital of his chronic pains helps to make sense, for example, of his behavior in 1944, in a bivouac of the American army on the allied march to Paris, where he calmly ate his dinner, helmet off, while German bombs poured down and every soldier took cover in the basement. At work in incidents like this was something much less happy than a formal display of stamina. Nevertheless, I agree with Lynn that none of the evidence suggests a process of deterioration which impaired his ability to write; on the contrary he produced, in the last two decades of his life, thousands of pages besides those of the posthumous works we have seen. What may in part have failed in him was a capacity for self-criticism. Yet he spent many months in the late fifties revising the sketches he had made years earlier for *A Moveable Feast*. And to judge even by the present, much foreshortened, version of *The Garden of Eden* (which Lynn rightly praises for its "brilliant, drastic editing" by Tom Jenks), his last effort as a novelist was also his most ambitious.

Lynn's theme, and he needs it less than he supposes, is what he calls the "cross-sexual experimentalism" that runs through Hemingway's work. He keeps a sort of running tally on the incidence of women cutting their hair short, or challenging men to approve their intention of cutting it short, and he observes that the outward change commonly goes with a reversal of sexual positions. There is a level at which all this is simply true. Catherine Barkley's "I want us to be all mixed up," in *A Farewell to Arms*, is only the clearest signal of a motif that touches many of Hemingway's stories, and that becomes the focus of the action in *The Garden of Eden*—a novel, from one point of view, about nothing but haircuts, breakfasts, and spirited talk concerning their finer points. This is at any rate a potent fantasy, but Lynn wants to honor it as something more: he is not quite sure what. In consequence, the reader is heaped with strange and unamalgamating materials, which suggest everything from a quirk to a compulsion, while the biographer stands to the side and implies that much will be made of it some day. Yet, for Lynn, the good of this hobbyhorse is that it keeps him from riding another as hard as he might have done. He belongs to the current crop of suspicious critics. They come in orthodox and heterodox varieties, and he is of the orthodox: those, namely, who know for sure that every impulse of social idealism is a form of political naïveté or worse. So, around the time of the Spanish War, he starts to hector his subject with caption-sentences like the following: "At no point during [Hemingway's] visits to Spain did he consider reporting the conflict from the Nationalist as well as the Loyalist side." But Hemingway never pretended to be a reporter in this debased, unreal and quite recent sense of the word—the sense according to which a reporter's duty is not only to be truthful but to fake a "responsible" tone of impartiality which, as a thinking being, he cannot possibly credit.

Hemingway had a keen sense of politics almost from the first. His masterly report in the early twenties of an interview with Mussolini is still worth looking up: it gets to the bottom of him fast (with the help of a wolf pup Mussolini had the poor judgment to try and use as a prop). One may also recall such things as the discerning remarks, made in passing in *Death in the Afternoon,* on the importance of cobblestones to revolutionaries, and how solid paving has done more for tyrannies than any weapon known to their police. In short, he used his eyes and ears, in politics as in everything. Nor was he ever a crier up of "two moralities"—one for the war whoop and one for the sermon. *For Whom the Bell Tolls* is proof of his steadiness here, with its dry portrait of the Stalinists, whom he had expected to admire, and the cold epigram about La Pasionaria. Hemingway, in these matters, had nothing to learn from his biographer, or from anyone living then or now. He was a man of fierce democratic instincts, like Whitman, who happened, unlike Whitman, not to care for most of the people he encountered in daily life. But their cause was real to him. Of the Spanish War itself, even before his first journey to the front, he observed that "the Reds may be as bad as they say," but "they are the people of the country" and the war is between them and "the absentee landlords, the moors, the Italians, and the Germans." Even Orwell's summing up in "Looking Back on the Spanish War" was a little more rhetorical than that. By contrast *The Fifth Column,* the one work he wrote *hors de combat,* is just a bad play with some good boasting. It accords to Spain all the reality of X, where X is any field of action offered by the times; and it was denied a more than moderate success on Broadway only because Humphrey Bogart was not on hand to utter its one great line: "We're in for fifty years of undeclared wars and I've signed up for the duration. I don't exactly remember when it was, but I signed up all right." This statement had its chief importance even then as a promise by the writer himself. Hemingway kept it and was still keeping it twenty-two years later, when Castro's revolution touched him closer to home, and he did not affect to greet it with dismay.

Johnson argued in the *Rambler* that there are times when a biographer is obliged to be a moralist. Famous men like Addison, or for that matter Hemingway, who are able to fashion a public character for themselves, have to be held answerable by posterity: that is part of taking them seriously. The principle still seems to me a good one, but as hard as ever to set fair limits to. Literary critics and sensational journalists tend to write biographies from opposite motives (misplaced custodial reverence or the hope of an opportune unmasking) but either way they get the lives of artists wrong and their moralism is noxious. Lynn, however, fits neither of these categories; his work is the slightly chastened homage of an old fan; so that his moral judgments, when they enter at all, are often very valuable. He has his fullest occasion in the account of Hemingway's break with Sherwood Anderson. From their first meetings in Chicago, Anderson had been cordial and generous to Hemingway, without any air of patronizing. He wrote a statement of praise to appear on the jacket of *In Our Time* and brought Hemingway together with his own publisher Horace Liveright. Yet in these first months of his public reception, Hemingway was growing heartily sick of hearing himself classed in the school of Anderson and Gertrude Stein, and seeing his reviewers pick out some of his early stories as imitation Anderson. This grievance joined his wish for a bigger publisher and provoked his writing of *The Torrents of Spring*, an out-and-out parody of Anderson's *Dark Laughter*. Hemingway's strategy was to force Liveright either to insult his most celebrated author (by publishing the book) or to give the disappointed parodist an opening to terminate his own contract (by refusing to publish it). The upshot was just as he planned: Scribner picked up *The Torrents of Spring* and stayed with Hemingway ever after. This sort of maneuver is common enough. What makes Hemingway's conduct peculiarly unpleasant to review is his wish, even as he was betraying Anderson, to keep up his friendship with him by working out an honorable explanation. In a letter written at the time he appealed to his friend's good nature, with the help of some sophistry: (1) he was just being the good critic that Anderson needed then; (2) he could think of doing it only because he was the lesser writer of the two; (3) anyway, he was right to want to withdraw from Anderson's patronage, even if an unsympathetic reader might see his gesture as somehow ungrateful. Lynn comments: "Quite possibly, this utterly grotesque argument was the work of a man who was drunk." What I think Lynn misses elsewhere is the drama of Hemingway's retractions. Other original writers whose egotism served them pragmatically—Wordsworth and Frost both come to mind—have also burned a path for themselves with methods just like these. But Hemingway, though he is often disingenuous when first confronted, is almost never so in the long run. His *Letters* contain a retrospective view, in another letter to Anderson, of the whole business of Liveright and *The Torrents of Spring*, in which he concludes of himself: "What a horse's ass."

He could say this without a fuss because he knew it was not the whole truth. But how did he look to others? Two observations have stayed with me through two thousand pages of Hemingway facts. One is from Gregory Clark, a war veteran who knew Hemingway at the *Toronto Star*: "a more weird combination of quivering sensitiveness and preoccupation with violence never walked this earth." The other is from Damon Runyon: "Few men can stand the strain of relaxing with him over an extended period." But what comes through in every report is the impression of a captivating energy. This worked its charm most tellingly on friends who never became quite intimate and who remained uncertain of his affection. Dorothy Parker wrote well, often, and always admiringly of Hemingway's work; but she made the mistake of talking to him once about an abortion she had had. By having done it at all she disturbed a part of him that was always less bohemian than his surroundings; but she doubtless offended a much deeper piety by alluding to it in the course of a social conversation. Some time later Hemingway composed a rancorous, painfully ugly, free-verse satire on her life (complete with anti-Semitic slurs, to please Ezra Pound), which he had the prudence not to publish and the ill grace to insist on reading aloud to several of their mutual friends.

Parker heard of this and forgave it; and her last words are recorded to have been: "Tell me the truth. Did Ernest really like me?" A similar attachment kept his first two wives, Hadley Richardson and Pauline Pfeiffer, close to him long after he had ruined the marriages with insult and infidelity. From the sheer force of his energy, their own self-love came to be linked with his. The psychoanalytic word for that kind of power is narcissism; it is said that in any battle of wills the narcissist always wins, for he has an unbeatable advantage: to him the other person's claims are never real. But there is another way of putting this. The narcissist loses the world for the sake of winning all the people in it (those, at least, who have the luck to meet him). From the preceding notes on Hemingway's writing, it ought to be clear why such a pattern of conduct suited his art. When, close to the age of fifty, he started to reflect on his life as a whole, he wrote two novels that resemble each other as allegories of narcissism: *Across the River and into the Trees* and *The Garden of Eden*. It is curious to realize that both of these books, one with a military hero in his fifties, the other with an artist-hero in his twenties, belong to nearly the same period of composition; and that Hemingway chose to publish the less impressive of the two, in which the problem is exemplified, rather than the more impressive in which it is fully understood and judged.

Given the dangerous consistency of Hemingway's self-trust, the most unexpected fact to emerge from this biography is the resourcefulness with which he accepted intelligent criticism. His best reader beyond any doubt was Fitzgerald. Of the long opening chapter of *The Sun Also Rises*, which gave the backgrounds of the characters, only a short sketch of Robert Cohn survived Fitzgerald's objection to the "elephantine facetiousness" of the tone. A less definite problem with the novel, he thought, was that Jake Barnes's pathos was still missing a last, low note; for, in his scenes with Brett, he did not really seem like an impotent man; more like a man in "a sort of moral chastity belt." Again, in the manuscript of *A Farewell to Arms*, he noticed that Hemingway was able to regard his hero with a degree of retrospective irony, while for the heroine he retained every solemn feeling he must once have cherished for the woman on whom she was based. "In consequence

unless you make her a bit fatuous occasionally the contrast
jars—either the writer is a simple fellow or she's Eleonora
Duse disguised as a Red Cross nurse." It remained an unequal friendship, however, partly owing to a streak of
hero worship in Fitzgerald, and partly to Hemingway's un-
concealed disgust at any hint of slack self-discipline. He
read *The Crack-Up* as the confession of a man who was
finished. By these reflections written close to suicide, Fitzgerald also violated an unspoken canon of Hemingway's
writing and action alike—one, however, that might have
been deduced by any careful reader of "A Clean, Well-
Lighted Place." It was about this time that Hemingway
worked into "The Snows of Kilimanjaro" the now-famous
anecdote concerning "poor Scott Fitzgerald" and his illusions about the rich. Fitzgerald commented with propriety
on the scandalous ease of that *poor*: "If I choose to write
de profundis sometimes, it doesn't mean I want friends
praying aloud over my corpse." Besides, as he knew, the
truth about the exchange was very different from the
anecdote. Fitzgerald was not present when it took place,
at a lunch in New York that brought together Hemingway,
Maxwell Perkins and Mary Colum. And, in fact, it was
Hemingway who said he had been getting to know the
rich and they were "different"; and Mary Colum who made
the reply he later took as his own, that the only difference
was they had more money. Of course, Hemingway's report improved both sides of the conversation. But as a
specimen of his practice, it is enough to make critics
permanently wary of interpreting his writing much in the
light of facts drawn from his life.

Yet that is what Lynn has tried to do; his subtitle should
have been "the life in the work." There is a general difficulty with his method of analysis, which is not quite
summed up by saying that writers sometimes do imagine.
Even if we could find a traceable source for every detail,
the fact would remain that life is less rigorously organized
than art. This does not mean that a thorough immersion
in archives may not yield a blunt and otherwise inaccessible wisdom about a writer's provocations. Thus, faced by
the three dozen variants Hemingway produced for the
end of *A Farewell to Arms*, one might say (though Lynn
does not) that anyway Catherine Barkley had to die, be-

cause Agnes von Kurowsky jilted the author and he never got over it. But the status of such remarks will never be critical; for they give no help at all in thinking about a book. Lynn's speculations on "the work" belong to the same limbo of possibly trivial secret knowledge. He says in a gloss of "The Battler": "At last, [Hemingway] had reason to hope that he was on his way to the literary championship of the world. But was his excitement unalloyed, or was it edged with an inexplicable dread?" The question is graceless, as well as rhetorical, in just the way the story is not. Similarly "Fifty Grand" is here interpreted as an apology for Hemingway's escape from his contract with Liveright: Benny Leonard (said to be the prototype of the dirty fighter in the story) is actually Horace Liveright, and "Behind the facade of a cynical and brutal boxing story lay Hemingway's ugly wish to believe that a Jewish publisher had hit him in the groin, so to speak, and that therefore it was all right for him to reply in kind." Notice how easily the first substitution (Leonard for the fictional boxer) shades into the second (Liveright for Leonard). If fictions were problems in algebra, these quadratic equations would solve them. *The Sun Also Rises*, obviously, affords the widest such opportunity in all of Hemingway's work; and Lynn has a very full day there. He comes close to suggesting that Jake Barnes is a male lesbian, on the grounds that Natalie Barney and Djuna Barnes lived, respectively, at 20 Rue Jacob and the Hotel Jacob, in Paris.

Still, this way of reading is in fact revelatory in two important instances. *The Torrents of Spring* contains a sexual triangle, with an old waitress and a younger one competing for possession of the hero, Scripps O'Neill. Lynn reads it as a straightforward diagram of Hemingway's transition, during the writing of the book, from his wife Hadley to Pauline, whom he was on the verge of marrying. As Meyers showed in his biography, the decision to publish the book at all was, evidently, associated in Hemingway's mind with the decision to make public his split with Hadley. And even at the time, both elements of the crisis were unmistakable—the more so because Hadley recommended against publishing the book and Pauline was staunchly in favor of it. What is odd is that none of them, including Hemingway, seems to have read the story as a *roman à clef*: the mask of parody was in this case authoritative and complete. A more patent instance in which a work served as a map of a still going relationship was *The Fifth Column*. There, as Lynn points out, Hemingway not only declared his new attachment to Martha Gellhorn, but gave a full portrayal of the temperamental discord that would end their marriage almost a decade later. *The Fifth Column*, however, remains his least rewarding work of any length, *The Old Man and the Sea* alone excepted. To decode, it may be agreed, is sometimes also to interpret, but only with writing in which the carpet is all figure.

"A master miniaturist, a poet essentially": such appears to be Lynn's final verdict on Hemingway as a writer. It is not false, but it sounds a little satisfied, and without more details one cannot know what to make of it. How the life and work accord with each other, rather than corroborate each other's data, is the subject that opens up when life and work have been rehearsed on separate stages. To take just one resistant piece of evidence: John Dos Passos, who by the end of his life had no reason to spare Hemingway any just reproach, made the unpredictable comment that he had been a "builder up" and not a "breaker down" of the women he married. One can explain this by supposing that, from the force of example, his constant and heedless activity gave an involuntary encouragement to some others, who did not always care if self-absorption was at the bottom of it. A point of rereading his work after reading about his life is to see how some such quality gets into writing. It seems to be there under enormous repression. The effect is "miniature" if you like; but nothing could be more wrong than the idea that it comes from *paring down*. His work, in the short stories above all, is an act of displacement and concentration, but it neither simplifies nor clarifies. It is worth repeating in this context what early readers like D. H. Lawrence and Virginia Woolf noticed immediately: that Hemingway's insistent concern with personal power derives from a fear of its opposite. His men of action are never far from inertia.

The most wounding truth ever published about Hemingway was in a chapter of Wyndham Lewis's *Men Without Art*. The heroes of Hemingway's books, said

Lewis, are *"those to whom things are done*, in contrast to
those who have executive will and intelligence." This
charge of passivity is so apparently counter-intuitive and
yet, as one reflects on it, so plain a fact about his work,
that one is not sure with what degree of paradox it was
uttered. By subtitling the same chapter "The Dumb Ox,"
Lewis did, however, imply that the impression left by
such characters was scarcely foreseen by the author himself. Hemingway, and not just the type he wrote about,
was here being denied intelligence. Now Hemingway
seems to me so much more intelligent a writer than Lewis
that the description of him as a primitive hardly calls for
refutation; and by "executive will" Lewis is very likely to
have meant that Hemingway would have been a wiser
citizen of the twentieth century had he been more of a
Fascist. So to see the worth of what Lewis was saying,
one has to turn from the political design of his criticism and
go back to the comment itself. I will do that presently but
I have first to deal with another obfuscation.

For Lewis, in the same place, attempted a broad char-
acterization of Hemingway's prose. He called it *Steining*.
In that one-word cartoon, he was hoping to nail down forever an opinion that had already become commonplace.
Versions of it have continued to appear in posthumous as-
sessments of Hemingway, and the judgment will therefore
bear some looking into. There is a trick of Hemingway's
early prose, from repetitions of rhythm, of emphasis, or of
single words, that was there for him in Gertrude Stein
if he needed it. But Stein's repetitions are logical: they
thicken the medium without adding to the representation.
Whereas Hemingway's repetitions always mean to con-
firm or darken the texture of the scene he is describing.
That is why hers seem a kind of rhyming in prose while
his carry an undersong of contest or excitement. Stein, also,
wrote according to a principle: "Prose is the balance the
emotional balance that makes the reality of paragraphs
and the unemotional balance that makes the reality of
sentences and having completely realized that sentences
are not emotional while paragraphs are, prose can be the
emotional balance that is made inside something that combines the sentence and the paragraph." Hemingway wrote
to no such principle. In every sentence, he retained a tact

for the weight of individual words; for him, their history was an almost audible measure of their weight. These generalizations may be tested against, for example, the opening and closing paragraphs of *A Farewell to Arms*, and any pair of comparable passages in a novel by Stein. The truth is that she, Hemingway and Sherwood Anderson all at this time shared a certain bias of *anti*-affectation, and occasionally it tended to produce in all their work sentences of a certain size and shape, roughly corresponding to the idiom of unhackneyed journalism. But they invented the style before the journalists got to it. And they were up to different things.

As a writer of prose, therefore, Stein is only instructive as Hemingway's antithesis. But in her lecture "What Is English Literature," she gave an accurate and original view of the situation they shared, as American writers coming after the last Victorians. Stein remarked there how the unit of vivid utterance in English had gone from the word in the Renaissance to the sentence in the eighteenth century (Swift and Goldsmith are her examples) all the way to the paragraph at the end of the nineteenth (in Swinburne, Browning and Meredith). In this last period, English literature has been so busy with its possessions, both linguistic and political, that its medium little by little has been refined to assure the registration of that fact alone. The result is that, in the twentieth century, it can describe a new thing only in passages that take on a certain vagueness from their very bulk. It is as if English writers needed ever-widening views to show how vision could be deployed as an instrument of possession. Original work, even when it gets done in this way, will be confined to "daily island life," understood as a habitual property. You can see the difference, says Stein, between this and American literature, if you compare all the English writers of the age with their contemporary, Henry James. He, too, writes in paragraphs rather than sentences, and needs that much space to achieve a single observation; but, above each of his paragraphs, there floats something impalpable, a certain heft in the atmosphere; and that diffusive ideal and reward come from the author's effort to construct a reality out of nothing given. American writing on this view is the reverse of imperial: rather it is unpropertied, and

chiefly original in that it shows the difficulty even of own-
ing itself. The analysis throws a new light on Stein's remark about San Francisco, "There's no there there." She
may have meant it to be an American compliment after all.

But let us return to the creations of this atmosphere—
those to whom things are done. Hemingway's characters
are men *and* women without a place. It is pertinent that
he wrote no novel with an American setting, and very few
stories after his earliest, unless one counts the border
operations of *To Have and Have Not.* Placelessness is a
condition of the nihilism I mentioned earlier, but it is also,
for the reasons that Stein gave, a kind of deliverance for
the writer. These characters, as much as their author, because they are always on the move, can build their lives
in keeping with a theory that belongs uniquely to them.
Nothing else will ever anchor them. A last comparison with
James may help to remove any trace of parochialism from
such a quest. James's men and women create a life for
themselves purposively, through the acquisitions of art and
artifice. Indeed, they are often preoccupied with works of
art as the final determinant of what their lives can mean:
the hero of "The Middle Years" and the heroine of *The
Spoils of Poynton* are in this sense remote examples of an
identical predicament. But Hemingway's characters have
to make their lives for themselves by impulse alone, and
with the means available to every man and woman. His,
therefore, is a leveling aesthetic, as Lewis sensed in the
twenties and as Communist reviewers would notice rather
late, with the appearance of *To Have and Have Not.* Anyone, Hemingway seemed to be saying, with normal human
equipment could live the richest kind of life that he as an
artist had imagined. Only, if they were not artists, they had
to do it by acts of inward and not outward creation. Here
we come back again to the distinction proposed in *Death
in the Afternoon,* between two sorts of art and two sorts of
discipline. That distinction now looks weaker, for it covers
not just major and minor arts but the work of individuals
in general, in all the uses they make of their lives. Yet at
this point Hemingway's interests contract, almost con-
vulsively, and he reckons that his story about the artist can
only be the story of a sacrifice. Once, he says, those who
are not makers of art begin to think about their lives, they

are not far from thinking about the death that unsettles every human design. They are then, under whatever name, interested in art. If, further, they come to resent the artist's privilege in "using" his life, they will want to take revenge however they can.

Hemingway wrote the story of such a revenge in "The Short Happy Life of Francis Macomber." The artist there is a hunter, a coward at first and aimless in his work, who recovers his courage and attains the mastery of a perfect kill, but at the cost of being murdered by his wife, who could endure his impotence until made jealous of his art. *The Garden of Eden,* in all but its surface properties, is another version of the same story. The hero is a novelist, David Bourne, whose early career has been paid for by his wife, Catherine; and the action covers their honeymoon, and their discovery together of a second woman, Marita. As we are shown from the start, David lives in his writing, and not in his life itself. Yet for the honeymoon, he joins Catherine in a regimen of bicycle trips along the Riviera, swimming, and picnics on the road or in the hills above. Apart from these outings, David and Catherine share a life of narcissistic fantasy. She is always cutting her hair shorter and bleaching it whiter, and having his cut and bleached to look like hers. They are pictured again and again, and speak of each other, as twins, or as the same person, and with that comes the exchange of sexual roles that is almost customary in Hemingway. But in this novel, at last, he gives the theme to the story it wanted all along.

There is a strong suggestion here that the novelist has taught his wife everything and made her part of his materials; and again, that his power followed naturally both from his isolation and from the command he enjoys in his work. The look-alike games play out the meaning of such a conquest, and give the first faint premonition of a battle. As soon as Marita enters the scene, she seems to attract both David and Catherine more than they do each other; she is, after all, the first addition of something different in a life that has become pure echo; and it is with this recognition that one sees how far David has overstepped a necessary boundary between the artist and his experience. Catherine's revenge has two phases: the seduction of Marita, and the burning of all of David's manuscripts. The last incident seems to have been drawn from Hemingway's experience as well as his reading. In 1922, when his marriage with Hadley was already in trouble, she lost a valise in which she had placed the originals, typescripts and carbon copies of all the writing he had done in Europe. The novel frames the catastrophe as an act of conscious aggression. But formally, the plot of *The Garden of Eden* repeats that of *The Light That Failed*, with a notable exception. The two women of Kipling's novel—the aspiring painter whose envy of the hero's gift stops her from loving him; and the vicious serving girl who scrapes his masterpiece to an illegible smear—are here collapsed into the single figure of Catherine. Close as Hemingway was to the actual and literary patterns for his story, his conclusion touches a surprisingly selfless vein of dramatic truth. We are left with the suspicion that this act of revenge was somehow, humanly, justifiable: it is a terrible way, but the only way, for Catherine to assert the claim of her life against David's art. And when their marriage ends abruptly and David takes up with Marita, the same story is poised to begin again. Marita may be dark and Catherine fair, but nothing can disturb the "inner core" David writes from, which "could not be split or marked or scratched."

One detail I think shows better than any other Hemingway's own understanding of what is at stake between Catherine and David. When she burns his manuscripts, she still manages to rescue from among them the *cahier* that is merely a diary of the time he has spent with her. Could this, she asks, now serve as material for stories to write in place of the lost ones? She has the pride and selfishness of an artist, without art. Thus, Hemingway's imagination of her fate is involved with his recognition of his own; and it is this that makes him able to write the catastrophe as well as he does. *The Garden of Eden*, it seems to me, provided a way for its author to admit something to himself which he had kept well hidden after *The Sun Also Rises*. His notion of a perfect pairing was really a treacherous game, after all, even though it helped to distract the people he kept near him. For it expressed his need to reduce all life to a kind of frictionless sheen. This may be consoling for an artist like David Bourne, whose imitative practice of love helps to conceal or protect an inner core. It is nothing like that for Frederic Henry when he becomes "the same" as Catherine Barkley. The relevant episode is near the end of *A Farewell to Arms*, when he has to spend parts of days alone; and the Catherine of that book tells him:

> "All you have is me and I go away."
> "That's true."
> "I'm sorry, darling. I know it must be a dreadful feeling to have nothing at all suddenly."
> "My life used to be full of everything," I said. "Now if you aren't with me I haven't a thing in the world."

All that can occupy such a vacancy is the work of art, and it commonly does so in the most unpromising settings. One recalls that in *Across the River and Into the Trees*, Cantwell's ecstasy is reserved not for his lovemaking with Renata in a gondola shrouded by the Venetian mist, but for the portrait of her which he keeps in his hotel and which has become more vivid to him than she is herself. It is the same with David and his manuscripts.

What is new in *The Garden of Eden* is the stinging clarity with which it portrays the condition of knowing such an abstract love while being unable to trust its permanence. Catherine, talking of the countryside they have been seeing, confides to David, "I don't want to die and it be gone." He replies, "You know what you saw and what you felt and it's yours." Yet it will not be hers when she dies; and that is the thought she cannot stand. "Then," he concludes, "don't let it happen till it happens. Look at the things and feel." It is a therapy offered by the author and his hero alike. But she is comfortless because she knows the terms of both sides of the sacrifice; and, after burning the manuscripts, she gives an explanation of her own:

> "I want to talk about them," Catherine said. "I want to make you realize why it was necessary to burn them."
> "Write it out," said David. "I'd rather not hear it now."
> "But I can't write things, David."
> "You will," David said.

The last reply is shaking, and it can only mean: she will write (if she will) because, having given useless pain, she

[*217*]

has come part of the way to being a writer already. It is thus in keeping with every tension of the story when, in its very last moments, David moves from love and hate to something like sympathy with Catherine, but only after reading a letter that she has written.

> He had never read any other letters from Catherine because from the time they met at the Crillon bar in Paris until they were married at the American church in Avenue Hoche they had seen each other every day and, reading this first one now for the third time, he found that he still could be, and was, moved by her.

Memory, of course, is never true, not even the memory of so many interlocked, undistinguishable days. But reading does for this hero just what living never can; and his returns to the letter hold more truth for him than any memory.

The Garden of Eden is the only novel Hemingway wrote in which he brought into the open something like the view of writing that he first declared in *Death in the Afternoon*. But the novel is emotionally daring for another reason: it goes some way to connect this attitude with the pathos of a single author's life. It may therefore supply the sort of master clue Hemingway's biographers have wrongly sought in Paris or Havana. For the novel has a story within the main story, a narrative of the hunt for a powerful elephant in which David, as a child, accompanied his father, and first came to know his father well. The story is told by paraphrase or indirect discourse, but the result anyway is marvelously suggestive. In narrating the hunt, by contrast with the outward chronicle of David's marriage, Hemingway all along stresses its differentness from common experience: a quality he tries to catch by returning to a time before sense impressions have closed into memories. Here, it is the father who is associated with the giving of death and with the recovery of something from life by words. The quest he leads is altogether as relentless as those Hemingway would later describe himself leading in Africa, when, at the age of thirty-five, he was already asking to be called Papa. So by writing this story, the son hoards all the weight of an old accusation against his father; the elephant they were chasing had seemed, when shot, "to sway like a felled tree and came smashing down toward them. But he was not dead. He had been anchored and now he was down with his shoulder broken. He did not move but his eye was alive and looked at David. He had very long eyelashes and his eye was the most alive thing David had ever seen." Compare, now, with these sentences given from a boy's perspective, the description of the dying bull in which Hemingway likens him to "the dry powder snow your skis cut through." The latter way of feeling belongs to the father. But it seems to be part of the moral of *The Garden of Eden* that the writer Hemingway was destined to be was always a compound of this father and this son.

> He had intended to ask his father about two things. His father, who ran his life more disastrously than any man he had ever known, gave marvelous advice. He distilled it out of the bitter mash of all his previous mistakes with the freshening addition of the new mistakes he was about to make and he gave it with an accuracy and precision that carried the authority of a man who had heard all the more grisly provisions of his sentence and gave it no more importance than he had to the fine print on a transatlantic steamship ticket.

Yet within *The Garden of Eden*, the motive of the African story remains buried quite deep. It is a "given"—wholly a matter between David and his father, and therefore between Hemingway and himself.

If a puzzle remains somewhere in the design of all of Hemingway's writing, it lies in the process by which this second story recedes into a stark background of daily phenomena, and we are left only with the one face of the hero and the actions that define him. But that, mostly hidden, work of reduction does seem related to a larger movement of Hemingway's writing, by which every reader comes to feel his distinction. Much of the drama of his work goes on in a transitory pause of action, where a human figure slips away from the scene that has held it provisionally, but the narrator's eye rests for an extra beat on the chance surroundings. Stories like "A Clean, Well-

Lighted Place" and "Hills Like White Elephants" even figure the effect in their titles. But, of course, it is more than an effect; it is almost the statement of a purpose for writing. In his Nobel Prize speech, which was not about man but about prose, Hemingway said: "Things may not be immediately discernible in what a man writes, and in this he is sometimes fortunate; but eventually they are quite clear and by these and the degree of alchemy that he possesses he will endure or be forgotten." This will serve as a defense of all that his work does salvage, now that the author himself has passed from the scene. His shadow has merged with the landscape, far outside the range of English, where one can feel it in Waugh, in Orwell and in Beckett. It is there in the closing montage of Antonioni's *The Passenger*, with the scene of death in a quiet room and the long look out to the drive, where a woman tramps slowly back and forth in the white dust. The composure of such moments was a temperamental necessity for Hemingway. That it should have become inseparable from the very idea of modernity is one of those accidents that are not less fateful than the choices of a life. A future that knows Hemingway from a distance will sort out better than we can now the proper fame of his words. By the focus of a body of work, no one has ever done more, or more swiftly or admirably, to change the way that writing was practiced and thought about. He belongs to the company—more select, in fact, than the masters themselves—of those who have made a whole period imaginable for art.

Please, Sir, May I Go Mad?

G. K. Chesterton, Self-Revelation and the Stage

P. J. Kavanagh

In 1913, G. K. Chesterton had an early success with his play *Magic*, but although he wrote a couple more theater pieces he did not seriously follow up this success. Nevertheless, these dramatic works throw such an unusually personal light on Chesterton, and on his thought, they are worth looking at closely; they are also very enjoyable. In order to examine them properly, we have to go forward to the posthumously published *Autobiography* and look briefly back at the English history in which his ideas were rooted.

In *Autobiography* (1936), Chesterton describes how he and his brother, Cecil, as young men, used to play with a planchette, or Ouija board. One day they asked it to say something about a rather dull acquaintance, a Member of Parliament. After a few struggles it spelled out the word, incomprehensible to them both, "orriblerevelationsinighlife." "If it was our subconsciousness, our subconsciousness at least had a simple sense of humour. But that it was our subconsciousness rather than our consciousness (if it was not something outside both) is proved by the practical fact that we did go on puzzling over the written word, when it was again and again rewritten, and really never had a notion of what it was, until it burst upon us at last."

The story comes in a chapter called "How to Be a Lunatic," in which Chesterton affirms that at this period of his life (though not on this occasion—with its "Orrible Revelations in Igh Life") he encountered the Devil. It is a light enough tale, that of the planchette, in an uncharacteristically somber and evasive chapter. He remarks about his contemporaries that when they say: "'Evil is only relative. Sin is only negative. There is no positive badness; it is only the absence of positive goodness'—then I know that they are talking shallow balderdash only because they are much better men than I; more innocent and more normal and more near to God." But he does not tell

[*221*]

us what form his "aberration" from normality took; ". . . there was a time when I reached that condition of moral anarchy, in which a man says, in the words of Wilde, that 'Atys with the blood-stained knife were better than the thing I am.' I had never indeed felt the faintest temptation to the particular madness of Wilde; but I could at this time imagine the worst and wildest disproportions and distortions of more normal passion." It does not matter if these fantasies were a part of Chesterton's delayed adolescence. The point is that he believed he had seen the power of evil, inside himself and outside, an external force, and believed it his duty to insist on the fact of it in a doubting world. In *Autobiography* he is summing up the aim of a lifetime: "Perhaps, when I eventually emerged as a sort of theorist, and was described as an Optimist, it was because I was one of the few people in that world of diabolism who really believed in devils . . ." [In order to avoid a consequent pessimism] "I invented a rudimentary and makeshift theory of my own. It was substantially this: that even mere existence, reduced to its most primary limits, was extraordinary enough to be exciting." Thus, his lifelong lightness of manner was a conscious decision, taken in the face of the enemy, evil; neither a mask nor a pose, it was a weapon. He was against pessimism because he had experienced it, and thought of it as the special spiritual disease of his "modern" times.

There is no clear sign that in his battle with the "modern" Chesterton had much success. Most of the prestigious literary and scientific names of his day belonged to the other camp. This is difficult to realize from his tone, which is that of a reasonable man, sure of his ground, talking to other reasonable men, who could be counted upon to agree with him—except for a mistaken few who happened, briefly, to have the floor. He was widely read, became hugely popular, as journalist, novelist, critic, poet. Yet he stood almost wholly alone, foursquare against the current of the time. The impression is that he has since been bypassed by the waters of it. The only serious question is whether he was always facing in the wrong direction.

Perhaps his use of the word "modern" was too wide in application to have meaning. Yet there is still a "modern" sensibility—as he would have used the adjective—that believes the more horrible something is, the more likely it is to be true. This is an assumption against which, among modern writers, Saul Bellow wages eloquent war. Also there is still current the idea, almost equally dangerous, that lightness, grace, humor, in a writer, inevitably conceal an absence of the profound.

By "modern" Chesterton meant atheism, fashionable pessimism, the wilder reaches of realism—"I never bought a pistol and shot myself or my wife, I was never really a Modern"—and so many other connected things that he contentedly annoyed all sorts of people. (Certainly he can be accused of philistinism. His views on modern art are the least interesting aspect of his writings but, fortunately, on the whole he steers clear of it.) Above all, or almost above all, he was aiming at something he detected in the national character of the English, which he believed not to be native but to have been implanted, to his countrymen's great loss. To discover what that is we have to go back to the beginning of modern England, the beginnings of Chesterton's "modernism," back to the English Reformation; which eventually led two highly intelligent Victorian young men to start playing about with a Ouija board in search of "spirits."

Whatever the English Reformation did or did not do, for good or ill, it was outstandingly successful during a remarkably few years, and as a coolly engineered part of political policy, in taking the "spirits" out of Catholicism at home, in order to protect England from the influence of abroad. The intention was to cut her off from the internationalism of Rome, and to create quickly, in the face of external and internal danger, a new, isolationist nation.

What was international about Catholic usages was their emphasis on the mysterious; so the process (abetted by native reformers, but the urgency remained political) was one of demystification. The Mass, instead of a Sacrifice, became a Commemoration; altars were proscribed and became merely tables. In 1549 there was commanded the destruction of all remaining religious statues and works of art.

S. T. Bindoff, in his *Tudor England*, describes how, in the attempt to erase the past, the vice-chancellor of Oxford University "earned the sobriquet 'cancellor'"; so

[*223*]

great was his zeal in destroying irreplaceable books and manuscripts, "the flower of the middle ages." There were rebellions, which were firmly put down. Forty years later Burghley was still coolly pondering, for Elizabeth, the possibility of exterminating the remaining Catholics; he concludes that they are too many, but there are other ways: to ask them whether, if the forces of the Pope invaded, they would fight for him or for her. If they chose the Pope they would be executed; if (the majority) chose her, their Papal loyalty would by so much be weakened, and they could be isolated.

Step by step England was being taught that loyalty to the old religious forms was both superstitious and un-English. There was still resistance. When the Jesuits Garnet and Southwell landed in England in the 1580s, they were soon writing to Rome for consignments of papally blessed objects because "people cryed out for these." They were both executed, and their names blackened, so successfully that to this day the word "Jesuit" can be used in mockery. The threat of the Spanish Armada (1588) helped unite England, then in 1604 came the Gunpowder Plot, a private, Catholic (Jesuit-forbidden) attempt to blow up the King and Parliament, and to this day in England Guy Fawkes is burnt in effigy every year. England had lost its mysteries, the old sense of a fruitful interaction between this world and the next; also, a sense of the external power of evil, and it had been taught that these things were the sign of a traitor and a foreigner. "Modern" England was born, skeptical, secular and, it must be admitted, publicly philistine: some dim memory lingering on in turnip ghosts at Halloween and in Ouija boards. So, at any rate, did Chesterton see the matter, and the average agnostic liberal Englishman can still be made uneasy by a whiff of incense or by too many candles. England had been turned around.

"The Elizabethan church," writes Bindoff, "was designed to appeal to the lukewarm multitude, and it enlisted their lukewarm support. . . . its chief merits were negative. It had no Pope, it had no Mass, it made no windows into men's souls, it lit no fires to consume men's bodies. The fact that it also kindled no flame in men's hearts, if hardly a merit, was less of a defect in that most men's hearts were not inflammable."

It was precisely this "flame in men's hearts" that Chesterton, the son of beloved agnostic parents, still not a "Romanist," was determined to rekindle in his countrymen. He believed that the ordinary people of England (who "have not spoken yet") had for political reasons been tricked into believing that the old observances, which had kept them in touch with the spiritual part of their natures, were merely foreign superstitions and magic. They had been led into materialism, therefore into working for the soulless excesses of capitalism and imperialism, robbed of their religion and their country—by the redistribution of church lands—and, because "people cryed out for these," into infinitely baser forms of superstition, like table rapping. There was power in the mystery they had been denied. In 1913 Chesterton called his first play *Magic*.

The audience is in no doubt of his theme. The professional conjurer turns on Smith, the smiling, skeptical Anglican clergyman ("one of the Christian Socialist sort"):

CONJURER: [*With a sort of fury*] Well, does anybody believe it? Do you believe it?

SMITH: [*With great restraint*] Your question is quite fair. Come, let us sit down and talk about it. Let me take your cloak.

CONJURER: I will take off my cloak when you take off your coat.

SMITH: [*Smiling*] Why? Do you want me to fight?

CONJURER: [*Violently*] I want you to be martyred. I want you to *bear* witness to your own creed. I say these things are supernatural. I say this was done by a spirit. The doctor does not believe me. He is an agnostic; and he knows everything. The Duke does not believe me; he cannot believe anything so plain as a miracle. But what the devil are you for; if you don't believe in a miracle? What does your coat mean, if it doesn't mean there is such a thing as the supernatural? [*Exasperated*] Why the devil do you dress up like that if you don't believe in it? [*With violence*] Or perhaps you don't believe in devils?

SMITH: I believe ... [*After a pause*] I wish I could believe.

CONJURER: Yes. I wish I could disbelieve.

He means he wishes he could disbelieve in devils. It is the same Chesterton who explains himself twenty years later. In that sense the play is autobiographical, and Chesterton is the Conjurer.

It is possible that he wrote it in response to the constant nagging of George Bernard Shaw. In 1908 Shaw is clearly returning to an old matter: "What about the play? . . . I shall deliberately destroy your credit as an essayist, as a critic, as a Liberal, as everything that offers your laziness a refuge, until starvation and shame drive you to serious dramatic parturition. I shall repeat my public challenge to you, vaunt my superiority, insult your corpulence, torture Belloc; if necessary call on you and steal your wife's affections with intellectual and athletic displays, until you contribute something to the British drama." Even, with typical Shavian cheek, he attempts to occupy Chesterton's own ground, and suggests that he led him there. "It is my solemn belief that it was my Quintessence of Ibsenism that rescued you and your ungrateful generation from Materialism and Rationalism. You were all tired young atheists turning to Kipling and Ruskinian Anglicanism . . ." He concludes with a sentence not strictly relevant but so profound that it has to be quoted: "Lord help you if you ever lose your gift of Speech, GKC! Don't forget that the race is only struggling out of its dumbness, and it is only in moments of inspiration that we get out a sentence. All the rest is padding."

In 1909 Shaw is at it again:

CHESTERTON.
SHAW SPEAKS.
ATTENTION!
I still think you could write a useful sort of play if you were started . . . Now to business. When one breathes Irish air one becomes a practical man. In England I used to say what a pity it was that you did not write a play. In Ireland I sat down and began writing a scenario for you.

It runs to about three thousand words (published in the second volume of Shaw's *Letters*) and is about the Devil and Saint Augustine visiting contemporary England and examining the present, nearly nonexistent, state of its

Christianity. Shaw concludes his letter (after offering to *pay* Chesterton to write it): "It is to be neither a likely-to-be successful play nor a literary lark. It is to be written for the good of souls."

Four years later, Chesterton's *Magic* had that intention.

The action takes place in the park and drawing room of an endearingly comic duke. His Celtic Twilight niece encounters a monklike stranger in the park. (Celtic Twilight=fairies=false superstition; the stranger's cowl= some dim folk memory of pre-Reformation monks.) She, of course, takes him for a magician, summoning fairies.

Enter into the drawing room an agnostic doctor and the "Christian Socialist" clergyman whom we have met, who wants the duke's subscription to a "model public house." The doctor wants the duke's subscription to prevent such a place. They each receive equivalent subscriptions: "The Duke is the kindest of men, and always tries to please everybody. He generally finishes by pleasing nobody." Moral: Make up your mind.

The cowled stranger turns out to be not a magician but a conjurer, invited by the duke to perform that evening. The duke's businessman nephew thinks he can see through all his tricks, and goads him, in a way directly reminiscent of the way Catholics were goaded during the Reformation: "I guess I wish we had all the old apparatus of all the old Priests and Prophets since the beginning of the world. I guess most of the old miracles were a matter of just panels and wires." A chair falls over, a picture moves—just panels and wires. Then, after an inner struggle (someone who saw the play is reported as saying that "sin as a simple *fact* had never been put so effectively on the stage") the conjurer changes the color of the lamp shining outside the doctor's surgery across the park. The young man runs out distractedly to see how this was done, and later his sanity is despaired of. The conjurer is implored to explain his trick, to save the nephew, but he refuses. He says it was done by magic, and it is at this point there takes place the dialogue just quoted: "In black blind pride and anger and all kinds of heathenry, I called on the fiends and they obeyed."

Later he relents, explains to the sick young man a way the color could have changed naturally. But he does not tell the others or the audience: "If I told you a natural way of doing it ... half an hour after I have left this house you will all be saying how it was done." The power of mystery, denied four hundred years before, will be denied afresh.

Preposterous in summary, like most plays, it reads at least as well as Shaw does, and as amusingly, but there is an intriguing vein of darkness in it, absent from the cheerful Chesterton of the essays, who always presents himself as the embodiment of common sense.

At the center of the play is the temptation of the conjurer to confound the overly reasonable by summoning devils, and his yielding to it. The types on stage, agnostic, rational, materialistic, Anglican, are ignorant of the evil powers at loose in the world. Their belief that such things are superstitions is not a source of strength, as they imagine, but a weakness, implanted in them not all that long ago. It is all quite clear. Said George Moore, "Mr. Chesterton wished to express an idea and his construction and his dialogue are the best he could have chosen for the expression of that idea; therefore, I look upon the play as practically perfect." It was, for Moore, his favorite "modern" play. . . .

With the compulsive modesty that has so much damaged his reputation, Chesterton described the play's weakness as the audience "not being in on the central secret from the start." He was talking technically, of dramatic irony; he might as well have said that the weakness of the play is that the audience *is* in on the secret, it knows that the doctor's lamp is not changed by devils but by the stage electrician. But it seems this matters less when the play is performed than when it is read. It was a considerable public and critical success, Shaw standing up in his box and shouting "Bravo!"

However—although Shaw nagged, and was still nagging in 1930 ("A chance for Gilbert," he wrote to Chesterton's wife, "who ought to have written *The Apple Cart*. He leaves everything to me nowadays")—Chesterton wrote nothing more in dramatic form until *The Judgement of Doctor Johnson* fourteen years later. It was not produced for five years after that, and then at the semi-private Arts Theatre, for only six performances. This is surprising. It is a profound and amusing piece. If *Magic* is autobiographical in its beliefs in devils, the second play, so much later, suggests Chesterton's disillusion with postwar politics in a way that is never made quite so personal in his other writings. Those who are put off by Chesterton's certainties would find him more tentative and shadowed in his plays.

His Dr. Johnson wearily, and pungently, prefers order, almost any sort of order, to its opposite. There is a sparkling portrait of "Liberty" Wilkes, whose political rationalism and radicalism has become, by an easy transition, a rationalization of sexual libertinage. Johnson/Chesterton has something to say about this which will not find favor everywhere today. When he reasons with the young revolutionary American Republican, who has left his wife, the young man answers that his wife agrees with his opinions about freedom. Johnson replies: "Sir, your wife has no opinions. She has as good a head as yours; and there is not and never has been a single opinion in it.... You will be surprised to find how large a proportion of your fellow-creatures live and die and do good works without being troubled even with good opinions.... It is you and your precious opinions that have boxed the compass from Puritanism to profligacy." The Reformation again!

In the closing moments of the play, Johnson comes to his sad peroration, about republicanism, about democracy. It is sad because Chesterton, for so long and in the widest sense a political liberal journalist, suggests a loss of hope for change, a loss of belief in anything practical at all, save kindness. "You have often reminded me that kings are only men.... Suppose your politicians are more hated than kings.... When your parliaments grow more corrupt and your wars more cruel ... do you in that day of disillusion still have the strength to say: these are no Yahoos; these are men; these are they for whom their Omnipotent Creator did not disdain to die."

Chesterton was too much of a propagandist (and too little a dramatist) ever to close a play with words, and from so authoritative a figure, with which he did not agree.

There is an admission in this, not to be found elsewhere in quite that form.

The plays should be studied, and even revived, for they are less wordy, and sparkle with a less hectic brilliance, than Shaw's; and contain as many ideas, which are deeper rooted.

His last attempt at a play, *The Surprise* (mistakenly dismissed by one biographer as "best forgotten"), reveals a further darkening, also absent from the rest of Chesterton's work contemporary with it.

To its first publication in 1952 Chesterton's secretary and devoted archivist put the note: "Written in 1932 . . . but it was put aside before revision and has never been acted."

In it he returns to his first love, the toy theater. The characters begin as puppets; the puppeteer is the Author who, rather disturbingly, in view of Chesterton's early fears about his own sanity which he confesses in *Autobiography*, cries out to a passing friar to see his play: it contains "A question about me. It might possibly be put in this form: Have I gone mad? Or it might be put in the other form: Please, Sir, may I go mad?"

In the first act the Poet is thrown into a cell and wakes in the morning to bread and water which he finds are cake and wine: this is the first "surprise." This goes back to Chesterton's earliest convictions and his self-rescue from morbidity. "At the back of our brains, so to speak, there was a forgotten blaze or burst of astonishment at our own existence. The object of the artistic and spiritual life was to dig for this sunrise of wonder," he says in *Autobiography*. Thus, his poet tastes wine as though for the first time. A Prince, unwillingly keeping an old promise to marry the Princess, finds instead that under the bridal veil the Princess has put her lady-in-waiting, whom he indeed loves: the second "surprise." "Many a man has been lucky in marrying the woman he loves. But he is luckier: in loving the woman he marries," says the Princess.

The second act begins with the Puppeteer bewailing the lifelessness of it all (although it has been lively enough to the reader). This he admits: "They are intelligent, complex, combative, brilliant, bursting with life and yet they are not alive." So he runs the whole action again; the Poet wakes to water that is water, the Prince breaks his marriage promise, the Princess marries him anyway, with a vengeful trick, the Poet falls upon the Prince with his sword, and the distressed Author is forced to intervene: "Drop it! Stop! I am coming down." The Author as God— a Christ, as Malcolm Muggeridge has pointed out.

It is an odd piece, presumably unfinished, and very dark indeed. Any reader with the feeling that Chesterton considers himself too much on the right side of things would be—Surprised.

To a cheering audience at the first night of *Magic*, Chesterton announced (the report is from *G. K. Chesterton* by Michael Ffinch) that "he did not believe he could write a good play, nor a good article, nor even a good picture postcard, perhaps the hardest task of all. But he did believe in his own opinions, and so sure was he that they were right that he wanted his audience to believe them too."

Too many have been put off by that modesty and that certainty; by the jokes, by the anti-Semitism which has been exaggerated but from which he cannot be absolved. This last could be explained as a hatred of imperialism and international capitalism, but the charge must stand, though it bears no relation to the anti-Semitism of Hilaire Belloc or T. S. Eliot. It is political, not racial. But some allowance, even in an expounder of such wide overviews as Chesterton—whose parish was Christendom, whose concern, behind every joke, was eternity—must be made for the prevailing atmosphere of a writer's time. He died in 1936, but had already warned against the rise of Adolf Hitler.

At least you always know where you stand with Chesterton. By contrast, the forthright Shaw is much more tricky. In 1908 Shaw writes to Chesterton, once more pre-empting Chesterton's ground: "Do you think it would be possible to make Belloc write a comedy? If only he could be induced to believe in some sort of God instead of in that wretched little conspiracy against religion the pious Romans have locked up in the Vatican, one could get some drive into him." But Chesterton, who changed little from the beginning, spells his position out in *Autobiography*: "I am very proud about being orthodox about the mysteries of the Trinity or the Mass; I am proud of believing in the Confessional; I am proud of believing in the Papacy.

"But I am not proud of believing in the Devil. To put it more correctly, I am not proud of knowing the Devil."

With such a litany, Chesterton sounds determined to put off all readers who are not coreligionists. He has almost succeeded in doing this, but not quite. He remains one of the most quoted of writers, often without acknowledgment. The darkness he suggests in his knowledge of the Devil is sometimes obscured by the hustings style of his essays, addressed to the back of the hall; delightful to some, maddening to others, for whom it conceals the earnestness beneath. But the darkness shows in his plays perhaps because the audience was more intimate; they are funny, but contain black strands. Shaw was probably right: for the sake of those "moderns" who cannot trust a light unless they see it streaked with darkness, Chesterton should have written more plays.

HOGGING THE CONSTITUTION
BIG BUSINESS & ITS BILL OF RIGHTS

Robert Sherrill

> *Everything which is properly* business
> *we must keep carefully separate from*
> life.   Goethe

> *[I]n a democracy, the economic is*
> *subordinate to the political, a lesson*
> *that our ancestors learned long ago,*
> *and that our descendants will un-*
> *doubtedly have to relearn many years*
> *hence.*
>
> William Rehnquist, dissenting in
> *Central Hudson* (1980)

There's a folk tale about a Western mining-town mob
that seized a young man and got ready to lynch him.
Placing a rope around the victim's neck, one of the mob's
leaders asked if he had any last words. "Yes, indeed," he
said. "I want to know, why are you hanging me?" The
leader replied, "Because you told someone you were
against the U.S. Constitution." "That's a damned lie," the
young man said. "I would gladly die in defense of the
Constitution. All I said was that I did not know what the
Constitution was about."

If that is a capital crime, most of us—including most
lawyers, right up through those sitting on the highest
benches—live in peril of the noose. During this two hundredth anniversary of the framing of the U.S. Constitution,
the most fitting way to celebrate it is to find the most immediate example of our ignorance. And I think I have done
so. I got my clue from an advertisement that was placed
in many magazines not long ago by Philip Morris, offering
to pay $15,000 to the essayist who best explains why the
First Amendment's protections should be extended fully
to commercial speech (particularly, of course, to cigarette advertisements), with another $65,000 going to
runners-up.

Naturally, there's a heap of self-interest involved in that
public relations stunt. Philip Morris, the largest cigarette

manufacturer in the country and the progenitor of the most famous of the killers, Marlboro, is nervous. The whole tobacco industry is nervous. There's a move in Congress to ban cigarette ads in newspapers and magazines. Naturally, ad managers for print journalism are pretty nervous, too, since a ban of that sort would deprive magazines of about $500 million and newspapers of about $200 million each year.

But there's nothing wrong with self-interest, after all, and in this case it might help stir up a useful debate. As one who heartily opposes First Amendment protection for commercial speech that originates with corporations, I don't expect to agree with a single point made by the Philip Morris essayists, but it is refreshing at least to have the debate finally going on among people in general and not left to the closet doodlings of the United States Supreme Court, which for most of the past dozen years has stumbled and lurched toward what I (while admitting a hanging amount of ignorance) consider a dangerously pro-corporation position.

M ost experts on the subject seem to agree that the wealthy men who wrote the Constitution gave little more than a passing glance over their shoulders at the First Amendment and the rest of the Bill of Rights, which they tacked onto the Constitution only to win support from those they considered to be radical soreheads.

The scholars seem to agree, also, that to the extent that the so-called Framers gave the First Amendment any thought, they meant it as a device to protect the press in its encounters with government and to protect the ordinary citizens' right to get together and petition government. That's all. Self-government was the thing. Not the price of jams in Bloomingdale's deli. "It seems safe to say," writes Jonathan Weinberg (*Columbia Law Review*, 1982), "that advertising was not speech specifically intended to be protected by the Framers. It appears, though, that the Framers in fact had no coherent theory of free speech, and paid little attention to the issue. Just as no specific meanings were intended, it appears likely that virtually no particular meanings were foreclosed—the very vagueness of the text was intended to delegate to future generations the task of developing an exact meaning."

He probably gives the Framers too much credit for being purposefully vague, but in any event, here we are, many generations later, still "developing an exact meaning"—and, when it comes to the proper treatment of commercial speech, doing it in a very sloppy fashion indeed.

Oddly enough for a nation where politics and commerce are so intertwined, commercial speech as a big issue, a federal case, is something new. For most of our history, the regulation of commercial speech was thought to be just one of those chores that the states and local governments handled, not much different from or rating much higher than the regulation of barbers' colleges. Not until 1942 did the U.S. Supreme Court hand down an opinion on whether commercial speech merited constitutional protection. Let us consider that as

ACT I
Valentine v. Chrestensen. 316 U. S. 52 (1942)

In 1940, a very small-time entrepreneur from Florida bought a surplus Navy submarine and moved it to New York City, where he moored it at a state pier in the East River. Then he started distributing handbills to promote tours of the sub. The cops stopped him. The Sanitary Code of New York City didn't allow the distribution of commercial advertising in the streets. He was told he could distribute a handbill solely devoted to "information or a public protest," so long as it didn't contain a commercial pitch.

Back to the print shop went our Floridian and ordered up a new batch of handbills. On one side he told about his submarine (but didn't list the admission price) and, on the other side, he protested in strong language the problems he had had with the City Dock Department.

The cops said the protest side was O.K. but not the commercial side. The Floridian went ahead with the distribution anyway. He was arrested, and he went to court. He sued for an injunction to stop the cops from violating his Constitutional rights. He won as high as the appellate court, which said the cops had no right to interfere with the spreading of information proper for the public to know about, and just because profits were involved didn't lessen the man's First Amendment rights.

But when the case came to the United States Supreme Court, the judges *unanimously* overturned the appellate court and ruled against the submarine entrepreneur. Its opinion was that "the streets are proper places for the exercise of freedom of communication" but "we are equally clear that *the Constitution imposes no . . . restraint on government as respects purely commercial advertising*" (my emphasis).

The Court went on to say that it was much too clever to be fooled by the submarine exhibitor's political kicks at the City Dock Department: "Affixing of the protest against official conduct to the advertising circular was with the intent . . . of evading the prohibition of the ordinance. If that evasion were successful, every merchant who desires to broadcast leaflets in the streets need only append a civic appeal, or a moral platitude, to achieve immunity from the law's command." No editorial gimmick would elevate advertising to the level of a constitutional issue. One and all, conservative members and liberal members (bear in mind, the two greatest free-speech advocates in Supreme Court history, Hugo Black and W. O. Douglas, were on the Court) agreed that the Constitution *did not protect commercial speech.*

Since this was the first time that the Supreme Court had ever handed down an opinion on the issue, it was, to put it mildly, an historic occasion. A monumental breakthrough. A watershed. And yet, so deeply entrenched in the collective judicial mind—accepted as a veritable truism—was the exclusion of commercial speech in those days, the judges didn't even know the import of their own case. They just tossed it off like a traffic cop writing a two-dollar summons. Later, Justice Douglas would admit that he and his colleagues had rendered the opinion with very little contemplation. "The ruling," he said in embarrassed recollection, "was casual, almost offhand."

But it would remain solid as a rock, rarely challenged, for more than thirty years, as indeed it should have stood, because it was a good decision.

And though *Valentine v. Chrestensen* may have been

decided casually, the Court on later reflection stuck to it. During the following three decades or so, the Court used several occasions to reaffirm its position, notably in 1951 (*Breard v. Alexandria*) when door-to-door magazine salesmen challenged an Alexandria, Louisiana, statute that interfered with their solicitations. The salesmen claimed that the local law abridged free press and free speech. Justice Reed spoke for the majority: "Only the press or oral advocates of ideas could urge this point. It is not open to the solicitors for gadgets or brushes." In dissent, Black said he thought that their merchandise—magazines—made them "agents of the press" and thereby gave them protection under the First Amendment, but even he acknowledged that there was nothing constitutionally wrong with a city's blocking a "'merchant' who goes from door to door 'selling pots.'" So, whether their example was gadgets or brushes or pots, once again liberals and conservatives on the Court agreed that hawking them was not covered by the free speech guarantees.

And so things stood until...

ACT II

Bigelow v. Virginia, 421 U.S. 809 (1975)

On February 8, 1971, the *Virginia Weekly* of Charlottesville, Virginia, published an advertisement that read:

Unwanted Pregnancy
Let Us Help You
Abortions are Now Legal in New York
There is no residency requirement
For immediate placement in Accredited
Hospitals and Clinics at Low Cost
Contact
Women's Pavilion
515 Madison Avenue
New York, New York
Or call any time [etc.]

The *Virginia Weekly*'s managing editor, Jeffrey C. Bigelow, was arrested and charged with a misdemeanor for violating a state law prohibiting the promotion of abortion. The Virginia Supreme Court upheld his conviction, but Bigelow, claiming the state had violated his free speech

[237]

and free press rights, took his appeal to the U.S. Supreme Court. There he won.

Although the Court once again admitted that "purely" commercial speech deserved little constitutional protection, it now attempted, almost farcically, to argue that there was a real difference between the submarine handbill and the abortion ads. But common sense easily illuminates the striking similarity. Both submarine tour and abortion placement were strictly commercial services. So why did the newspaper ad deserve more protection than the handbill? Because, wrote Justice Blackmun for a hefty 7-2 majority, "Viewed in its entirety, the advertisement [for the abortion clinics] conveyed information of potential interest and value to a diverse audience—not only to readers possibly in need of the services offered, but also to those with a general curiosity about, or genuine interest in, the . . . law of another State and its development, and to readers seeking reform in Virginia. The mere existence of the Women's Pavilion in New York City, with the possibility of its being typical of other organizations there, and the availability of the services offered, were not unnewsworthy."

Hey, wow! What a singularly bulging treasure trove of information the justices found in only two lines: "Abortions are now legal in New York. There is no residency requirement." Blackmun made it sound like a treatise on abortion.

If the Court had been as creative in 1942, and inclined to use its creativity in that direction, it could have argued that the handbill information about the submarine tour was at least as useful to those who, say, wanted to make a career of the Navy and were thinking about going into the sub service, or to those who wondered what their tax dollars were being spent for at the Pentagon.

Anyway, as Justices Rehnquist and White pointed out in a brilliant dissent, all of the pious talk about the importance of a discussion of abortion was totally beside the point: ". . . the subject of the advertisement ought to make no difference. It will not do to say . . . that this advertisement conveyed information about the 'subject matter of the law of another state and its development' to those 'seeking reform in Virginia,' and that it related to abortion, as if these factors somehow put it on a different footing from other commercial advertising. This was a proposal to furnish services on a commercial basis, and since we have always refused to distinguish for First Amendment purposes on the basis of content, it is no different from an advertisement for a bucket shop operation or a Ponzi scheme which has its headquarters in New York. . . . [S]uch information might be of interest to those interested in repealing Virginia's 'blue sky' laws."

If the abortion ad was trivial in information, it should also have been trivial in importance as a test case. Indeed, one might fairly wonder why the Court bothered with it at all, for the Virginia statute under review had never before been used since it was passed in 1878. It was one of those statutes, easy to find in every state, that become quaintly obsolete and remain forgotten unless resurrected by some crackpot prosecuting attorney. Nor would the law ever again be used. No sooner had Bigelow been arrested than the Virginia legislature changed the law so that it could apply only to Virginia abortions, not those performed out of state. And yet the Supreme Court snapped up the dispute, obviously, or so it seems to me, because a majority of the justices were just itching for a case, any case, in which to bring commercial speech more fully under the First Amendment, no matter what contortions were necessary to get it there.

Even so, the Court was curiously timid. "We conclude, therefore," quoth the majority, "that the Virginia courts erred in their assumptions that advertising, as such, was entitled to no First Amendment protection. . . ." Why stop there? If not *no* protection, the Court must mean *some* protection. How much of a "some" did it have in mind? The Court wasn't saying.

Timorous and vague though it was, the Court's decision was nevertheless a landmark in one respect: it said positively (through a double negative) that commercial speech *could* be covered by the First Amendment, but clearly left the impression that this protection depended on the content of the message (it should be "interesting," of social concern, etc.). That sort of hedging, however, left the Court's conspirators (as I count them) dissatisfied, and so the majority screwed up its nerve and in the very next term shoved commercial speech much further under the "possible protection" of the First Amendment, and the wily justices did it in an even more elaborately manipulative way. Let us raise the curtain on what could be considered the real turning point in our tragicomedy.

ACT III
Virginia State Board of Pharmacy v. Virginia Citizens Consumer Council. 425 U.S. 748 (1976)

Virginia had a statute prohibiting drug-price advertising by pharmacists. Consumer groups could buy ads listing the different drug prices; so could labor unions, or associations of retired people, or anybody else—the prohibition was strictly aimed at pharmacists. But the Virginia Citizens Consumer Council Inc. and the Virginia State AFL-CIO challenged the statute, claiming that it deprived them of useful information. They did not ask the Court to let *them* discover and advertise the prices (they didn't need permission); they did not ask for First Amendment protection as speakers. They asked for First Amendment rights for the pharmacists as speakers (who, by the way, were not asking for it, since it would obviously not have benefited them financially) and also they were asking for their own First Amendment rights as—a much more esoteric group— *listeners*.

Does a listener have standing in a First Amendment suit?

The Court's majority (with Blackmun once again writing the opinion) said yes. "Freedom of speech presupposes a willing speaker. But where a speaker exists, as is the case here, the protection afforded is to the communication, to its source and to its recipients both."

Okay. But the central question still remained: Is *absolutely pure* commercial speech—in this case, nothing more than a price list of drug commodities—covered by the First Amendment? The advertisement in *Bigelow* didn't mention prices. It mentioned a service, and furthermore it mentioned a service for something (abortion) that in itself was a constitutional issue. But now, in *Virginia Pharmacy*, the Court was facing the question of whether some share of First Amendment protection should be given an advertisement for, say, sleeping pills or gout pills or tetracycline—with virtually no intellectual content.

"Here, in contrast [to *Bigelow*]," wrote Blackmun, "the question whether there is a First Amendment exception for 'commercial speech' is squarely before us. Our pharmacist does not wish to editorialize on any subject, cultural, philosophical, or political. He does not wish to report any particularly newsworthy fact, or to make generalized observations even about commercial matters. The 'idea' he wishes to communicate is simply this: 'I will sell you X prescription drug at the Y price.' Our question, then, is whether this communication is wholly outside the protection of the First Amendment. [Notice the waffling "wholly."] . . .

"Our question is whether speech which does 'no more than propose a commercial transaction,' . . . is so removed from any 'exposition of ideas,' . . . and from 'truth, science, morality, and arts in general, in its diffusion of liberal sentiments on the administration of Government' . . . that it lacks all protection. Our answer is that it is not."

Ah, what a stretching of the blanket of free speech was there! What a change of mood since the days when even that old First Amendment radical Justice Black had refused its protection to purveyors of pots. Now the Burger Court, which had never shown much hospitality to the political and social uses of the First Amendment, was suddenly eager to make not only the peddling of pots but the peddling of aspirins and Band-Aids worthy of its protection.

Its argument, which appeared to have been typed on a cash register, with Blackmun again doing the honors, went like this:

To be sure, the Framers saw the First Amendment as filling a vital need: the spread of the kind of political speech that makes for an informed populace and thereby a better government. But why limit the First Amendment to protecting what the citizen *needs* to know? Who's to say what's vital? Why not make it also protect what he *wants* to know? Using that standard, the Court must recognize that the consumer's interest in the price of cigarettes and sanitary napkins "may be as keen, if not keener by far, than his interest in the day's most urgent political debate." An advertisement for a political debate for which admission is charged should not receive any more protection than an advertisement for a massage parlor, for "no line between publicly 'interesting' or 'important' commercial advertising and the opposite kind could ever be drawn. Advertising, however tasteless and excessive it sometimes may seem, is nonetheless dissemination of information as to who is producing and selling what product, for what reason, and what price." The main point to remember, said Blackmun, is that no matter how crappy the product or worthless the service, if the advertisement makes the commercial wheels go round, if it brings in the buck, it deserves protection because the buck is at the heart of the American body politic. "So long as we preserve a predominantly free enterprise economy, the allocation of our resources in large measure will be made through numerous private economic decisions. It is a matter of public interest that those decisions, in the aggregate, be intelligent and well informed. To this end, the free flow of commercial information is indispensable. . . . And if it is indispensable to the proper allocation of resources in a free enterprise system, it is also indispensable to the formation of intelligent opinions as to how that system ought to be regulated or altered."

Twelve years have passed since that ruling, and although the exact status of commercial speech is still cloudy, for the most part advertisements have fared very well at court. The most confusing, and yet perhaps the most important opinion handed down during that period was *Central Hudson Gas & Electric Corp. v. Public Service Commission* (1980). The utility company had placed advertisements encouraging the use of electricity; the power commission had forbade such ads because of the energy crisis. A majority of the Court said that states do indeed have the right to suppress commercial speech that goes against public policy, but that states are bound by very strict rules in exercising this power: (1) the suppression must be supported by a "substantial government interest," (2) regulation has to "directly advance" state interest, and (3) the regulation cannot be "more extensive than necessary to serve that interest."

How was that to be interpreted? Exactly whose side was the Court on? Some lower courts were hopelessly baffled. One appellate panel spoke for many of these suffering judges when it said, citing *Central Hudson*, "We respectfully decline to enter the thicket of attempting to anticipate and to satisfy the *subjective ad hoc* [their emphasis] judgments of a majority of the United States Supreme Court."

But to one key participant, Justice William Rehnquist, *Central Hudson* was not at all difficult to decipher. To him (he was a bitter dissenter in the case) the three-point test "adopted by the Court thus elevates the protection accorded commercial speech that falls within the scope of the First Amendment to a level that is virtually indistinguishable from that of non-commercial speech."

And he was right. After all, editorial speech can also be suppressed by the state if doing so serves a "substantial government interest." To be sure, it has to be a very substantial interest indeed, but the state can do it. *Central Hudson's* support of state regulation was not nearly so important as the hurdles it raised against regulation—hurdles so high, in fact, (if the Court chose to interpret them in that fashion) that commercial speech could become virtually as removed from state regulation as was editorial speech.

If that were the end of our tragicomedy, we could conclude that corporations—and it is from them that most commercial speech flows—finally had won the ultimate majestic status symbol they had been conniving to obtain for many years—full citizenship, with all the rights of free speech stemming therefrom.

Fortunately, that wasn't the end. Still to come were some exciting developments in

ACT IV

The Framers of the Constitution could not have meant for the blessings of the First Amendment to be extended to corporations as we know them today because such monstrous things were as alien to them as the atomic bomb, and if those gallant men of the eighteenth century by some miracle had foreseen the eventual creation of the modern corporation, the vision would doubtless have frightened them into planning ways to bind the leviathans with many chains rather than extend human freedoms to them. How could they have reacted otherwise than in fright? After all, as David Ewing, managing editor of the *Harvard Business Review*, has pointed out, "Some of our corporate and public organizations have larger 'populations' than did the thirteen colonies. General Motors, with 681,000 employees, is nearly two and one-half times the size of the second largest colony, Pennsylvania, which had a population of about 284,000 people in 1776. Westinghouse, the thirteenth largest corporate employer with 166,000 employees, is four times the size of the thirteenth largest colony, Delaware, which had a population of 41,400. In fact, 125 corporations have larger 'populations' than did Delaware in 1776." (*Big Business Reader: On Corporate America*, 1983)

The modern corporation did not move out of the primordial economic slime and onto the land, and begin to propagate in any great numbers, until just before the Civil War. Once established, however, they multiplied in awesome numbers and with awesome power. The government, and particularly the courts, did virtually nothing to control them; on the contrary, from the seedy Gilded Age up to the 1930s the courts often literally and always figuratively were in the employ of the corporations; laws which might otherwise have held them in check were "interpreted" out of existence. Even the antitrust laws, Congress's only serious effort to control giant business, were promptly killed and stuffed by the Supreme Court and exist today only as museum exhibits.

The most profitable collaboration between the Supreme Court and the corporations came in 1886. That was the year they pulled off the biggest literary heist in history. That was the year they stole the Fourteenth Amendment.

As everyone knows, the Fourteenth Amendment was created to force the sullen, recalcitrant Southern states to treat the recently freed slaves not merely as black bodies taking up space, not as unwelcome apparitions, but as real *persons*, as *citizens*. "No state shall make or enforce any law which shall abridge the privileges or immunities of citizens of the United States," it reads; "nor shall any state deprive any person of life, liberty, or property, without due process of law; nor deny to any person within its jurisdiction the equal protection of the laws."

As soon as the Fourteenth was ratified in 1868, the corporations began trying to purloin those lovely words for their own use. No wonder they found the Fourteenth so attractive. It specifically addressed the *states*, and when corporations fought health laws, child-labor laws, sweatshop laws, or when they manipulated land and right-of-way laws, they were usually dealing with state laws. Naturally, it would be to their great advantage to have the full use of the Fourteenth. But to get it, they would have to qualify as *persons*, which would be difficult inasmuch as the Fourteenth obviously was aimed only at protecting flesh and blood. For hundreds of years corporations had been correctly viewed as nothing but a legal mass of assets, as a legislative concoction of government. They had never been thought of as something alive. The great jurist Edward Coke said in 1605, "Corporations . . . have no souls." This was the traditional view of them. But ah! if that view could be legally changed; if the corporations could, so to speak, put soot on their faces and mingle with the ex-slaves as they moved across the threshold into citizenship, if little ol' Standard Oil and humble Union Pacific could be seen by law as no different from the lowliest of citizens, justifiably receiving the same protections from the courts, requiring no more regulation than a sharecropper, worthy of the same mercy as an impoverished miner—what a grand and glorious difference that would make!

Eventually, big business got what it wanted. Arthur S. Miller reconstructs the moment: "The Supreme Court in its infinite wisdom saw new light in 1886. In an otherwise obscure case about railroad regulation, when the lawyers were again trying to convince Their Serene Highnesses that corporations should be persons within the meaning of Section 1 of the 14th Amendment, Chief Justice Waite stopped oral argument and announced to counsel that he need not discuss the point further. Waite said that all the justices were of the opinion that corporations were indeed legal persons." (*Corporate Power in America*, 1973)

That one court action, Justice Black correctly said, "has had a revolutionary effect on our form of government." The inequality between white and black that the Fourteenth Amendment was supposed to cure has instead been transformed into perhaps an even greater inequality between the corporate "person" and the natural person.

"It is difficult to pretend any longer," wrote Jerry S. Cohen (*Power Inc.*, with Morton Mintz, 1976), "that there is 'Equal Justice Under Law,' or even that this is an ideal destined someday to be achieved. The law simply cannot bestow equal justice so long as there are two separate and unequal classes of citizens—one that cannot be imprisoned and another that can, one for whom the most severe penalty is the punishment of its capital, and another that can receive capital punishment."

The terrible ruling of 1886 may have given corporations an overwhelming protection and procedural power in lawsuits, but did it extend all the *liberties* of the natural person, including free speech, to them? There was considerable doubt about that, and the doubt increased in 1906 when, under the pressure of the Progressive Era, the Supreme Court ruled that the liberty protected by the Fourteenth "is the liberty of natural, not artificial persons." (*Northwestern Natural Life Ins. Co. v. Riggs*)

Since then the corporations have been trying to persuade the courts to extend the generosities of 1886 in such a way as to let them wallow in the First Amendment just as you and I can. That, of course, would magnify their advantages in political and economic and health and safety debates to a fearsome degree.

The imbalance is already impressive. No judicial statement of the past seems so giddily unrealistic and outdated today as Justice Holmes's oft-quoted notion that "the best test of truth is the power of the thought to get itself accepted in the competition of the market." It is absurd to think that a natural person has the wherewithal to compete with a "corporate-person" in the marketplace of ideas. When airbags for autos were under debate in Congress, letters from consumers supporting the bags were no match for the full-page advertisements placed by Ford Motor Company in twenty-seven of the largest newspapers (ads that were so deceptive that the Department of Transportation publicly disputed every point in them).

As Fred Harris once said, "You don't have to believe that somewhere there are twelve bankers, politicians, and corporate executives who meet once a week to decide the future of America—there aren't—to see that General Motors has more to say [through "their regular channels of communications, advertising"] about air pollution standards than you or I or even millions like us do." (*Corporate Power in America*)

That is so obvious that it has penetrated the thinking of some members of the Supreme Court who ordinarily are not rated as champions of the little guy. Justice White, for example, who said in *First National Bank v. Bellotti* (1978) that because corporations wield such vast economic power and speak independently of the views of their individual shareholders they "may be viewed as seriously threatening the role of the First Amendment as a guarantor of a free marketplace of ideas."

Bellotti involved a critical issue: Can a state prevent corporate management from spending corporate money to circulate political propaganda that has no connection with its corporate business? The majority of the Burger Court said no, the state cannot. White (joined by Brennan and Marshall) said yes, it could.

Most important to the future of this continuing debate, joining these three in dissent, in a separate opinion, was none other than Brother Rehnquist, who promises to be the unlikely star of this show.

I almost said unlikely hero, but that may be going too far. Rehnquist has such a dismal record on some other issues that he does not deserve to be rated that high for his service on this one alone. And besides, he may be on the right side for the wrong reasons: perhaps he does not abhor corporations (the right reason) so much as he loves the state too much. He is an extreme statist, with a reputation among some Court observers as a rather slavish cheerleader for government. Nevertheless, he will be enormously useful in this fight, and perhaps can turn the Court around, not only because he has a marvelously dashing, Captain Blood style of writing opinions but because he has a deep reservoir of the right instincts, as I think can be shown by what he said in a number of cases.

• Rehnquist is particularly contemptuous of the infamous 1886 decision to make corporations "persons," noting with prudish disapproval that this decision was taken "with neither argument nor discussion." Corporations—which he describes with Chief Justice Marshall's words: "The mere creature of law, it possesses only those properties which the charter of creation confers upon it"—will never win from him the right to play without restriction in political debate. ("... the 14th Amendment does not require a State to endow a business corporation with the power of political speech." *Bellotti*)

As for bringing "purely" commercial speech—stuff such as price lists—under the First Amendment, he feels that to be a disastrous mistake, the inevitable consequence of the Burger Court's having taken that first step down the "slippery slope" of protecting commercial speech. "A Pandora's box," says he, was thereby opened. It was not only bad law, it was bad taste. "The First Amendment speech provision, long regarded by this Court as a sanctuary for expressions of public importance or intellectual interest," he wrote, "is demeaned by invocation to protect advertisements of goods and services." And advertisement, he said, is simply "not the sort of expression that the Amendment was adopted to protect." (*Bates v. State Bar of Arizona*, 1976)

• When Blackmun argued in *Virginia Pharmacy* that protecting drug price lists was good for the economy and therefore good for the body politic, Rehnquist's dissenting opinion fried him in sarcasm: "There is certainly nothing in the United States Constitution which required the Virginia Legislature to hew to the teachings of Adam Smith in its legislative decisions regulating the pharmacy profession."

• And when Blackmun argued that the "consumer's interest in the free flow of commercial information ... may be as keen, if not keener by far, than his interest in the day's most urgent political debate," and went on to argue that the majority's catering to that interest was "consistent even with the view that the First Amendment is 'primarily an instrument to enlighten public decisionmaking in a democracy,'" Rehnquist once again had exactly the proper reply: "I had understood this view to relate to public decisionmaking [on] political, social, and other public issues, rather than the decision of a particular individual as to whether to purchase one or another kind of shampoo. It is undoubtedly arguable that many people in the country regard the choice of shampoo as just as important as who may be elected to local, state, or national office, but that does not automatically bring information about competing shampoos within the protection of the First Amendment."

• Rehnquist scorns the "marketplace of ideas" concept when applied to commercial speech, believing that "although the 'marketplace of ideas' has a historically and sensibly defined context in the world of political speech, it has virtually none in the realm of business transactions." To him, the difference between the two is quite clear. In the commercial bazaar, ideas are often fraudulent, and their correction, if correction can be achieved, involves complex lawsuits. But "in the world of political advocacy and *its* marketplace of ideas, there is no such thing as a 'fraudulent' idea: there may be useless proposals, totally unworkable schemes, as well as very sound proposals that will receive the imprimatur of the 'marketplace of ideas' through our majoritarian system of election and representative government."

• And finally, Rehnquist believes that state-chartered, state-propped, profit-making enterprises can't have it both ways. Fair's fair. If they insist on being coddled by the state—seeking and receiving "the blessings of potentially perpetual life and limited liability"—then they must accept state control, including control of their speech, for "liberties of political expression are not at all necessary to effectuate the purposes for which States permit commercial corporations to exist." He reduces the commercial speech of such enterprises to the status of charity, particularly when it relates to activities and products that exist at the whim of the state. In *Posadas de Puerto Rico Associates v. Tourism Company of Puerto Rico* (1986), Rehnquist came out on top—5 to 4, his first victory for his commercial speech position—with an opinion that the government of Puerto Rico had a perfect right to ban casino gambling advertisements on the island even though gambling is legal there. "It would," he wrote, "surely be a strange constitutional doctrine which would concede to the legislature the authority to totally ban a product... but deny the legislature the authority" to reduce demand for the product by banning advertising.

Brrrrr. Philip Morris and pals must have felt a deep chill when *that* opinion came down. Obviously cigarette companies (and liquor companies eventually?) have good reason to fear that if Congress outlaws or greatly subdues their print advertisements to protect the nation's health, appeals for First Amendment protection will arouse scant sympathy from Rehnquist and his allies on the Court.

And that, I think, would be a wonderful eventuality, if in the process of upholding the restrictions on corporate speech, Rehnquist et al take extra pains to emphasize that at least so far as the First Amendment is concerned, it is high time to reverse the Mistake of the Century and stop pretending that corporations are persons. The beauty of the commercial-speech debate is that nowhere can the corporation's differences from a natural person be so clearly shown. The main differences have to do with motivation and freedom. Size is only incidental. (See, for example, C. Edwin Baker, *Commercial Speech: A Problem in the Theory of Freedom.* Iowa Law Review 1 [1976].) Justice Douglas once said that only in the home should the Constitution recognize individuals who have the kind of freedom to follow personal values and "prejudices" that merit First Amendment protection. (*Bell v. Maryland,* 1964) Contrasting corporations with homes, however, may overdramatize the point, which can just as well be made by comparing corporations with groups such as the AMA, the UAW, and the NAACP. In the latter, as Andrew Hacker has pointed out, "in spite of tendencies toward bureaucratization... the power of these associations is simply an extension of the individual interests and wills of their constituent members." On the other hand, "when General Electric, American Telephone and Telegraph, and Standard Oil of New Jersey enter the pluralist arena we have elephants dancing among the chickens. For corporate institutions are not voluntary associations with individuals as members but rather associations of assets, and no theory yet propounded has declared that machines are entitled to a voice in the democratic process" (*Corporate Power in America*).

To be sure, individuals and groups of individuals are interested in making money, but they combine this with other reasons for associating, conversing, writing, and tossing ideas around. They do these things because of a multitude of values. A corporation has only one: profit. Granting that corporate dollars help support some admirable social activities (let us pause here to pay the required thanks to Exxon's and Mobil's support of PBS and Philip Morris's support of the Joffrey Ballet); nevertheless, these things are completely incidental to the corporations' real goal: forever profits. Neither Frank Resnick, head of Philip Morris, nor his efficient peers in corporations anywhere are permitted to have any other drive. As Justice White put it, correctly, "the principal function of the First Amendment, the use of communication as a means of self-expression, self-realization, and self-fulfillment, is not at all furthered by corporate speech. It is clear that the communications of profit-making corporations . . . do not represent a manifestation of individual freedom or choice" (*Bellotti*). And this simply eliminates them from the First Amendment game.

The exclusion of corporate speech from the First Amendment should not be because of content but because of source. It isn't what they say but who says it that really matters. If corporate speech gets protection, let it come from the commerce clause or the due process clause or some other part of the Constitution. The First Amendment belongs to human beings and the press, and it should be secured for their use *only*, before the nonsense planted by the Burger Court becomes any more dangerously rooted.

CHEZ L'OXYMORON

Anne Carson

Oxymoron: [ancient Greek ὀξύμωρον, substantive use of neuter of ὀξύμωρος pointedly foolish, from ὀξύ sharp + μωρός dull, stupid, foolish] a rhetorical figure by which contradictory or incongruous terms are conjoined so as to give point to the statement or expression; an expression, in its superficial or literal meaning, self-contradictory or absurd, but involving a point.

Oxford English Dictionary

"I am Heathcliff."

Catherine Earnshaw

Once I went to South America to look at the edges of shadows. It was July. I was living in a small town near New York. The moon waning. Night after night unable to sleep because of the shadows, I got up, followed them along the wall, down the stairs, outside. They lay stretched across the lawn like a sound, blacker than any sound. They lay having a solidity like objects and a hard, whole life in them that is withheld from us. The edges cut away from us back into a world of a different kind. Can you stand there, I thought, can you balance, can you glance in? It became my endeavor to stand on the very edge of shadow. Night after night I practiced my attempt. Night after night I failed. There is shadow and there is no shadow and you can see the difference between them— you can stare at it, measure it, describe it, you can show it in a mirror, but to stand on that edge—no, you can't do it. I traveled to South America hoping that, in the inverted relationships of that hemisphere, edges might assert themselves differently, shadows would be as solid as categories, but no. The edge where shadow and no shadow come together and lie side by side is a point without space. A contradiction without terms.

Yet we do have terms for such things, if the world of phenomena does not. We do contrive, in forms of language, to balance on the edge between shadow and no shadow, seeking a point of insight that is to be found nowhere else. One of the forms we contrive is *oxymoron*. "How far is oxymoron, so dear to tragic texts, essential to the representations that the city gives of itself in drama?" asks Nicole Loraux in *Tragic Ways of Killing a Woman* (Harvard University Press). Her answer is an inquest of pleasure, the special pleasure we take in watching women die on the stage of fifth-century Greek tragedy. Oxymoron informs every aspect of this pleasure, she finds. Female death, as we see it enacted in classical drama, is a rhetorical compound of masculine and feminine idioms forced together at high pressure into certain anomalous shapes and unthinkable thoughts: pleasurable to the extent that they remain unthinkable even as you think them, remain anomalous as they take shape. Balanced on the edge between male and female, and arguably unique to the tragic response, is a pleasure that sways in the mind like fragrance—a whiff of cool sweat as the actor lifts the female mask to place it over his face.

Oxymoron is a word that enacts itself. Its two components, the adjective ὀξύ (meaning "sharp" or "pointed") and the adjective μωρόν (meaning "dull" or "foolish"), lie contiguous but distinct, like rooms on either side of a connecting door. So too the ancient tragic stage is composed of two spaces and a connecting door. Through this door the tragic heroine purposing to die conventionally disappears, into the interior of her house, so as to do the deed in private; some time later a messenger or servant arrives on stage to report her death in a lengthy set-speech. But, as Loraux is not the first to observe, tragic protocol is a curious business. The messenger-speeches that announce women's deaths in fifth-century tragedy are raw and alarmingly beautiful narratives, much more intrusive than plain performance could ever be. Here you see women in physical and mental extremity, exposing themselves to ultimate violation—as if they thought themselves unwatched. Words betray the dying woman to you. Words withhold her death from dramatization in order to exhibit it all the more fully on the screen of your imagining mind. Words wrap the woman herself out of sight and at the same time thrust you into the private parts of her suffering. Words render her as tragic pleasure, a pleasure contingent upon a closed door.

Behind a closed door was where ancient opinion preferred to locate the feminine presence; Greek propriety, in general, denied to women the public caress of fame. A reputable woman lived her life out of sight and vanished at death into her husband's memory. As Pericles put it, "The glory of a woman is to have no glory." Except on the tragic stage: here you see women strut and die as darkly as men, more darkly in fact. For death can impart a manly glory. But, to be feminine, glory must blot itself out: suicide is the match with which most tragic heroines kindle their own fame. Tragedy takes special pleasure in staging this oxymoron of female glory, Loraux claims. She traces its etiology to the deepest places of the Athenian sociocultural imagination, where you see one image replicate itself again and again. It is the image of a woman hanging up a noose.

That hanging is "a woman's way of death" was a truism of ancient aesthetics, but why? The sword makes practical and symbolic sense as the typical instrument of masculine destruction, but what is particularly feminine about the rope? Loraux offers several explanations. Hanging was, in Greek eyes, the ugliest form of death, called ἀσχήμων ("formless"), λώβη ("multilation"), μίασμα ("pollution") and incurring utmost dishonor. Yet a certain physiological appropriateness can be claimed for this ugly act: "As it closes forever the too open bodies of women, hanging is almost latent in feminine physiology," says Loraux. In dramatic practice, moreover, hanging gives infinite play to feminine artifice, for the suicidal women of tragedy commonly replace ropes with some item of female accouterment—veil, girdle, headbinder—and so end their lives hoist by their own allure. At the same time, hanging preserves both feminine allure and feminine physiology from the intrusion of "weapons that cut and tear, those that draw blood."

[254]

But the Athenian tragic aesthetic was not interested in making a clean distinction between male and female deaths on grounds of gore. Loraux draws our attention to a deliberate confusion of sexual styles at the moment of decision. There are, for example, women who seize the sword and die in blood like men (Sophocles' Deianira and Eurydice, Euripides' Jocasta). There are womanish heroes who entertain notions of hanging themselves (Euripides' Admetus) or die by inadvertent strangulation (Euripides' Hippolytus). More interesting, there are locutions that refuse to make a choice between rope and sword, like the untranslatable φόνιον αἰώρημα of Euripides' Helen. This heroine flirts with mortal possibilities in the terms:

> I shall put my neck
> in a deadly dangling noose (φόνιον αἰώρημα),
> or in a mighty effort sink the whole blade of a sword
> into my flesh. . . .

"Deadly dangling noose" is a fudged translation of the adjective φόνιον ("bloody") and the noun αἰώρημα ("hanging" or "suspension" or "hanged object"). Balanced on the edge between blood and bloodlessness, Helen's oxymoron is a microcosm of the female relation to dramatic death, Loraux seems to suggest. For the female is at liberty (as the man is not: no man actually hangs himself in tragedy) to "play the man" in her death if she chooses. No small part of your tragic pleasure consists in watching her engaged in that play with the sexes of death.

Playing with death by play upon language is a game you have learned to enjoy as a spectator of the Greek theater. Women play the game best, perhaps because they are, in the ancient assumption, preternaturally devious. At any rate, Helen's tricky word αἰώρημα ("suspension") provides another example of the oxymoronic logic of female death. Tragic diction uses this word of motion in two opposite directions: both the woman who hangs herself up in a noose and the woman who hurls herself down from a rock (for example, Evadne in Euripides' *Suppliants*) call their action αἰώρημα. By comparing with this usage the tragic convention of "escape odes," in which despondent heroines or female choruses voice a desire to find death by flight through the air, Loraux unfolds an important mythopoeic distinction between male and female in terms of fixity and movement.* "Identified as he was with the hoplite model, a man had to hold his ground and face death head on." And again she demonstrates that tragedy realizes this distinction by playing with it, asserts categories by confusing them. Thus Sophocles' Ajax exacts a queer compromise from death: planting his sword firm as a hoplite, this hero hurls himself upon it like a woman leaping into the void. Deianira, too, mixes the options of tragic suicide tellingly. She seizes a sword and plunges it into her side, as if to escape female categorization once for all, only to be caught by the heel of a Sophoclean word play. "She has set off for her last journey on a foot that does not move," is the sentence in which the chorus report Deianira's death by the sword. Deianira's "motionless foot" (ἐξ ἀκινήτου ποδός) is an interpretational crux to which Loraux gives an entirely original reading. The locution is intended to evoke, she believes, a conventional background of tragic heroines swaying in nooses and so to contrast Deianira's manly preference for a death with both feet on the ground. Fastened to death by an oxymoron that deserves comparison with Helen's "bloody suspension," Deianira brings you again to that unique point of balance, between a wound and its own blood, where your intensest tragic pleasure seems to lie.

It is this same keen edge of pleasure that cuts the throats of female heroines like Iphigenia, Polyxena, Macaria. Virgins in fifth-century tragedy do not generally kill themselves, Loraux tells us, for they have less autonomy than mature women. Virgins instead are slaughtered by men,

---

* It is odd that Loraux does not engage the precisely contrary findings of her countryman Jean-Paul Vernant, whose celebrated study of Greek social space, *"Hestia-Hermes. Sur l'expression religieuse de l'espace et du mouvement chez les Grecs"* in *Mythe et pensée chez les grecs* I (Paris 1974) identifies woman with the fixed principle of the hearth and man with the infinitely mobile Hermes. Perhaps we are meant to understand that death reverses all such categories; perhaps a deeper (in?)coherence deserves examination. *"Les mythes se-représentent entre eux,"* Lévi-Strauss warns.

in fictive transgression of taboos against human sacrifice. Their maiden status gives a ghastly inverse realization to traditional Greek metaphors associating marriage with the funeral rite. For these girls, to be put to death is indeed a kind of wedding, in which Hades plays the role of the waiting bridegroom and the sacrificial knife performs an act of surrogate defloration. And once again, in a different sense, you see the tragic heroine balanced on an edge between blood and bloodlessness, in this "paradoxical image of the sacrificed virgin whose virginity is taken from her at the very moment when she is being exalted for purity." Oxymoronic modifiers like νυμφὴ ἄνυμφος παρθένος ἀπάρθενος ("maiden lacking maidenhead, virgin not virgin," Euripides' *Hecuba*) adorn these heroines as they face death, in order that they may "satisfy at once the anger of the gods and the dreams of the spectators."

Loraux's final chapter is an autopsy of the female body as constituted by the tragic imagination of the Greeks. According to her finding, death comes to women primarily through the throat (δέρη), a locus of beauty as well as of greatest vulnerability—whether to noose or knife. The male body, in contrast, is much more diversified for access by death. A man's side, stomach, chest, lungs and liver are all fatally vulnerable. Thus, when Sophocles' Deianira pierces her side "with a two-edged sword rammed home between the liver and the diaphragm" (*Trachinae*), she is usurping not only the weapon and action, but the anatomy of masculine death. Deianira's blow is problematic, however. In order to strike herself below the liver, Deianira uncovers the *left* side of her body. Various explanations of this anomaly, more and less insulting to Sophocles, have been proposed; Loraux reads it, ingeniously, as a "textual ruse." Sophocles knew Deianira's liver to be on her right side but also shared a common fifth-century understanding of the left side of the body as "the female side" and the right as "the male side." The poet is creating a deliberate anatomical oxymoron in order "to emphasize that a woman's death, even if contrived in the most manly way, does not escape the laws of her sex."

Oxymoron is mapped out as theatrical choice, at the climax of Euripides' *Hecuba*, upon the anatomy of Polyxena. At the moment of being sacrificed, and having just declared herself ready to proffer her throat to Neoptolemus' knife, the maiden suddenly changes her mind. Exposing her flesh from neck to navel, she drops to one knee and cries out:

> Here is my chest, young man.
> Strike there, if you like.
> Or if you prefer the neck,
> here is my throat ready.

Neoptolemus hesitates, as do commentators on this text, to take Polyxena's point; in the end he decides to go for the throat. While commentators traditionally proceed to claims of Euripidean "eroticization," Loraux prefers to see in Polyxena's alternative a graphic female claim upon ἀνδρεία, the masculine virtue of martial courage. Euripides celebrates the contradictory quality of this "manly woman" by juxtaposing two *loci* of death: in the chest like a warrior or in the throat like a victim of sacrifice. With her throat cut, Polyxena is "reclaimed at the last moment for feminity," and so a tragic heroine had to be, Loraux argues, for reasons of cultural stability. "Tragedy does transgress and mix things up—this is its rule, its nature—but never to the point of irrevocably overturning the civic order of values." In other words, the oxymoronic confrontation of male and female within individual psyches on the tragic stage is a luxury bought at the price of genuine aberration—a cage gone in search of a bird, Kafka would say. To good citizens like yourselves, tragedy offers "the controlled pleasure afforded by an enjoyment of the deviant when it is acted out, reflected upon and tamed"—the deviant maintained as deviant. Female glory asserted as a paradox. Shadow as nullity. I think it was in a bar in South America a man said to me, "By means of a box of matches you can represent everything, except a box of matches."

Remembering E. M. Forster

Santha Rama Rau

A t various times in his long life he was described as
dowdily dressed and physically awkward but with
"fine eyes . . . and a most expressive and sensitive mouth,"
and as a "very pale, delicately-built young man, slightly
towzled and very shy, with a habit of standing on one
leg and winding the other round it." Lytton Strachey
nicknamed him "the Taupe," another friend said he
looked "like a whim." A *New Yorker* reporter found "a
shy, apprehensive Edwardian gentleman with a long sensitive nose and tousled tan moustache," and Frank Hauser, who directed the first production of the play *A Passage to India*, saw a "stooping spry old buffer in a grey
tweed suit, glasses glinting, . . . the familiar rabbit-face
. . ."* He considered himself "physically ugly—red nose
enormous, round patch in middle of scalp . . . Face in the
distance [seen in the mirrors of his club] is toad-like and
pallid, with a tiny rim of hair along the top of the triangle.
My stoop must be appalling . . ."

By the time I met E. M. Forster, in 1957, I was reasonably familiar with his appearance from photographs, including the astonishing figure in Indian court dress
in *The Hill of Devi*, and paintings, notably the much-
reproduced portrait by Roger Fry. So, although he was
neither so tall nor so thin as I had supposed, I would
easily have recognized him. What I hadn't expected,
standing in his living room in King's College, Cambridge,
was the startlingly shrewd look of appraisal in the eyes
behind the steel-framed spectacles, nor the unshakable
courtesy that elevated good manners to the level of
charm. It was a curious feeling to be welcomed and
judged at the same time.

The events that led to this meeting began a couple of
years before. Cheryl Crawford, one of the founders of
the Group Theatre in New York and a producer in her
own right, remarked to me over dinner one night that
there had never been a play on Broadway either by an

* *Grand Street*, Autumn 1984.

Indian or about India. Casually, I replied that the first should be a dramatization of *A Passage to India.*

"Well, why don't you write it?" Cheryl asked.

I answered that I'd never written a play, and anyway Forster would never permit that sort of messing about with his work. But the idea nagged away at me, and I decided to try. Just as a literary exercise, I told myself. No one need know that I had had the impudence to take such liberties with one of the century's most celebrated novels. I needn't, in fact, show it to anyone, certainly not to Forster, who must be swamped with any number of far more professional adaptations.

I spent that summer absorbed in Forster's Indian landscapes—Chandrapore, Marabar, Mau; the English Club, the Indian homes, Fielding's garden house in the Government College grounds. They gave the Connecticut countryside around me an air of unreality, the deep green woods and meadows seen through the dusty heat haze of a distant Indian Hot Weather. The whole scene was improbably peopled by Forster's cast: the volatile, endearing, touchy and sometimes elegantly dignified Dr. Aziz; the old and enigmatic Mrs. Moore, a fascinator and a pivotal character; the queer, thorny and honest girl, Adela Quested, whose hallucination of attempted rape sets off the central dramatic action; Professor Godbole, funny and profound; Fielding, liberal, accessible, intelligent; and all around them, the tight English community of colonial rulers and the large number of their Indian subjects.

Predictably, when I had typed THE CURTAIN FALLS at the end of the last act of the play, I couldn't resist sending it to Forster. I drafted and redrafted a dozen versions of the covering letter assuring him that I didn't expect an immediate reply and that I wouldn't be surprised by his rejection of the whole idea of a dramatization. At that time I didn't know that Forster always answered letters and requests, particularly from writers, with extreme promptness. Within the month I received a letter from him, in an almost illegible longhand, in green ink, saying he had read my play, liked it, had a few minor changes and suggestions to make and would I consider coming to Cambridge to talk with him about them?

Dazed and incredulous, I accepted his invitation and, one spring afternoon, found myself (shaking with nerves) exchanging the usual greetings with this famous stranger. I gazed around at the comfortable, unpretentious, sometimes surprising furnishings with which he surrounded himself. Scattered about the room on any convenient surface were souvenirs of his visits to India, a coin collection, Victorian knickknacks, some lovely pieces of china, vases of flowers, an open book, letters all over the place. The pictures on the walls ranged from family portraits through landscapes I couldn't identify to a print of Picasso's "Boy Leading a Horse." A shabby sofa draped with a shawl and two armchairs faced a fireplace with an elaborate chimneypiece full of pigeonholes and niches holding copper and china plates and jars.

We sat at a table which he used as a desk set under one of the tall Gothic windows, heavy curtains pulled back, and went over my script, line by line, including stage directions. The fitful English sunlight mottled the pages and spasmodically illuminated the grandfather clock in the corner, the upright piano against the wall, the bookcase beyond it. I lost some of my nervousness when I saw that Forster was equally ill at ease; and besides, there seemed nothing to dread in his careful kindness, his hesitant voice seeming only to suggest, never to dictate, changes.

The major impression that remains with me from that afternoon is of the immutable reality that his characters, invented or not, had for him. Sometimes he demonstrated this in the alteration of a word or a gesture. In the first act, at Fielding's tea party, where I had written that Mrs. Moore "bows" when she is introduced to Professor Godbole, Forster had substituted the word "nods." "She's the kind of woman," he explained, "who would nod rather than bow—do you see?"

Sometimes his attitude made for more intractable difficulties. I asked him, for instance, for help with the character of Mrs. Moore, in many ways the most compelling figure in the book and unlike anyone I've ever met on paper. In the novel one can listen in on her thoughts, observe her intuitive understanding of India, and even share her disturbing mystical experience in the Marabar caves. But a play does not, of course, allow such literary eavesdropping and Mrs. Moore, describing the famous echo that "undermined her hold on life," has to say *out loud*, " 'Boum'—or something like that. Whatever is said, the same monotonous noise replies. 'Boum' is the sound as far as I can express it, or 'bou-oum,' or 'ou-boum' . . . utterly dull. Hope, politeness, the blowing of a nose, the squeak of a boot, all produce 'boum.' "

Now it's all very well if, on stage, the English Club members think Mrs. Moore batty, but the audience shouldn't. Even more important, they mustn't find her comic. What, I asked, should I do about this? Forster thought a moment and then said, "Mrs. Moore was always a very tiresome woman," as if that ended the matter. And for me, in a way, it did. Mrs. Moore couldn't be revised, made more coherent just because I wanted to present her through another medium. She had to remain who she was.

There were other matters on which Forster showed a remarkable grasp of stage requirements. I had described the young City Magistrate, Ronny Heaslop, to whom Adela Quested is half-engaged, as "an extremely good-looking man" rather than the "red-nosed boy" of the novel. Forster recognized at once that this was a kind of theatrical short-cut—a way of explaining why a thoughtful, somewhat unconventional but plain girl like Adela would consider marrying a hidebound stick like Ronny. In the margin of my typescript Forster had written, "Thank you for rescuing my poor Ronny." Again, when we talked at length about the structure of the play, he saw the omission of the last section of the novel, entitled *Temple*, as "inevitable." Even though, as he told me, this made his story more "melodramatic" than he had intended, clearly it was "better theater."

The exhilaration of that first meeting, and of finding that Forster liked my dramatization, was followed by months—stretching into years—of deflating experiences. He and I had signed an agreement allowing me to arrange a production and he had written to Cheryl Crawford giving my play his formal approval. Only then did I come up against the reality of Broadway economics.

Cheryl pointed out that a play needing at least twenty-five actors and four sets was somewhat less than financially feasible. Almost worse, it didn't contain a starring role that might attract a "bankable" actor. The closest thing to such a part was the young Dr. Aziz, who more or less had to be played by an Indian.

Her verdict was echoed by producers on both sides of the Atlantic. It wasn't until 1959 that I first heard from a man I had never met, Frank Hauser, director of a company I had never heard of, The Meadow Players, requesting permission to produce *A Passage to India* at the Oxford Playhouse, which I had never visited.

Meanwhile, whenever I happened to be in England, I tried to see Forster either at King's or in London if he could manage it. As he had no telephone, these arrangements often involved a heady confusion of messages left with the college porter or with London friends. One letter that I saved is dated only "Thursday." "Dear Miss "Rau" (I knew him for almost fifteen years, but we never became Morgan and Santha to each other):

> I have just returned to Cambridge to find your messages.
> This is to confirm my phone message, in return, to you:
> I will come up tomorrow (Friday) and will call on you
> at 3.0 o/c at 98 if I hear that it suits you. We *must* meet
> if it is possible, and I shall be happy to make the journey
> though I shan't come unless I am sure of finding you in.
> In haste
> Yrs sincerely
> E. M. Forster.
> I need to know your answer before 10.30. A.M. tomorrow
> (Fri), on account of train.

"98" was Lindsay House at 98 Cheyne Walk which belonged to an old friend with whom I often stayed. It is a beautiful house and Forster particularly enjoyed the view over the Thames and Battersea Bridge as we sat over tea and Fuller's walnut cake and talked about India, about new writers, about the ballet.

Disconnected moments from those meetings remain, for some reason, especially clear: Forster, in Cambridge, telling me about a concert he had recently attended, ex-

[263]

plaining that it was held in a church and the audience had been told not to applaud, shaking his head in bewilderment that no expression of delight or appreciation was appropriate in church. "Don't you think it odd to suppose that God would *mind?*" Forster flattering my young son extravagantly by offering him sherry one morning when he had nothing on hand more suitable for a little boy. Forster, in London, at a cocktail party given by my father, who was then the Governor of the Reserve Bank of India. Several of the guests were from the higher echelons of English banking, and when Forster was introduced to Sir Cameron Cobbold, the Governor of the Bank of England, almost simultaneously the two men said, "I have always wanted to meet the author of A *Passage to India,*" and "I have always wanted to meet the Governor of the Bank of England."

Frank Hauser has written that, in the winter of 1959, he and Forster discussed my dramatization and found they were "in total agreement"; rehearsals were begun. I decided not to go from New York to Oxford for the opening largely because the expense seemed unjustified for what sounded like a sort of semiprofessional university production. Forster took the endeavor more seriously. On January 10, 1960, he wrote to me from King's:

> It is wretched that you will not be either at Oxford on the 19th or here on Feb. 1st. [The opening at the Cambridge Arts Theatre] Things seem going well and I am most excited at Frank Hauser bringing an Indian back to play Aziz. [In fact, Zia Mohyeddin is Pakistani.] He has shown me his cuts: the only important one concerns Miss Quested before she goes into the Cave. I did not object to it, and hope and think you won't. My own disappointment is over the Punkah: there is not to be one in the Trial Scene, for technical reasons.

On that distant afternoon of our first meeting, Forster and I had agreed that the beautiful, almost naked Punkah-wallah, the young man who rhythmically pulls the rope to work the fan in the courtroom, was a crucial figure symbolic of an eternal India impervious to the small and transitory disturbances of Britons or Indians. It was important that the final curtain should fall on a courtroom empty except for the Punkah-wallah impassively working the fan over the deserted scene of so much emotional turmoil.

Forster also took his own contribution to that first production seriously. He had been asked to give a sort of official blessing to the venture by writing a program note. He sent me a copy and added, "hope you will think it is on the right lines." *On the right lines?* He had written:

A PASSAGE TO INDIA

I have always thought of my novels as novels, and have never written them with any other medium in view. So it is a surprise as well as a pleasure to encounter this excellent and sensitive dramatic version of *A Passage to India*. It is the work of an Indian writer of celebrity and distinction, Miss Santha Rama Rau, and naturally this has increased my pleasure and promoted my pride. Miss Rau has given up her time and her creative work in order to dramatise a novel written by a foreigner on the subject of her own country. If international generosity exists anywhere, it is here, it is here, and most warmly do I thank her.

The note went on to give some very interesting insights into his own view of a novel that had caused such a tempest of controversy when it was first published:

I began to write the novel in 1913, but the first world war intervened and it did not get published until 1924. Needless to say, it dates. The India I described has been transformed politically and greatly changed socially. I also tried to describe human beings: these may not have altered so much. Furthermore—taking my title from a poem of Walt Whitman's—I tried to indicate the human predicament in a universe which is not, so far, comprehensible to our minds. This aspect of the novel is displayed in its final chapters. It is obviously unsuitable for the stage, and Miss Rau—most rightly in my judgment—has not emphasised it, and has brought down her final curtain on the Trial Scene.

In a way I am glad that I wasn't at the first night. I don't suppose I would have written my own account. Instead I have Frank's letter which told me:

> . . . last night went off better than any of us could have hoped. It was one of those lucky nights in the theatre when everyone—audience, actors and O.M.'s—seemed to come together in a sort of delighted absorption. Mr. Forster rounded it off by the best curtain speech I've ever heard. After a most graceful, and obviously sincere, tribute to you, he congratulated the company "not only for being so good but for being so many." From then on he had the audience in the palm of his hand, and juggled them into wild applause. A happy evening.

In his admirable biography of E. M. Forster, P. N. Furbank quotes an entry from his own diary describing that night:

> After the performance M. came on the stage to make a speech, holding his arms drooping in front of him, in an odd posture: was struck by the commanding upper-middle-class voice emerging from the slightly awkward figure. He said: '. . . How good the actors were. And how pleased I was that there were so many of them. I am so used to seeing the sort of play which deals with one man and two women. They do not leave me with the feeling I have made a full theatrical meal. They are excellent in many ways, but they do not give me the impression of the multiplicity of life . . .' Talking today, he said it was absurd to say, as the *Times* review had done, that he was writing about the incompatibility of East and West. He was really concerned with the difficulty of living in the universe.

I hadn't expected that all the London critics from the daily and the Sunday newspapers, as well as the weekly magazines, would travel up to Oxford for the opening. (How could I have forgotten how famous Forster was?) Their reviews were favorable and Frank cautiously wrote that "it does not seem out of the question that the play should now travel to London."

Less than three weeks later, Frank wrote that "agents

and managements are working themselves up into an agreeable lather" bidding for West End and Broadway rights. A number of these new enthusiasts had turned down the play in the first place. But before the opening in London, the Club scene in the second act would need some rewriting. This is the occasion when the English community of Chandrapore gathers to discuss what shall be done about Miss Quested's accusation of Dr. Aziz of assault and attempted rape. "Many people," Frank reported, "felt and still feel that the English were 'caricatured.'" Something would have to be done to make these people more convincing and complex, less black and white. He added the daunting sentence, "I've talked to Mr. Forster, who says he is quite content to leave any changes to you."

Letters and fragments of dialogue, rewritten speeches and explanations flew back and forth across the Atlantic. Somehow Frank incorporated the changes into the script. Somehow he got the actors and the new lines rehearsed. After a provincial tour, *A Passage to India* opened in London in April 1960, and once again I wasn't present, though some members of my family who happened to be in London were.

On April 27 Forster wrote to me:

I went to the opening performance at the Comedy. Very splendid: everything tightened and clarified, good reception and *most* enthusiastic press. I think all must now be set fair for New York

Mrs Pundit [Mrs. Pandit, then Indian High Commissioner in London], who ignored the letter I wrote her about the Oxford performance, arrived at this one late, and informed the actors afterwards that she had advised you not to dramatise the novel! Well content with herself, she then departed. More important, I managed to have a glimpse of your mother and sister in the general confusion.

Well we are doing well. The pity is we are never together.

A letter from Frank on the same day opened deliriously with an account of the money we were making ("Monday night £300, Tuesday night £400, and the advance up from about £500 to £800 in one day"), and went on to say:

> Forster is obviously very happy about it all now: I got an enchanting letter from him after the first night blaming the management ("those commission-gatherers" he calls them) for preventing me from appearing with him on the stage. They didn't of course; I could have easily walked on if I had wanted, but it is excellent that his natural reaction should be to hold them responsible for anything that displeases him!

Things were indeed "set fair for New York." I wrote to Forster telling him that Lawrence Langner of the Theatre Guild, the American producer, was now ready to make plans for Broadway. I enclosed a letter from my nine-year-old niece, Nina, who had been the only person to count the curtain calls on the first night. His reply was my first indication of how strongly he felt about his own work and any representation or interpretation of it. (Not at all the popular picture of the self-effacing, unworldly artist.)

> Thank you so much for your letter and for "Nina's" charming one. I can't remember the curtain rising and falling all that often
> Your words are confirmed most agreeably: I have just had the papers about the New York production and will work through them tomorrow   I do hope they will let Frank Hauser produce, and as for Zia Mohyeddin—they are *MAD* if they don't have him. He *is* the part—please tell them so from me, with all the eloquence at your disposal. I think too that they ought to have Norman Wooland [who played Fielding]. For the two women parts they will probably insist on substituting actresses with names.
> Here the play goes better and better, and the College Porter has just rushed up to tell me that 'Women's Hour' says it is the only play worth seeing in London.

Even when it had been running seven months, Forster's detailed concern with the London production continued. On October 20 he wrote:

I went to see the play last week. With one exception it is greatly improved. The action is much more tense and exciting, and the weaknesses in the club-scene have been almost entirely eliminated. The exception, oddly enough, is "Fielding". Something has gone wrong with him. He shouts and he responds too quickly to his cues and is quite losing the spontaneous and dignified effect that he had at first. I cannot think what has happened—Dadie [George Rylands, Fellow of King's and Chairman of the Cambridge Arts Theatre] says that Frank ought to speak to him.

In between, it had been a cheerful and profitable spring and summer for all of us. Forster's old friend, Joe Ackerley (whom he later asked to represent him at the New York opening), wrote in August to another friend:

The first thing dear Morgan did when I met him on my return from Paris was to press another £ 200 into my hand (five-pound notes in an envelope). Shrieking with laughter he told me that he was making £ 5000 a year out of the dramatisation of A Passage to India, doing excellent business still at the Comedy.

In a way, this "excellent business" and a long London run was not really what Forster most wanted. When, late that autumn, box-office receipts began to slacken, Donald Albery, who with Tennant's was the London producer, asked us all to take cuts in royalties. Forster wrote explaining his refusal.

I have suddenly several things to say.
(i) *Congratulations.* I did so enjoy your introduction to the excerpt of the play in Time International or whatever the paper's called. [*Life International*] so readable, perceptive and generous.
(ii) *Suggestions.* I do hope you'll agree to write an introduction to the 'reading'-text which Harcourt Brace is issuing. I have written that little programme-foreword. Now I hope you'll write for the book—and at much greater length.
(iii) *Confession.* Mr. Albery here has asked me to accept half-royalties if the takings fall below a certain sum, telling me (correctly I think) that you have consented to

such an arrangement, and (incorrectly) that Frank
Hauser has also consented. I have discussed it with F.H.
and have come to a conclusion which I hope will not dis-
please you: I have refused D.A.'s request. I have done
so for two reasons [a] highminded: I dislike people wrig-
gling out of agreements, especially when they have made
pots of money [b] practical: I have no wish to prolong
the run here—the bait he offers me. The sooner it ends,
the sooner can Zia etc. get over to the States, and the
Broadway rehearsals begin.—So I hope you will not feel
displeased with my refusal.

(iv) *Confidential.* I have just had a letter from a Miss
Elizabeth Hart, whom I don't know, wanting to dramatise *Where Angels Fear to Tread* and saying that she has
been in touch with you. Before I reply, I want to get
quite clear that you have no wish to dramatise it yourself. I would prefer to wait any length of time for your
work (which I so unreservedly admire) rather than get
involved in someone else's.—Could you send me a line
about this.

[Here two lines are heavily crossed out.]
I am getting muddled; and will stop: with apologies for
so long a letter

That last sentence was the only clue he gave to the state
of his health. During that winter, P. N. Furbank records
in his biography, Forster began to feel acutely, and with
a kind of resignation, that his life was "Going to Bits." In
January 1961, he wrote in his Commonplace Book:

> This phrase describes me today and is indeed the one I
> have been looking for: not tragic, not mortal disintegra-
> tion, only a central weakness which prevents me from
> concentrating or settling down . . . I have plenty of in-
> teresting thoughts but keep losing them like the post-
> cards I have written, or like my cap . . .

About the American production of *Passage*, with all
its complications of directors, casting, Equity requirements, script changes and so on, he showed no sign
of any such "central weakness." He wanted to know
exactly what was going on and expressed strong opinions
on everything I told him. Only occasionally did he remark on a deterioration in health, sometimes obliquely,

"I am . . . on the tired side, and am clear that I shall not be coming over for the U.S. production." Sometimes he was more direct. Acknowledging a copy of a newly published book of mine, *Gifts of Passage*, he wrote:

> . . . now here come your Gifts themselves in their pleasing U.S.A. dress. I have been in hospital, and they, with their attractive mixture of recollections and rearrangements, are the very thing for a convalescent.

Sometimes he made a joke of it:

> I wish I could be there [at the New York opening] too, but much as I should like to emulate the appearance of Voltaire at Irène I think I had better not try. It is no good cracking up, even in Mrs. Kennedy's arms.

But where any aspect of the play itself was under discussion, he was crisp and to the point. Lawrence Langner decided that Frank Hauser was not well enough known in America to direct the Broadway production. Instead, he suggested Tony Richardson, whose films had a wide audience, and Donald McWhinnie, who had recently directed *The Caretaker* in New York. As Forster had foreseen, the Theatre Guild insisted on "names" for the leading roles. On October 23, 1961, he wrote:

> Here are some notes
> Donald McWhinny *not* preferred to Tony Richardson, but acceptable. I saw The Caretaker over here—an odd little affair I thought it, and not nearly as good as The Birthday Party, still what there was to direct in it went all right.
> Gladys Cooper—not really right, but I've always admired her greatly, and if she would be so good as to get herself up as dumpy as she can bear and to mug up a little mysticism or poetry she would do for Mrs. M[oore].
> E[ric] Portman preferred to R[alph] Richardson, on the whole.
> Now for our questions and comments,:—
> Who does Adela? Immensely important, I think. Please may I be informed before it is settled.
> Very important: Scenery. The Court Scene unsuccessful in the ~~London~~ the original, is said to have been most

impressive in one of the provincial shows—Bristol I
think—where the building was ~~flimy~~ flimsy, made as it
were of wattle, ~~through~~ which the tropical sunshine
~~burnt~~ pierced. And in connection with this scene
MOST IMPORTANT OF ALL
the nude beautiful punkah wallah. Without him, Mr.
Rylands says, the play must be cancelled! He can easily
be contrived—he was at Nottingham, though neither
beautiful nor nude there, and a punkah was seen working
which blew off no one's wig. Will you please impress
this on all whom it may concern.

Zia—we all repeat—is imperative and must remain so
even if poisoned by some aspiring Porto Rican.

In a halting way, things were gradually coming together
in New York. Most of Forster's requests were met, though
his choice of Mary Ure for Adela Quested was not possible under Equity rules. With so many non-Americans in
the cast, a certain proportion of the roles had to be reserved for Americans. On November 12, he wrote saying
he felt "idle and non-contributive," but continued:

The news sounds good, my only outstanding anxiety
being Adela. She is difficult and essential—strange that
her part should not be listed as "star"—though when I
come to think of it stars have no necessary connection with
parts. I have also had a nice letter from D. McWhinnie,
and hope he may manage to see me before he goes.

Then, already looking ahead to the First Night, he wrote:

. . . my friend Joe Ackerley intends to come over for the
play, and I should be glad if he could represent me so
far as is feasible. Could you secure for him the seat that
would have been assigned to me at the opening performance?—not necessarily 'the' seat, but 'a' seat and
one to the front as he is a bit deaf. He once met you with
pleasure at Lionel Fielden's, he says, and I expect you
know his play [The Prisoners of War] and his more recent 'dog' efforts [My Dog Tulip: Life with an Alsatian],
and may have heard his excellent broadcast on the Oxford production. Whether he will do any publicity for the
N.Y. one I don't know, but his determination to be present seems fixed. . . . I do wish I could come myself but

with last year's illness and next year's 83 it is obviously impossible.

Finally, with the director and casting settled, the rehearsals complete, the play opened in Boston on January 16, 1962. Directed by Donald McWhinnie, Gladys Cooper played Mrs. Moore, Eric Portman played Fielding, and a young American actress, Anne Meacham, who had received excellent notices in an off-Broadway production of *Hedda Gabler*, played Adela Quested. Zia, of course, was Aziz.

I think I tried to spare Forster the nightmare of the previews in Boston. I remember them only as the most exhausting two weeks I have ever spent. Twenty minutes of playing time had to be cut from the script to avoid paying overtime to stagehands and the theater staff. After every performance, the producers, the director and I met to discuss what more should be cut, what rewritten, what inserted. I would retreat to my hotel room and type out the changes. These would be put into rehearsal the next morning and in the evening we watched to see how they "played." And then the routine was repeated.

But K. Natwar Singh, a member of the Indian Mission to the United Nations, a friend of both Forster's and mine, had seen one of the previews and written to Forster about it. Promptly the reply came back to me with both brisk suggestions and the usual measure of generous encouragement:

Natwar kindly sends me a line about the Boston performance, and I gather that Godbole is poor. If you agree perhaps you will make representations in the relevant quarter. They would have all my support, for I'm sure that part *need* not be played by an Indian. Both in London and Nottingham I found an Englishman quite satisfactory, and there must be equally satisfactory Americans. A 'mystic' part isn't necessarily a subtle or difficult part, is it?

You must be having much excitement and I hope some pleasure. Come what may and tumble what can, (for I gather the 'mechanics' aren't right yet) you have done a marvellous piece of work for which I shall never cease to be grateful.

For January 31, 1962, the opening night on Broadway, he had promised that "I shall keep my fingers crossed," and added, "I am so delighted that you got Godbole right." But by then I was too numb to register much of what happened at the opening. I do remember the shock of seeing the posters which announced: A PASSAGE TO INDIA by SANTHA RAMA RAU and in tiny letters underneath, Based on a novel by E. M. Forster. I wrote to him the next day, mostly about the lavish after-theater party that my agent, Helen Strauss, gave, in the conventional way, at Sardi's, the delight on Zia's face when all the guests at Sardi's applauded his entrance, and his thrill when Helen assured him, after the first reviews singled him out for special praise, that now he would get star billing. On the marquee and advertisements his name would appear, like Gladys Cooper's and Eric Portman's *above* the title.

The reviews were rather better than I had expected though not the sort that would give the play the kind of success it had had in England. I thought the cuts had coarsened and weakened the play. The snatches of dialogue intended to make it more "relevant" to an American audience and inserted, at the producers' insistence, during the frantic nights of rewriting in Boston, seemed hopelessly out of tune with Forster's work. Still, we were playing to almost full houses, so both Forster and I were somewhat taken aback when, in March, the Theatre Guild asked us to consider the same sort of royalty cuts that the London producers had wanted, again in the interest of a longer run.

Forster wrote to Helen Strauss:

> I was of course surprised that when (according to all my advices) booking was so good business should be so bad. But business is a mystery into which I will not attempt to penetrate.

But Helen recommended that I agree, explaining that this was a standard arrangement in the theater. Forster, predictably, objected. On March 7, 1962, he wrote:

. . . I do wish we could meet and talk. With your greater
knowledge of America and of its stage you may well be
making the right decision, and a few minutes conversation might lead me to share it. As it is, do please write me
a little line, and I am sorry to bother you.

I have only to add that, though of course I like money,
my two chief objectives in an American production have
already been attained. In the first place New York—the
best of it—has seen your wonderful dramatisation of the
novel. In the second place Zia has gained the larger audience he so richly merits and should go forward triumphantly in the future. So I am not bluffing when I tell
Miss Strauss that, as far as I am concerned, the play can
come off at once.

However, on the advice of the Society of Authors, he
accepted a modified version of the royalty reduction, remarking sourly:

I always assumed, in my naivete, that it was the job of
one's agent to get one the best possible terms, but apparently one has sometimes to struggle for them oneself,
in the face of their opposition.

Through all these elaborate negotiations, his interest
in the play itself never slackened. He heard

. . . that the longer the play runs the more it is being
altered to meet the supposed wishes of the American
public, and that the alterations are often for the worse. I
cannot of course test this. Have you observed deterioration—apart from the inevitable deterioration that comes
from repetition? If you have, and if you think well to
protest, you will have my warmest support and thanks.

In the same letter he gave a small sample of perhaps
his most profound and best-known characteristic—the
immense and enduring importance he placed on friendship.

To turn to a very different matter—the *Passage* as you
know was dedicated to and partly inspired by my great
Moslem friend Syed Ross Masood [who died in 1937].

> Old friends of Masood, and indeed of my own, have founded an 'Urdu Hall' in Hyderabad Dn. [Deccan] to promote Urdu Culture . . .

He went on to ask, very diffidently, whether Zia or I, because of our connections both with India and the play, might care to make a small contribution to it. When I assured him that of course we would, he replied with warmth and surprise:

> How very gracious of you to consider the possibility of a small donation to that Urdu Hall. I hadn't supposed you would, and told my Hyderabad friend that I would pass the suggestion on, but thought it unreasonable. If you and Zia decide to combine in a sympathetic gesture in honour of Masood, it might be a good idea to write to him and explain why you are doing so. You can't be expected to be passionately interested in the enclosed "appeal", nor am I—: but it would have had the approval of Masood

In spite of our various accommodations, the play closed in May 1962, still—mysteriously—playing to nearly full houses.

But that was not the end of the story of Forster's embroilment in show business. From the time of the first London reviews we had been receiving offers for the film rights. Forster's unwavering position was, as he wrote to me, " 'No go,' I am afraid." This did not, in any way, halt the dozens of inquiries and pressures to allow a movie sale. In New York many of these requests came to me and mostly I managed to follow Forster's advice—"I think the simplest thing is to say 'No.' " On one occasion, though, when a representative of a major Hollywood studio telephoned offering what seemed to me a staggering sum, I hadn't the nerve to turn it down on Forster's behalf and suggested that the studio get in touch with him directly at King's College. I later heard the rest of the story from a Cambridge friend.

The studio representative telephoned Forster and, naturally, the call was received in the Porter's Lodge. The porter asked the caller to wait while he walked across the front court and up the first staircase and knocked on

Forster's door. "There's a Mr. Hollywood on the line for you, sir."

"Hollywood?" Forster said in his most innocent, donnish manner. "I don't think I know any Mr. Hollywood. You'd better tell him I'm out."

The porter returned downstairs, walked back across the courtyard to the telephone, and said, "I'm sorry, sir, Mr. Forster is out."

Even when I wrote him that Satyajit Ray wanted to film *A Passage to India*, Forster was inflexible. "I didn't and I don't want *A Passage* filmed. I am so sorry."

Strangely enough, he did not feel the same aversion to television. Forster readily gave permission to the BBC though he knew that the program would be recorded on film—or videotape. I think this was partly because he felt that the TV version would be, in essence, a film of the play, and broadly speaking, he was right. A few scenes were included—the meeting of Mrs. Moore and Aziz in the mosque, the train journey to the Marabar Hills and so on—where the TV camera gave us a wider scope than the stage allowed, but largely the TV adaptation stayed very close to the play. Another factor that made the TV arrangement attractive was that Sibyl Thorndike, whom he greatly admired, was to play Mrs. Moore. She had told him that she would have loved to perform the part in London, but had felt she was too old to be able to appear in eight performances a week. In the TV studio the work was much less exacting and she eagerly accepted the role—one of her last. Zia again played Aziz, and Cyril Cusack and Virginia McKenna were Fielding and Adela Quested.

As before, Forster took a deep interest in the casting and the production, though by then (1965) his health was uncertain and his faculties weakening. From 1961 on he had a series of falls, illnesses and strokes which eventually affected his speech, his memory and his ability to write. They were interspersed with periods of good health and moderate activity, but it was all, inevitably, on a descending scale. His attitude was expressed in a letter to his close friend, Bob Buckingham, "We must not worry about my failing powers . . . To me decay is so natural in a universe that admits growth . . ."

Forster made it hard not to share his own philosophical acceptance. There seemed to be no self-pity in his rigorous demands on himself, and never a hint of complaint in the later letters I received from him, even though they had to be written by Joe Ackerley or other friends when all he could manage was a scrawled signature—sometimes only initials—at the end.

The last letter in his own hand came in response to an article I had written about his work in a book of tributes collected and edited by K. Natwar Singh for Forster's ninety-fifth birthday on January 1, 1964.

A hasty line from the Christmas turmoil which—since this is the Welfare State—seems likely to persist eternally—to thank you for contributing to this welcome book. Reading it, I have had the feeling that you were talking with me—not 'to' nor of course 'at',—but *with.* Strictly speaking I ought to join the merry rout below and get some ink, but to persist with what I've got seems wiser. It means so much to me that Indians should still read the *Passage* and find sympathy and sense in it, and I am able too to tell you I'm glad that it is still read in Pakistan—I so appreciate Natwar's inviting Ahmed Ali. [a writer and fellow-contributor]

I so enjoyed all you write in it. And it explains to me why I so liked your play.

When you have spare time in England, please let me know, and I shall hope to see you and to come to see you. Like every one else I am older, but feel well for my age and get around in moderation.

Warmest wishes for 1964 and for the future generally and affectionate thanks,

Morgan Forster

A postscript: Helen D. Willard, Curator of the Harvard Theatre Collection in the Houghton Library at Harvard, asked me, after the play opened in New York, whether I would donate any correspondence, early or late manuscripts, programs or other material concerning *A Passage to India* to the Harvard Library. I sent her whatever I had, and asked Forster if he would do the same. He couldn't find any such material at the time and promised to search further. "My main trouble," he wrote, "is untidiness; where for instance at this very instant is my pen?"

To Miss Willard, when she approached him directly, he replied:

> . . . I fear that I have not to hand any of the documents to which you refer. I rather tend to destroy matter which does not seem to me of primary importance, and this may have happened here.
>
>   With many regrets
>   Yours very sincerely
>   E. M. Forster.

KHODASEVICH AND TRADITION

Henry Gifford

Vladislav Khodasevich was born a little more than a century ago in Moscow; he died in Paris shortly before the outbreak of the Second World War. The dates, and the places, are significant. Any Russian poet living through those years could not fail to concern himself with tradition—to experience it even as for some a matter of life and death. And for one who spent his last seventeen years in the cruel dislocation of exile, to know where he belonged as a writer and to maintain a belief in the viability of Russian culture was the next most important thing to survival in the flesh. It is more than fortuitous, one feels, that the very last fragment among the unpublished and unfinished poems in the edition of his verse by Malmstad and Hughes should end with the line: "Russian poets are wiped out."

In the second and third decades of this century, as we know, throughout Europe innovation seized all the arts. In Russia Futurism, which offered a brutal challenge to all inherited modes and conventions, allied itself, too rashly, with the forces of violent political change. Khodasevich did not lack sympathy with the Revolution, but his hostility to the Futurists was unmitigated. He could never forgive Mayakovsky for what seemed to him the betrayal of poetry in order to achieve personal domination—a charge he also laid against Bryusov, whom he had once, like many of his generation, admired as an upholder of fine craftsmanship. Khodasevich could write movingly about the last disordered phase of Esenin's life, recognizing a kind of nobility in his feeling for Russia and in the seriousness that underlay all the deliberate courting of scandal. But he could find no words of compassion for Mayakovsky's suicide. It was not merely dislike of the man: Khodasevich never lost sight of principle when making his judgment on a poet's performance. He protested rather against the mindless subversion of everything that mattered to himself. The Futurists' call to throw Pushkin

[*280*]

and Lermontov off the ship of modernity seemed an incitement to mutiny which could end only in shipwreck.

When the train carrying him in June 1922 out of Russia crossed the frontier, Khodasevich showed his companion, Nina Berberova, an unfinished poem. It speaks of his predicament as the son of a Polish father and a Jewish mother, who could not, like other émigrés, bring away a handful of native soil to remind him of his origins:

> To Russia a stepson, and to Poland—
> Who I am to Poland I don't know myself.

All the motherland he can claim is the eight volumes of Pushkin's collected works in his traveling bag. Later the poem would be concluded with the assurance:

> But wherever I am, to me will whisper
> Those hallowed African lips
> About a land of fable

—a country that lived in his imagination, with a splendor of its own. The Pushkin who vouches for it is presented as an alien like himself: the lips that speak the Russian language to such perfection are African, those of an *arap* or Negro, which is how Pushkin described his Ethiopian ancestor Gannibal, the "Negro" of Peter the Great.

The sense of being a stepson makes Khodasevich in his homelessness very much a modern poet, a spokesman of our century. Whether as internal emigrant or as the outsider who finds after all that he stands at the center of things, the stepson has seen often more clearly than the native-born. Mandelstam, like Khodasevich, had not one drop of Russian blood in his veins, but they both lived intensely in the Russian language. Khodasevich wrote a poem (completed not long before he left Russia) in grateful acknowledgment of his debt to the peasant woman from Tula who had nursed him. She it was who gave the child "her bitter motherhood," bitter since the baby he displaced did not survive the foundling hospital. With her milk he also imbibed "the tormenting right" both "to love and to curse" Russia. Pushkin, "the wonder-working genius" of Russia, he declares has been his teacher; the field

in which he performs the "honorable exploit" of writing
verse with entire dedication is the "marvelous language"
of Russia:

> And before your weakling sons
> I can moreover boast at times
> That this language, bequeathed by the ages,
> I guard more lovingly and more jealously . . .

In a prose memoir of his earliest years Khodasevich admits to the fault of impatience "which has caused a lot
of unpleasantness in my life and constantly vexes me." He
accounts for it by the fact of "having been born late," a
long way the youngest in his family, and so trying uncon-
sciously to make up for lost time. Certainly it was frustrating for him to come midway between two literary
generations. Had he taken his due place in the family immediately after the sister who preceded him, Khodasevich
would have grown up in the full flowering of Symbolism;
but instead he began writing verse when that moment had
already passed and no successor had yet appeared to the
school which gave in its time so powerful an impulse to
Russian poetry. Khodasevich was the exact contemporary
of Gumilyov, who shared his predicament; and he compares himself with the most isolated Russian poet of the
next wave, Marina Tsvetaeva, condemned, both of them,
to "remain forever solitary, 'outlandish.'" In 1933, when
he made these observations, it would have been hard to
say whether Tsvetaeva or Khodasevich faced the greater
hardship, material as well as spiritual. The kind of poetry
each wrote was almost totally different from the other's;
but their common problem had been, as he remarks, that
of having "emerged from Symbolism." In Moscow its
atmosphere had been much heavier, more suffocating,
than in the Petersburg of Gumilyov and Akhmatova.

Khodasevich reflected deeply on the effects of a Symbolist upbringing after he had left Russia. A little poem of
1927 called "The Cliff" invokes, as so often with him, a
comparison with Pushkin, who, exactly one hundred years
before in the poem "Arion," had described himself as the
singer alone surviving the shipwreck of the Decembrist in-
surrectionaries, to dry his wet garment in the sun beneath

the cliff. Khodasevich likewise surveys the disaster of a generation:

> For you I have not a word,
>   Not a sound in my heart,
> Poor visions of the past,
>   Friends of the vanished years!
>
> Perhaps I have died, perhaps
>   I was cast up into a new age,
> While the one we lived together
>   Was only the coursing of the waves,
>
> And I, dashed on the rocks,
>   Am bloodied yet alive,
> And from afar I see
>   How the ebb bears you away.

Actually he had already found words to write of one friend, Muni, his closest in early years, who had been destroyed by Symbolism, and he would very soon record the wretched story of another victim, Nina Petrovskaya, which he placed at the head of the collection of literary memoirs called by him *Necropolis*. In the preface to this book, Khodasevich affirms that everything he has to tell about these writers, all known to him but now dead, is founded on what he has seen for himself. His account of Nina Petrovskaya, shamefully treated by Bely and by Bryusov, yet even so her own worst enemy, is unsparing but compassionate, in the manner of Samuel Johnson's *Life of Savage*. Savage and Petrovskaya were both victims of their situation and of themselves.

Khodasevich says elsewhere that to have lived "in the Symbolist dimension" was to have participated in "a real case of collective creation." It left an indelible mark on all who had passed through that experience. The great "truth" of Symbolism, which he defines as the endeavor to merge art and life, was also in his view its great "sin." He could see a certain heroism in the attempt to make art "a kind of philosopher's stone." But the result was too often a failure of the art, since some of the energy leaked into the poet's life—he compares it with poorly insulated electricity— and the "talent for living" was prized as much as the "talent for writing." However, the living itself became strangely unreal and ecstatic; it could never be experienced as having significance in its own right, but was changed by entering the "symbolic dimension."

He admits that art and life are not divisible: this is for him an "eternal truth, experienced by Symbolism in the most profound and vivid way." It led to the great error, the heresy that destroyed many of its followers. Symbolism in Russia demanded that those who joined the order (for such Khodasevich insists it was) should burn with an unceasing frenzied fire. All that mattered was to be possessed, no matter whether by good or evil in conventional terms. The artist turned into an actor. "They knew they were acting; but the play became life. The reckoning was not theatrical."

K hodasevich saw very clearly the decadent aspect of Symbolism, particularly in some of the precepts formulated by its leading exponents Balmont and Bryusov, in the first, self-proclaimed "decadent" phase. There was indeed "a poison in the blood" from which not one of the Symbolists was wholly immune. He recalls too how immensely complicated was the world he and Muni had to adjust themselves to in the oppressive and storm-laden atmosphere of Moscow Symbolism. Very early in his career he came to know Andrey Bely, of whom Mandelstam was to record that no other writer in Russia before the Revolution had been more agitated and troubled by premonitions. "I by no means shared all Bely's views," Khodasevich said, "but he influenced me more strongly than anybody I have known." Khodasevich had to find his own way out of the "forest of symbols." The wonder is that, having been so deeply involved with the movement, he was yet able, as his very sensitive critic Weidlé has said, to purge Symbolism of its luxuriance and pretentiousness, and sometimes its latent disbelief, and to live through its theme as his own, "in its truth, actually and not in words."

Writing on the centenary of *Pan Tadeusz* in 1934, he tells of an experience that came even before his "irreversible russification" at the kindergarten. Khodasevich's mother, a Catholic convert who outdid any Polish patriot in romantic devotion to her husband's country, made him say his prayers in Polish every morning. Then she would talk to him about Poland, and sometimes read him the opening lines of Mickiewicz's poem, always breaking down at the same point where the hero alights from the carriage joyfully at his old home. The little boy sensed that Mickiewicz was somehow different from poets like Pushkin, Lermontov, Maykov (the first poet he actually met, reciting one of Maykov's own lyrics to him), and Fet. This was a different thing altogether, "not just poetry" which you must try to understand, but "somehow indissolubly linked with prayer and Poland," and with the Catholic chapel they attended in Moscow. Mickiewicz and Poland were invisible like God, and they dwelt with God, "behind the low grille, upholstered in red velvet, in the thunder of the organ, the fume of incense and the golden brilliance of the sun's slanting rays that fell on the altar." The altar itself was the "vestibule" to another world, in which he had once been, and to which he would return.

Khodasevich calls these "the confused imaginings of a child." He could have received no more solemn a preparation for making Symbolism his own theme. But, unlike his seniors Bely and Blok, he did not apparently take much note of Vladimir Solovyov, even though he read Solovyov's *Three Meetings* at the age of sixteen. Khodasevich, as he insisted, was always a solitary, and his interests were not those of the day. He tells us that he came "to art in general and to poetry in particular" by way of the ballet. "Ballet exerted a decisive influence upon my whole life, and on the later formation of my tastes, passions, interests." As a young boy he became expert in "all the subtleties" of "an exquisite art." It has been noticed that Gumilyov, always a perceptive critic of verse, wrote in 1914 about Khodasevich's second volume, *The Happy Little House*:

> The reader's attention follows the poet easily, as though in a flowing dance . . . as yet he is only a ballet-master, but the dances he teaches are sacred dances.

The control and ease of movement Khodasevich had appreciated in ballet were exemplified for him in poetry by one of his early models, the late-eighteenth-century verse fabulist Dimitriev. This pallid precursor of Krylov was the ally of Karamzin in imparting a Gallic urbanity and precision to Russian writing. Those qualities appealed very strongly to Khodasevich, who was to claim many years later that he had been able (though with difficulty) to "graft the classical rose / On the Soviet wilding." In his essay on Dimitriev (1937) he shows a full awareness of the limitations in Dimitriev and Karamzin. At its conclusion he quotes a letter of Pushkin's: "I don't like to see in our primordial language traces of European affectation and French refinement. Rudeness and simplicity suit it better."

That Khodasevich had learned the same lesson for himself is attested by a comment of Mandelstam's in an essay of 1923. By this time Khodasevich had published the two volumes of verse in which he demonstrates his maturity and independence as a poet, *The Grain's Way* and *The Heavy Lyre*. Mandelstam observes that "Khodasevich brought into the 20th century the intricacy and caressing rudeness of the common people's Moscow speech, as it was used by literary circles of the landed gentry in the last century." He placed Khodasevich in a line that descended from "the best period of Russian poetical dilettantism, from the family album, the verse epistle to friends, the epigram of everyday life." One such "amateur poet" mentioned by him is Countess Rostopchina, about whom Khodasevich wrote a long essay in 1908, the same year in which he published his own rather weak first volume of poetry, *Youth*. Rostopchina, like Pushkin's friends Baron Delvig and Prince Vyazemsky, all of them aristocrats who wrote engaging verse, had varying degrees of talent which Khodasevich estimated exactly. In the final reckoning they may be termed dilettantes, whereas Baratynsky in the same period shows an original force and penetration beyond theirs. Khodasevich's innate seriousness did not interfere with his pleasure in the simplicity and even the banality of Rostopchina. They were all the more to be appreciated, he said, "in our days, deliberately complex, living spiritually beyond their means . . ." The Symbolist "poison" was virulent in 1908. Much later a poem of his would recall that seeing the turbid waters of Byron's and Pushkin's romantic Brenta in 1911 made him prefer "prose in life and in verses." What Mandelstam overlooks in his

essay where he describes Khodasevich as a minor poet of
real distinction is the actual importance to him of Pushkin.
Khodasevich was of course fascinated by Pushkin's milieu.
To his friend Sadovskoy, whose political views had come
to oppose his own, Khodasevich insisted that they would
always be in a sense citizens of the same country, quoting
the line from Pushkin: "Our fatherland is Tsarskoe Selo."
The palaces and gardens of Tsarskoe Selo are inseparable
from the presiding image of Pushkin. It was above all, and
unquestionably, a lifetime of minute attention to Pushkin's
work that enabled Khodasevich to stand on his own as a
major poet and (in his own phrase) to be an "enduring
link" between the past and a possible future.

He also came to admire Pushkin's rugged and majestic
predecessor, Derzhavin, whose formality combined so
easily with outspokenness and a home-loving innocence.
Derzhavin had been fortunate in living at a time when
cultural and poetic activity meant "a *direct* participation
in building the state." Khodasevich suggests an interesting
parallel between him and Suvorov (each of whom dedicated verses to the other). It happens that he had to write
on the twenty-fifth anniversary of Chekhov's death when
deeply immersed in preparing his biography of Derzhavin.
He compared the two wholly to the advantage of Derzhavin, who had lived in an age that was "constructive,
harmonious, for all its polyphony," and he believed that if
Russia were to arise once again it would find more inspiration in the strenuous Derzhavin than in the contem-
plative and resigned Chekhov. This view was expressed in
1929. By then Khodasevich had known all the frustrations
of exile. To contemplate the vigor and hopefulness of
Catherine's age, and also the sturdiness of Derzhavin in
his vicissitudes, must have been the one tonic available.

It took Khodasevich a decade of feeling his way for
mastery increasingly to show in the years after 1914.
This he recognized when publishing in 1927 his *Collected
Poems* which omitted the two volumes of 1908 and 1914.
By the latter year Symbolism was in marked decline; the
Futurists had stormed onto the stage; and Gumilyov was
leading the alternative movement of Acmeism, which
Khodasevich viewed with less sympathy than might have

been expected, since it favored measure and clarity, and, in Mandelstam's view, restored a moral dimension to verse. But Khodasevich seems to have judged it by Gumilyov, whom he regarded as never having freed himself from the influence of Bryusov, and as being essentially an unpoetic person. Whereas Blok "was a poet always, in every minute of his life," Gumilyov, he said, "was one only when writing verse." Khodasevich belonged to no school, and had few supporters. Muni until he died in 1916 offered extremely severe criticism of his poetry, and was succeeded by a judge no less candid, the Pushkin scholar Gershenzon. "His criticism was always well-disposed—and without mercy." But Khodasevich's achievement depended largely on himself.

It was recognized in an unexpected quarter by Bely, who reviewed *The Heavy Lyre* in 1922 under the title "Rembrandtesque Truth in the Poetry of Our Days." What he admired in Khodasevich's work was its ability to catch the only truth possible in a time "when everything . . . has disintegrated (the earth does not nourish, nor the soul intoxicate)"—a truth that consists in "spirituality, and sobriety, and sternness, and precision."

There could be no better account of Khodasevich's quality. Bely adds to it the observation that like Baratynsky's Muse, Khodasevich's also startles by "the unusual expression of her face," as Baratynsky put it. Khodasevich does indeed often grimace in his poetry; he can be caustic and savage with a sudden twist of the knife; but, as he maintained in a poem of 1923 that expresses his poetics,

> I walk among my verses
> Like a strict abbot
> Among the subdued monks . . .
>
> Given to me from generation to generation
> I love my human language:
> Its stern freedom,
> Its flexible law . . .

The language was "human," unlike *zaum'*, the trans-sense idiom of the Futurists, appropriate he thought only to angels or brutes. In the interplay of freedom and regularity, it embodies that literary conservatism which he refused to identify with reaction. The literary conservative he describes as "a perpetual arsonist: the keeper of the fire, not its extinguisher."

In *The Grain's Way*, and more pronouncedly still in *The Heavy Lyre*, it is clear that Khodasevich remains true to the Symbolist vision. But his belief in a transcendent order is balanced by a steady apprehension of the natural world in all its uncompromising and often oppressive reality. His strong sense allies him with Pushkin and Pushkin's predecessors in the eighteenth century.

The Grain's Way, though written against a background of increasing hardship and illness, is deliberate in its affirmation of hope. The poem he set at the beginning, from the last week of 1917, proclaims that his soul, and the people itself, since they must go through darkness, do so to revive like the grain that must perish to yield fruit. The final poem, written a few months later, when shortages must already have been presaging the near-famine conditions of the next years, celebrates the baking of bread, with cherubs assisting, as they shed an occasional feather upon the glowing domestic scene. In another poem of the same year he says that "the mute growth of the grain / Fills the soul with a sweet fullness." This was not to be the characteristic note of Khodasevich in his hard-pressed later years.

The most interesting poems in *The Grain's Way* are five blank-verse narratives in five-foot iambic lines occasionally lengthened or broken off. It is a meter derived from Pushkin's poem on his return in 1835 to Mikhailovskoe, his place of exile ten years before. Pushkin almost certainly appropriated it from Wordsworth; the calm meditative movement is evocative of those eighteenth-century poems of solitary thought that Wordsworth built upon. All but one of Khodasevich's pieces has at its center an epiphany; and the shadowy connection with Wordsworth enables us to see a quality in Khodasevich that separates him from the Symbolists. Like Wordsworth, he seeks to establish the exact circumstances in which his revelation came to him. Pushkin provides the bridge between them, with his capacity, noted by Khodasevich, to render things in their "fullness of being," with the palpability and many aspects, as he says, of "objects in the real world."

The first of Khodasevich's narratives, "Episode," describes the strange experience known to anthroposophists as "separation of the ethereal body." It happened—and Khodasevich is scrupulous in giving the details—"on one of those despondent, wintry, blizzard-swept mornings" of 1915 (a tactical disguise for the real date, 1918), and the poet, staring blankly at the bookshelf, the yellow wallpaper, the mask of Pushkin with closed eyes, and hearing the cries of children outside, is detached from his body—below on the sofa, "with a cigarette gone out between the fingers, / Altogether thin and pale." It is a moment of extraordinary calm and well-being, only to be succeeded by the hard struggle to enter his body again, like a snake resuming its cast-off skin.

The next of the poems, "November the Second," describes the aftermath of the Bolshevik seizure of power in Moscow.

> Seven days and seven nights Moscow tossed
> In fire, in delirium. But the rough doctor freely
> Bled her, and, weakened on the morning
> Of the eighth day, she came to.

It is noteworthy that the image is drawn from *The Bronze Horseman* in which the disastrous flood of 1824 in Petersburg is similarly described:

> The Neva tossed like a sick man
> In his uneasy bed.

This, by the way, is one of Khodasevich's very few poems that deal directly with public events, although their pressure can be felt in at least two of the other blank-verse narratives. In "The Monkey," where this animal's touching gratitude for a drink of water revives in Khodasevich a mystical awareness of life in its legendary past fullness, the closing line casually remarks:

> On that day war was declared.

And the last of the series, about a ruined house, refers to times "When war, or widespread death, or revolt / Suddenly swoop down and shake the earth."

In "November the Second" the scene of havoc, when

the anxious inhabitants emerge like rats after a storm, is depicted with a stark vividness. But all this leads up to the epiphany. A pair of doves are released from a basket, and among the watchers a small boy looks on entranced:

> And hears in himself the beating of the heart,
> The movement of juices, growth . . . In Moscow
> —Suffering, torn apart and fallen—
> Like a small idol he sat, indifferent,
> With a senseless and beatific smile.

And Khodasevich bows to him, in recognition of his right to happiness.

The Heavy Lyre opens with the last completed poem by Khodasevich in this measure. It is entitled "Music," and is carefully set against the concluding poem of the book, "Ballad," in which the music of poetic creation descends upon the narrator rocking in his chair under the sun of an electric light bulb. The first poem begins with a calm morning after a snowstorm. The poet and his matter-of-fact neighbor are chopping wood in the yard. The vapors in the sky resemble "wings of gigantic angels," and this prompts the poet to ask his neighbor if he cannot hear the music, which is later defined as that of a cello and, it may be, harps in the sky. Sergey Ivanych, straining but baffled, grudgingly concedes that it could be the funeral of a military man. At last he is spared further teasing and they resume their work:

> But the sky
> Is lofty as before, and still up there
> The feathered angels are shining.

Bely had admired in another poem of this book particularly its concluding line—"The almost liberated soul." "In the word 'almost,'" he said, ". . . is the essence of Khodasevich's poetry." In it lay "the magical beauty of truth" in the stanza he quoted. "Music" is a poem that deliberately hovers between fantasy and conviction. Sergey Ivanych is being gently mocked. But he also represents the philistine who cannot share the poet's vision; and these last two and a half lines of the poem seem to validate, or better, they "almost" validate, the reality of the "unheard symphony."

A small group of poems early in *The Heavy Lyre* is devoted to Psyche, the poet's soul, or creative being, which exists in the height with no relation whatsoever to the sufferings of the man on earth, from which it even shrinks away. His editors note that elsewhere he had equated Psyche with Blok's Beautiful Lady, and there are allusions in these poems to Tyutchev, and to the Symbolist poet Sologub. Another poem of the same year, "Elegy," which describes the soul as "my exiled one" entering her "native, ancient abode," states that

> . . . for ever she has no need
> Of him who under slanting rain
> In the alleys of Kronverksky park
> Roams in his paltriness.

Nichtozhestvo, "nullity" or "paltriness," recalls Pushkin's famous account of the poet, in a lyric of that name. Until Apollo summons him, "among the paltry children of the world / Perhaps he is the most paltry of them all."

Apollo (and not, as the editors point out, the frenzied Dionysus) summoned Khodasevich to become an Orpheus in the much admired "Ballad," the poem of 1921 that sealed his reputation. It delineates the creative process in the same way as Pushkin did in his poem "Autumn." "Ballad" gives incontrovertible evidence that Khodasevich had not abandoned the Symbolist vision. Bely, Blok and even Bryusov are presences in its background; there is allusion to Pushkin's "The Prophet," which exalts the poet as seer in a way taken up by the Symbolists; and the measure is from their forerunner Tyutchev's "Sleep at Sea." But again the circumstances are given in their banality, the plaster ceiling in his round room for the sky, a sixteen-candle-power electric light as the sun, the table, chair and bed, those "wretched things" of his that are caught up in the dance, as he transcends, "grows out above," himself, rising from a condition of death to find his feet "in the flame below ground," his head "in the coursing stars." It is a celebration of the poetic word in all its glory, its power to transform:

> And there is no plaster sky
> Or sixteen-candle sun;
> On the smooth black steps
> Orpheus has set his feet.

There is, of course, a darker side to this collection, or the title *The Heavy Lyre* would have lost some of its resonance. A poem from the same year, "The Motorcar," contrasts the white wings of the car's headlights in the darkness with the black wings projected by another, demonic vehicle that appears to him by day:

> I forget, I lose
> My radiant Psyche,
> I stretch out blind hands,
> And I know nothing:
>
> Here stood a world, simple and whole,
> But ever since *he* rode this way
> In the soul and the world are blanks,
> As if acid had been spilt there.

The acid, which had long been latent in Khodasevich, corrodes more powerfully in his final volume, *European Night*. He had undergone the same hardships as others in Moscow during the civil war. Though he accepted the Revolution, if only because it seemed to promise the cleansing of philistinism (which came back as grossly as ever under the New Economic Policy), he found working with the authorities in the cultural field deeply frustrating, though with its ludicrous aspects. Finally on Gorky's advice he escaped from hunger and officialdom at the end of 1920 to the much less regulated Petersburg. The period throughout 1921 and early 1922 until his decision to go abroad in the latter year was propitious, as never before, to Khodasevich's work. The city was half-deserted and silent; it had the same tragic beauty that Joseph Brodsky would encounter there after the ravages of the Second World War. "The combination," Khodasevich says, "of this inner freedom with the harsh tragicalness of surrounding life gave to art a keen, even tormenting but still powerful impulse . . . those to whose lot there fell the bitter happiness of living then in Petersburg knew that in spite of everything—it was happiness." In the "Russian" Berlin of 1922–23, in the Russian colony of a Parisian working-class suburb thereafter, he would find little that could be called even a bitter happiness.

Berlin, styled by him in one poem "stepmother of Russian cities," then packed with more than a hundred thousand of his fellow countrymen, made an unfortunate prelude to the years of emigration. In this transit camp of ponderous stone, where many were unsure whether they would stay or return, his first impressions of the émigrés he met were discouraging. To a friend he wrote: "You would want to sing the 'Internationale' here for days on end." He was disgusted to find that the crass materialism of NEP Russia had become rampant here too. Maxim Gorky, with whom his relations were very much those of a family friend, shared with him in the enterprise of editing a journal *Beseda* to which both émigrés and writers at home could contribute; it was finally sabotaged by the Soviet government. After some rather desperate traveling round western Europe and some months at Gorky's villa in Sorrento, Khodasevich and Berberova settled in Paris, to a life of constant poverty and a diminishing future for his own art.

The émigré journals and newspapers were largely in the hands of public figures who were not interested in poetry; and soon all the activity of the Russian press and publishing houses began to fall off. Nowhere could he find that quickening of the pulse of life which had been so evident in Petersburg. There the shock of the Revolution, the dangers and uncertainties that followed, had brought about a new seriousness in the public, a concern to find out in what ways literature could help them. Émigré Paris had nothing of this. It was oriented towards the irrecoverable past; the writers with established reputations merely repeated themselves; the young writers had little encouragement from them and gradually became demoralized. Khodasevich complained that Russian literature in the emigration had failed, because it never recognized its mission. In 1933, when the "European night" had noticeably drawn nearer, he gave this explanation of the failure: "It [the literature of the emigration] has not known how to experience in full depth its own tragedy, as though seeking shelter amid catastrophe. . . ." And the outcome had been "complacency, the spirit of philistinism."

He lived the tragedy as best he could in his poetry, but this grew more bitter, more desperate, and gradually the ability to write it began to fail him. A particularly bleak little poem of 1927 reveals his weariness of spirit:

> Through the foul wet winter's day—
> He has a case, she a bag—
>
> Over the parquet of Paris puddles
> They hobble along, man and wife.
>
> I paced after them on and on,
> And they came to the railroad station.
> The wife was silent, and silent the man.
>
> And of what could they speak, my friend?
> She had a bag, he had a case.
> Heel clattered with heel.

In the February before he left Petersburg, Khodasevich had taken part in an anniversary celebration of Pushkin. His speech was as notable as the famous one given by Blok at this time on the necessity for writers to enjoy that "peace and freedom" longed for by Pushkin. Khodasevich's concern was different. He feared that the moment had approached when Pushkin would cease to be for a new generation the intimate presence that he was for Khodasevich and some of his contemporaries. The young, who had lived through "the din of the last six years," he said, "have become slightly hard of hearing." The nuances of Pushkin, his allusions, were lost upon them as mere archaisms. Nor could they feel that sense of nearness to him, that tenderness for Pushkin, which Khodasevich's generation had felt.

There was one triumph demonstrating his own power to close that gap in *European Night*—a poem of one hundred eighty or so lines entitled "Sorrento Photographs." During his stay at Sorrento, Khodasevich often rode round the coast in the sidecar of a motorcycle belonging to Gorky's son Maxim. The latter appears to have been an eager but inexpert photographer who imposed one scene accidentally on another. And this is the technique Khodasevich allows memory to use in his poem. Pacing a hillside near Amalfi, he "stumbles on a foreign stone," while he visualizes the funeral in Moscow of a floor-polisher. The women carrying his coffin seem to walk through the prickly agaves; the dead man's "curly forehead / floats through the blue air" of Italy. Then the poet and Maxim are away in the motorcycle; it zigzags into Sorrento, where they witness at night a procession carrying an image of the Virgin in Holy Week, and she is borne past, with a lace handkerchief in her waxen hand, but no tears on her serene face. In a final episode, as the motorcycle rattles on above the bay of Castellammare, he sees there the vision on a November dawn of the Fortress of Peter and Paul overturned in the waters. And in all this Italian landscape we are not allowed to forget the dominance of Vesuvius, which had once destroyed Pompeii and arrested its civilization.

In this sustained and vivacious poem, which has adopted the brisk iambics and the rhyme scheme of Pushkin's narrative verse, Khodasevich manages to hold two worlds in interplay—a thing he had always been aiming at in his best previous work. But here the complexities are greater, the facets more various, as in Pushkin's poetry. The lightness and flexibility of "Sorrento Photographs" are a gift to him from Pushkin; but the voice in the poem is at once familiar and new, that of a poet who keeps faith with the past but lives in the present. Khodasevich is not an archaizer, a brilliant hand at pastiche; he can still be innovative even in his preference for the forms of Pushkin's day; his idiom is true to himself, spare and sensitive.

Khodasevich achieved no more on those lines. The next year he wrote his own epitaph, with a title that derives from Pushkin and Derzhavin, "The Monument":

> In me is the end, in me the beginning.
> So little was accomplished by me!
> But still I am an enduring link;
> To me that happiness has been given.
>
> In a Russia new but great
> They will set up my image double-faced
> At the intersection of two roads,
> Where there is time, the wind and sand . . .

Time was cruel to Khodasevich; it took away most things he held dear. The wind that raged in the Petersburg of

Blok's vision in *The Twelve* has been blowing ever since; the sand of the desert is creeping up on our civilization. Khodasevich had another twelve painful years to live after writing that poem. He could see no future for Russian literature in its divided state; there seemed to be no impulse left for his own poetry. But his work as critic and as it were moralist of culture, in his major writings on Pushkin and Derzhavin, in the memoirs gathered in *Necropolis*, in countless essays and reviews, most of them still to be collected, make him in another way an "enduring link." He is among the very best Russian critics of his age, comparable, despite all the differences, with Mandelstam. It is astonishing to see how well placed he was to feel the pulse of the time. He wrote, as nobody else has so discerningly, on Maxim Gorky; he had an understanding of Bely in all his contradictions which delighted Tsvetaeva, who also wrote finely on this poet; he happened to meet Blok only a few months before his death, and to spend an hour and a half with him in revealing talk; he once walked round the streets at night in surprising harmony with Esenin. Khodasevich was always on the alert for the essential truth in a man, as he had found it in the admirable Gershenzon; and without any attempt to idealize, he often recognized this in Russian writers. Gorky's self-deceptions were not lost upon him, but he discovered that this jealous guardian of his own legend—Khodasevich calls him "a consistent hater of the truth"—wanted no false praise of his writing, which he knew to have many weaknesses. Here, Khodasevich says, "he sought manfully for the truth."

In his poem about Elena Kuzina, his nurse, Khodasevich described his continual service to poetry as an "honorable feat." Of his vigilance in this endeavor, the extreme sensitivity to any kind of falsehood or self-seeking in writers, Weidlé in particular has spoken. This passion for the literature of his country, meaning Tsarskoe Selo and all that stemmed from it, never died in Khodasevich. His own verse faltered, and virtually came to an end. But not entirely. His last completed (or nearly completed) poem, written in 1938 to celebrate the classical four-footed iambic line, affirms it to be "stronger than all the fortresses of Russia." It is rash to conclude that, because the first wave of emigration was scattered, and Khodasevich fell silent, his career proves no more than the penalties of exile, or of a crippling aversion to the dominant trend of his time, the modernist movement in poetry. The progress of any art depends more than is often recognized on revivals. Poets are unpredictable in their liking for predecessors whom to-day's fashion has overlooked, and from whom they make a fresh beginning. There may yet be discoveries for them in Khodasevich.

My Short Life with Seferis

Kostas Taktsis

The summer of 1954—a very important year for me—I printed at my own expense a small group of poems entitled *Symphony at the Brazilian Café*. The cover was designed with excessive good will by the painter Tsarouhis. The idea for it was my own, but he chose the type and the angel lamenting under a weeping willow on the back cover. It was an announcement of death. My most arrogant intention was to suggest the death of poetry in general, but it really referred to the death of my own poetry, which in any case was stillborn. Tsarouhis was already quite well known by then and much admired, and I was naive enough to believe that his underwriting my poetic gesture would in some way give it authority, legalize it. The delusions I generally nurtured at the time made my reentry into reality that much more painful. The public was shocked by the poems. The bookstores refused to accept any copies. One or two dismissed me rudely (even though they don't know it, I've never forgiven them). Also, people in our small circle to whom I tried to give a copy would pick it up like a live coal or a snake, then touch wood and cross themselves. With a few exceptions they all thought I was crazy, and Tsarouhis seemed quite pleased. This is the way I look at it now: at that time I lived in constant rapture, and the fact that people were scandalized by something I thought very natural and innocent was simply a great mystery to me.

I can't say how people who didn't know me personally reacted as they took my collection of poems out of the manila envelope. At least the late Embirikos invited me to his home and made me read all the poems into a tape recorder. Three or four others, Penzikis among them, sent very warm letters. I also received some conventional thank-you notes. From Seferis, who was then ambassador to Beirut, I received neither a letter nor a card. The omission on the part of a man who was Greece's greatest living poet after Sikelianos's death made me quite bitter, and maybe it speeded up, just a tiny bit, the decision I made

[299]

two years later—and what a good decision that was—
never to write poetry again. Anyway, from that time on, I
felt an irrational aversion both to Seferis personally—
whom I didn't know—and to his poetry, which I knew
rather superficially and didn't like. Besides, a little later I
cut every link with poetry, at least in the strictest sense of
the word, and left Greece—forever, I thought. Seferis
didn't interest me any more; I forgot him, or anyway believed I had.

During a Sunday afternoon in the fall of 1959—spring
in the Southern Hemisphere—I was sitting in the
garden of my house in Australia under the blooming jaca-
randa with a friend who is now the director of the greatest
museum of art in that country, and we were reading. I was
reading a book on Mithra and how that religion almost
became the official one of the Roman state instead of Christianity. He was reading an American art magazine. At
one point he said: "There's something here that will interest you," and he gave me the magazine. Heading the
page was a photograph of Seferis. He was sitting stooped
in front of the broken reliefs on the stage of the Dionysus
theater in Athens, and was looking dreamily at a wild
flower that he held between his fingers. An English translation by Rex Warner of "Memory I" from *Log Book III*
followed. I couldn't remember the original at all, and the
translation didn't say much to me. But I was startled. My
feelings were mixed. I was proud that the radiance of a
Greek poet reached as far as that end of the world and
that he was read by an Australian, even though he was a
poet who had "rejected" me. At the same time, my obligation to recognize that Greek poetry was still alive after
the "funeral" I had administered to it was a double wound
to my overblown ego. But it was also a bugle call. So life
was still going on over there—without me! I must give up
my sloth and my loose living, I thought, and sit down to
write. I returned the magazine to Daniel. "What do you
think of him?" I asked. Daniel was a graduate of Oxford,
unusually cultured even for a European. "It's a translation," he said, shrugging. "I don't know what it's like in
Greek, but it's a good poem." I made a face and returned
to my book about Mithra and Mithraism, but I couldn't

concentrate. That same night I wrote to Athens and had all my Seferis books sent to me.

So, about ten days later, I was reading him carefully for the first time, and I was forced to swallow my pride and confess that some of the poems were very good. Cavafy was great, but after all he wasn't the only great Greek poet. At that moment I needed to get in contact with the whole of Greece, even with those parts of it that didn't suit my temperament, and it was that Greece which I now found in Seferis. I read—in Greek this time—the marvelous "Memory I," so full of Cyprus, so bitterly full of Cyprus those dreadful days:

> So I continued along the dark path
> and turned into my garden and dug and buried the reed
> and again I whispered: some morning the resurrection
>   will come,
> dawn's light will blossom red as trees glow in spring,
> the sea will be born again, and the wave will again
>   fling forth Aphrodite.
> We are the seed that dies. And I entered my empty
>   house. *

Suddenly I felt the deep nostalgia for Greece that had secretly been burning inside me for some time now—like a hand that gets hold of you and pulls you with fierce strength. At that time (it isn't totally true that I was being slothful) I was trying desperately to give shape to my book *The Third Wedding*, and the thing was resisting me. I attributed this to my three-year absence from Greece: "I've forgotten my Greek," I thought, "I can't write any more." Seferis confirmed my fears and livened the great need I had to return to my roots, my country, my language. That's why, later, I was able to understand and share the feeling of asphyxiation that must have been felt during the seven-year dictatorship by those of our writers who found themselves cut off from their country. I too felt that asphyxiation, but with a difference: I could get into a plane whenever I chose to and return to Greece. In theory, of course. Because practically it wasn't so easy. I would have

---

* Translations of Seferis's poetry are from *Collected Poems*, trans. Edmund Keeley and Philip Sherrard (Princeton).

had to spend the savings of three years for a simple spiritual journey. It was a great decision to make and I never
had the coolness needed to make great decisions. Every
time I had to, some external factor was needed to force me
to decide what I couldn't decide on my own. And if one
is naturally impatient when one has to wait a long time for
this external factor, one makes sure to bring it on. More to
the point, one lets one's subconscious take care of it. This
was pretty much how I found myself back in Athens in the
spring of 1960.

It seemed to me I was seeing it for the first time, and
through Athens, I was clearly seeing all of Greece and
all the Greeks: without prejudice, or malice, only with
love. And I fell into ecstasy. Whatever it was that had
been preventing me from writing for so long disappeared.
I tore up the innumerable pages that had accumulated for
four years and started my novel again the way it is now.
For this, as well as for my escape three years earlier, Seferis was responsible without knowing it. I see it now as
a blessed coincidence. But at that time I still did not know
him personally, I still imagined him as my friend Nanos
Valaoritis had described him to me. Nanos, together with
Bernard Spencer and Lawrence Durrell, had been the first
to translate Seferis's poems into English (*The King of
Asine and Other Poems*, London, 1948). When Seferis won
the Nobel Prize, Nanos felt that he too had contributed a
little to it and that nobody recognized this, and he wasn't
totally wrong. Strangely enough, when the time came for
me to meet Seferis, Nanos was the first to introduce me
to the poet. It was the winter of 1965, a short while after
Eliot's death. The British Council had organized an evening to commemorate him, a small requiem. Seferis was
to take part. It was the first time I would see him in the
flesh, and my curiosity was understandably strong. An
Englishman and a Frenchman spoke about the life and
work of Eliot. Seferis read a passage from *Murder in the
Cathedral* that he had translated earlier. His voice was
deep and masculine, warm and musical; he spoke with a
very slight lisp. It's true that he read somewhat monot-
onously, but this made the reading more suggestive. I
studied him, listened to him totally absorbed, and God

[*302*]

knows, I'm not one of those who are easily impressed. At one point I whispered to Nanos, who was sitting next to me: "But he's very good!" Nanos made a face as though to say: mm, he has his good points. A little later, on the fifth floor where we had been invited for drinks, Nanos came over and pulled me away from a lady I was gossiping with and guided me to Seferis triumphantly, like a trophy: "Here he is!" Seferis looked at me as though something in my appearance amused him, as though he wasn't expecting me to look the way I did. "*Bré!*" he said. "Are you Taktsis?" I nodded stupidly. "Do you know," he said, "that I'm an admirer of yours?" My heart beat fast. His words went to my head like strong wine. So my efforts had not gone completely wasted. . . . What could I say? "Me too," I stammered, "me too . . ."—and nobody could tell whether I was returning the compliment or was being perverse: Did I too admire him or did I too admire myself? Seferis waited patiently for me to go on, but I was dumbfounded, I'd swallowed my tongue. Then he turned toward an Englishman who had approached him very discreetly, with awe, and I was left alone, flooded by guilt feelings, which somehow had always been for me the unique source of whatever love I ever felt for a person, a love that very often came too late for me to tell and for that person to want or be able to hear me tell.

A few months later he sent me, via Nanos, his *Three Secret Poems.* That same day I dropped off a package in his mailbox (I too lived behind the Stadium then): a copy of the first edition of *The Third Wedding,* with a warm dedication—but maybe not as warm as it should have been. A few days later, I ran into him and his wife in the street. Maró Seferis now tells me that I was holding an enormous watermelon in my arms and looked very funny. I only remember that I asked them if they were looking for a taxi, that Seferis looked at me again as though he was amused and then made a pun that I had gotten used to since childhood. He said: "Yes, we're looking for a Taktsi."

I don't know what brought about my first visit to their house. I only remember that I spent two very human hours there during which—I don't have to emphasize this—Seferis learned a great deal more about me than I about him (rather easy, since I have such a passion for talking continuously about myself). Maybe it would be fairer for both of us to say that his curiosity was natural: he belonged to a world that was known to both of us, there was no need for me to ask him questions. I belonged both to his world and, at the same time, to a world he was totally ignorant of. After that meeting I called them now and then but not too often. I knew how many others were making demands on his precious time. His wife would answer the phone. I would say: "It's me!" And she, invariably: "Bah? Good to hear from you. George, it's Taktsis." Two out of three times they would invite me to come over.

We usually sat in the room where his desk was. Mrs. Seferis worked on her embroidery and listened to us talk, intervening in the discussion very rarely and—supreme example of good behavior—not always on her husband's side. What did we talk about? About everything, including literature. But our most memorable discussions, which I must admit I always initiated, centered around erotic love in all its forms: it is the most effective method of penetrating into the labyrinth of a man's soul and coming out alive—a real Ariadne's thread. And something else: it is a way to become familiar enough with a person to be able to speak freely with him, in other words to love him. I don't know if all these things interested Seferis, but I'm sure they amused him, made him feel "unbuttoned" with me, and younger. "*Bré*, Taktsi," he would say with tender tolerance, "are you mad? What are you saying? Do you know that every time you come here Maró ends up having bad dreams that night?"

I suspect that he was the one who had the bad dreams. His wife once recalled that during the war, when they were newlyweds, in Egypt, and were staying in a hotel in Cairo, she sometimes snored very loudly and Seferis would cover her face with a pillow because he was afraid that the people in the room next door would take her snoring for erotic moaning. "Don't you remember? You almost suffocated me." Seferis of course was neither prudish nor puritanical. Behind the façade of the diplomat, quite apart from the poet, there hid the man from Asia Minor with a fiery temperament. I'm quite certain that Seferis did not idealize his libido by lining up words on paper like Kazantzakis; otherwise his poetry, juicy and untidy, would not have its superb economy—a result of constant subtraction—and the balance that distinguishes it. But he was upper-middle-class by upbringing and occupation. Wounded maybe, but not neurotic, and without a trace of unhealthiness in his outlook. He was a discreet man of the world, the kind of person who entrusts his love life to the woman he happens to love, and who could not conceive, out of a feeling of shame and human dignity, of sharing these secrets with anyone else. The memorable poet Nikos Kavvadias, now dead, told me that once in Beirut he tried to lure Seferis to the red-light district. When Seferis realized where he was, he sped away and was rather angry.

So, what I told him disturbed his sleep? If so, I don't blame him. I think it brought him into contact with mysterious worlds which, even if they interested him theoretically, he now had neither the disposition nor the time to investigate, so close was he to the end of the road. The world he knew was already mysterious enough, and he had expressed that beautifully in the "Sensual Elpenor" section of "Thrush."

> I saw him yesterday standing by the door
> below my window; it was about
> seven o'clock; there was a woman with him.
> He had the look of Elpenor just before he fell
> and smashed himself, yet he wasn't drunk.
> He was speaking fast, and she
> was gazing absently toward the gramophones;
> now and then she cut him short to say a word
> and then would glance impatiently
> toward where they were frying fish: like a cat.

Does it help to know the love life of a poet or novelist in order to understand his work better? In some cases, like Cavafy's, yes. In others much less, and Seferis belongs to the second category. A careful reading of his poems reveals all. Seferis didn't need to hide anything because he had nothing to hide, the erotic element in his poetry coincides with that of any heterosexual person and for this reason presents no interest. But I insisted on treating him without respect. I wanted to enter his soul like a surgical knife, even if this killed him a little every time. And Seferis suffered me stoically, without protest.

It wasn't enough that I treated him without respect during his waking hours; I did the same during his sleep. Late at night, when a friend would give me a ride home in his car, I would ask him to stop a little farther beyond my place, at dimly lit Agras Street, and there I would nail my eyes to Seferis's house while we concluded our evening's conversation, as though I were trying to pierce the walls, reach his bed and stand over him like Proust's hero over the sleeping Albertine who was really Albert: what was the poet dreaming about at that moment? Then I would come down the steps to Euphorionos Street. So a year went by, and on one of these nights, again late—two o'clock in the morning—at the corner of Euphorionos and Automedontos, just as I was getting ready to enter my home, I saw the tanks going down Vassileos Konstantinou Street.

I'm trying to get to those first months after the Colonels' 1967 coup and my mind stops working. It isn't strange at all. It had stopped working then too. I had fallen into a quasi-catatonic state and was the better for it. Because every time I recovered and realized what was happening, I fell into black despair. The information that came to me, at least in the beginning, was confused and of the same kind that everybody else heard: resistance movements that collapsed even before we learned of their existence, hotel-prisons on the outskirts of Athens for some political prisoners—usually center-rightists—or some fruitless visit by Pattakos* to the home of Mrs. Eleni Vlachos to persuade her to publish her newspapers again. Now and then we gathered at a friendly house to listen to foreign broadcasts and, of course, gave ourselves over to political talk, but at that time still without hatred for the Colonels: they hadn't yet shown their real face, nor did any one of us ever imagine they would stay in power for seven whole

* Brigadier Stylianos Pattakos, a leader of the Colonels' Coup (1967).

years, much less that they were brought in to betray us. The fact that they had cornered King Constantine and his crew even made them a bit attractive. For the first victims of that disaster—excluding the leftists, who were paying for the mistakes of the rest of our political world and had been herded into the Hippodrome as scapegoats, and also excluding Mandilaras, who was murdered, we were told, in cold blood—we didn't have any superfluous tears to shed. Those first victims had had a hand in messing things up: with that hand they had torn out their own eyes, and along with their eyes, they had torn out ours as well. What we were trying to understand was who finally had hold of the invisible strings in that strange puppet theater out there. Most of the people, including those who had always been close to the centers of power, didn't have the slightest idea. Besides, King Constantine's attitude created some confusion. The palace on the one hand and the Colonels on the other gave the impression of two mules fighting in a stranger's barnyard, and the average man didn't yet know what to make of it all or what position to take. As Seferis belonged to the category of the average man in terms of eroticism, so I belonged to the same category in terms of politics.

Meanwhile, although life had gone back to its natural rhythm, the situation was becoming more and more suffocating. Pattakos had given up his tanks and had taken on schoolgirls who wore miniskirts, and Ladas was beating up totally heterosexual journalists in his office because they had reported that some famous ancient Greeks were homosexual. In the area of Arts and Letters, deadly silence reigned. The more substantial magazines had stopped publication—naturally not *Nea Estia*—and quite a few intellectuals had either been arrested or had escaped abroad. After they arrested the writer Elly Alexiou, I wrote a letter of protest to a newspaper, but they chose to publish a similar letter from a well-known architect. When I complained, I was told: "He has a name—you don't." One day, at the Brazilian café—where we still went out of habit—I asked the late Rodis Roufos why some of us writers didn't get together and compose a statement of protest. He thought it was too soon. The Right was waiting to see how things would develop and what role the palace would finally play. But not only the Right. Even the average democratic citizen now turned to the palace— how ironic—for a solution to this impasse. Finally, when that comic abortive coup by King Constantine was in progress, even those who disliked him took courage. When it failed, our sorrow and anger had no limits. So he couldn't even pull this off? The only positive element that came out of that whole unsuccessful theatrical show was that it made us realize the new régime was not as temporary as the Colonels were proclaiming it to be and as many naive people believed. It was time then for some kind of action. But what action?

I was never politically oriented. My almost uninterrupted absence from Greece for ten years, from 1954 to 1964, had cut me off from many old contacts. And my unorthodox love life, which I never lost an opportunity to proclaim, made my presence in any resistance organization rather undesirable. Not only because they considered me corruptible, which was understandable, but because on the subject of unorthodox eroticism, the phallocrat resistance fighters and their wives differed only to a degree from Ladas in their attitude, and not always even to a degree. I could of course write and be critical of the régime indirectly. Besides, wasn't that the only thing I knew how to do, whoever was in power? So I sat down and wrote a short story: "A Few Pennies for the Salvation Army." By coincidence, the printer to whom I went was the same one who had printed my poems, *Symphony at the Brazilian Café*, thirteen years earlier. In the meantime he had moved to a more central part of Athens. The owner of the press was very happy to see me again but refused to print the story. Apart from its central theme—that those whose job it is to save us end up making life worse for us—there was a postscript at the end: "I wrote this story when we recovered from that dreadful blow that struck us down and our minds started working again more or less normally...." Much later I managed to get the cultural attaché of the American Embassy to make fifty photocopies of the story for me, and I distributed these to friends and acquaint-

[*308*]

ances. I think it was the first illegal literary text that circulated during those days. After that I stopped writing. I gave myself to late nights. During the day I sat absentmindedly at my desk holding my face in my hands. The fact that *The Third Wedding* had been published by Penguin Books in England three months earlier was no great solace. The news of this publication had gone totally unnoticed in the Greek press; I wasn't one of those people who can take care of their own public relations. Besides, who had the heart for things like that at the time?

Did I see Seferis during those days? Yes, Mrs. Seferis now tells me. Did we talk about politics? No. I recall our meetings starting from the spring of 1968 and after. One night the three of us went to the house of a friend, the late Tiggy Ghika. From start to finish we talked about the Colonels' coup, which we considered even then a second Asia Minor disaster. That whole evening I felt a strange pain in my stomach. As we left Tiggy's we stopped at an all-night pharmacy on Voukourestiou Street and I bought some aspirins. But I didn't think that day or the next that I ought to go see a doctor.

Then the story of the Ford Foundation grants started, which was to create such turmoil later. I refer to it because my life with Seferis is involved in that affair also. A high official of the Ford Foundation had come to Athens. It wasn't the first time. For years before the coup, the Foundation had given grants to Koun's Art Theater and to Dora Stratou's Ballet. This time the Foundation official asked the assistant cultural attaché of the American Embassy what Greek writers he thought were good and also needed some financial aid. The attaché had no idea. The Foundation's assistant, Katie Myrivilli, was sick in the hospital. So he asked some common friends of ours, George and Lydia Vassilopoulos, and they suggested me.

I met the official at the Brazilian and we chatted about this and that. "Are you sure," I finally asked, "that you could give me, *me*, a grant?" He smiled. "We're not interested in your private life, only in your work." So I signed a printed application form. But added to all my other anxieties was the worry that something would happen suddenly and they would end up giving me nothing. The pains I had in my stomach were getting worse and I continued not to go to the doctor. One day at noon I met Nanos Valaoritis outside Zonar's. He was angry. "I went to see Seferis," he said, "to ask for a letter of recommendation for Alec Schinas, and the old man refused—damn it!"

We were walking up toward Kolonaki. "Nano," I said, "I never thought of asking him for a letter of recommendation for the Ford grant." "Don't waste any time," Nanos said. "Seferis will give you a letter right away." I called him. Seferis said: "Come by tomorrow afternoon and we'll write it together." I sent the letter and waited. Two months, three months. Then one evening as I was walking in the street I hemorrhaged from my bleeding ulcer and was taken to the hospital. When I came out, I received a phone call saying that I had been awarded the grant and that it wasn't two or three thousand dollars, as I had expected, but fifteen. "What are you going to do with so much money?" Seferis asked when I went to see him and thank him. "I would like to go as far away as possible." "Why don't you sit down and write?" "I can't." He shook his head sadly. "Neither can I . . . At least try to be ready when the time comes . . ." After that we saw each other more frequently. In August I took him, his wife, and her granddaughter out to the Heraeon for a swim. He didn't complain that I was driving like a madman, but he reprimanded me for smoking. "You smoke too much. At least avoid smoking while you're driving." He turned to his wife in the back seat. "I never used to smoke when I drove, did I, Maró?"

That noon I talked to him about his obligation to make a statement of protest. Of course I wasn't the only one to do that. Everybody was pressing him. But Seferis demurred. "Bré, Taktsi," he said, "do you too really believe in that sort of thing?" "No, but this isn't the time for holding back. We've got to do what we can." "And you think I could have any effect?" "Hell," I said, "you won the grand Nobel prize. Besides, what counts is the gesture." But he continued to demur. Now that I've read that excellent poem of his called "Helen," with the epigraph from Euripides (". . . in sea-girt Cyprus, where it was decreed/ by

Apollo that I should live . . ."), I think I can guess some
of the feelings he must have had. Seferis knew Greece
well, and it was natural that he should have wavered. He
was afraid that once again one day a messenger would
come to say that this time too we had fought for "an empty
tunic," for something which was "just a phantom image."
Maybe that was why he was so deeply disillusioned. He
just wanted to be left alone to die peacefully in Greece.
When he went to the United States in the fall of 1968, and
the protestations of American students made him over-
come his last doubts about speaking out, he still waited to
return to his country first and then speak, because apparently he was afraid that if he spoke while abroad he
might not be allowed to return. Then, back in Greece, he
issued that statement which stirred all of us and gave
young men the incentive to continue the fight and some
intellectuals the incentive finally to do their duty. So two
more years went by, and one day in August, while I was
vacationing on Amorgos, I learned that he was very sick.

When I got back to Athens I hurried over to the Evan-
gelismos Hospital. He was under intensive care, and no
visitors were allowed to see him, but I managed to slip
in, picked up a white robe from a hanger, put it on as best
I could and went into his room. Mrs. Seferis was sitting
by his bed holding his hand, yellow as wax, the intravenous
needle in his arm held by a Band-Aid. When she saw me,
she opened her eyes and mouth wide, aghast. I reassured
her with a gesture and came closer. He seemed half his
normal size. My eyes filled with tears. His were closed.
But maybe he sensed our dumb gestures or felt another
presence in the room; anyway, he came out of the depths.

"Who is it?"

Mrs. Seferis leaned over him. "Taktsis."

His lips moved. He made some unintelligible hoarse
sounds.

"What did you say, George?"

"True friend, that Taktsis . . ."

"It did him good," Mrs. Seferis said to me when we
came out. How could it have done him good? Two weeks
later he was gone from us. He didn't live to see the end of
the seven-year dictatorship which had so poisoned his last
years. But luckily for him, he also didn't manage to witness

the betrayal of his beloved Cyprus. He didn't live to taste our first unadulterated joy but, again luckily for him, he didn't come to know the reservations we eventually had about this eternally rumored but never realized better future of ours.

Translated from Greek by Mary Keeley

This article was first published in the newspaper *Kathimerini* in September 1974 as a memorial three years after Seferis's death.

TRIAL BALANCES

ELIZABETH BISHOP AND MARIANNE MOORE

David Kalstone

Elizabeth Bishop left unfinished at the time of her death a long memoir of Marianne Moore, a piece she had been eager to do. Of course, she had written to and about Moore all her life: hundreds of letters, tributes in the form of a poem and three critical essays, informal talks about Moore and her work, anecdotes saved and polished over the years, tales told out of school. That critics linked their names both flattered and irritated, amused and puzzled the women—seemed an evasion of what mattered most, the stubborn particular. So, when yet once again a magazine, this time French, spoke of Moore's influence on Bishop, the younger woman wrote to her old friend:

> Everyone has said that—I was going to say, all my life—and I only wish it were truer. My own feeling about it is that I don't show very much; that no one does or can at present; that you are still too new and original and unique to *show* in that way very much but will keep on influencing more and more during the next fifty or a hundred years. In my own case, I know however that when I began to read your poetry at college I think it immediately opened up my eyes to the possibility of the subject-matter I could use and might never have thought of using if it hadn't been for you. —(I might not have written any poems at all, I suppose.) I think my approach is so much vaguer and less defined and certainly more old-fashioned—sometimes I'm amazed at people's comparing me to you when all I'm doing is some kind of blank verse—can't they *see* how different it is? But they can't apparently. [October 24, 1954]

And Moore, with an equally polite and generous irritability, replied:

> As for indebtedness, Elizabeth, I would reverse everything you say. I can't see that I could have "opened your eyes"

to subject matter, ever, or anything else. And a stuffy
way of appraising us by uninitiate standards blankets all
effort with impenetrable fog! I roam about in carnivorous
protest at the very thought of unimaginative analyses.
Alexander Pope to the rescue!

Even allowing for Bishop's deferential tone and for
Moore's playful archness, the two women show a healthy
respect for the distance between them and for the complex of feelings we call "indebtedness." Moore, who had
had no tutelary older poet in her own life, must have
sensed Bishop's talent and independence from the start.
Her role in Bishop's emergence as a poet is more mysterious than any simple comparison of texts could suggest. In
a relaxed moment of her memoir, Bishop writes:

> I have a sort of subliminal glimpse of the capital letter M
> multiplying. I am turning the pages of an illuminated
> manuscript and seeing that initial letter again and again:
> Marianne's monogram; mother; manners; morals; and I
> catch myself murmuring, "manners and morals; manners
> *as* morals; or is it morals *as* manners?" Like Alice, *"in a
> dreamy sort of way,"* since I can't answer either question,
> it doesn't much matter which way I put it; it *seems* to be
> making sense.

Moore is taken up in an alliterative blur of childhood
associations with the remote Nova Scotia village where
Bishop grew up: the coiling initial letters that fascinated
Bishop in her beloved grandfather's Bible; his old-fashioned village lessons in behavior revisited in at least one
of a planned series of poems on "manners"; and beneath
it all the unspoken fact of Bishop's childhood, an absent
mother. Thinking about Moore must have been in part
like recognizing fragments of her Nova Scotia life "through
the looking glass." What must it have been like, for example, for a young woman who had not seen her mother
since she was five to know an older poet who was by contrast inseparable from hers? And to have met Moore in
the very year when Bishop's long-hospitalized insane
mother had died? The apartment at 260 Cumberland

[*314*]

Street in Brooklyn where Moore lived with *her* mother was "other-worldly . . . as if one were living in a diving-bell from a different world, let down through the crass atmosphere of the twentieth century." Bishop always left there feeling happier, "uplifted, even inspired, determined to be good, to work harder, not to worry about what other people thought, never to publish anything until I thought I'd done my best with it, no matter how many years it took—or never to publish at all." Moore's world was in part a vanished sustaining maternal world transposed into another key; it nourished Bishop's writing life, yet could be contradicted with impunity. It was as if Bishop had in Moore both a model and a point of departure, an authority against which she could explore, even indulge, her more anarchic impulses.

Bishop was still in college when she met Moore in 1934. She first heard of the poet from her "more sophisticated" friend Frani Blough. There was no copy of Moore's *Observations* on the shelves of the Vassar library, so Bishop tracked down the poems to early issues of *The Dial* and *Poetry* and began a determined study not only of the verse but of reviews of Moore's work and of Moore's reviews of other poets. Almost by accident she discovered that Miss Fannie Borden, the Vassar librarian, knew Moore, had known her from the time Moore was a child, and in fact had the only copy of *Observations* at Vassar. Bishop, in telling how she met Moore, always dwelt on Miss Borden, as if she were an appropriately eccentric, somewhat Gothic herald to the story: the tall thin librarian, almost inaudible, who rode a chainless (!) bicycle, was said to be a cousin of *the* Lizzie Borden, a fact that some felt had ruined her life. Miss Borden offered to introduce Bishop to Moore, and it was arranged that the two meet one Saturday afternoon in March outside the upstairs reading room at the New York Public Library. Bishop, years later, didn't remember their conversation but she "loved her immediately." Within a few weeks she had sent Moore Father Lahey's life of Gerard Manley Hopkins, written to ask her if she might be interested in an excellent book on tattooing, and invited her to the circus.

[*315*]

The Moore Bishop met was forty-seven, her red hair mixed with white, her eyes pale blue, her "rust-pink eyebrows frosted with white." It was an odd moment in the older poet's life. She had ceased being editor of *The Dial* in 1929. It had been almost ten years since she had published a book of poems, and the royalties on *Observations* up to that point totaled fourteen dollars. In *Hound & Horn*—the same issue in which Bishop read Moore's wonderful "The Jerboa"—Yvor Winters was remarking, "Miss Moore, indeed, seems to have exhausted the possibilities of her style and to have abandoned writing." That image would be challenged by the appearance in 1935 of Moore's *Selected Poems*, with an introduction by T. S. Eliot. At their meeting a year earlier, Bishop observed that Moore was "poor, sick, and her work is practically unread I guess" but "amazing." Moore was "very impersonal," spoke "just above a whisper," but could "talk faster and use larger words than anyone in New York." From the very start, their correspondence shows an unexpected parity between the older woman and the younger. Nevertheless it was four years before Moore invited her to call her by her first name, something Bishop celebrated in electric capitals: DEAR MARIANNE. Her tone with Moore is always respectful, grateful, thoughtful, but even at the beginning bold—"a flicker of impudence," Moore said. Bishop is always trying to lure Moore out into the world: come to the circus, come to the movies (*Son of Mongolia*, for example), come to Coney Island (she did), come to Spain (she couldn't). Though the two women were to be friends until Moore's death in 1972, it would be the early years, 1934–1940, that were richest in implication of quirky family ties and professional challenge.

Aside from some detailed exchanges about Wallace Stevens, Bishop seems uninterested in Moore's modernist connections. Rather, what attracted her were the older poet's manners and mannerisms, her fusion of old-fashioned domesticity—the kind Bishop knew with her aunts and grandparents during her early childhood in Nova Scotia—with forthright notions about writing and style. Both Marianne and her mother ("Mother is a rabid advocate of the power of suggestions versus statement") "corrected" many of Bishop's stories and poems between 1934 and 1940. More provocative, more daunting, were Moore's poems and letters. "Why had no one ever written about *things* in this clear and dazzling way before," Bishop was to remark of Moore's work. "Although the tone is frequently light or ironic the total effect is of such a ritualistic solemnity that I feel in reading her one should constantly bear in mind the secondary and frequently somber meaning of the title of her first book: Observations." As Eliot was to say of the *Selected Poems*, "For a mind of such agility, and for a sensibility so reticent, the minor subject, such as a pleasant little sand-coloured skipping animal, may be the best release for the major emotions. . . . We all have to choose whatever subject-matter allows us the most powerful and most secret release; and that is a personal affair."

Bishop was a keen observer before she met Moore; learning that this could be a way of life identified with a way of writing was another matter. Every detail of the letters Bishop sent from Europe and Key West, every gift was "inspected"; even Bishop's postcards provided Moore "a veritable course of study" and provoked detailed comments and verbal images in return. Bishop remembered a fifth- or sixth-grade teacher who confounded her by saying that some people preferred a description of the forest to the forest itself. "I never believed her, but now I know that to send you a postcard is to get back something worth a thousand of them!" The Moores' habit of scrutiny, appropriating the exotic to their self-contained world, was challenging, intriguing, amusing—and must also have posed something of a conundrum. It was tied to a life that, even in the Thirties, was valetudinarian. Increasingly, the mother and daughter, in a manner worthy of a Victorian ménage, were bound to one another by illnesses, a tie that in the 1940s became acute. Marianne's letters are ringed with care, siege, tribulation. She is constantly in awe of Bishop's travel; apart from visits to Marianne's brother, Warner Moore, in Virginia, the Moore women always seemed too ill or beset to travel. Bishop, on the other hand, was in these years almost always on the move. After Vassar she settled in New York for almost a year, then, in July 1935, set out on her first trip to Europe. She traveled in Spain and North Africa, lived in France until the summer of 1936. She returned to France in 1937; and then after a series of yearly trips to Florida, bought, with her friend Louise Crane, a house in Key West, her first real "home" since childhood. Alongside the Moores' life of domestic economy and effort, Bishop felt herself something of a truant. The contrast, the tension, between the two ways of life, posed in sharpest relief, and in the most human terms, literary questions about place of observation and the observer. Moore's descriptions, as Bonnie Costello points out, were mostly mediated for herself, a lens of print focusing her subject; she did much of her exploring through catalogues, journals, museum documents, exhibitions. On the other hand, Bishop was, in her poems, less the poised researcher, less the orchestrator of a varied ensemble of fact. In the role of traveler, she used observation as a kind of tentative anchorage, as a way of grasping for presence in the world. The "powerful and secret release" that description offered her, however much it owed to Moore, would be of a different order from the older poet's.

Bishop only slowly discovered her traveler's observations to be a poetic strength, rather than a dereliction or a self-indulgence. We are accustomed to thinking of her lively clarity, her openness to the world—attitudes she had mastered in her later poems—but we are largely unaware that these blithe strengths were the product of tensions and fears. Her commitment to the *illusion* of physical presence—her hallmark—was hard won. She observed because she had to. Moore's precise style ran counter to what Bishop thought of as "the dreamy state of consciousness" she lived in just after college, "the time I was writing the poems I like best." Moore's secure bravado in dealing with the physical world was something Bishop instinctively valued, though she only gradually absorbed it into her writing. It was not simply the *fact* of her response to

[*318*]

Moore, but the miraculous and instinctive timing of it that mattered.

Bishop's early notebooks (1934 and 1935) are in part dedicated to concentrated descriptive exercises:

> the soft combed and carded look of the flames in the gas oven

> the rain came down straight and hard and broke into white arrow heads at the tips

> These last mornings the street-sprinkler goes around about 9:30. The water dries off very rapidly but very beautiful-ly, in *watermelon* patterns—only wet-black on grey, in-stead of darker green on lighter green.

Yet her observer's instinct cuts across a more deeply rooted inclination, an interiorizing interest. When, not long after, the passage about the street sprinkler finds its way into a poem ("Love Lies Sleeping"), it is with a psychological and subjective cast that Moore would not have been likely to give it. As with so many of Bishop's poems of this period, "Love Lies Sleeping" (first called "Morning Poem") is set on the edge of waking:

> Along the street below
> the water-wagon comes

> throwing its hissing, snowy fan across
> peelings and newspapers. The water dries
> light-dry, dark-wet, the pattern
> of the cool watermelon.

> I hear the day springs of the morning strike . . .

The accuracy is of a very special sort, less after the fact, less explicit visually than the notebook entry (no colors, no ad-verbial stage directions). Instead, the rhythm ("light-dry, dark-wet") suggests an impression only just gathering be-fore she finds an image for it. The protagonists of many of these early poems ("The Weed," "The Man-Moth") have trouble accommodating the claims of the world. The pre-cision of a passage such as this one is colored by the effort of "coming back to life." Hence the provocative "hissing"

and the eventually comforting context as the water wagon's "snowy fans" turn human discards—the peelings and
papers—to wholeness, "the pattern / of the cool watermelon." The frailty of human arrangements and recognitions is one of the subjects of "Love Lies Sleeping," and
one of its most haunting images is of the mind just barely
reassembling the world but pleased with its own ingenuity:

> From the window I see
>
> an immense city, carefully revealed,
> made delicate by over-workmanship,
>   detail upon detail,
>   cornice upon façade,
>
> reaching so languidly up into
> a weak white sky, it seems to waver there.
>   (Where it has slowly grown
>   in skies of water-glass
>
> from fused beads of iron and copper crystals,
> the little chemical "garden" in a jar
>   trembles and stands again,
>   pale blue, blue-green, and brick.)

Among Bishop's notebook entries of 1934–35 are many
that, if not directly indebted to surrealism, show a mind
disposed to accept its lessons:

> The window this evening was covered with hundreds of
> long, shining drops of rain, laid on the glass which was
> covered with steam on the inside. I tried to look out, but
> could not. Instead I realized I could look into the drops,
> like so many crystal balls. Each bore traces of a relative or
> friend: several weeping faces slid away from mine; water
> plants and fish floated within other drops; watery jewels,
> leaves and insects magnified, and strangest of all, horrible
> enough to make me step quickly away, was one large long
> drop containing a lonely, magnificent human eye, wrapped
> in its own tear.

The monitory eye wrapped in its own tear is an appropriately riveting image for Bishop's writing at the time: the odd combination of observation and alienation that makes her early poems, especially, different from Moore's. She had, by the time she discovered Moore's work, an already matured metaphysical taste, had read sixteenth- and seventeenth-century English lyrics; George Herbert was—and remained—her favorite poet. Many of her best poems of the 1930s can be read as versions of seventeenth-century poems about the soul trapped in the body. Sometimes the predicament is comic. Her Gentleman of Shalott accepts with a shrug being half mirror, half man. More often the versions are troubled, as with "The Man-Moth" and "The Weed." The claims of the world come to the protagonists as an almost physical shock, embodied in the rushing subway and the poisonous third rail of "The Man-Moth," and in "The Weed," in the rushing waters where the weed grows "but to divide your heart again."

"The Weed," like "Love Lies Sleeping," takes place on the edge of dream and waking. It is the poem in which Bishop most sees the world through George Herbert's eyes. But unlike Herbert's "The Flower," for example, "The Weed" is a dream of grim release which substitutes for heavenly joys a sense of the wild persistence of life. The call to the physical world is involuntary and takes the speaker back not so much from a world of grace as from a prized state of withdrawal, static and final:

> I dreamed that dead and meditating,
> I lay upon a grave, or bed,
> (at least, some cold and close-built bower).
> In the cold heart, its final thought
> stood frozen, drawn immense and clear,
> stiff and idle as I was there.

Bishop experiences these glacial comforting states often in the early poems and stories. Here change intrudes as a psychic explosion, "prodding me from desperate sleep," in the form of a weed that divides her cold heart's "final thought." From the "immense" clarity of this moment the allegorical scene becomes more animated. A flood of water, then two, divide the heart, but now into "half-clear" streams. In the strangest moment of this strange poem a few drops of water are shaken from the struggling weed into her eyes and onto her face; so that she sees

> (or, in that black place, thought I saw)
> that each drop contained a light,
> a small, illuminated scene;
> the weed-deflected stream was made
> itself of racing images.
> (As if a river should carry all
> the scenes that it had once reflected
> shut in its waters, and not floating
> on momentary surfaces.)

The few drops falling upon her face are like tears, and they contain the most precise, arrested visions of the world the speaker permits herself. ("Illuminated" suggests not only "lit" but also bedecked and pulsing with the illuminist's meaning, a moment of arrested glory for the "racing images.") But the overriding impression of the poem is the passivity with which she undergoes both the trance-like state close to death and the nervous gaiety with which the weed draws her back to life. Physical vision seems twinned with separateness, loss, and somehow with guilt. Awareness, a state to which the speaker only reluctantly abandons herself, is "weary but persistent . . . stoically maintained," as Lowell was to say in reviewing her first book.

"The Weed," written in the summer of 1936, is obviously related to the dreamlike notebook entry of 1934 in which, on the window coated outside with raindrops and inside with steam, Bishop has the hallucination of a "lonely, magnificent human eye, wrapped in its own tear." The image is unusual enough, as is the mixture of alertness and withdrawal it implies. ("I tried to look out, but could not," Bishop says of her dream.) But where many young poets would have been crippled or confused, Bishop was able, at that early stage of her writing, to make successful and moving poems of this disposition. In her notebook, naturally, emotional contradictions are more jagged and exposed. On one hand we see her as spirited and confident, full of the modernist spunk that Mary McCarthy in *The Group* attributes to Vassar women just settling in depression New York. "We were puritanically pink," Bishop writes, "and perhaps there seemed to be something virtuous in working for much less a year than our education had been costing our families." (She herself was briefly employed at fifteen dollars a week by the USA School of Writing, a shady sad correspondence course for hopeful— and hopeless—writers.) "I think that it is in the city alone, maybe New York alone, that one gets in this country these sudden intuitions into the *whole* of contemporaneity. . . . You catch it coming toward you like a ball, more compressed and acute, than any work of 'modern art.'" But alongside the outgoing modernism and receptivity in this, her first New York journal, are strong suggestions of guilt, reserve, and withdrawal. Contrary qualities which would much later come together as strengths in her writing were initially dispersed—and yet, in her best poems and stories of this early period, dispersal of energies was itself her subject.

Mary McCarthy once said of Bishop's writing, "I envy the mind hiding in her words, like an 'I' counting up to a hundred waiting to be found." The analogy is apt even down to the expectant concealed child. What one often hears "hiding" in Bishop's poems—especially the early ones she wrote in and about New York—is an instinctual self resisting a nervous seductive adult persona she associates with city life. "The Man-Moth" dates from her first New York stay, "Love Lies Sleeping" and "From the Country to the City" from a second stay in 1936 and 1937 after she returned from a year in France. In each of them, metropolitan excitement is transposed into a still wondering but more sinister key. The language of these early poems allows us to take them almost as Renaissance dialogues of soul and body. The prepositions in the title "From the Country to the City" are not just spatial, mea-

[323]

suring a return from a weekend, but also suggest an epistle addressed from one realm to the other with the force of an interior drama. "Subside" is the body's erotically tinged plea against the urban brain "throned in 'fantastic triumph'" (the latter a phrase borrowed from Aphra Behn's "Love Arm'd").

"The Man-Moth" and "Love Lies Sleeping" involve similar messages and pleas from submerged figures resisting the encroachments of the febrile adulthood of the city. Except for his infrequent frustrated romantic ascents, the man-moth is doomed to ride the rushing subways always facing the wrong way. His residual purity goes all but unobserved:

> If you catch him,
> hold up a flashlight to his eye. It's all dark pupil,
> an entire night itself, whose haired horizon tightens
> as he stares back, and closes up the eye. Then from the lids
> one tear, his only possession, like the bee's sting slips.
> Slyly he palms it, and if you're not paying attention
> he'll swallow it. However, if you watch, he'll hand it over,
> cool as from underground springs and pure enough
> to drink.

In "Love Lies Sleeping" the poet intercedes ("Queer cupids of all persons getting up") on behalf of city dwellers whose speechless representative is the dead staring proto-visionary at the end of the poem:

> for always to one, or several, morning comes,
> whose head has fallen over the edge of his bed,
> whose face is turned
> so that the image of
>
> the city grows down into his open eyes
> inverted and distorted. No. I mean
> distorted and revealed,
> if he sees it at all.

Poems of this period seem to allow Bishop simultaneously to be a keen observer—the figure who "tells" the poems scrutinizes every detail to extract her meaning—and yet to identify with figures absent, withdrawn, practically lifeless. A submerged self is variously imagined and identified. But in what Bishop wrote after she left college it is clear that she was drawn to fables that gave body to a divided nature; alongside a hectic modernity one senses a shadowy space for the absent or unrealized figures of a buried or inaccessible childhood.

This is more explicit in a journal entry that connects similarly suspended states with moments of crisis in her life. On her first trip to Europe, aboard the *Königstein* in late July 1935, Bishop underwent a series of disorienting experiences. One evening she sees patches on the waves: "these are *men on rafts*, poor wretches clinging to a board or two. . . . I am *positive* I see them there, even a white body, or the glitter of their eye-balls rolled toward us." Twice at dinner she is

> overtaken by an awful awful feeling of deathly physical and mental (mortal?) *illness*—something that seems "after" me. It is as if one were whirled off from all the world and the interests of the world in a sort of cloud-dark, sulphurous gray, of melancholia. When this feeling comes I can't speak, swallow, scarcely breathe. I knew I had had it once before, years ago, and last night on its second occurrence I placed it as "*homesickness*." I was homesick for two days once when I was nine years old; I wanted one of my Aunts. Now I really have no right to homesickness at all. I suppose it is caused actually by the motion of the ship away from New York—it may affect one's sense of balance some way; the feeling seems to center on the middle of the chest.

Readers who know a poem Bishop wrote about her childhood almost forty years later—"In the Waiting Room"—will recognize the collocation of feelings: the sense of being engulfed, drawn under the waves, or literally whirled off the globe, losing one's grip of discrete particulars and having to reassemble the world anew. Whether the childhood illness she refers to in her notebook (she says she was nine then) is the same one she recounts later in her poem (in which she says she was seven), the circumstances are similar, and this notebook entry made when she was twenty-four marks the moment when she begins to understand the vertigo and connect it with loss. Of course, and typically, she veers away from home-sickness, says she has no "right" to it, and lays the cause to seasickness and moving away from the familiar New York. But are they indeed so different? The fainting spell of "In the Waiting Room" occurred very soon after the seven-year-old Bishop was moved away from her maternal aunts in Nova Scotia. Of the attack at age nine, she remembers that she wanted one of her aunts. The threat of abandonment and disorientation are very close in her mind; and the notebook entry suggests that she is beginning to connect her observer's powers with a constant and urgent need to fend off the something that was "after" her; that reconstructing the world was a way to combat or express what in 1936 she identifies as "homesickness."

The young woman who felt, when she sailed to Europe in 1935, that she had no right to homesickness, spent much of her life overcoming it. Anne Stevenson, the author of the first full-length book on Bishop, is correct in saying that Bishop's poems are not conventional travel poems and have much more to do with re-establishing the poet's own sense of place. Bishop was to say that she always liked to *feel* exactly where she was, geographically, on the map. A whole train of displacements had marked her youth, and the plain facts that set them in motion are recorded in several chronologies Bishop was asked to prepare for publication and in the autobiographical stories she was eventually able to write once she had settled in Brazil. She advised Stevenson to print this entry: "1916. Mother became permanently insane, after several breakdowns. She lived until 1934." Bishop went on to say, "I've never concealed this, although I don't like to make too much of it. But of course it is an important fact, to me. I didn't see her again." The shattering reserve of that comment (down to the careful comma before "to me") is a warning to critics. Bishop never traded on her losses. At least one of her close friends from the Vassar years, Louise Crane, was unaware that Bishop had a living mother until her own mother told her that Gertrude Bishop had just died. One of her college advisers, who knew that Bishop was "on her own," found her "in a perfectly polite and friendly way, very reticent. . . . When I opened a door, she would turn the talk to her work, about which she was intelligent and resourceful." Long before she ever wrote directly about her childhood, Bishop seemed aware of the fact that she would in one way or another do so. A notebook entry written just before sailing to Europe in 1935 reads:

> A set of apparently unchronological incidents out of the past have been reappearing. I suppose there must be some string running them together, some spring watering them all. Some things will never disappear, but rather clear up, send out roots, as time goes on. They are my family monuments, sinking a little more into the earth year by year, boring [?] silently, but becoming only more firm, and inscribed with meanings gradually legible, like letters written in "magic ink" (only 5 metaphors).

The little self-protective parenthesis at the end suggests that for the moment these were feelings best distanced as a *literary* problem.

Bishop had spent much of her parentless childhood in Great Village, Nova Scotia, where her mother had taken her after the death of her father. Gertrude Bulmer Bishop was twenty-nine when her husband died, only eight months after the birth of their daughter and only child, Elizabeth. They had been married three years, and the family always felt that the shock of his early death (he was thirty-nine) brought on the series of breakdowns his wife then suffered. (Bishop herself believed that, though there was no history of insanity in the family, her mother had shown signs of trouble before.) For the first five years of her life the young child was effectively in the care of her mother's parents and her aunts. Her mother was hospitalized most of the time; first in McLeans' sanitorium outside Boston and then, after a final breakdown, in a mental hospital near Dartmouth, Nova Scotia, for the last eighteen years of her life.

[327]

To an unusual degree the child's attention was deflected toward the village itself, its rhythms and familiar figures. Great Village was at least fifty years behind the times: no electricity, no plumbing. Whether the village represented external stability and safety, or whether the child's losses prodded her to scan everything habitually for clues and meanings, the smallest details of Great Village life remained with her: the tanners' pits, the blacksmith's shed behind their house, the dressmaker, the milliner, the routine of taking the cow to graze. The decisive shock of her early life must have come when she had to give up the reassurances of Great Village and her mother's family to live in Worcester, Massachusetts, with the more solidly established Bishop grandparents. Not that they were unkind. But it is from this displacement that she dates the first of the fits of vertigo she much later identified as shocking her into an awareness of her own human pain. She began to suffer the severe illnesses—bronchitis, asthma, symptoms of St. Vitus's dance, severe eczema sores—that plagued her until her late teens. The Bishops sent her to live with a maternal aunt in Boston; she could go only fitfully to school, and spent most of her young girlhood "lying in bed wheezing and reading." Years in the Walnut Hill School, a private high school, and at Vassar seem to have revived and strengthened her, but she emerged into young adulthood feeling that she had always been a guest in other people's houses.

When Bishop first used the Nova Scotia of her childhood as a setting for a short story, "The Baptism" (1937), it was with an eerie sense of a youthful life vanishing, withdrawing before her eyes. In "The Baptism" three young sisters, orphaned, face their first Nova Scotia winter on their own. The almost unspoken fact of the story is that the mother and father have only recently died. The parents' elided disappearance is taken for granted, as if it were perfectly natural for three young women to be living alone in a tiny remote village without some adult presence, some relative, to oversee them.

Lucy, the youngest, becomes increasingly obsessed with

a guilt whose sources she cannot identify and almost convinces her sisters that "she must have been guilty of the gravest misdemeanors as a young girl." One night she hears the voice of Christ above her bed and another evening has a vision of God burning, glowing, on the kitchen stove. "His feet are in hell." The growing ecstasy and alienation from her sisters ends in her decision—they are Presbyterians—to become a member of the Baptist church. She is only heartsick that for total immersion she must wait until the ice leaves the river. At the first thaw she is baptized, catches cold, develops fever, and dies.

Childhood images that Bishop was to look back on with affection in later works—the religious engravings in the family Bible, the singing of hymns around the piano—turn up here in a more dangerous context. Reading one of their father's old travel books, *Wonders of the World*, Lucy becomes overstimulated by a depiction of the Nativity: "the real, rock vaulted Stable, the engraved rocks like big black thumb prints." Readers will anticipate the return of those images ten years later in "Over 2,000 Illustrations and a Complete Concordance." In that later poem Bishop remembers the engraving with yearning for simple belief in the domestic warmth it recalled. Lines of the engraving beckon magically to the eye, move apart "like ripples above sand, / dispersing storms, God's spreading fingerprint." But in 1936 and for the obsessive Lucy of "The Baptism" the "big black thumbprint" seems to mock, if not besmirch, the scene. The engravings draw her away from her family, deeper into her mania, until finally, terrifyingly, the child disappears.

Early deaths—several in Nova Scotia—are subjects to which Bishop was frequently drawn, as if scrutinizing the horizon for her own childhood. "The Farmer's Children," probably begun at the time of "The Baptism" but published ten years later, deals with two boys who die of exposure, frozen to death in a barn. "Gwendolyn" (1953) recounts the death of a valued young playmate; and the poem "First Death in Nova Scotia" is about the laying out of a child, her dead Uncle Arthur. One of the books she borrowed from Moore, read and reread in 1935, was the diary of Margery Fleming, a Scottish girl, born in 1803, who wrote these journals as part of her tutelage in her sixth, seventh, and eighth years and was dead before she was nine.

In the 1930s Bishop did not think of herself exclusively as a poet. Much of her writing energy was absorbed by short stories. It was through surreal narrative such as "The Baptism" and through the fables of her early "non-descriptive" poems that she instinctively sought some way to represent her conflicts. That she understood the need to "place" her childhood is suggested in a very grown-up essay she did as an undergraduate. "Dimensions for a Novel" suggests that she was an attentive reader of Proust or that some of the novels she had read prodded her to at least an intellectual grasp of how personal loss enters into one's writing:

> If I suffer a terrible loss and do not realize
> it till several years later among different surroundings,
> then the important fact is not the original loss so much
> as the circumstances of the new surroundings which
>   succeeded in
> letting the loss through to my consciousness.

Or again:

> The crises of our lives do not come, I think,
> accurately dated; they crop up unexpected and
> out of turn, and somehow or other arrange themselves
> according to a calendar we cannot control.

The stories or poems she was describing were far from the ones she would be writing the year she left college. But the essay presents itself as a kind of literary preparation for releases that were to come later. It draws on a reserve of patience, a faith in the indirection that will allow urgent feelings to appear, the slow reordering of sensibility in which events are understood not chronologically but in a new psychically accurate or revealing formation. "The process perhaps resembles more than anything the way in which a drop of mercury, a drop to begin with, joins smaller ones to it and grows larger, yet keeps the original form and quality."

When the young Bishop says that the important thing was not so much one's original loss as the new surroundings that admit it to consciousness, she seems to be deflecting her energies from narrative to description and to anticipate the ways she would slowly, obliquely, absorb, through her writing, feelings too painful to face head on. In certain surroundings—Key West in the late 1930s and again in 1946 and 1947 after revisiting Nova Scotia; or Brazil after 1951—she would be stimulated by circumstances that reminded her of her childhood in Great Village, the intimacies and improvisations of village life, and the parentless years she spent there. It was only in the protection of and prompted by a life both exotic and domestic in Brazil that she wrote directly about the losses of her childhood: two remarkable stories, "In the Village," which tells of her mother's insanity and early disappearance from her life, and "Gwendolyn," the story of the death of a young playmate.

But those stories were twenty years in the future, and a writing life is more and less than direct expression. The subject matter that allowed Bishop "the most powerful and secret release" in the Thirties and Forties reflected in part Marianne Moore's poetry and scrutinizing friendship. When Bishop met Moore, we know, she had already struck out on a course independent of the older poet. Moore's influence was less a passion to be outgrown—the case with many apprenticeships—and more a steady slow infusion to the bloodstream. Gradually, in response to Moore's example, Bishop's narrative ambitions were being dispelled in favor of description and observation. Not that she radiated authority the way Moore did. In Moore's poems the observations hung in the air like charged particles in her magnetic field. Or, sometimes, like dispersed flashes of a distant storm. They help us locate an intellectual or emotional impulse, a center of energy. In Bishop's poems, time and movement are more important; her observations grow

[*331*]

out of travel and exposure to landscape. Her assertions are more provisional; the poems are "situations" that help her explore and voice her frail claim to presence in the world.

Bishop's *Complete Poems* might well have been called by the title of her first book, *North & South*, as Stevens wanted to call his life's work *The Whole of Harmonium*. In the village intimacies and domesticities of Key West and especially of Brazil, she found the "new surroundings" that both replaced and reawakened her northern childhood. "What I'm really up to is recreating a sort of deluxe Nova Scotia all over again in Brazil. And now I'm my own grandmother." In 1946 and 1947 she visited Great Village and Cape Breton for the first time in many years. The great poems that resulted—"At the Fishhouses," "Cape Breton," "Over 2,000 Illustrations and a Complete Concordance" among them—revived her sense of the ancient emptiness, the dwarfed intimacies of their human communities, as if relearning a forgotten harmonic scale. We have to learn to read these "observations" as, for Bishop in the writing and at the time, more potent than narrative and preceding it. It was a skill for which Moore had prepared her, but she put it to uses different from Moore's. Bishop's eye for detail, as Howard Moss suggests, is a dramatic eye: she often experiences traditional dramatic problems—character, comic or tragic action—by fitting out a stage for them, a stage on which the protagonists will not necessarily appear.

In 1935, with very little evidence to go on—Elizabeth Bishop had written only a few poems and published fewer—Marianne Moore wrote a prophetic note (an anticipatory defense against feminist critics as well?):

> Some feminine poets of the present day seem to have grown horns and to like to be frightful and dainty by turns; but distorted propriety suggests effeteness. One would rather disguise than travesty emotion; give away a nice thing than sell it; dismember a garment of rich aesthetic construction than degrade it to the utilitarian offices of the boneyard. One notices the deferences and vigilances in Miss Bishop's writing, and the debt to Donne and to Gerard Hopkins. We look at imitation askance, but like

the shell which the hermit crab selects for itself, it has value—the avowed humility, and the protection. Miss Bishop's ungrudged self-expenditure should also be noticed—automatic apparently, as part of the nature.

The occasion was an anthology called *Trial Balances* in which thirty-two young poets between the ages of twenty and twenty-five were introduced by more established poets. Louise Bogan presented Roethke, Stephen Vincent Benet introduced Muriel Rukeyser. Moore's presentation of Bishop was an act of extraordinary vision. Faced with a young poet of dissimilar temperament and needs, she sensed that a kinship of method would eventually liberate Bishop's energies and define her difference from Moore. Moore put her faith in a thoughtfulness that is also oblique, does not bluntly purvey ideas, and is not "like the vegetable shredder which cuts into the life of a thing."

Excerpts from the writings of Elizabeth Bishop used by permission of Alice Methfessel, Literary Executor of the Estate of Elizabeth Bishop.

Excerpts from the writings of Marianne Moore used by permission of Clive E. Driver, Literary Executor of the Estate of Marianne C. Moore.

The Day Laborer and the Queen

Barbara Jones

*E*llen Terry, Player in Her Time, by Nina Auerbach, recently published by Norton, tells the story of an actress who let herself be seen and cast as others (chiefly men) wished to see and cast her, and who lost her boyish vigor as a result. I'm not sure that the story this book tells is the story of Ellen Terry, or that to lose boyish vigor is so bad a thing for a woman. But the book makes it easy to believe that people used Ellen Terry inordinately. People continue to use her. Her biographer uses her to illustrate some feminist themes. And I will use her to suggest some things about Geraldine Page, who died in June last year and who seems to me never to have let herself be used by anybody.

Ellen Terry was a beautiful actress in an era when the theater was pictorial and when art in general was all about seeing and beauty. Auerbach quotes Henry James lamenting that "the theatre just now is the fashion, just as 'art' is the fashion and just as literature is not." Terry was queen of the London stage; Henry Irving was king. At the time of her jubilee in 1906, Terry was, as Auerbach says, "as awesome an emblem of power as Queen Victoria had been." There is nothing in Terry's life to suggest that she wanted to be anything other than an adored, popular object. She took care in letters and interviews to speak generously of everyone: of George Frederic Watts, whom she married and who cast her out, of Edward Godwin, by whom she had two children and who abandoned her. She presented so warm-hearted an aspect to everyone that it would have been difficult for criticism of her temperament to stick: "All the world seems to say kind things about me. I am happy in knowing it; and thus I love the world and all who live upon it. Why shouldn't I?"

Watts and Sargent painted her, Lewis Carroll and Julia Cameron photographed her. She liked being a model and she was good at it. Of the year she spent in Watts's studio, she said she "was happy, because my face was the type which the great artist who had married me loved to paint.

I remember sitting to him in armour for hours and never realising that it was heavy until I fainted." In at least one instance, she was better able to achieve her artistic aim as a model than as an actress. In 1888, after her failed stage portrayal of Lady Macbeth, Terry trotted over to Sargent's studio in full costume to have her portrait done and the portrait (which adorns the cover of Auerbach's book) was a success, expressing "all that [she] had meant to do" on stage.

She liked modeling wholeheartedly; about acting she was ambivalent. Raised in a theatrical family and employed as an actress from the age of nine, she left the stage at seventeen to marry and model for Watts. That union lasted only a year; she went back to the stage, but ran away again when she was twenty-one to live with Godwin. The affair with Godwin was scandalous and cut her off from her family and friends, but it reaffirmed her sense of herself as an object of beauty. She was beloved by Godwin, whom Max Beerbohm dubbed "the greatest aesthete of them all." She was queen, a decade before her association with Irving, to the man Oscar Wilde called the "general king." They lived in a house of medieval and Japanese influences: "a temple of art." Terry left this life when Godwin's career faltered, he left her, and she needed money. Virginia Woolf believed money was merely Terry's excuse for returning to the stage, but in later years, Shaw thought Terry acted because her son, Gordon Craig, was draining her money, "not because she was an actress who needed to act."

Here are some of the things Ellen Terry said about acting:

> Never had any ambition. . . . Not at all. I was a paid servant and had to, at least try to do it . . .

> I have always been more woman than artist.

> The looking forward for me is pretty blank—I don't mean in the theatre, that's nothing—I care for that least of all.

> [Irving's] soul was not more surely in his body than in the theatre, and I, a woman who was at that time caring more about life and love than the theatre, must have been to him more or less unsympathetic.

I can't write now about the play, & I've no other news—
but I do wish I cd get away to fresh air somewhere, the
last months day & night at the theatre has made me sick
of it.

Terry's stage image was fixed. "She is always," Max
Beerbohm wrote, "whatever she does, the merry bonny
English creature with the surface of Aestheticism—always reminds me of a Christmas-tree decorated by a Pre-
Raphaelite." But her acting was a blur to remember. "The
memory of the Lady's Portia," W. Graham Robertson recorded "... is like a dream of beautiful pictures in a scheme
of gold melting one into another.... but of Irving's Shylock
I seem to remember every movement, every tone."

Geraldine Page was an actress in an era when movies,
not plays, were the fashion. Actors show-cased their
talent in New York theaters, then flew off to Hollywood
forever. (After success on Broadway in *Sweet Bird of
Youth*, Paul Newman, an Actors Studio member in good
standing, offered that he hoped to do a play "every third
year.") Good looks were at least as important to an actress's
stage employment as they were in Ellen Terry's time, yet
Page, who was never beautiful, forged a signal place for
herself in American theater with her commitment to the
actor's work. Terese Hayden, an assistant to producer/di-
rector Herman Shumlin in the fifties, says of Page at rehearsals for *The Immoralist*, "What I saw was somebody
able to roll up her sleeves and work almost like a day la-
borer, a kind of monumental gift of energy and concentration . . . just methodically setting about evolving this
character with her flesh and blood."

Ellen Terry forgot her lines and fooled around on stage,
throwing in asides, ad-libbing. To Shaw she gave "an impression of waywardness; of not quite fitting into her part
and not wanting to. . . ." But Page would have impressed
Shaw differently. As a child, she had wanted to be an artist.
First a pianist, then a painter; then, after performing in a
church play when she was seventeen, she found what she'd
"been trying to find since [she] first heard that piano," acting. Onstage, Page said, she felt a "freedom and power"
she'd never felt before. After the church production, she

studied at the Goodman Theater in Chicago for three years and performed for another six in stock companies in Illinois—Lake Zurich, Woodstock, Marengo, Rockford and Springerton—before coming to New York.

In her early New York days, when she was slender, in *Summer and Smoke, The Rainmaker* and *Separate Tables*, and in television work like the adaptation of Faulkner's "Old Man," Page had the face of a wooden puppet: hard shiny cheeks that looked stuck on, like apples or rubber balls. She had a long, sloped chin, and in profile in those days her head looked like one of those cartoons of an animated crescent moon. She had beautiful hands, thin wrists and elegant, slim fingers, and with her fluttery high voice and her womanly body, she offered up a distinctly female presence. Still, when she first arrived in New York from the Middle West, Vincent Canby, though admiring of her talent, was convinced "this girl . . . should go home." Even at her most glamorous, as the aging beauty in *Sweet Bird of Youth*, she sported bangs and a soft, jaw-length permanent that made her look like Shirley Booth. Later she grew jowly and heavy and had underarms that flapped. Lewis Carroll chose Ellen Terry as one of his favorite little girls; at a climactic moment in *Agnes of God*, Page as Mother Superior, her giant head framed in a wimple, looked like Tenniel's enraged Duchess.

Page appeared in several dozen movies and television shows over forty years, and she performed in five hundred plays. Here are some of the things Geraldine Page said about acting:

I'm going to do this for the rest of my life and nobody is going to talk me out of it.

I'd rather have people think I was a great actress than a bankable one.

Theater is dress up, it's fooling people, it's being someone else—which is what actors want to do.

Like every other female ever born, I want a family. It's difficult. It's difficult under ordinary circumstances, but I'm determined. I may be sixty before I get there, but I'll achieve it. It'd be simpler if I could just not act any more, but that's really ridiculous.

Page chose her roles upscale and down, regardless of commercial considerations. In 1956, she replaced Margaret Leighton on Broadway in *Separate Tables* at a time when American actresses didn't get parts in English plays, especially talky ones. The actress Jaqueline Brookes says, "It simply wasn't done for a star to replace a British actress. It spelled career disaster. But Gerry wanted to do it and she did." When Anne Bancroft won the role of Regina in *The Little Foxes*, Page, still wanting the part, agreed to do the package tour. She performed in *Agnes of God* on Broadway and on the national tour and later at the Westport County Playhouse. She called herself "greedy gut" and "the greediest actress who ever lived" because she "want[ed] to play everything." She believed actors could fully develop their talents only with performance, and that a lack of stage experience was the reason American actors had a lesser reputation than British ones. With Rip Torn, her husband for twenty-three years, Page tried repeatedly to found a repertory theater. Finally, after over thirty years in New York, Page signed on with the fledgling Off-Off Broadway Mirror Repertory Company; and come movie contract or Broadway offer, Page's commitment to the Mirror Rep came first. In 1985, she performed nightly in *The Madwoman of Chaillot* at the Mirror Rep while rehearsing by day for the Off-Broadway debut of Sam Shepard's *A Lie of the Mind*. She was working from 10 A.M. until midnight. She was sixty-one years old and had high blood pressure. When Ann Wedgeworth (who was married to Rip Torn before Page) fell sick during previews for *A Lie of the Mind*, Page said, "Well, I'll play both parts, if you want." So she performed her role stage right, then ran behind the scenery to stage left where she took up a script and played Ann Wedgeworth's part.

Ellen Terry's watchword was "useful." She wanted to be a "useful" actress. Only an actress whose motto was "use" could be the kind of actress that Page was. Her wilfulness and willingness gave her access to the richest array of resources for her work—she *used* everything. She is known to have grabbed a hunk of cellulite under her arm as if it weren't part of her and say to the costume designer, "The character can use this." At Page's memorial service, Anne Jackson said, "She used the stage like no one else I've ever seen. It was like playing tennis with someone who had twenty-six arms."

She was notorious for selecting costumes and props for her characters. "Most of the costumes were too fancy," she said of the costume hunt for *Separate Tables*. "But when I saw that slinky thing, I just gasped." And she had an unusual capacity and eagerness to wear everything if everything was apt. When the costume designer for *Blithe Spirit* (Page died after a Friday performance of this production) brought a number of possibilities to Page's dressing room, she said, "I'll take them all." In *The Pope of Greenwich Village*, as a mourning but immovable mother, Page stole the movie in one tightly shot scene, with a drink in one hand, a cigarette in the other and rosary beads wrapped around her wrist like a whip. When, as Carrie Watts, Page sneaked from her son's apartment for *The Trip to Bountiful*, her steps were entirely furtive but her body was a walking hat tree of telltale paraphernalia: a shiny gold locket chain, a crinkled straw hat, a worn suitcase, a pocketbook, a pair of gloves, an old coat slung over her arm.

Ellen Terry, no matter the play, portrayed one character, one compliant yet goddesslike heroine, and audiences loved her. Preparing for her portrayal of Lady Macbeth, a part in which she was unusually involved, Terry worried that her interpretation would clash with her popular image. She penned troubled, preemptive letters to friends and theater critics:

> It is not a very pleasant prospect for *me*—For I rather anticipate folk will hate me in it . . .

> —to try to do what is expected by so many people or to do what I want to do—That is the question. . . .

But Page said she was her own biggest fan. After her splash in *Sweet Bird of Youth*, she pretended surprise at everyone else's "discovery": "What's everybody making a fuss about? I don't have a new voice or anything. I've just sort of been scraping the dust off what was there all the time." She chose her roles to please herself: "What I like most is violent contrasts. If I play a lowdown wicked drunk, I like to play a saintly, good, generous, modest person next." She played elderly women repeatedly, but this also satisfied her drive for variety—"all my favorite roles are older characters. The older a character gets, the more choice you have in playing her—as life progresses, experience accumulates." After *Summer and Smoke*, she turned down spinster roles; after *Strange Interlude*, she turned down revivals; after *Black Comedy*, she turned down farce. She turned down the original production of *Who's Afraid of Virginia Woolf*: "I'd like to play a part like that, but in a better play."

Offstage, Terry took on numerous personas, the better to please everyone; Page would not dissemble. As a starlet on the Hollywood set of *Hondo* she told the admiring John Wayne that he couldn't buy her contract unless he gave her script approval, and she flaunted her association with Uta Hagen and her admiration for Lillian Hellman. (She didn't make another movie for ten years.) In print, she said she "hated" all of Sam Shepard's previous work (while she was appearing in Shepard's *A Lie of the Mind*), that audiences were "bloodthirsty voyeurs coming to watch someone spill his guts out on the stage." She told a young interviewer, "If you feel strongly about [Tennessee Williams], it's probably best you never met him."

For Terry and other Victorian actors, the great hope was assimilation into polite society, but Page wouldn't assimilate in the simplest ways—she disassimilated, if anything. She bought her clothes at Lamston's, accepted her Academy Award in a thrift-store cloak, attended a fancy-dress museum dinner where some of her television work was being celebrated wearing an old aviator's cap, the cracked leather flaps pulled down over her ears. In New York everyone I know has a story about mistaking Page for a bag lady. One time a photographer waited fifteen minutes in a restaurant for Page to arrive before realizing she was the down-and-out-looking lady at the bar.

Page's wilfulness made her an actor of authority and did not at all require her to forfeit that responsiveness which the stage offers us most particularly, that thing we "bloodthirsty voyeurs" attend the theater to see. Shaw observed that Terry "had to stop too often and wait too long to sustain her part continuously when [Henry Irving] was on the stage," but when Geraldine Page was on the stage the other actors waited for her. Actor Darren McGavin told *Newsday*, "She was alive every minute, with so much detail that you'd just have to wait until she got finished what she was doing." "Gerry is never ahead," an actor told *Time* in 1960. "She is always reacting as if she did not know what the other actor was going to say."

Page's performances were not always exemplary; sometimes they weren't even good. Audiences tired of her mannerisms—the wavery voice, the excited hands. But whereas audiences loved Ellen Terry because she gave them what they wanted, Page's audiences never knew what they were going to get and that was precisely the reason to go. And in the end Page's independence meant something to the theater of our time.

Ellen Terry's family believed acting was a good trade because, among other things, actors could not be replaced by industrialization, but today theater is overrun with machines. Mechanical sets and costumes are the stars of the biggest West End and Broadway hits. And theater as popular entertainment has been replaced entirely by the movies. According to Peter Masterson, who directed *The Trip to Bountiful*, film distributors argued against casting Page in that film, after she had worked thirty-six years as a leading actress, because "no one knew who she was—she wouldn't be box-office." In Ellen Terry's time, there were day laborers all over and Terry was exceptional for looking ethereal: as her daughter's lover, Christopher St. John, put it, "all earthiness purged away by time." But in our time, there are pretty pictures all over and not so many day laborers to be found. To our happiness, for a while, Page presented a live body at work, not the image of one.

THE CONSTITUTION—OUR PONDEROUS ARK

Nicholas von Hoffman

Every fifty years, from the time of the writing of the American Constitution, the nation has paused, hiccupped and tried to celebrate it. None of these efforts at memorializing the great charter has been especially successful. The last time out, in 1937 at the time of the one hundred fiftieth anniversary, the occasion degenerated into a squabble about whether the Chairman of the House Judiciary Committee, who was in charge of the celebrations, was planning to put his picture on copies of the document to be distributed to the country's schoolchildren. So, like its predecessors, the two hundredth is turning out to be a botched, unachieved affair at which lawyers, politicians, professors and drama critics complain that the thing isn't being done right.

The two hundredth Fourth of July came off nicely with gongs, firecrackers and dance extravaganzas, but the Constitution's birthday celebrations fail because people don't think just throwing a party and having a good time is enough. Comes the Constitution, a need is felt for *gravitas*, solemnity, pomp. The attitude toward this revered eighteenth-century document is worshipful. A time for seminars, meditation and good taste, for old oak and stained glass. Across the spectrum, the posture is reverential and religious. To a Jerry Falwell, it's a divinely inspired set of laws for God's second chosen people to live by, and to Bill Moyers it is nothing short of "miraculous." The Constitution in our culture is too big and too elaborate an idea for a simple anniversary fête. It's no more fitting to have a birthday party for the Constitution than for the Bible.

Constitution worship is neither new nor phenomenal. NBC had no sooner put together the first radio network in the 1920s than a patriotic speaker was heard to tell listeners that the Constitution was "our holy of holies, an instrument of sacred import." The Macon (Georgia) *Telegraph*, January 27, 1893, reporting the funeral of Supreme Court Justice Lucius Quintus Cincinnatus Lamar, told its readers that "Justice Lamar had for many years carried in his inside vest pocket a small copy of the Constitution of the United States. Next to the Bible, it was the book he loved the best, and he referred to it often. In life he was never without it, and yesterday the little book was buried with him. It lies close to the heart that loved its teaching and upheld its rights at all times." As early as 1834 Congressman Caleb Cushing had named the Constitution "our Ark of Covenant."

Hence to call the Constitution in our political culture sacred scripture is to employ a figure of speech greater than mere metaphor. Many Americans do actually think of the Constitution as a divinely inspired document. It follows from Protestant thinking that long antedates the American Revolution and holds, with early eighteenth-century preachers like Jonathan Edwards, that the Calvinist God of strict Biblical interpretation had chosen North America as the special instrument of His providence. This wondrous land was to be the New Jerusalem and, in the intervening centuries, this analogy has been elaborated and repeated until it is the everyday stuff of oratory and political thought. In the unrolling of time, it began to seem as though the story of America was something akin to the story of the New Testament as viewed through the eyes of the more severe forms of Protestantism.

The Founding Fathers, now frequently capitalized, have taken on the aspect of the Holy Apostles, and the meeting hall in Philadelphia where the Constitution, now almost universally capitalized, was written has taken on the emotional and theological character of the upper room where the disciples waited for the descent of the Holy Ghost. This was, after all, the very place where Bill Moyers's miracle took place. As Peter, Thomas and the others tarried for the bird-shaped spirit to come down from Heaven, so Madison, Washington and their collaborators worked behind closed doors until that same spirit made them its instrument and inspired them to bring forth this unique addendum to Christian Holy Scripture, the Constitution of the United States of America.

The sense of the Constitution being revealed truth is reinforced by other unspoken elements in the American political theme park. Abraham Lincoln has long since become the Christ figure of our history, the gentle, wise, strong and God-sent Son of Man, whose true nature was only made clear to us after his crucifixion at Ford's Theater when Stanton beheld his lifeless body and told the others gathered in the room of sorrows, "Now he belongs to the ages."

In this enormous, panoramic religio-political metaphor We, the People, play the role of the Holy Paraclete and sometimes, though less often and less recognizably, the role of the congregation. The former is the case when We the People are extolled for our ultimate wisdom, our lasting good sense, love of justice and ability to know truth from falsehood, etcetera. Then We, the People are the true spirit and the final truth of America. In the latter sense We, the People see ourselves as members of the congregation, and often as wayward and sinful ones, in our roles as jurors, voters, taxpayers, conscripts.

Not only is this imaginary embroidery of nationhood vast in vision and detailed in its workings, but it is strongly Protestant in its origins and its themes. Millions of a vague, somewhat Protestant background, who do not go to church, recognize and respond to it. It comes out of the unspoken culture. It also attracts others besides Protestants, dormant or practicing.

In the nineteenth and early years of the twentieth century, Roman Catholicism saw the underlying, essential Protestantism and recoiled from it. Accommodation with the American secular religious vision was specifically condemned as heretical by the Vatican, which called the aberration "Americanism" or "Modernism." But the last fifty years, which have seen Roman Catholicism in America embrace so many Protestant attitudes, have also seen Catholics come to believe in the great Protestant political metaphor.

Of the three major religious groups, only American Jewry has restrained itself from accepting the vision. Jewish politicians and lawyers hang back from joining in this "fetishism," as Constitution worship has occasionally been called for a century or more. They are able to see that the grand American political metaphor is a Christian one, and so they understand whose God would be honored in the one minute of nondenominational silence if the courts ever allow this prayerful pause into the schools.

[*344*]

The vision that has made the American Constitution an inspired document makes it unlike anybody else's written Constitution. The parchment lodged in its shrine in Washington is, in the psychology of our people, the received word, and man may not rewrite the word of God. Thus "tinkering" with the Constitution had become an editorially condemned form of profanation by the early 1900s. Flibbertigibbet peoples like the French or the Italians, not the chosen people, might change their Constitutions on whim, but theirs, of course, are neither very old nor at all inspired. The states in our own federal union have frequently torn up their Constitutions and written themselves new ones that seemed more useful for the needs of the day, but The Constitution was, is and always will be a changeless document.

In like manner, Americans have coined the word "unconstitutional," a deeper, more serious sin than unlawful or illegal. A companion phrase is "constitutional confrontation" or "crisis," which to the American mind is something different from the pedestrian political impasses other governments and peoples find themselves in from time to time. The idea behind such phrases derives from the mysterious power central to the sacred writings themselves, for we too are, like the Moslems, the Jews and the Christians, "people of the book."

The transformation of the Constitution into a quasireligious document and its superstitious reverence by the masses and the classes were long ago noted and mocked. "The Constitution became for them a sort of abracadabra which would cure all disease," wrote Thurman Arnold fifty years ago. "Copies of the Constitution, bound together with the Declaration of Independence and Lincoln's Gettysburg Address, were distributed in cigar stores; essays on the Constitution were written by high school students; incomprehensible speeches on the Constitution were made from every public platform to reverent audiences which knew approximately as much about the history and dialectic of that document as the masses in the Middle Ages knew about the Bible—in those days when people were not permitted to read the Bible. The American Liberty League was dedicated to Constitution worship. Like the Bible, the Constitution became the altar whenever our

best people met together for tearful solemn purposes, regardless of the kind of organization. Teachers in many
states were compelled to swear to support the Constitution. No attempt was made to attach a particular meaning to this phrase, yet people thought that it had a deep
and mystical significance, and that the saying of the oath
constituted a charm against evil spirits."

The better part of two centuries has been taken up
comparing Britain's unwritten Constitution with America's
written; and in due course it was often noted that the
American Constitution is, by its own provisions, hard to
change. In fact, as a Biblical document, it is next to impossible to change.

In the beginning, when the ink was still fresh on the
parchment, and the authors of the document were still
alive and in politics, Constitution worship was a phenomenon of the future. Hence ten very significant amendments
could be quickly proposed and ratified. The evolution of
the notion of the Constitution's divine origins takes place
in the second half of the nineteenth century, but enough
people still did not believe in the document's infallibility
to make it possible to pass the income-tax amendment and
the direct election of senators in the early years of this
century. Since then, with the interesting exception of the
Prohibition amendment, the only amendments to pass are
essentially perfecting amendments. The definition of We,
the People was expanded and fulfilled by giving women
and teenagers the vote. The two-term amendment, passed
by an angry and resurgent Republican Party smarting from
national defeats at the hands of Franklin Roosevelt, only
made it through the ratification process because it seemed
to fulfill George Washington's view that two terms are
enough for a President. Prohibition was inscribed in the
Constitution in large measure because of the same kind
of militant Protestantism which elevated the document to
the level of Holy Scripture.

As far as ordinary changes in political process and government structure go, the Constitution has been frozen
for three quarters of a century. It has become unamend-
able. Thus it was as much horror at allowing epigones to
doodle marginalia on the written word of God as it was
conservative discomfort over the proposal that sank the

Equal Rights Amendment. Similarly, a few years ago the balanced-budget people came within a hair's breadth of triggering a never-used provision in the Constitution for calling for the convocation of a second constitutional convention. Two thirds of the state legislatures must pass a resolution for this to happen, and the balanced-budget people were within a state or two of succeeding when the reaction set in. Liberals and conservatives alike fell into a panic of consternation at the thought that America, after an interval of two centuries, would again meet in convention assembled, for Pentecost comes but once to the chosen people.

Though the culture may have made the fundamental charter of government a lapidary document, the society changes, and in one fashion or another the Constitution has been made to conform to the needs of the times. The ordinary instrument for accomplishing this is the Supreme Court, where an astonishing, priestly ritual precedes the changing of the Constitution.

This is done by a process of divination through which the true meaning and intention of the Founding Fathers or "the Framers" is determined as it would apply to such un-eighteenth-century topics as the multinational corporation, the application of the First Amendment to television broadcasting or the education of black children, who were, of course, in James Madison's time, kept wholly illiterate as a matter of prudent public policy. Anyone coming from another society to ours and arriving, therefore, without the gift of belief in the American civic religion would find the whole exercise as exotic as Gulliver did when he visited Lagado and observed the learned professors extracting sunshine from cucumbers.

The procedure's working depends on an act of trust and belief by the citizenry similar to that needed when the Vatican promulgates a new article of faith. Whereas we call changing the Constitution "ascertaining the Founding Fathers' real intent," the Papacy calls its act of legislation "defining doctrine." The doctrine has been lying there all along, from the hour Christ said, "Peter, upon this rock I will build my church." It had gone unnoticed and unextracted from the legacy of received truth. When

Christ died, he left a perfected faith to which nothing can be added or subtracted, and thus the body of revealed truth can only be refined and defined to bring out what was already there but hadn't been seen. The Supreme Court does the same thing when it discovers that the death penalty is cruel and unusual punishment or that abortion is a constitutionally accorded right. None of this is new, just heretofore unrecognized.

This sacerdotal approach to fundamental legislation has given public controversies over questions touching the Constitution a mandarinlike obscurantism. The air is often heavy with pedantic assertions about what Madison and his collaborators really meant and/or how this phrase or that paragraph in the venerable parchment should properly be construed. The debates bear similarity to those of a Baptist convocation, locked in dispute between the liberal constructionists and the fundamentalists of the strict interpretation. Should the right to bear arms be taken literally or not? Does the coinage clause constitute a lawful designation of Congressional authority to another branch of government? On and on the convolutions go, as they must in a society straining to put distorted gloss on a few thousand words of eighteenth-century prose because its religious-political scruples prevent its taking up a topic and dealing with it by some simpler legislative process.

Whether there may be a simpler legislative process for Americans, with their history and their political culture, is a subject for another time, but we may speculate that the longer the history and the passage of time, the more impossible it has become for Americans to get out from under the dead weight of their Constitution, not that they show any signs of wanting to. The government in Washington is one of the oldest continuous institutions in the world; its antiquity has taken hold of the popular cultural imagination. Its age, the long American past, old days, ancient or ancient-appearing traditions are praised and emphasized at every opportunity; we are told to live up to a heroic past, to keep our liberty, to preserve our freedom. The emphasis is always on conserving what we've been given, not on exploring new possibilities. The political culture has come to have a built-in bias against the new and in favor of the old-time religion of Thomas Jefferson and the other worthies in silk britches and powdered wigs in our pantheon.

The preference for the appearance of changelessness has given rise to what may be a unique form of debate in an advanced democratic society. Since they can't change their Constitution, Americans accuse each other or the government of failing to live up to it. The civil-rights movement was able to invoke the Bill of Rights, which serves as the ten commandments to the Holy Book of the American religion, to demand and get many of its objectives. Dr. Martin Luther King, Jr., was not seeking to establish new rights and new values, but to give life and force to those which he claimed had been there and had been sinfully ignored all the time. Blacks were at long last to be sheltered under the umbrella of the Constitution by claiming they had always had a place prepared for them, but that it had been usurped. In effect, the Constitution was amended by somewhat fraudulently insisting that nothing more was being done than restoring and giving due prominence to the old. It's a device other societies with imperfect legislative mechanisms, such as Rome in the Republican period, have resorted to.

Thus, although most of the words of the Constitution are as they were when written, by one contrivance or another the government for which they stand as fundamental law is completely changed. Regardless, the holy text remains a statement of Jeffersonian idealism and Jefferson himself, as the minister whose sermons best express the old-time religion, has been made at least an honorary "Framer." Millions apparently think it was his pen through which God spelled out the words of the hallowed political contract. Yet, though the Jeffersonian view blots out all others, Hamiltonian principles actually guide public policy. America dreams a Jeffersonian/constitutional idyll in a day-to-day existence of harsh Hamiltonian necessity.

From the first, Hamilton's brand of federalism never found acceptance in the nation's political culture, and, from John Adams to Walter Mondale, politicians who espoused it have had tough sledding. Alexander Hamilton himself is down the memory hole, a nonperson, honored only in the act of ordering affairs as he might have ordered them, but these incongruities don't matter to Americans, who don't notice them. If the language of the Fourteenth Amendment was tortured by the late nineteenth-century Supreme Court to charter and enfranchise modern corporate America, it's little noted and never objected to.* In like manner, the commerce clause has been bent, molded and sculpted into unrecognizability. Such feats of exegesis were needed to preserve the integrity of sacred scripture, while a new structure of law and government was built.

These strange and oblique ways of proceeding help explain the tentative, partial and tardy quality in much that American government does. Things must be arranged to correspond with the sacred text, while at the same time ex parte groups and individuals use the constitutional argument for delay, obfuscation and complexity. Nevertheless, over the centuries, little by little, the legal exegetes have found the formulas that permit change and adaptation to allow things as diverse as government loans to exporters and clean air. It is in the arena of politics that the Constitution remains largely uninterpreted and therefore unchanged.

With all deference to Madison's oft-described reading of Montesquieu and the political philosophy of the ancients before writing the first draft of the great document, what emerged from the convention and was ratified by the thirteen states is something not too dissimilar from the British constitution as it existed during the Hanoverian dynasty. During much of the eighteenth century, Britain could be said to have had a triune government functioning under the separation of powers among Crown, Parliament and the courts. The most distinctive political feature of the age of the Four Georges, a powerful bicameral legislature, separated from a strong, independent throne, was crudely recreated by the Englishmen who wrote the American Constitution. They took the salient features of the monarchy, as it had evolved up to the late eighteenth century, and, converting king to President, set up again in North America. There are various little telltale features in the American Constitution that betray the model from which it is drawn, the most revealing of which is placing

* But see Robert Sherrill on page 95 of this issue.—Editor.

the origin of all money bills in the House of Representatives. This was perhaps the hardest-fought-for right and the most important gained by the House of Commons in the bloody struggles of the seventeenth century. Only Englishmen of this period would include this detail, because only they had had the political experience to make it relevant. Nobody else would have thought it up.

By the nineteenth century, the kings of England had given up the attempt to govern without ministers selected by Parliament. Throughout the century, British polity changed to make it impossible for the prime minister to come from the House of Lords, and by the beginning of the present century he or she had to be a commoner and come from the Commons. With that, the modern fusion of the legislative and executive that is characteristic of the world's advanced democracies took place. The United States, however, equipped with its unchangeable Constitution, met the modern world with its strangely archaic political institutions and arrangements.

Not surprisingly, American politics has a familiar smell to anyone with a little knowledge of eighteenth-century British politics, where the strongest partisan tensions were between the throne and Westminster, between the king's party and the parliamentary party. That same set of tensions was translated across the seas and has embedded itself in American politics for all time. The two most durable political parties here are the Congressional party and the White House party. Other parties have come and gone, à la the Federalists and the Whigs, or have literally exchanged principles and outlook, like the Democrats and the Republicans. But what has always endured is the American version of the ancient struggle between Crown and Commons. For two centuries, from George Washington's administration to Ronald Reagan's, President and Congress have wrangled over prerogatives and spheres of power. Thus American history shows that neither a Jefferson nor a Reagan, committed as they may be to the dispersal of power, will yield an inch of it to the five hundred thirty-five adversaries at the other end of Pennsylvania Avenue. In like manner, when the Iran-Contra affair was made public, Republicans in Congress were as zealous as

Democrats in attacking a President who had broken the law and ignored policy as laid down by the Senate and the House of Representatives.

Of course, if the radical Republicans had found one more vote in the Senate and thereby been able to eject Andrew Johnson from the presidency, American political institutions might look quite different on the Constitution's two hundredth anniversary. That angry clash was as close as the American Congress has come to emulating its British parliamentary parent by trying to wrest control of the running of the government from the White House. The battle was waged over Johnson's legal use of his prerogative in firing Edwin Stanton, his Secretary of War. Congress wanted Stanton to remain, and if it had prevailed, the eighteenth-century Constitution would have been overthrown and the United States would have moved toward some version of parliamentary government.

It was not to be, and for the health and power of Congress it may have been just as well. One of the characteristics of modern parliaments is that, while they are omnipotent in theory, in actuality they are so unswervingly subservient to the prime ministers and cabinets they create that they have no life, no independence of their own. To this day, being a member of the British parliament isn't a full-time job; there isn't enough for a member to do, so that the House of Commons still often sits at night or late afternoon at the end of the business day.

By contrast, membership in Congress is a full-time job and then some. Moreover, the institution itself is like no other national legislature, with its research and investigative arms and thousands of staff people, many of whom are experienced specialists in every field of human activity. Wherever anything is transpiring on the globe, you will shortly see a Congressional staff person taking notes, asking questions and paving the way for a visiting delegation of inquiry. While remaining recognizably the institution the people who wrote the Constitution may have had in mind, Congress has metamorphosed itself into something no one foresaw. Its size and its permanently adversarial position vis-à-vis the White House might have been anticipated, but not the role it has come to play in the era of decline of electoral politics.

The Electoral College arrangement provided for in the
Constitution has been a dead letter for more than one hundred years; most Americans are probably unaware even
that it exists, but everybody knows that every four years
we vote for President and many of us know that every two
years we do the same for Congress; but knowing it isn't the
same as doing it. For the last seventy-five years voter participation rates have floated downward. The enfranchise-
ment of blacks and older teenagers in the 60s and 70s has
not pushed the number upwards. One out of two, or perhaps more, of the people who may vote for President,
don't. The voter participation rates for Congress are much
lower than that. Thus a majority of the citizenry habitually
do not play the part assigned to them by the Constitution.
Of those that do, the meaning and intent of what they do
isn't obvious. They may, in the issueless sort of way en-
visioned by the Constitution's writers, be choosing the best
person, or they may be performing a symbolic rite, living
up to the duty required of them by the words in the sacred
writings.

In a political culture in which wealthy people customarily contribute to candidates running against each other,
in which there are no political parties to speak of, and in
which the faces and sentiments of the candidates are
scarcely more than electronic flashes on the screen, it's
easier to speculate about why people don't vote than why
they do. In Chicago last winter, it was reported that more
than 90 percent of the eligible electorate cast ballots to
decide between black male Harold Washington and white
female Jane Byrne. We can infer that those voters knew
what they were about, but the clarity of their intention
only makes what goes on in an ordinary presidential election all the more murky.

If the quadrennial exercise of suffrage has evolved into
a constitutional solemn high mass, a liturgical expression of nationhood, the document itself has taken on the
taste of a slightly sourish egalitarianism. Americans believe
it's the Constitution that makes them equal, less, one sometimes thinks, for immediate benefits and privileges than
the abstract sense of personal dignity it bestows. One
man/one vote has been grafted into the Constitution, but

now that it's there, two thirds of the population don't use it. Equal access to bad schools, bad hospitals, bad jobs or no jobs is acceptable as long as these inadequacies are distributed with fine impartiality.

The equal citizen who doesn't vote and has only a passing interest in who occupies the constitutional offices is, nevertheless, in daily contact with his government through its multifarious agencies, commissions and departments. In addition, the members of Congress have been converted into their constituents' Washington agents to get them jobs, contracts, regulatory exemptions, loans, hospital beds, and on and on. Nothing like it was imagined by the men who wrote the Constitution, but apparently these new, extra-constitutional duties are more important than a member's party or policy proclivities. (This may explain why members of Congress are seldom beaten for reelection by opponents offering voters new policies and different approaches. When members of Congress are defeated for reelection, which only infrequently happens, it is usually ascribed to their being "out of touch," or providing inferior constituent services or in some other way failing, not in Constitutional responsibilities, but the extra-constitutional ones.)

All these activities are carried on extra-constitutionally, out of sight of the ark and the sacred scrolls; the political activities prescribed in the Constitution have little bearing on the aspect of government citizens are most interested in. Even a Ronald Reagan learned that mandates garnered through the constitutional election processes are of limited value, for policy victories won in the polling place don't translate easily into legislation or administration. The Constitution's decision-making machinery whirs, turns over and kicks out its verdicts, but they have only a tangential effect on the real decision-making, which is carried out by other processes.

Americans grow up comfortable in the thought they live with many levels and kinds of government, none of whose jurisdictions are exactly clear. So in addition to the fifty state governments, there are two federal ones, the formal, textbook Constitutional government, which can be changed or modified only with excruciating difficulty and painful slowness, and the other federal government, which goes along in great complexity but with suppleness and adaptability. It makes for confusion and expense and more litigiousness in an already lawyer-saturated society. Other governments and other ways may be cheaper and more effective, but a people not only get the government they merit, they often get the only one their political culture can tolerate. Would American society countenance any significant "improvements" in the present constitutional system? Not very likely.

The question is not whether there are cheaper, more expeditious ways to run a democracy, even one whose elections are chiefly symbolic, but how well the system will run when the *Sturm und Drang*, anxiety, crisis and massive unhappiness reappear, as they inevitably do from time to time. Then things may crack apart or the power of the Constitution, the Ark of the American Covenant, may yet, in its strong Calvinist way, keep us one and together.

SAME AS IT EVER WAS

Daniel Wolff

Watching David Byrne promote himself as a popular artist and, at the same time, try to maintain his avant-garde credentials, is one of the more instructive political and moral spectacles you're likely to see these days. "For years we have been taught not to like things," is how Byrne puts it. "Finally, somebody said it was O.K. to like things. This was a great relief. It was getting hard to go around not liking everything." As the most visible member of the new avant-garde, Byrne is speaking not only about his own work but about a broader problem: how to keep selling modernism.

In a recent cover story, *Time* listed among Byrne's creative community the minimalist composer Philip Glass, performance artist Laurie Anderson, choreographers Laura Dean, Lucinda Childs and Twyla Tharp, and theater artist Robert Wilson. (Byrne has collaborated with all but Dean and Childs.) What these share is an aesthetic transposed from the 1960s visual-arts scene and a desire, in Byrne's words, "to show their stuff to a wider audience and be accepted." Byrne's band, The Talking Heads, received their avant-garde badge of approval in 1983 when artist Robert Rauschenberg designed the cover of their record, *Speaking in Tongues*. But the Heads have always played art-rock. Byrne and band members Tina Weymouth and Chris Frantz met in 1975 at the Rhode Island School of Design where they were art students, and were later joined by Jerry Harrison, a graduate of Harvard. After playing at downtown New York City punk clubs and touring Europe, they cut their first album, *77*. Its opening song, "Uh-Oh, Love Comes to Town," revealed not only Byrne's ironic, intelligent voice, but the aesthetic formula that he's retained throughout his career. "I'm the smartest man around/ . . . Where is my common sense?/ . . . I believe in mystery." Intelligence gives way to confusion gives way to mystery, all to a driving beat and a purposefully eccentric vocal. As main songwriter and singer for the band, Byrne made clear early on The Talking Heads' ambition to be rockers for the intelligentsia. If rock and roll came about through the marriage of black R & B with country music, Byrne was going to fuse the funkier aspect of dance music to the tradition of Andy Warhol and John Cage.

Songs like "Psycho Killer" and "Don't Worry About the Government" show Byrne's emerging song-writing skills. His main approach is to take an idea or persona (like the psycho killer) and describe it through tiny bits of information: a collage technique that's the verbal equivalent of the 529 Polaroid close-ups which composed the band's portrait on the 1978 *More Songs About Buildings and Food.* It's an appropriate cover since *More Songs,* their second album and first of a series of collaborations with producer Brian Eno, firmly stakes out The Talking Heads' artistic turf. The album begins with love songs—the staple of pop music—but love songs from a depressive's point of view. "What does it take to fall in love?/ . . . I'm not in love/ . . . I believe that we don't need love." The record's oppressive, fragmented, end-of-the-world atmosphere— where nothing makes sense and everything's seen through the artist's ironic, distant perspective—resolves itself through the album's saving grace: rhythm. "Take Me to the River," a remake of soul singer Al Green's earlier success, was The Talking Heads' first hit. If being an artist is Byrne's idea of the only viable way to deal with the modern world (as in "Found a Job" where "people fighting over little things/might be better off/ . . . making up their own shows."), the ecstatic release is art's payoff. "Especially when there's a rhythm," Byrne has said, "you're kind of lifted and put more in touch with some sort of collective sensibility." Byrne traces his interest in "naïve" art to its ability to connect with this group unconscious and sees modern art as having the same power, "except [in naïve art] you know that the person doing it is not trying to trick you."

This aesthetic—shared with the trancelike, repetitive music of Philip Glass and the slow motion, otherworldliness of Robert Wilson's theater pieces—can be traced back to the early founders of modernism. Essentially, Byrne's approach to making art follows André Breton's definition of surrealism from the '20s: "The dictation of thought, in the absence of all control exercised by reason, and outside all aesthetic and moral preoccupations." Or, in Byrne's own words, "Stop making sense." Surrealism originally embraced fragmentation, the unconscious and the eccentric point of view, for political reasons. As Tristan Tzara wrote in 1916: "There is a great negative work of destruction to be accomplished." In response to the horrors of modern warfare and the reordering of power in the West, surrealists set out to shock and overthrow the bourgeoisie. They embraced Freud and quoted Trotsky, who called inspiration "the creative union of the conscious and unconscious" and revolution "the inspired frenzy of history."

But Breton's idea that authentic art leads to the confusion and destruction of capitalist society didn't pan out. Instead, modern art's permanent revolution became essentially self-referential. The aesthetic held, but avant-garde artists like Cage, Merce Cunningham and Rauschenberg came out of the Black Mountain School in the '50s with the belief that the object of the dictum "Make it new" was art, not society. Along with The Velvet Underground and David Bowie, The Talking Heads brought these values to the working-class world of rock and roll. Instead of the straightforward emotion of "Heartbreak Hotel," Byrne champions the fragmented and the disconnected. "When the house is finished," he's written, "you'll never be able to see [it] all again." Rather than being "new wave," this art-school cubism is, by now, a third generation paraphrase of Giacometti's *Palace at 4 A.M.* The result is songs like "The Good Thing," where a string of Confucianlike one-liners are thrown together and we, the audience, are left to make sense or not of these cut-up, incomplete fragments.

This superimposing of modernist values onto rock helps explain Byrne's attitude to black dance music: as the way out of the apocalyptic, modern-art *angst* which is his speciality, and the equivalent of the studied innocence of a Gauguin. But *More Songs* doesn't end with the ecstatic "Take Me to the River." Byrne's art is, finally, too dependent on the alienated perspective to be resolved by the sociability of dance. Though part of The Talking Heads' appeal has always been their apparent enthusiasm for what they're doing ("I'm living in the future/And I feel wonderful."), Byrne's shouts of "Work it out!" can always be read as ironic. And his goal of making "high art" keeps him at the same cultural remove from Al Green as Picasso was from African sculpture. *More Songs* ends, instead, with "The Big Country": an indictment of middle-America as seen from a great and cold distance. "I have learned how to look at these things, and I say/I wouldn't live there if you paid me." The hint of slide guitar behind the lyrics serves as ironic comment on the sappiness of country music. And while Byrne concedes that "those people have fun with their neighbors and friends," his last line is that "it's not even worth talking about," and then he fades out chanting baby talk: "Goo goo ga ga ga." The Talking Heads may be amused by the activities of regular people, but Byrne can't help but echo Tzara's "All action is vain."

And so it goes through the Heads' records of the late '70s and early '80s. Continuing to collaborate with Eno, Byrne introduces more exotic African and Arabic music while maintaining his point of view. Serious, wonderfully danceable songs like "Living in Wartime" snap back into ironic distance with the chorus: "This ain't no party/This ain't no disco/This ain't no fooling around." The everyday world is the enemy, where "air can hurt you, too," the animals are laughing at us, and heaven, naturally, "is a place where nothing happens." Is Byrne a sincere naïf or is he trying to "trick" us? His eccentric vocals and absurdist sense of humor make it impossible to tell, and the seductive, often beautiful music serves to carry us past caring. With the 1980 *Remain in Light*, the African funk-groove cranks up a notch, and the improvised rhythm tracks (now supplemented by additional musicians like Adrian Belew and singer Nona Hendryx) highlight what a fine dance band The Talking Heads have become. "Once in a Lifetime" is Byrne's own "Take Me to the River," in which he's matured enough to write an original and convincing trance dance to take us "into the blue again/after the money's gone." And still, the record ends with "The Overload": "The center is missing/The gentle collapsing."

Part of what wasn't holding together very well at this point was the band. While Byrne continued to receive all the song credits, bassist Tina Weymouth and drummer Chris Frantz went off and proved they had more than a little influence on the Heads' driving sound by making their own, strong dance record under the name of The Tom-Tom Club. Byrne turned deeper into pure Art. He and Eno cut *My Life in the Bush of Ghosts* (1981), a series of sampled vocals taken from radio evangelists, Lebanese singers and black gospel choirs and then put over multitrack party rhythms by Byrne, Eno and various studio muscians. Never as convincing as the Heads' own music, the album nevertheless strengthened Byrne's reputation as an avant-gardist who could take the innocent and render it into the ominously ridiculous. Byrne's ethnocultural tourism reaches new heights here. "There's nothing wrong with stealing little bits," Byrne has said, supporting his definition of the artist as transcendent. But without the push of the Heads' rhythm section, we begin to notice that here, as in all his work, the bits are stolen from working-class or other, to him, "naïve" cultures. The inspired frenzy of Elvis—which was created by *crossing* racial, sexual and social barriers—becomes in Byrne's hands a way of subtly reemphasizing the differences between us.

In the same year, Byrne released *The Catherine Wheel*: his score for the modern-dance piece by Twyla Tharp. The pattern remains the same. In the early parts of the dance, a "typical" family fights, fucks and self-destructs until, in what was called The Golden Section, all disappear into ecstasy. It's hard to determine whether the mean-spiritedness of the piece comes originally from Tharp—whose choreography is even more disdainful of everyday people than the music—or Byrne, who sets the scene as "a great big house with nothing in it," judges that "these people are savages," and concludes "there's nothing we can do."

Defended by critics as "a dazzling bit of aw-shucks virtuosity," *The Catherine Wheel* nevertheless seems to have marked a turning point in Byrne's musical history. Divorced from Weymouth and Frantz and their convincing, enveloping beat, Byrne's music was simply less appealing. One immediate result was that these more experimental records didn't sell as well. While Byrne would go solo again to write *The Knee Plays* with Robert Wilson and has never abandoned his modernism, when The Talking Heads reformed for the 1983 *Speaking in Tongues*, it was to make a lighter, more danceable, more acceptable brand of pop.

Part of the changed approach was Byrne's assertion that he was "an ordinary guy." "These are just people," he's now decided, "and I'm not afraid." There are even positive love songs like "Better than That," where the narrator seems almost capable of maintaining a relationship. And the apocalyptic question of "Who's driving?" in "Swamp" is buried more and more regularly in the oblivion of the trance. "I get wild/It's automatic/ . . . I'll survive the situation." The music is closer to mainstream rock and roll, and the album concludes with a "naïve melody" where Byrne offers an avant-garde paraphrasing of The Beach Boys: "I feel numb/ . . . so I guess I must be having fun." "Whatever happens," Byrne sings now, "is fine."

Little Creatures, the Heads' next album, is even poppier. The hit, "And She Was," elevates the mystical and distant observer into an archetype. Byrne seems to have concluded that, while still a modernist, he wants his art to read in the marketplace. Asked in *Equator* magazine what it felt like to be part of the avant-garde, Byrne pauses "long enough for anyone else to smoke a cigarette," and then begins backing away. "I guess people nowadays wonder whether that exists anymore," he says. He guesses it must mean "art that would have a small audience, but that would be innovative." The catch, as he sees it, is "if you're really doing things that are way ahead of your time, hardly anyone would like it."

Here we see the metamorphosis of David Byrne in the Reagan era. His dilemma is his own aesthetic, which is based on keeping a distance from the very people he's trying to reach. How do you shock the bourgeoisie and still have them buy the product?

Little Creatures ends with the celebratory march, "Road to Nowhere," where we are all heading merrily towards nothingness. Throughout the album, Byrne sings that "ecstasy is what I need" and, triumphantly, "See me put things together/Put them back where they belong." He has begun to switch the emphasis in the surrealist formula from how alienating it is to be among an educated, artistic elite to how much fun it can be. "I know that I like a lot of the same things yuppies are supposed to like," he says in an interview in the *New Musical Express,* and this philosophy of pleasurable elitism helps make young urban pro-

fessionals his core audience. But for mass appeal, he has
to reach beyond that. *True Stories*—this year's film, book
and soundtrack—is his solution.

"The thing about it is," he writes in *True Stories*, "all of
these people are right. None of them is wrong. They are
setting a good example, and in this film and book I'm
teaching myself to appreciate them." To sell his vision to
a wider audience, Byrne has to retailor his perspective,
and modernism makes the necessary shift in values easy.
An aesthetic which holds to no moral positions and puts
maximum value on "the new" not only lends itself to the
marketplace, but can effortlessly *become* fashion. "Democracy," Byrne concludes in the *New Musical Express* interview, "is just a license to manufacture or sell anything
you please or dress however you want."

Byrne's strategy in *True Stories* appears to be to expand Breton's credo "Only the marvelous is beautiful" into
"Everything is marvelous." His role as The Narrator is an
extension of his voice in The Talking Heads' music. He
is the alien stranger who rolls into a Texas town and starts
examining the locals. There's The Lying Woman (who
never tells the truth), a Musica Chicana band led by Tex-
Mex star Esteban Jordan, The Lazy Woman (who never
leaves her bed), and a black servant who's also a voodoo
doctor. These characters, based on "true stories" in *Weekly
World News* and other tabloids, are, finally, all the same
to Byrne. Admitting in a postscript to the book that a lot
of the stories aren't, in fact, true, he confesses that he
doesn't care. "What's important is that I believed they
were true. . . . I hope that the people in these articles are
real because they certainly did inspire me." To Byrne,
the value of tabloid eccentrics and minority cultures is
equal: they are colorful, odd, and therefore fuel for his
creativity.

Even beautifully shot and artfully directed, *True Stories*
reveals what has always beat beneath Talking Heads'
music: the heart of a snob. Because Byrne defines himself
as an artist in terms of his distance from the norm, to treat
his audience as equals—to take *any* openly comprehensible
position—is too threatening. "I stay away from loaded
subjects," Byrne writes about the movie, "—sex, violence,
and political intrigue—because as soon as you get on

[*362*]

those subjects, everybody already has preconceived ideas about them. I deal with stuff too dumb for people to formulate opinions on." The film's culminating scenes of a small-town parade and talent show make it clear that it is *our* lives, people's everyday lives, which are "the dumb stuff." We can either join Byrne in laughing at and being perplexed by the shopping malls, tract housing and baton twirlers—or reject his irony and remain on the outside among the ordinary people. Presented by Byrne as being apolitical, that choice is in fact defined when Louis, the film's hero, ends up singing: "We don't want freedom/ We don't want justice/We just want someone to love." That about sums up, as the song's title confirms, "People Like Us."

"David is one of those people," says Philip Glass, "who has forced us to redefine what we mean by popular culture and serious culture, commercial art and noncommercial art. He so resolutely does his own work regardless of whether it is commercial or noncommercial, and with so little regard for the canons of either of those fields, that he creates something uniquely his own." It's this profile that Byrne seems to most want: the man who never considers fashion and, yet, is always fashionable. Rather than redefining popular culture, he uses it the way Rauschenberg uses newspaper photos: undercutting it, abstracting it, taking away its meaning under the guise of an ironic humor which is all that remains of the surrealists' social criticism. Even the sweat-soaked performances in the concert film *Stop Making Sense* are calculated and self-conscious: the dance moves borrowed from Tharp and Dean, the big suit Byrne wears from Japanese theater. At the bottom of Byrne's style, even at its most engaging, lies disdain. "I discovered that it was easier to like things," he repeats in one of *True Stories'* publicity interviews. But asked in another if he's changed his mind about the line from "The Big Country"—"I wouldn't live there if you paid me"—his answer is an unambiguous "No."

"For the first time in the history of postwar experimental performance," trumpets playwright Robert Coe in *Time*, "serious artists have ceased to assume an attitude of indifference or superiority to the culture-at-large." But a review of Byrne's career makes it clear that his "seriousness" is based on values exactly the opposite of this promotional statement. No matter how it's packaged, the meaning of David Byrne's art remains, in his own words, "same as it ever was." To embrace that meaning—to be so won over by his artistic talents as to accept Byrne's perspective—ends up being little more than an act of self-hatred.

In Praise of Illiteracy

Hans Magnus Enzensberger

Can we dispense with the written word? That is the question. Anyone who poses it will have to speak about illiteracy. There's just one problem: the illiterate is never around when he is the subject of conversation. He simply doesn't show up; he takes no notice of our assertions; he remains silent. I would therefore like to take up his defense, although I don't hold any brief for him.

Every third inhabitant of our planet manages to get by without the art of reading and without the art of writing. This includes roughly 850 million people, and their numbers will certainly increase. The figure is impressive but misleading. For humanity comprises not only the living and the unborn, but the dead as well. If they are not forgotten, then the conclusion becomes inevitable that literacy is the exception rather than the rule.

It could only occur to us, that is, to a tiny minority of people who read and write, to think of those who don't as a tiny minority. This notion betrays an ignorance I find insupportable.

On the contrary, all things considered, the illiterate begins to seem like a figure. I envy him his memory, his capacity for concentration, his cunning, his inventiveness, his tenacity, his sensitive ear. Please don't imagine that I am dreaming of the noble savage. I am not speaking about romantic phantoms but about people I have met. I am far from idealizing them. I also see their narrow horizons, their illusions, their obstinacy, their quaintness.

You may ask how it comes about that a writer should take the side of those who cannot read.... But it's obvious!—because it was illiterates who invented literature. Its elementary forms—from myth to children's verse, from fairy tale to song, from prayer to riddle—all are older than writing. Without oral tradition, there would be no poetry; without illiterates, no books.

"But," you will object, "what about the Enlighten-

This article is taken from a talk by the author on receiving the Heinrich Böll Prize from the City of Cologne.

[365]

ment? . . ." Agreed! "The dullness of a tradition that excluded the poor from advancing their lot . . ." No need
to tell me! Social distress rests not only on the rulers' material advantages but on immaterial privilege as well. It
was the great intellectuals of the "*dix-huitième*" who discerned this state of affairs. The people had not come of
age, they thought, not only because of political oppression and economic exploitation but also because of their
lack of knowledge. From these premises, later generations drew the conclusion that the ability to read and
write belongs to any existence fit for a human being.

However, this suggestive idea underwent a succession
of noteworthy reinterpretations in the course of time. In
the twinkling of an eye, the concept of enlightenment was
replaced by the concept of education. "In terms of the
education of the populace," according to Ignaz Heinrich
von Wessenberg, a German schoolmaster in Napoleon's
time, "the second half of the eighteenth century marks a
new epoch. The knowledge of what was accomplished in
this regard is joyous news to any friend of mankind, encouraging to the priests of culture, and highly instructive
for the leaders of the commonwealth."

Not all of his contemporaries agreed. Another educator
of the people, Johann Rudolph Gottlieb Beyer, wrote
about reading books: "If it does not always cause insur-
rection and revolution, it does make for malcontents and
discontents, who always regard with jealousy the undertakings of the legislative and executive powers, and who
do not favor the country's constitution."

All this seems familiar to us. The fear of enlightenment
has outlived the enlightenment itself. It survives not only
in the twentieth century's dictatorships, but in West German democracy. We have always had a few legislative
or executive idiots who would like to abrogate the constitution in order to protect it from the harmful effects of
certain publications.

But even conservative cultural criticism has learned
very little on this score in the last two centuries. It keeps
its index finger perpetually raised in warning. "Why,"
wondered Johann Georg Heinzmann as early as in the
days of Goethe, "why [should] things always be written
and published for the ruined species of man who wants to

be ever entertained, ever flattered, ever deceived?"

"The results of such tasteless and thoughtless reading are . . . senseless waste, unconquerable reluctance to exert oneself, limitless itch for luxuries, suppression of the voice of conscience, boredom with life, and an early death," complained Johann Adam Bergk in his pamphlet *The Art of Reading Books.*

I quote these long-forgotten texts because their themes haunt us to this day. Anyone listening to our cultural/ political Sunday talks and panel discussions would have to get the impression that in two hundred years hardly any new arguments have been invented.

As far as the project of literacy goes, we've made great strides. Here, it seems, the philanthropists, the priests of culture and the leaders of the commonwealth have scored triumphantly. Who could contradict Joseph Meyer, one of the most capable of the nineteenth-century publishers, who invented the slogan "Education shall make you free!"? Social democrats raised this watchword to the status of a political demand. Knowledge is power! Culture for everyone! To this very day they fight on indefatigably against educational privilege and for equal opportunity. Since the time of Bebel and Bismarck, one set of glad tidings has followed the other. By 1880, illiteracy in Germany had already fallen below one percent. In other European countries, it lasted somewhat longer. But the rest of the world has also made enormous progress since UNESCO raised its flag in the fight against illiteracy in 1951. In a word: Light has conquered darkness.

Our joy over this triumph has certain limits. The news is too good to be true. The people did not learn to read and write because they felt like it, but because they were forced to do so. Their emancipation was controlled by disenfranchisement. From now on learning went hand in hand with their State and its agencies: the schools, the army, the legal administration. When the children of Ravensburg entered an award ceremony in 1811, they already had a song on the topic:

> Good burghers at their duty strive:
> To show a prompt obedience.

[*367*]

But who can teach us so to thrive
And do our work with diligence?
Only schools can mold our hearts
Teaching us these useful arts.

We dedicate ourselves to Good
And love new knowledge as we should.
Our schools for this we thank and praise:
Now may we thank them all our days.
And so for our good schools we sing,
Hail the State and Hail the King!

The goal pursued in making the populace literate had nothing to do with enlightenment. The friends of mankind and the priests of culture, who stood up for the people, were merely the henchmen of a capitalist industry that pressed the state to provide them with a qualified work force. It was never really a question of the Good, the True and the Beautiful, of which the patriarchal publishers in the Biedermeyer period spoke and to which their current descendants still eagerly refer. It was not a matter of paving the way for the "writing culture," let alone liberating mankind from its shackles. Quite a different kind of progress was in question. It consisted in taming the illiterates, this "lowest class of men," in stamping out their self-will and their fantasy, and in exploiting not only their muscle power and skill in handiwork but their brains as well.

For the unlettered human to be done away with, he had first to be defined, tracked down and unmasked. The concept of illiteracy is not very old. Its invention can be dated with some precision. The word appeared for the first time in a French publication of the year 1876 and quickly spread all over Europe. At the same time, Edison invented the light bulb and the phonograph, Siemens invented the electric locomotive, Bell the telephone, and Otto the gasoline motor. The connection is clear.

Furthermore, the triumph of popular education in Europe coincides with the maximum development of colonialism. And this is no accident. In the dictionaries of the period we can find the assertion that the number of illiterates "as compared with the total population of a country is a measure of the people's cultural condition." "This [is] lowest in the Slavic countries and among the blacks of the U.S.A. . . . At the highest level there are the . . . Germanic countries, the whites of the U.S.A. and the Finnish race." And they do not fail to instruct us that "Men . . . [stand on a level] higher, on the average, than women." (Meyers Grosses Konversationslexikon 1905)

This is no longer a matter of statistics, but a process of discrimination and stigmatization. Behind the figure of the illiterate, we can discern Hitler's concept of *des Untermensch*, the subhuman who must be eliminated. A small, radical minority has reserved civilization for itself and now discriminates against all those who will not dance to its tune. This minority can be described with precision: men rule women, whites rule colored races, rich rule poor, the living rule the dead. What the "leaders of the commonwealth" never suspected in the early days of the Reich must be apparent to their great-grandchildren (once burned, twice shy): enlightenment can end in persecution; culture can turn barbaric. You will ask why I should concern you here with problems of merely historical interest. But this history has overtaken us. The revenge of the excluded is not without a certain grim irony. The illiteracy we smoked out has now returned, as you all know, in an all but venerable form. A new figure has conquered the social stage. This new species is the second-order illiterate.

He has come a long way: the loss of memory from which he suffers causes him no suffering; his lack of self-will makes life easy for him; he values his own inability to concentrate; he considers it an advantage that he neither knows nor understands what is happening to him. He is mobile. He is adaptive. He has a talent for getting things done. We need have no worries about him. It contributes to the second-order illiterate's sense of well-being that he has no idea that he is a second-order illiterate. He considers himself well-informed; he can decipher instructions on appliances and tools; he can decode pictograms and checks. And he moves within an environment hermetically sealed against any infection of his consciousness. That he might come to grief in this environment is unthinkable. After all, it produced and educated him in order to guarantee its undisturbed continuation. The second-order illiterate is the product of a new phase of industrialization. An economy whose problem is no longer production but markets has no more need of a disciplined reserve army. Along with the classical production-line worker and the office employee, the rigid training to which they were subjected also becomes redundant, and literacy becomes a fetter to be done away with as soon as possible. Simultaneously with the development of this problem, our technology has also developed an adequate solution. The ideal medium for the second-order illiterate is television.

Probably most theories proposed to explain this phenomenon are false. I know what I'm talking about, since less than twenty years ago, I ascribed amazing emancipatory potential to the electronic media. Such hopes, even if unfounded, had at least the advantage of temerity. We cannot say as much for the observations of the American sociologist Neil Postman that are now causing such a stir: "When a people allows itself to be led astray by trivialities, when cultural life is newly formulated as an endless suite of entertainments, as a gigantic amusement park; when public discourse becomes an indistinguishable blather; in short, when citizens turn into viewers and their public events turn into variety shows, then the nation is in danger—the extinction of the culture becomes a real threat."

Only the vocabulary has changed: otherwise the American of 1985 argues exactly like the good Swiss of 1795 who sent an "Appeal to His Nation" to warn it of the menace of cultural collapse. Of course, Postman is right as far as his main point is concerned: Television is junk with a cherry on top. Strangely enough, he seems to think that this is a drawback. But junk is what the networks are about. Television has its mindlessness to thank for all its charm, its irresistibility, its success. Still more remarkable is another tic observable in the apologists for the reading culture. It seems extremely important to them to note by which media mindlessness is produced. If it's printed in black and white, it's a cultural treasure; spread by antenna or cable, it puts "the nation in danger." Well, anyone who takes cultural criticism for gospel truth has only himself to blame.

For me, in any case, it is hard to believe a Cassandra

whose ominous cry serves to protect her own sales and at the same time gropes blindly for new markets. Let's not forget: it was a printed product, the *Bildzeitung*, that proved you can sell the abolition of reading as reading matter and provide a printed medium for second-order illiterates. And, naturally, it is publishers who are falling over each other to put in cables, fling up new satellites and blanket the continent with programs that have been purged of any programmatic content. They can still rely on state support now that it's a matter of putting an end to literacy, just as they could two hundred years ago, when the idea was to make the populace literate. Meanwhile, the project of compulsory cabelization corresponds exactly to the "compulsory education" as referred to in the laws of that time. It is fitting that West German industry has, as its interlocutor, a minister who incarnates the very type of the second-order illiterate with all the clarity we could wish for.

The educational policy of the state will have to align itself with the new priorities. By reducing the library budget, a first step has already been taken. And innovations are to be seen in school administration as well. It is well known that you can go to school now for eight years without learning German, and even in the universities this Germanic dialect is gradually acquiring the status of a poorly mastered foreign language.

Please do not suppose that I would want to polemicize against a situation of whose inevitability I am fully aware. I desire only to portray and, as far as I can, explain it. It would be foolish to contest the secondary-illiterate's *raison d'être*, and I am far from begrudging him his pleasures or his place in the sun.

On the other hand, it is safe to say that the project of the enlightenment has failed. The slogan "Culture for everyone" begins to sound comical. And a classless culture is even further from view. On the contrary: we can look forward to a situation in which ever more sharply divided cultural milieus are created that no longer share a common public forum.

I would like to risk the assertion that the population will split up into more and more distinct cultural castes. (Naturally, I use this term descriptively, with no systematic pretensions.) These castes cannot be described as of the traditional Marxist model, according to which the ruling culture is the culture of the rulers. The divergence between economic position and consciousness will continue to grow.

It will become the new rule to see second-order illiterates occupying the top positions in politics and in business. In this connection, it is sufficient to indicate the current President of the United States and the current Chancellor of the Federal Republic. On the other hand, you can easily find—both in Germany and in the U.S.A.—whole hordes of cabdrivers, newspaper hawkers, manual laborers and welfare recipients whose thoughtfulness, cultural standards, and wide-ranging knowledge would have taken them far in any other society. But even this kind of comparison falls short of portraying the true state of affairs, which admits of no clear analysis. For even among the unemployed you can find zombies; even in the presidential office there are people who can read and write and even think productively. But that also means that, in questions of culture, social determinism has become obsolete. The so-called privileges of education have lost their fearfulness. If both parents are second-order illiterates, then the well-born child has no advantage over the worker's son. One's cultural caste will henceforth depend on personal option, not origin.

From all this, I conclude that culture in our country has come into an entirely new situation. As for the claim it always made, but never made good, of providing a common denominator for all people—that we can simply forget. The rulers, mostly second-order illiterates, have lost all interest in it. As a result, culture cannot, and need not any longer, serve the interest of a ruling class. It does not any more legitimate the social order. In this sense, it has become useless—but there is a kind of freedom in that. Such a culture is thrown back on its own resources, and the sooner it realizes this, the better.

Where does all that leave the writer? In terms of power, he may seem to have become an anadromism. But as far as literature goes, I think it has been less deeply affected than it might seem. At base, it was always a minority concern. Probably the number of those who really live with literature has stayed about the same over the last two hundred years. Only the composition of this minority has changed. For some time now it has no longer been a class privilege—or requirement—to be concerned with literature. The victory of the second-order illiterate can only radicalize literature: it contributes to a situation in which people will read only out of their own free will. When it has lost its value as a status symbol, as a social code, as an educational program, then literature will be noticed only by those who cannot do without it.

Whoever wants to can bemoan all this. I have no such desire. Finally, weeds have always been a minority, and every city gardener knows how hard it is to do away with them. Literature will continue to thrive as long as it commands a certain agility, a certain cunning, a capacity for concentration, and a good memory. As you recall, these are the features of the true illiterate. Perhaps he will have the last word, since he requires no other media than a voice and an ear.

Translated from German by Michael Lipson